The
1910s

The 1910s

David Blanke

American Popular Culture Through History
Ray B. Browne, Series Editor

GREENWOOD PRESS
Westport, Connecticut · London

Library of Congress Cataloging-in-Publication Data

Blanke, David, 1961–
    The 1910s / David Blanke.
       p. cm.—(American popular culture through history)
    Includes bibliographical references (p.   ) and index.
    ISBN 0–313–31251–6 (alk. paper)
    1. United States—Civilization—1865–1918. 2. United States—Civilization—1918–
    1945. 3. Popular culture—United States—History—20th century. 4. Nineteen tens.
    I. Title. II. Series.
    E169.1.B634 2002
    973.91'3—dc21   2001040598

British Library Cataloguing in Publication Data is available.

Library of Congress Catalog Card Number: 2001040598
ISBN: 0–313–31251–6

First published in 2002

Greenwood Press, 88 Post Road West, Westport, CT 06881
An imprint of Greenwood Publishing Group, Inc.
www.greenwood.com

Printed in the United States of America

The paper used in this book complies with the
Permanent Paper Standard issued by the National
Information Standards Organization (Z39.48–1984).

10 9 8 7 6 5 4 3 2 1

To Alexander and Benjamin

Contents

Contents

Acknowledgments

I wish to acknowledge my debt to the many historians who have contributed to the creation of this book. I have tried to conserve their enthusiasm for the era and their particular subjects. In addition, I attempted to synthesize their views into a coherent and meaningful overview of popular culture in this most active of decades. As with any survey, the danger of misappropriating or over-generalizing such a complex mixture of research and writing can be great. While their works are cited in the notes and in the further reading section, I again express my appreciation for their dedicated efforts.

This book was greatly aided by the advice, ideas, and encouragement of many people. In particular, I would like to thank Tricia Currans-Sheehan, Phil Hey, Jim Redmond, and Bill Welu for their opinions and feelings about American popular culture both in the 1910s and today. A special note of thanks goes to Sr. Mary Jane Koenigs at the library of Briar Cliff University and the Inter-Library loan staff of the Mary and Jeff Bell Library at Texas A&M University–Corpus Christi. The support of Texas A & M University–Corpus Christi, and especially that of my colleagues in the College of Arts and Humanities, was essential for the completion of the final manuscript. Debby Adams, Emma Bailey, copyeditor for Greenwood, Lynn Wheeler, and series editor Ray B. Browne offered essential criticism throughout the project. The book has been significantly improved by their efforts. Finally, I am also indebted to LeAnn Krysl, Kristi Lenz, Diana Villarreal, Noemi Ybarra, and Sonya René Witherspoon for their administrative assistance in completing this project. Any errors or omissions that remain are my responsibility alone.

    To my wife, Janet, I again offer my love and gratitude for her unflagging support and encouragement. To our children, Alexander and Benjamin, I dedicate this book with love.

Series Foreword

Popular Culture is the system of attitudes, behavior, beliefs, customs, and tastes that define the people of any society. It is the entertainments, diversions, icons, rituals, and actions that shape the everyday world. It is what we do while we are awake and what we dream about while we are asleep. It is the way of life we inherit, practice, change, and then pass on to our descendants.

Popular culture is an extension of folk culture, the culture of the people. With the rise of electronic media and the increase in communication in American culture, folk culture expanded into popular culture—the daily way of life as shaped by the *popular majority* of society. Especially in a democracy like the United States, popular culture has become both the voice of the people and the force that shapes the nation. In 1782, the French commentator Hector St. Jean de Crevecouer asked in his *Letters from an American Farmer*, "What is an American?" He answered that such a person is the creation of America and is in turn the creator of the country's culture. Indeed, notions of the American Dream have been long grounded in the dream of democracy—that is, government by the people, or popular rule. Thus, popular culture is tied fundamentally to America and the dreams of its people.

Historically, culture analysts have tried to fine-tune culture into two categories: "elite"—the elements of culture (fine art, literature, classical music, gourmet food, etc.) that supposedly define the best of society; and "popular"—the elements of culture (comic strips, bestsellers, pop music, fast food, etc.) that appeal to society's lowest common denominator. The so-called "educated" person approved of elite culture and scoffed at popular culture. This schism first began to develop in Western Europe in the

fifteenth century when the privileged classes tried to discover and develop differences in societies based on class, money, privilege and life
styles. Like many aspects of European society, the debate between elite
and popular cultures came to United States. The upper class in America,
for example, supported museums and galleries that would exhibit "the
finer things in life," which would "elevate" people. As the twenty-first
century emerges, however, the distinctions between popular culture and
elitist culture have blurred. The blues songs (once denigrated as "race
music") of Robert Johnson are now revered by musicologists; architectural students study buildings in Las Vegas as examples of what Robert
Venturi called the "kitsch of high capitalism"; sportswriter Gay Talese
and heavyweight boxing champ Floyd Patterson were co-panelists at a
1992 SUNY New Paltz symposium on literature and sport. The examples
go on and on, but the one commonality that emerges is the role of popular culture as a model for the American Dream, the dream to pursue
happiness and a better, more interesting life.

To trace the numerous ways in which popular culture has evolved
throughout American history, we have divided the volumes in this series
into chronological periods—historical eras until the twentieth century,
decades between 1900 and 2000. In each volume, the author explores the
specific details of popular culture that reflect and inform the general
undercurrents of the time. Our purpose, then, is to present historical and
analytical panoramas that reach both backward into America's past and
forward to her collective future. In viewing these panoramas, we can
trace a very fundamental part of American society. The "American Popular Culture Through History" series presents the multifaceted parts of
a popular culture in a nation that is both grown and still growing.

Ray B. Browne
Secretary-Treasurer
Popular Culture Association
American Culture Association

Introduction

The events of a decade can significantly influence how we understand the past. Often to the frustration of historians, Americans are quick to interpret events as part of the "Roaring Twenties" (1920–1929) or the "Go-Go Eighties" (1980–1989), for example, rather than attempting to unfold the complex threads that make up the patterns of history. In the process, the historical record is artificially flattened as causes are separated from effects. Upon reflection it should be obvious that the Great Depression, beginning in 1929, or the conservatism of the Reagan administration, from 1981 to 1989, were not episodes contained within a single decade which, like a parking meter, suddenly ended after ten years. Apocryphal warnings about the end of the world at the close of the last millennium (whether this occurred in 2000 or 2001) serve as a useful reminder of the limits of such a strict, numerical approach to history. Still, the use of decades to delimit the past is not without justification. The very fact that these units *are* visible and legitimate reminders of the passage of time underscores the sense that they have real meaning for most Americans. Ten years may not be enough time to evaluate the grand sweep of U.S. history, but it certainly is a significant amount of time in the life of an average human being. Any study of popular culture needs to be particularly attuned to these earthly realities.

The 1910s, then, are no different than any other ten-year period as a unit of analysis. While elections were held, wars were fought, lives were lived, and fortunes were made, Americans were as captured by the clock and calendar as we are today. When stated this way, the changes that were recorded in the nature of popular culture throughout the era become even more remarkable. For it was during the 1910s that America as a nation came to embrace and nurture its own particular form of modern popular culture; one, we shall see, that was more inclusive of this country's diverse citizenry and less influenced by the cultural patterns of Europe. It can be said with some justification that Americans "did more" with popular culture in these ten years than in almost any other decade of the modern era.

THE "TEENS"

The second decade of the twentieth century was regarded by many contemporaries as a watershed between the old and new. Beginning ominously with the return of Halley's comet and concluding with the shameful Chicago "Black Sox" Scandal—whose players were found to have thrown the 1919 World Series—the period was witness to some of the most transformative events of the modern era, including the introduction of large-scale assembly line manufacturing (also known as Fordism), women's suffrage, Prohibition, Progressivism, and World War I, to name a few. Recollecting the shifts in the fine arts, British writer Virginia Woolf concluded, somewhat colorfully, "On or about December, 1910, human character changed."[1]

Of course, not everyone agreed as to whether this change was good or even whether it was occurring quickly enough. Frustrations by contemporaries and historians alike have tinged our understanding of the 1910s like the patina on a copper roof. In essence, these disappointments were rooted in how closely one defended or despised the established status quo in American popular culture. For example, in architecture, enthusiasts have wrestled for years with the proper appreciation for the shift away from European classicism toward a more modern American style. Given that most major construction projects took many years to progress from the drafting table to the construction yard, the buildings that appeared over the decades while this shift took place often appear embarrassingly tentative in their break with tradition. Architectural historian James Marston Finch believed that the 1910s were nearly an "esthetic wasteland" because of a strong and often overpowering reliance on preexisting styles (contemptuously termed derivative because it emanates or is derived from the work of others). Yet by focusing on the subtle alterations in popular culture, we are able to appreciate the creative and, at times, revolutionary changes that took place during the decade. The fact that many of the architectural forms first introduced in the 1910s—such as the bungalow, Stickley, or Prairie style—remain extremely popular today suggests that these slights shifts had the potential for significant and long-lasting change.[2]

UNDERSTANDING A DECADE OF POPULAR CULTURE

The term "popular culture" has been used to describe a grab bag of events, personalities, and phenomena, but here but it is defined as a cultural expression that is public, usually consumed or connected to the commercial marketplace, exists in a separate space or requires special technologies, and is generally accessible to all, both in content (that is, it does not require special training to appreciate or understand) and locale. This book is divided into two parts to explore these various aspects of American popular culture. In the first part, which reviews everyday America and the world of youth, the broad themes and demographic trends of the decade are surveyed. Here popular culture can be placed in the context of Progressivism, evolving women's rights, World War I, urban and rural America, and crime, for example. Moreover, a critical separation between the rights and responsibilities of children, adult society, and parents, is revealed, suggesting that modes of the decade's popular culture were greatly influenced by a new appreciation for the child.

In the second part, as indicated by the chapter headings, autonomous and, at times, seemingly contradictory subjects are explored. As a result, a review of the visual arts, for example, includes forays into magazine artists such as Norman Rockwell, cartoons such as "Krazy Kat," and the influence of the modern art unveiled at the 1913 Armory Show. Similar "odd couples" exist in other sections as well. The approach casts a wide net, incorporating many levels (from the producers and critics of culture to the individual performers and audiences who received it), subjects, and voices into the narrative. For nearly every topic, the historiography is vast, and the debate surrounding popular culture in the 1910s is still hotly contested. The chapter notes and suggested further reading are intended to provide a sample of useful secondary sources—books that can provide additional depth into the various topics introduced in each chapter.

Three broad themes help unify our understanding of these complex issues. The first is that popular expression experienced some degree of cultural synthesis in the 1910s as a result of modernization. While native-born white men retained their dominance throughout the decade, women, people of color, religious and national ethnics, and the lower and working classes gained an increasingly influential role in the expression of popular culture. These supposedly powerless people (often referred to in contemporary studies as subaltern groups) were usually closer to the immediate, and generally negative, effects of modernization, which included a rapid commercialization of their surroundings, a feeling of isolation within a bureaucratized, uncaring state, and a sense of frustration with the numbingly "proper" values of the Victorian era. Freed from these Victorian, Protestant, and largely middle-class values, new musical forms, slapstick comedy and vaudeville, adventure novels, and movies virtually exploded onto the scene in the 1910s. Even traditional components of American society—such as the role of children— gave way to a more global, progressive, academic, and legalistic understanding of early development that was based on the experiences of the country's poorest and least powerful citizens. In many ways, the efforts made at child welfare reform during the decade were the first sustained attempt to relieve the distress caused by modernization for those unintentionally victimized by change. In this way, a study of youth and popular culture is really a commentary on how America redefined itself as a plural nation in the modern era.

The omnipresent (and often prescient) writer and social critic Randolph Bourne ably identified this sense of cultural fusion when he argued in favor of a greater voice for America's youth. Bourne's resolution, which remains as relevant today as when he wrote in 1912, was to accept fusion as a natural process of social evolution. He wrote,

Youth does not simply repeat the errors and delusions of the past, as the elder generation with a tolerant cynicism likes to think; it is ever laying the foundations for the future. What it thinks so wildly now will be orthodox gospel thirty years hence. The ideas of the young are the living, the potential ideas; those of the old, the dying, or already dead. This is why it behooves the youth to be not less radical, but even more radical, than it would naturally be. It must be not simply contemporaneous, but a generation ahead of the times, so that when it comes into control of the world, it will be precisely right and coincident with the conditions of the world as it finds them.[3]

Such sentiments reflect a growing acceptance of cultural change, often aimed at the powerful, throughout the 1910s.

A second general theme is that cultural change was usually resisted, often quite forcibly, by the traditional guardians of taste and morals. Coupled with the emerging voice of women and non-whites, such conflict took on predictably bigoted and racist qualities. Less objectionable, but possibly more effective, was the economic neglect faced by many innovators. For example, Arthur Farwell, a white composer who tried to advance African American, Native American, and Western folk music among academic circles, complained that one willing to synthesize these sounds "finds himself [sic] in a perplexing situation; he discovers that his country will accept and pay readily enough for his services as a teacher, performer, etc., but that it apparently has no use for him as a composer, the very thing he has been educated to be."[4] For symphonic compositions or other examples of the fine arts, the old guardians of taste generally held sway in the 1910s (although, in the case of the high visual arts, this authority gave way during the decade). In less well-structured or newer forms of cultural expression, such as the movies, cultural conflict expanded the menu of "acceptable" entertainment, further widening the pool of talent, and led to an even greater experimentation in the years ahead.

Finally, popular culture evidenced a perceptible and significant shift away from European influence and authority, toward a more consciously American style in the 1910s. The rising confidence of ethnic, class, and racial cohorts within the country lent credibility to these first steps away from the traditions of the Old World. Progressive ideals, mass marketing and new technologies, and especially the tragedy of World War I convinced many Americans that their country was indeed on the right side of history. Ironically, when the modern art of Pablo Picasso and Paul Cézanne arrived in America, critics were successful in attacking their works by appealing to this growing sense of national cultural pride. European authorities, to these critics, were decadent and effete while the new modern style of the United States was lean, virile, and realistic. While such a trend worked against the immediate acceptance of these modern masters, by and large the rejection of the European influence greatly accelerated the pace of cultural change throughout the 1910s.

THE SIGNIFICANCE OF POPULAR CULTURE

Ultimately, as with any study of everyday life, we are left to judge the significance of change. What, exactly, can movies, comics, new eating patterns, clothing, and other seemingly trivial aspects of American life tell us about this country's past? Surprisingly, to many, the answer is quite a lot. For example, the growing conflict over the acceptance of many mass cultural events paved the way for a greater willingness on the part of Americans to criticize themselves and their traditional institutions. While this could quite easily take unproductive detours down dead-end paths—such as America's habitual low regard for intellectuals and the fine arts—popular culture often opened new avenues and opportunities for collective understanding. For example, the rise of the motion picture industry gave a powerful voice to forms of social criticism through the work of Charlie Chaplin, Mary Pickford, and D.W. Griffith. Mack Sennett's film success was based more broadly upon the growing rejection by Americans of the outdated, nativist views of social acceptability. Through his success as an actor and director, Sennett was able to establish the Keystone Company in 1912, which he led and inspired for the next five years. Calling themselves the Fun Factory, Sennett's firm recruited and signed some of the funniest and most ingenious comedic writers and performers of that or any other decade, including Mabel Normand, Fatty Arbuckle, and Charlie Chaplin. While Sennett relied heavily on situational comedy and the natural abilities of his company, he also trusted his audience to understand that film is an illusion, which suspends disbelief while staying connected to the viewers' commonsense experiences. The zany Keystone comedies were successful because they more closely related to the realities of American life than the self-righteous proclamations of most dramas. The most famous of Sennett's creations was the Keystone Kops. While pies in the face, banana peels, and car chases were (and remain) simply funny to watch, Sennett was able to frame the madness around strong symbols of social authority: the police, native-born elites, Victorian women, and religion, for example. No group was spared in his films. By 1915, Sennett was even parodying Hollywood itself. If one views these later shorts today, it is possible to dismiss Sennett's style of comedy as belonging to films detached from the problems of everyday Americans. The period from 1912 to 1917, however, demonstrated the strength of comedy as a form of mild social protest. Economic success sustained the format and brought a much-needed vitality and diversity from vaudeville to the movies.

In addition to diffusing the sting of social commentary, popular culture eased the tensions between conflicting groups. Listening and enjoying the work of African American or immigrant artists, subconsciously (albeit slowly) reduced the bigotry and racial fear of native-born whites. The needs of the modern family, particularly the "new woman," were explored in everything from advertising to popular songs. Even the "funny papers" provided evidence that married life and parenting had changed. Strips by George MacManus ("Bringing Up Father," 1913) and Jimmy Murphy ("Toots and Casper," 1918) addressed issues of women's suffrage and the war. Cliff Sterrett's "Polly and Her Pals" (1912) pioneered the depiction of the modern girl in ways that prepared the country for such strips as Martin Branner's "Winnie Winkle" (1920, which dealt with a working-class girl), and Chic Young's "Blondie" (which formally premiered in 1930 but was a derivative of strips Young had begun in 1922 with "The Affair of Jane"). Murphy's "Toots" was a fully liberated woman who drove cars, smoked cigarettes, and was deeply interested in popular entertainment such as music and the movies. Cartooning also provided real opportunities for women in the workplace. Edwina Dumm ("Cap Stubbs and Tippie"), for example, was a paid editorial cartoonist for the *Columbus Monitor* years before women were legally allowed to vote.

In a similar vein, popular culture provided a common vocabulary allowing very different members of society to converse. This happened figuratively, as millions of Americans began to watch the same shows, follow the same artists, or dress the same way, as well as literally. American speech was changed as a result of the linguistic fads that developed throughout the decade. The popular Model T was referred to as either a "Tin Lizzie" or "flivver" by everyone from the bank president to the street sweeper. Military terms, sadly more colloquial in the 1910s, such as ace, chow, and civvies came to mean someone who was cool, food, and casual clothes, respectively. Other words—dud, torpedo, and shell-shocked—were completely disassociated from the deadly meaning that gave them such vital importance to those who were "over there."

Coupled with a growing ability to both recognize new populations as well as to converse in a common language, popular culture in the 1910s clarified the challenges of everyday life. Freed from a genteel tradition that often avoided grim realities, the trend toward realism was infused in every mode of cultural expression. Such realism supported the arguments of progressive reformers who wanted to expose the caustic environmental atmosphere (crowded tenements, poor educational opportunities, and vice) that enveloped most of the working poor.

All told, the connections between popular culture and more traditional historical narratives (such as political, economic, and social history) are strong. The expressions of Americans in the 1910s were both the product of and helped to drive change in these other realms. Returning to the question of using a decade as a unit of analysis, we are reminded that history is the study of events that had meaning and consequence to those who lived them. Decades are important because that is how they (and we) track time. Equally, the popular culture that was expressed within the 1910s provided them with a way to make sense of the world around them. So it was then, as it is today.

Timeline of Popular Cultural Events

1910

Death of writers Mark Twain (April 21); O. Henry (June 5); painter Winslow Homer (September 29); and evangelist Mary Baker Eddy (December 3).

Postal Savings Bank established (June 25).

The Mann Act passed (June 25), outlawing the transportation of women across state lines for any "immoral purpose" (i.e., prostitution). Also known as the "White Slavery" Act.

Jack Johnson becomes the first black heavyweight champion of the modern era with a 15th-round knockout of Jim Jeffries (July 4).

Return of Halley's comet passes sun May 18 without disastrous consequences that were predicted.

Former president Theodore Roosevelt delivers his "new nationalism" speech at Osawatomic, Kansas (August 31).

Washington State adopts women's suffrage (November 8).

The Boy Scouts of America is chartered by William D. Boyce (February 8).

The Camp Fire Girls is chartered by Dr. & Mrs. L.H. Gulick (March 17).

Florence Lawrence declared the first genuine movie star as the "Vitagraph Girl."

Architect Frank Lloyd Wright completes work on the Robie House, Chicago, Illinois.

The National City Planning Association founded to help designers better coordinate architectural and landscape designs into American cities.

Morris and Rose Michtom found the Ideal Novelty & Toy Company.

1911

The electric self-starter for automobiles is first demonstrated (February 3).

Triangle Shirtwaist Fire (March 25) kills 146 workers in Lower Manhattan.

Supreme Court orders dissolution of Standard Oil Company (May 15).

Temperance reformer Carry Nation dies (June 6).

Roald Amundsen of Norway bests Robert Scott to the South Pole (December 14).

Edith Wharton publishes *Ethan Frome*.

The magazine *Masses* is rechristened with Max Eastman as editor.

Walter Dill Scott publishes *Influencing Men in Business*, which defines the methods of modern advertising.

Crisco shortening is introduced by Procter & Gamble.

The Children's Bureau is established.

Gordon Craig publishes *The Art of the Theatre*, describing the latest trends in staging and performing live theater.

Irving Berlin publishes hit song "Alexander's Ragtime Band."

The Kewpie doll, created by Rose O'Neill, appears.

The state of Illinois becomes the first to pass laws providing aid to mothers with dependent children.

Frank Lloyd Wright completes Taliesin, his home, studio, and retreat, near Spring Green, Wisconsin.

The Mona Lisa is stolen from the Louvre, in Paris, France.

Pennsylvania Station completed in New York City by architects McKim, Mead, and White.

Galbraith Rodgers takes 82 hours over seven weeks to fly across the United States in an airplane.

The Gideon Organization of Christian Commercial Travelers begins placing more than 60,000 Bibles in hotel rooms.

President William Howard Taft goes on a diet, his weight dropping from 340 to 267 pounds, in an effort to appear "healthy" for the upcoming presidential election.

1912

The ocean liner *Titanic* strikes an iceberg and sinks (April 14–15), killing 1,523 passengers and crew.

The Girl Scouts of America are founded by Daisy Gordon (May 12).

Clara Barton, founder of the American Red Cross, dies (May 15).

Eight-hour labor law extended to all federal employees (June 19).

Poetry, a Magazine of Verse is first published in Chicago, Illinois.

Percy MacKaye's publication of the *Civic Theatre* outlines new possibilities in public theater.

Maria Montessori publishes *The Montessori Childhood Education Method*, describing new techniques in preschool education.

Mack Sennett founds the Keystone Company to produce comedy motion pictures.

Carl Laemmle forms Universal Pictures.

Richard Hellman begins marketing his "Blue Ribbon" mayonnaise.

Will Marion Cook composes and publishes *A Collection of Negro Songs*.

Julia Lathrop named head of the U.S. Children's Bureau.

Novella *Tarzan of the Apes* is published by Edgar Rice Burroughs.

1913

The Armory Show of Modern Art is staged in New York City (February 17).

The Sixteenth Amendment to the Constitution is passed (February 25) allowing for a federal income tax on those making more than $3,000 per year (fewer than 600,000 of 92 million Americans are affected).

J.P. Morgan, financier, dies (March 31).

Congress designates second Sunday in May Mother's Day (May 10).

John D. Rockefeller donates $100 million to create the Rockefeller Foundation (May 14).

Sigmund Freud and Carl Jung engage in speaking tour of the United States.

Vernon and Irene Castle debut in America.

Frank Stella paints *Battle of Lights, Coney Island*.

A third professional baseball league, the Federal League, is founded to compete with the National and American Leagues. The Federal League folds in 1915.

Horace Fletcher creates a national sensation through his "cure" for obesity and stomach ailment, called Fletcherism, which advocates chewing one's food at least 100 times before swallowing.

The Oreo cookie is introduced.

James Reese Europe becomes one of the first African Americans to secure a record deal, with Victor Records.

Clarence Crane introduces a hard candy called the Life Saver. His first flavor is Pep-O-Mint.

A.C. Gilbert begins marketing the erector set.

Amateur Francis Ouimet, the 20-year-old son of a recent immigrant, defeats two British professionals to win the U.S. Golf Association Open, propelling the game of golf into a national sensation.

George Herriman's cartoon strip "Krazy Kat" premieres in the *New York Journal*.

The Mona Lisa is recovered in Florence, Italy, and returned to Paris unharmed.

Willa Cather publishes *O, Pioneers!*

The Height of Buildings Commission of New York City regulates the city's skyscrapers, mandating the famous "setback" design of the decade.

The Woolworth Building is completed in New York City.

1914

Tin Pan Alley songwriters organize the American Society of Composers, Authors, and Publishers (ASCAP) to protect their financial interests through royalty payments (February 13).

World War I begins in Europe (July 28–August 26).

First transcontinental telephone service between New York City and San Francisco is successful (July 29).

Robert Frost publishes *North of Boston.*

The magazine the *New Republic* is first published.

Charlie Chaplin becomes a national star after the release of *Kid Auto Races at Venice*; "Charliemania" sweeps the country.

Tinkertoys are introduced.

W.C. Handy introduces America to the blues with the publication of "The St. Louis Blues."

Women in eleven Western states and the territory of Alaska are allowed to vote in state and local elections.

Construction begins on the Lincoln Memorial, Washington, D.C.

Mary Pickford becomes a national sensation after starring in D.W. Griffith's *Tess of Storm County.*

By the end of the year, it took the Ford Motor Company only 1 hour, 33 minutes to construct a new Model T; the firm produced more than 300,000 vehicles this year.

Margaret Sanger publishes *Family Limitation*, introducing many to the values of birth control.

Thomas D. Eliot publishes *The Juvenile Court and the Community*, a new form of jurisprudence intended specifically for child offenders.

Mary Mills West publishes a booklet titled *Parental Care* for the Children's Bureau, which provides practical advice for mothers.

The Harrison Drug Act is passed to restrict access to narcotics in the United States. The federal government estimates that 4.5 percent of the American public is addicted to drugs.

Gold is discovered in Alaska, leading to the last gold rush in American history.

1915

Panama-Pacific exposition held in San Francisco (February 6–20).

D.W. Griffith releases his landmark film *The Birth of a Nation*.

The *Lusitania* is hit by torpedoes fired from a German U-boat (May 7), killing 1,193 passengers, including 128 Americans.

Telephone calls in New York City reduced to a nickel (July 1).

The *Eastland* steamer capsizes in Chicago killing 841 people (July 24).

The first transcontinental telephone call is placed. Direct wireless service is established between the United States and Japan (September 29).

Booker T. Washington dies (November 14).

Widower President Woodrow Wilson marries widow Edith Bolling Glat at her home in Washington, D.C. (December 18).

Vice President Thomas R. Marshall suggests, "What this country really needs is a good five-cent cigar."

Edgar Lee Masters publishes *Spoon River Anthology*.

Carl Sandburg publishes *Chicago Poems*.

Mary Mills West publishes a second important pamphlet for the Children's Bureau, titled *Infant Care*.

"Jelly Roll" Morton publishes the "Jelly Roll Blues."

R.J. Reynolds creates one of the most successful brand-name advertising campaigns in modern history in introducing Camel cigarettes.

The Victor Talking Machine Company begins selling phonographs to the public.

Ford Motor Company produces its one-millionth Model T.

The state of Nevada passes the first no-fault divorce law, but requires six months of residency in the state.

1916

First permanent annual Rose Bowl football game (January 1).

Writer Henry James dies (February 28).

Louis Brandeis becomes the first Jewish person selected to serve on the U.S. Supreme Court (June 3).

Poet James Whitcomb Riley dies (July 22).

The National Park Service is created (August 25).

The Keating-Owen Child Labor Act (September 1) regulates working conditions for many child laborers and, through penalties to industry, severely limits the employment of children under fourteen years of age.

Margaret Sanger opens the first birth-control clinic in Brooklyn, New York (October 16), and is arrested for distributing "obscene" materials.

Architect Irving Gill completes the Dodge House in Los Angeles.

Piggly-Wiggly, the first self-service grocery store, is founded by Clarence Saunders in Memphis, Tennessee.

D.W. Griffith films and releases the motion picture *Intolerance*.

Georgia O'Keeffe premieres at Alfred Stieglitz's New York Gallery known as 291.

The Provincetown Players move from Cape Cod, Massachusetts, to Greenwich Village, New York, and become the most influential Little Theatre of the decade.

Jeannette Rankin, of Montana, becomes the first women elected to the U.S. Congress.

Norman Rockwell illustrates his first cover for the *Saturday Evening Post*.

Fortune cookies are introduced to the world by David Jung, a Los Angeles noodle maker.

A polio epidemic strikes the United States; more than 29,000 are affected and more than 6,000 die.

1917

The Smith-Hughes Vocational Education Act (February 23) provides federal money to found many of the nation's first professional vocational schools.

Ragtime pioneer Scott Joplin dies (April 1).

The United States enters World War I (April 6).

The Committee on Public Information is created (April 14) to censor news and issue propaganda for the war effort.

The Constitutional amendment prohibiting the manufacture, sale, and use of alcohol passes Congress and is sent to the states for ratification (December 18).

The National Birth Control League, later Planned Parenthood, is created by Margaret Sanger.

The New Orleans group known as the Original Dixieland Jazz Band is "discovered" while playing at Reisenweber's Restaurant, New York City, introducing the town to the jazz sound.

The *Saturday Evening Post* earns more than $17 million in advertising revenues alone.

1918

Historian Henry Brooks Adams (March 27) and famed prize fighter John L. Sullivan (February 2) die.

Dancer Vernon Castle is killed in a plane crash (February 15).

The first airmail flight occurs between Washington, D.C. and New York City (August 12).

A national outbreak of influenza begins in September and kills 588,000 Americans.

World War I ends in an armistice (November 7).

The first installment of Irish writer James Joyce's *Ulysses* is banned by the U.S. Post Office.

The Raggedy Ann doll, created by Johnny Gruelle, is introduced.

1919

The Eighteenth Amendment, prohibiting the manufacture, sale, and consumption of alcohol, is ratified (January 29).

United Artists is founded (April 17) by Charlie Chaplin, D.W. Griffith, Douglas Fairbanks, and Mary Pickford.

Musician James Reese Europe dies (May 9).

Steel magnate and philanthropist Andrew Carnegie dies (August 11).

Severe civil and economic unrest shake the United States. More than 3 million are unemployed while more than 4 million workers participate in 2,665 strikes. Race riots affect 26 cities and 70 lynchings are confirmed.

Sherwood Anderson publishes *Winesburg, Ohio*.

John Reed publishes *Ten Days That Shook the World*.

Eight members of the Chicago White Sox take bribes to throw the 1919 World Series, resulting in the "Black Sox scandal."

The first transoceanic flight is successfully completed.

George "Babe" Ruth hits 29 home runs, shattering the old record. The next year Ruth will hit 54 homers, more than any other single *team* previously.

The Actors' Equity Association goes on strike.

D.W. Griffith releases *Broken Blossoms*.

Peter Paul Halajian introduces the Konabar.

Edward W. Bok retires as editor of the *Ladies' Home Journal*.

Lincoln Logs are introduced.

Part One

Life and Youth During the 1910s

The 1910s

1

Everyday America

For the average American, everyday life seemed to be in a constant state of change during the 1910s. In almost every way—from such mundane issues as eating and dressing to more exciting options in entertainment and travel—people were presented daily with choices that carried certain financial as well as cultural costs. But while the commercialization of everyday life during the 1910s was greater than that in previous decades, it was the challenge to America's traditional sense of itself that was the most significant. In a country that was consciously aware of its rural, democratic, and largely Western European heritage, the growth of an urban, commercial, and multiethnic popular culture generated deep anxieties and tensions in many citizens. In almost all sectors of the population—including immigrants, native-born whites, African Americans, and existing ethnic communities—everyday life became an everyday affirmation of what it meant to be an American.

Driving this modern impulse was the conspicuousness of change. New technologies and old were made more common and more vital to the average American. For example, motion pictures changed from being an interesting, but relatively trivial, pastime to a $735 million industry by 1920, which altered trends in fashion, public opinion, and even conversation. In 1910 458,000 automobiles were registered in the country; by the end of the decade, this number exceeded eight million. While the population grew at a moderate rate (from 92 to 106 million in ten years), the economic output nearly tripled (from $35 billion to $92 billion) and the average salary almost doubled (from $750 to $1,226 per year) which furthered the pace of commercialization.[1]

PROGRESSIVISM

That most Americans were aware of these changes and were actively engaged in deciphering the meaning of them is a key characteristic of the decade. While Progressivism meant different things to different people, it is important to recognize that it was driven by the forces of everyday life, was experienced by all sectors of the American public, and, by extension, was expressed more forcefully at the local level. Progressivism, largely an optimistic faith in the ability of science and rational thought to address the worst abuses of modern life, also advanced traditional racial, ethnic, class, and gender prejudices. The tragedy of the Triangle Shirtwaist Company fire, in 1911, was a good example. While New York City workers and labor organizations had vocally identified the dangerous working conditions, low pay, and health problems associated with the garment industry, it was not until the fire, which started in a container of waste fabric, claimed the lives of 146 people (mostly young women) that reform of the trade became a national issue. Once stirred, however, reformers such as Florence Kelley, Frances Perkins, and Al Smith radically redesigned both the inspection and operation of other work sites in the city, state, and throughout the country. Once under way, Progressive reforms expanded rapidly.

Broadly defined, the Progressive movement sought to accomplish three goals, the first of which was to limit the worst abuses of power associated with the concentration of capital. Reformers, using trust-busting, workplace inspections, and organizing workers, attempted to identify monopolies, in all their guises, and to empower interest groups. Second, Progressives hoped to amplify "social cohesion," or the tendency of Americans to see ourselves collectively, as a nation and a people, rather than as competitive individuals struggling against each other for survival. Jane Addams and Florence Kelley pioneered settlement houses in an effort to lend the talents of educated, active American women to those immigrants (mostly women) who were trapped by the environmental realities of poverty. Kelley and Lillian Wald brought the same ideals to the U.S. Children's Bureau in 1912. Finally, Progressives intended to benefit from the abilities of technical specialists to reorganize and improve society. Seeking efficiency as a means to this end, reformers created a number of institutions, associations, commissions, and other bodies to lend authority to America's professionals. In business, efficiency experts, such as Frederick W. Taylor who published *The Principles of Scientific Management* in 1911, improved management techniques, wages, and working conditions to get the most out of industry, thereby maximizing profits, improving quality, and creating a better work environment. While all three goals of Progressivism addressed specific areas of concern, often reforms were a mixture of these and other factors.

LIFE IN RURAL AND URBAN AMERICA

While the decade saw a rapid increase in the population of urban, industrial laborers (from 16 to 29 million) and a slight decrease in rural workers (from 11 to 10.4 million), the period was one of the few truly affluent times in modern rural America. Dating back to the turn of the century and lasting until the end of World War I, this golden age was nearly national in scope and resulted in the doubling of gross farm income and the tripling of farm values. The reasons for the boom were complex, but it was led by productivity enhancements (such as fertilizers, improved breeds, and machinery), easier access to world markets (which had become a near monopoly with the start of war in Europe), and generally an improvement in farm living conditions (due to the use of automobiles, electricity, and water pumps).

As had been their practice for generations, commercial farmers were active consumers. In addition to capital goods, then, home improvements and entertainment took an increasing share of the farm family's earnings. Local civic improvements, most notably in roads and schools, increased, and greater investments were made in local churches and other private functions. These efforts augmented the Progressive Country Life Movement, which began as a investigation into why, in spite of such good times, Americans were continuing to move from the countryside to the city. A 1909 commission, created by President Theodore Roosevelt, asked farmers to redouble their efforts at efficient agriculture and to develop more cultural pursuits in order to shore up the nation's countryside. Of course, those who did not directly benefit from by commercial farming, such as black tenant farmers and day laborers, were not greatly affected by the reforms. Stagnant rural incomes for African Americans in the South was one of the reasons for the Great Migration north during World War I.

The Country Life Movement carried with it themes that went to the heart of Progressive anxieties during the decade. The fear of lower agricultural productivity was the gravest concern. Not only would rising farm prices make it more difficult for America to trade abroad, but cheap food prices were essential to maintaining prosperity at home. Moreover, a general consensus emerged that rural people were not properly educating their young, preferring instead to use children as unskilled family laborers. An urban curriculum, which included a greater emphasis on the arts and humanities and, especially galling to rural people, physical education, was intended to offset the worst problems of provincialism. Formal vocational training, rather than the practical experience gained on the farm, was initiated with the passage of the Smith-Hughes Act of 1917, and aid for established farmers was granted in 1914 with the Smith-Lever Act.

New York City tenement yard. Courtesy of the Library of Congress.

Urban America was dominated by the millions of working-class people who called the nation's cities home. By the end of the decade, 60
percent of urban dwellers were immigrants and their children, arriving
most recently from Italy, Poland, Greece, and Eastern Europe. Few of
these people had a desire to settle in the countryside—many were fleeing
rural poverty or persecution—and many hoped to earn enough cash to
improve their lot in Europe, where they hoped to return. It was during
the first two decades of the twentieth century that Progressives became
aware of the difficult conditions that these Americans faced in their daily
lives. From unsanitary conditions and less than subsistence wages to
crime and substance abuse, the urban working poor were forced to build
a home within an environment that was nearly inhospitable to sustain-
able living.

Muckraking journalists and reformers lit on the topic of housing reform and sanitation less to benefit the working poor and more as a way
to highlight the corruption of big-city machines. Of course, the profits

generated by book sales and increased magazine circulation helped convince editors to publish these exposés. Even with their confused and often self-defeating agendas, reformers were successful in giving a face, a name, or a story to what had become routine suffering in the modern American city. When, in the 1910s, Progressive arguments suggested that the government had a stake in "saving" urban children or in providing "decent" recreational facilities, more and more of the citizenry found themselves in agreement.

Somewhere between rural and urban lie the suburbs, a growing and extremely significant portion of the modern American demographic. For the most part, suburbs were split between regions that were serviced by regular streetcar (light rail) facilities, populated largely by the native-born working class, and areas that required personal means of transportation, dominated by professionals, owners, and the upper-middle class. Suburbs favored single-family detached homes. With the growth of the automobile industry, higher industrial wages, and cheaper, more functional domestic architecture (such as the bungalow home, which first appeared in the 1910s), the suburbs had become an increasingly popular and affordable option for many by the close of the decade.

PROGRESSIVE POLITICS

For all the impressive and substantial legislation to be passed or adjudicated at the federal level, Progressive politics remained a fundamentally local phenomenon throughout the era. Once problems of urban and rural life were identified, it was the local city or county governments which became the focus of reformers. Such reform took many shapes, from the environmental improvements of housing and sanitation to such far-reaching projects as the City Beautiful campaign, which sought to redesign urban America, infusing parks and playgrounds for the social betterment of its citizens.

Most directly, the turn toward city commissioners, managers, or other administrative officials—directly elected and held responsible by the public—attempted to "rationalize" the operation of city government. By 1917, more than 500 American cities and towns had opted for such a structure. The result was a host of efficiency and social welfare programs that had a direct and immediate effect on everyday life. Saint Louis prosecutor Joseph Folk, who later was elected Missouri's governor, was typical in cleaning up the city council, passing pure food legislation, curbing organized crime, setting standards for industry and labor, and promoting the transfer of ownership of many utilities (such as the streetcars) to municipal governments.

At the state level, leaders such as Wisconsin's Robert La Follette Sr., expanded these initiatives onto the national stage. La Follette, whose

Wilson and Taft in an open carriage arriving at the U.S. Capitol for Wilson's first inauguration. Courtesy of the Library of Congress.

career included stints as a local district attorney, as a U.S. congressman, and as governor, was able to cobble together effective coalitions of voters which included farmers, small businessmen, and industrial workers. From this base, he promoted issues such as tax reform, the direct election of U.S. senators, primary elections, and railroad regulation. He trusted and relied on experts in higher education, beginning a tradition of tapping into these academic resources for public service.

Inevitably, when Progressivism entered the national political stage, it become the central platform for change. In 1912 four candidates vied for the presidency, each claiming a mandate to lead based on their Progressive agenda. While the incumbent president, William Howard Taft, had considerable Progressive credentials—appointing activists such as Philander Knox, Henry L. Stimson, and Charles Evans Hughes to his administration—he was not progressive enough to withstand a challenge from Theodore Roosevelt, Woodrow Wilson, and Socialist Eugene V. Debs. Roosevelt even left the Republican Party and formed the Progressive Bull Moose Party in 1912 based on his vision of New Nationalism (which he premiered on September 1, 1910, in a speech given at Osawatomie, Kansas) calling for a chief executive dedicated to the distribution of social justice.

Woodrow Wilson, the victor in 1912 and again in 1916, was the dominant Progressive force at the national level for most of the decade. While Wilsonian ideals in foreign policy, which are based on self-determination, free trade, and moral rectitude by each nation, have ebbed and flowed over the years, domestic reform under Wilson's watch, termed New Freedom, had an almost equally significant legacy. Wilson wanted government at all levels to be more open and representative and for business to be free from the evils of large, influential corporations. His administration reformed tariffs, advocated a national income tax, extended loans directly to farmers, established the Federal Reserve system and the Federal Trade Commission, passed banking and investment reform, banned child labor and mandated an eight-hour day in many industries, and helped pass the Clayton Antitrust Act, which legalized the formation of unions. Ironically, it was Wilson's cold personal style, his inability to compromise with Congress, and his sense of self-righteousness that doomed many of the policies most closely associated with the president, including the League of Nations. When he retired from public view, following a serious stroke suffered in 1919, he left a number of important new policies but no political coalition to further his causes.

INTEREST GROUPS AND THE "NEW WOMAN"

Just as local political leaders were instrumental in national Progressive policies, so too were interest groups, and not political parties, more influential throughout the 1910s. The formation of associations by professionals and other like-minded individuals was part of the Progressive impulse to rationalize and bureaucratize social organization. While groups like the American Medical Association and the National Association of Manufacturers were clearly created to protect specific economic or specialist niches, other interest groups formed to provide a more powerful voice for traditionally underrepresented populations. Two sectors in particular, African Americans and women, were especially active in the 1910s.

Since emancipation, blacks had struggled in vain to find equality in America. Following the advice of Booker T. Washington, many African Americans were willing to sublimate their own values and traditions, and to suffer quietly the outrage of segregation, in order to achieve economic self-sufficiency. By 1910, however, many black intellectuals, including W.E.B. Du Bois and William Monroe Trotter, were finding it hard to accept the strained arguments of racists. This growing awareness and acceptance of black culture—in the forms of religion, entertainment, and history—paved the way for a monumental meeting at Niagara Falls, Ontario, in 1905, where leaders vowed to develop methods to challenge and overturn the oppression that faced people of color. The Niagara movement began slowly, but in 1909, Du Bois and a number of white supporters founded the National Association for the Advancement of Colored People (NAACP) and a monthly journal titled *Crisis*. Spurred by contemporary events, such as the success of the openly racist film *The Birth of a Nation*, segregation and unfair practices during World War I, the Great Migration north, and the race riots of 1919, the NAACP provided a rallying point for citizens unwilling to continually accept second-class status. The group's focus on constitutional protections, most notably the fourteenth Amendment, set in motion the long history, which today we refer to as the modern civil rights movement.

Equally significant was the emergence of the "New Woman" in American life. This woman, who was increasingly engaged in public life, was both a political force and something of a stereotype. She was portrayed in popular culture as a cigarette smoking, dancing, sexually liberated, free spirit, but the rank-and-file "members" of the movement were more typically average working women and women's club members from around the country. Certainly, demographic trends suggest that something was afoot in the 1910s, as the marriage rate fell and the divorce rate increased, both by sizeable margins. To understand, for example, Margaret Sanger's crusade to provide birth control to working women during the decade as an expression of sexual freedom for the middle-class misses the deeper meaning. Sanger hoped to free all women, but particularly the working poor, from the primary biological factor (i.e., reproduction) that had limited female independence in generations past. Settlement houses added to the number of committed activists, which included Jane Addams, Florence Kelley, and Alice Paul, to name only a few, and expanded the types of reforms into child care, urban pollution, global peace, and consumer protection.

Women's suffrage both reflected and limited the effect of the New Woman on American society. Piloted by a number of different organizations, such as the National American Women's Suffrage Association and, later, the National Women's Party, the suffrage movement created a heightened awareness in American women of their unique circumstances. When, in November, 1910, the state of Washington passed a referendum legalizing women's suffrage (again, reform originated at the local level), it reanimated a movement that had been present in the United States since at least 1848. Over the next two years, California, Arizona, Kansas, and Oregon enacted similar legislation. When Illinois became the first state east of the Mississippi River to pass women's suffrage, it was clear that the movement was more than simply a Western

Suffrage Parade, New York City, May 6, 1912. Courtesy of the Library of Congress.

remedy to a low voter base and that class and ethnic differences were no longer as strong as the desire of a majority of men to enfranchise women.

Still, the push for universal female suffrage, which was finally accomplished in 1920 with the ratification of the Nineteenth Amendment, was not without considerable compromise. "Radicals" like Alice Paul picketed, paraded, and underwent hunger strikes to demand equality based on the promises made in the Constitution. (Paul first proposed the Equal Rights Amendment, in 1923, which was to acknowledge this pledge formally.) More numerous moderates, like Carrie Chapman Catt and Anna Howard Shaw were willing to use less dramatic means and to link women's suffrage to a host of previously unconnected issues, such as the war in Europe, immigration, and nativism, to secure their goals. While, ultimately, the right to vote was earned, the manner in which it was obtained splintered the women's movement after 1920, leaving little but the cliched images of the New Woman intact.

CRIME, VICE, AND PERSECUTION IN EVERYDAY AMERICA

While human nature can be seen as a relative constant, particularly for a period as short as a decade, the ways in which society *defines* criminal behavior can change over time. This was true of the 1910s, when "victimless crimes"—such as prostitution—became intolerable but mob violence proceeded without much opposition. While traditional capital offenses certainly occurred, there was little change of note from previous decades. Probably the lone indicator of more significant problems to come was the rising murder rate, which grew by nearly 50 percent from 4.6 to 6.8 deaths per 100,000 people (in 1990, the figure was 10.2).[2] No doubt, this was aided by the rapid pace of urbanization during the decade.

Prostitution, while illegal, had been a regular feature of everyday life in the United States since its inception. By 1910 reformers increasingly took note of the red-light districts (places where sex was commercialized), seeing them as a sign of the dangers and moral depravity of the inner cities. Vice fighters, such as the prominent Anthony Comstock, tried to save women they believed had been trapped into a life of prostitution by using police crackdowns and by publicizing the men who frequented the brothels. There were many other reasons for these campaigns, ranging from the growing real estate values of the inner city and better wages for female industrial laborers to changes in the family and an increase in premarital sex by America's youth.

The Mann Act, also called the White Slave Traffic Act, passed in 1910, was typical of the Progressives solution to a crime like prostitution. Assuming that all women who engaged in the trade were coerced either by violence or drugs, the act used federal resources to locate and break up the rings which, supposedly, abducted women, ruined them (the assumption was that they were raped repeatedly until they would be too ashamed to return to their homes), and then transported them across state lines to serve as prostitutes. Between 1910 and 1918, more than 2,000 were found guilty of violating the Mann Act.[3]

The combined effect of federal and local enforcement of these new vice laws was not generally beneficial for the women who practiced prostitution. While few brothels were still owned by women in the 1910s (unlike in previous years), the vice districts did allow for some form of protection for the average professional. Following the crackdowns, many of the most noteworthy (i.e., best run and highest paying establishments) brothels were closed by forcing the women out into the streets. Such women were increasingly exposed to greater physical dangers from small-time pimps, corrupt policemen, and the general public as a result.

Understanding alcohol use also underwent a profound change in the 1910s. Abuse of the addictive substance had been a recurring problem in the United States. Aided in part by the vast grain surpluses of the country as well as traditional alcohol use by native-born and immigrant alike, the drink was readily available to both men and women, adults and minors. While efforts to spread temperance (abstinence) and prohibition (legal bans) date back to at least the 1830s, the rise of the Women's Christian Temperance Union and the Anti-Saloon League, as well as the efforts at women's suffrage provided the necessary catalysts for the passage of a number of state-based alcohol reforms. Tinged with nativist fears of immigrant (largely Catholic and Jewish) cultures that did not object to the periodic use of alcohol, reformers were successful in portraying the waste and inefficiency of turning one's wages into inebriation as well as the social costs of family violence, absenteeism, and chronic poverty. Beginning, as usual, at the local and state level, by 1916, twenty-three states and a large number of municipalities had prohibited the manufacture of alcohol. World War I probably provided the final incentive for national action—rationing undermined using scarce resources for the production of alcohol, and many prominent German families were at the fore of the brewing industries—which occurred with the introduction of the Eighteenth Amendment to the U.S. Constitution in December 1917. Ratified two years later and enforced through the Volstead Act, passed in 1920, the "noble experiment" of prohibition made the manufacture, sale, and transportation of intoxicating liquors (more than 0.5 percent alcohol) a federal crime.

The unintended, but predictable, result of such criminalization was that average citizens began to accept greater lawlessness in order to secure a casual glass of beer (the preferred drink of most who broke the law). Because of the complexity and capital-intensive nature of manufacturing, selling, and transporting the now-controlled substance, organized crime was the beneficiary. Most notable were the various syndicates which emerged in the larger cities and the men who rose to prominence, including Frankie Yale in New York City and the notorious "Big Jim" Colosimo, John Torrio, Dion O'Banion, and Al Capone in Chicago. The insidiousness of a simple drink led to real corruption; Chicago's municipal government fell under the influence of such men as "Bathhouse" John Coughlin and "Hinky Dink" Michael Kenna. These, and many others, rationalized away police corruption and gangland murder, expanded racketeering, and rigged elections all for the sake of providing a thirsty public with the "hospitality" they craved. With Prohibition in force until 1933, such criminality has had a deep and lasting effect on many American cities in the modern era.

A willingness to turn a blind eye to outright criminal behavior had a lasting effect on other crimes. Unlike the victimless criminality of alcohol use, violence targeting racial and ethnic groups was widespread throughout the decade. Lynchings in the South and a revival of the Ku Klux Klan (which found greater acceptance in the North) created a tense atmosphere between blacks and whites which frequently escalated to violence. Two infamous examples, race riots in East Saint Louis (1917) and Chicago (1919), resulted in the deaths of hundreds, the destruction of entire black communities, and racial scars that would last generations. Few were ever held to justice—certainly none of the mobs who tortured and hung their hapless victims—but there were unintended benefits from such displays. Following the war, the NAACP was increasingly vocal about the prevalence of summary justice and racial violence. Their rising membership funded a Legal Defense Fund, which was used to eat away at the ambivalence that held a vice grip on America's legal system.

Fear of ethnic radicals, especially socialists, was another excuse to resort to violence. Inspired by exciting new publications, like the *Masses*, and intellectual trends, American socialists were mobilized by the Progressive movement, victories at the ballot box (socialists won hundreds of public offices, including nearly thirty mayoral seats), and a rebirth of labor activism. From journalists to artists to labor leaders, social activists were unforgiving in their attacks on the power of concentrated wealth. Radical strikes in Paterson, New Jersey (1913), and in Ludlow, Colorado (1914), and the success of the Industrial Workers of the World (IWW) led to a conservative backlash. Again, under cover of the war (which many socialists regarded as a struggle between capitalists), civil liberties were summarily suspended as hundreds of people were arrested, beaten, or killed in violence for being "un-American." The Bolshevik Revolution in 1917 unnerved many legislators, who authored a rash of laws aimed as such seditiousness. By 1920 hundreds of people, including presidential candidate Eugene V. Debs, were rounded up, arrested, or deported as a result of the Red Scare. During that same year, Nicola Sacco and Bartolomeo Vanzetti were tried and convicted of first degree murder on evidence that established little more than their immigrant status and radical social views. Their execution, in 1927, was such a travesty of justice that there was a worldwide condemnation of America's seemingly warped sense of justice. Such repression had a profoundly chilling effect on the nascent women's, labor, and civil rights movements in the United States.

THE GREAT WAR

World War I looms large over the narrative of everyday life in the 1910s. While the United States did not formally enter the conflict until April 6, 1917, the thoughts and actions of most Americans remained fixed on Europe after Gavrilo Princip, a Serbian nationalist, assassinated Archduke Franz Ferdinand, the heir to the Austrian empire, on June 28, 1914, precipitating the "Great War" several weeks later. Questions of American neutrality greatly affected the average citizen. The fact that America emerged from nearly 100 years of isolation and committed itself to forming a new world order speaks volumes for the long-lasting effects of this global tragedy. The effects to the United States pale to near insignificance when compared to Europe: the total war dead was about 116,000 for the United States and more than 24 million for Europe; moreover, the governments in Russia, Austria, and Germany were totally destroyed.[4]

When President Wilson called on Americans to be neutral "in thought as well as in action," he knew that the request was an ambitious one. The country was closely linked to English traditions and home to a large number of immigrants from Germany and Ireland (a nation seeking independence from England with a long history of hatred and violence between the two). Still, the public saw through many of the efforts by the belligerents to exploit ethnic hatred and often became more supportive of American isolation as a result. Humanitarian efforts to ease the suffering in Belgium, a neutral country which was mercilessly invaded by the Germans, suggest a general pro-Allied stance by the public, but nothing more. Most believed that the fighting should remain "over there."

By contrast, American businesses (and by extension the American public) were quite deeply involved in the conflict. U.S. banks were increasing loans to England and France who, in turn, would use the money to buy American food and manufactured goods. Orders seemed to expand exponentially in the first few years of the war, and soon the United States had an economic incentive to see that the Allies were capable of repaying their loans. An effective blockade of trade with Germany, as well as a near monopoly in trade to Latin America, expanded the gap. By 1917 U.S. loans to the Allies neared $2.6 billion; less than $35 *million* was extended in credit to Germany and its compatriots.

The effect of U.S. supplies on what was already, by 1915, a war of attrition was not lost on German military leadership. When it became clear that an embargo of war munitions from the United States was ineffective at stopping the flow of munitions to England, the Central powers announced a policy of unrestricted submarine warfare near and around the British Isles. On May 7, 1915, a German submarine sunk the passenger liner *Lusitania* killing 1,153 people, including 128 Americans.[5] That the ship was warned about a potential attack and that it was probably carrying munitions (which quite likely aided in its demise) was ignored by an American public who suddenly personally felt the loss of war. Repeated confrontation with the Germans in 1916 heightened tensions.

During that presidential election year, the question of America's involvement in the war became paramount. Strong isolationist and peace movements, led by Progressives and women's suffrage advocates, helped to propel Wilson to reelection under the banner that "He Kept Us Out of War." Unfortunately, the situation in Europe had deteriorated to the point that the nations at war were willing to risk any gamble in an effort to gain the upper hand. Germany reasoned that a final, massive assault in the spring of 1917 could turn the tide. In order to prevent supplies from reaching the Allies, total submarine warfare would be unleashed on all vessels in the Atlantic. Hoping to win the conflict before an inevitable declaration of war was made by the United States, German official Arthur Zimmermann secretly approached the state of Mexico with an offer of post-war assistance (and a fanciful claim to restore Mexico to its pre-1848 stature) in return for their attack on the United States. Coupled with a more aggressive naval policy, which resulted in the sinking of seven U.S. merchant vessels in March alone, the publication of the Zimmermann Telegram turned the tide against isolation. On April 6, 1917, the United States formally declared war on Germany and its allies.[6]

THE WAR OVER HERE AND OVER THERE

Although more than 24 million Americans registered to serve in the armed forces, and more than 2 million did serve, America's involvement in the conflict was relatively minor. Fresh troops, abundant supplies, and a renewed sense of ultimate victory certainly buoyed the spirits of the Allied powers and had the reverse effect on the Central powers. Still, it was Russia, an ally, that was the first to crack politically (France and Italy were barely maintaining their political stability) while German territory remained unoccupied when the armistice was finally signed. More than 52,000 Americans were killed in action in the short time that they were engaged, nearly the same number as all the servicemen who were killed in Vietnam.

By contrast, the effect of the war at home was considerable. Federal oversight of the economy began almost immediately, with Bernard Baruch heading the War Industries Board, which dictated prices, profits, wages, and supply of materials. Such a heavy hand gave credence to many of the Progressive principles of a "scientific management" of the economy, which would return during the New Deal. The Congress began massive war-bond and rationing programs that directly influenced the everyday lives of the citizenry. The government borrowed nearly $22 billion from the American public through the sale of Liberty bonds. Income tax reform (expanding the number of those who were required to pay), a federal police force (the FBI [Federal Bureau of Investigation], which was founded in 1917), and an active propaganda division (Committee on Public Information, which distributed more than 75 million pamphlets throughout the war) were examples of how the government expanded its role in and helped to standardize modern American life. While it is impossible to pinpoint the exact birth of the bureaucratic state in the United States, its conception most certainly occurred during World War I.

More directly, the lives of women and certain minorities were greatly changed. Benefiting from wartime industrialization, blacks, Mexican Americans, and women all found greater employment opportunities after 1917. Many relocated to Northern industrial cities in an effort to take full advantage of the favorable circumstances. During the Great Migration, more than 500,000 African Americans left the rural South. Women earned the right to vote largely as a result of their support of the administration during the war. Even moderate labor unions, like the American Federal of Labor (AFL), benefited by the sense of common cause that was generated in the United States. On the other hand, those who opposed the war, including the IWW, were treated harshly and summarily by the same government. Issues such as an eight-hour workday, a minimum wage, and collective bargaining were resolved by those willing to support the war effort.

Given the enormity of World War I, the peace process accomplished very little. When the exhausted nations agreed to an armistice on November 11, 1918, they had little notion of how to deal with the devastation wrought by the war and no idea of how to deal with the Bolsheviks in the newly christened Soviet Union. Wilson's proposal was to reshape international politics to "make the world safe for democracy." Such high ideals (intentionally) contrasted sharply with V.I. Lenin's call for a worldwide social and economic revolution but did little to quell Allied bitterness over the war. The Wilsonian doctrine—calling for self-determination, free speech, an international body of arbitration, and new ethnic nations in Europe—remained U.S. policy for much of the twentieth century, but it could not prevent a punitive peace treaty from alienating and pauperizing Germany. The result was the rise to power of Adolf Hitler only fourteen years later.

At home, peace forced Americans radically to retool their economy. Layoffs and shrinking profits led to a series of bitter strikes which affected almost a fifth of the nation's workers in 1919. In Seattle, New York, and Boston, notable strikes shut down key segments of the economy, even entire cities, for long periods of time. The rising fear of bolshevism led to a Red Scare which withdrew many of the gains in civil liberties that had been secured by the Progressives. Racial and ethnic violence erupted across the country. When Warren G. Harding called for a "return to normalcy" in the 1920 presidential election, he reflected the fear that something had been lost in America as a result of America's experiences in the war.

CONCLUSION

Harding's wish was never granted. In almost every way, the United States was a different country by the close of the decade. Certainly, much of the immediate cause was the European war, but the changes that occurred throughout the decade were only accelerated as a result of the war. The pressure on the country to address issues such as women's rights and the expanding ethnic and racial consciousness was already building, as seen by many examples of change in popular culture throughout the decade. While the 1920s would prove to be an era during which conservative, even reactionary, forces held the upper hand, the changes could not be stopped. In the 1910s Americans redefined themselves as a people and as a nation. There was no turning back.

2

World of Youth

By the close of the first decade of the twentieth century, officials within the federal government came to believe what child welfare workers had known for decades: there were fundamental problems with the way in which youth were treated in modern American society. Unable to protect themselves through the courts, children proved to be particularly vulnerable to the vast social and economic changes that swept through the United States during the Gilded Age and Progressive Era. President Theodore Roosevelt, in keeping with his forceful and often grandiose pronouncements, told the 216 attendees of the First White House Conference on the Care of Dependent Children, "The problem of the dependent child is acute; it is large; it is national."[1] The conference, convened in Washington, D.C., in January 1909, ushered in a ten-year period termed the Decade of the Child by many activists and later historians. During this energetic, optimistic, and generally inventive era, lawmakers and reformers took on such pivotal issues as school reform, dependent child care, infant care, child labor laws, and juvenile delinquency, to name only a few, which fundamentally altered the nature of youth in America.

Yet in examining *how* the United States defined and probed solutions to solve its problems, and not simply noting that they were *aware* that challenges existed, we are better able to understand what Americans in the 1910s perceived as the essential issues. For example, industrial pollution is clearly a concern for all citizens today. Do we regard the leading cause of this problem as being corporate greed, our limited ability to control the chemical by-products of production, or a seemingly insatiable consumer desire? If, as most would argue, it is a combination of these and other causes, which do we reform first? Where do public and private rights collide? During the 1910s, Americans from across the political, economic, and regional spectrum forwarded what they believed were solutions to the problems of youth.

The scope of reform was seemingly as wide as the nation's landscape. At root, these efforts hoped to question, describe, and improve upon many of the country's most basic institutions. For example, what role existed for the family in the new age? Was this traditional structure the best place for a child if the family proved incapable of economic survival? Who, ultimately, had the right to interfere in the family, regardless of its economic status? When was intervention warranted? Was there a special role to be played by mothers in the development of the child? Were there "good" and "bad" mothers and, if so, how did one tell the difference? Would science and, more important, experts in the fields of sociology, psychology, and child development have a prominent voice in drafting policy to rectify problems, or should this function remain within a more democratic structure? Plainly, definitions of normal child development loomed large in the proposed solutions. Normative values worked to devalue many racial, ethnic, and regional traditions in ways that left many children with even less protection, control, or sense of place in America. When added to the growing contention between local and federal authorities, or even whether the state had the right to regulate society and business, it is a wonder that any significant change at all occurred during the 1910s.

It is important to remember that it was the adult population, and not the children themselves, who researched, reported on, and reformed youth culture. Why, in an age that witnessed revolutionary social change, such as the birth of the modern consumer culture and the expansion of women's role in public society, did the subject of child dependency become so important? Jane Addams, an activist most noted for her work with settlement houses, suggested that it was the "Spirit of Youth," which merited such close attention by the nation. She regarded "youth's iridescent dreams" for social betterment and progress as a reflection of the broader goals of the Progressive movement. If children could be swept away by the isolation, hopelessness, and decay of modern living, then there was little chance for improvement on less emotionally compelling issues such as an eight-hour workday or tariff reform. To Progressives like Addams, the stakes for the country were much greater than youth alienation or petty violence. After attending Roosevelt's conference, Addams wrote in 1910 that it was the duty of all Americans to "moralize" upon child welfare, "to discipline it, to make it operative upon the life of the city." The penalty for not doing this, she concluded, was tantamount to national suicide, "for it is but too true that Democracy ... no longer stirs the blood of the American youth, and that the real enthusiasm for self-government must be found among the groups of young immigrants who bring over with every ship a new cargo of democratic aspirations."[2]

BEING YOUNG

When using the word "youth," it is well to remember that the term refers to all minors or those whom the state defines as having limited legal rights and responsibilities. Usually, states expanded these rights and responsibilities for citizens who were 18 to 21 years of age or older, as minors became legal adults. There clearly were vast differences between the needs and desires of youths depending on where they might fall along the spectrum from newborn to legal adult. Exceptions are the rule, as is clear when one considers that many young children routinely worked outside the home while many young adults continued to attend school or to live at home. Still, the divisions are useful because they outline the type and scope of reform that occurred during the decade.

While claiming that youths in the 1910s lived lives that were nasty, brutish, and short would be an overstatement, it is certainly true that the formative years of many Americans were less guarded and more imperiled than today. By 1910 more than 140 infants per 1,000 died within their first year of life. Those who survived could expect to live for an average of 50 years. Today, fewer than 14 infants per 1,000 perish at birth, and the average life span has expanded to about 73 years. Despite these shocking comparisons, children then were still significantly healthier, on average, than those reflected in the mortality figures reported during the late nineteenth century, when nearly one in four infants died.[3] These improved odds led to stronger emotional ties between infants and parents, which would combine with a resurgent and assertive middle-class sensibility in new and powerful ways in the 1910s.

As expected, race, class, region, and ethnicity were all key factors in the quality of life led by various young Americans. Rural African American children could expect to live lives of hard work and poverty, as had their parents before them, with little or no assistance from the state. It was certainly a good thing that the rural South provided strong African American communities and extended family ties because little attention was paid by white America. As Booker T. Washington reported, only 301 of Alabama's 900,000 black children received any form of state aid by 1910. He went on to marvel that the state of Massachusetts alone outspent every state in the South *combined* for the care of their dependent, overwhelmingly white, children.[4] Given the economic importance of these children to the regional economy, Southern legislators' thrift seems misplaced.

Adventuresome reporters who actually traveled to the region, such as the renowned muckraker Lewis Hine, saw the universal need for child labor to tend for and harvest the agricultural produce. Hine wrote in 1914 that children as young as four years old worked "six days in the week, five months in the year, under a relentless sun." One four-year-old "pick[ed] eight pounds [of cotton] a day when I saw her," while her sister, one year older, collected more than "thirty pounds a day."[5] The migration of blacks to the North in search of jobs and greater social freedom failed to alleviate these children's burdens. While their parents were paid better wages, thereby negating the need for constant child labor, children no longer benefited from the welfare provided by an extended family. According to Washington, after "the negro is brought into contact with an artificial civilization and newer surroundings, as he leaves his normal, regular, and best life in the South . . . and comes into contact with the artificial life of the city . . . [the child's] condition is changed" and problems arise.[6] While his accommodationist theories worked no better at generating reform, Washington understood that the corrosive effects of urbanization would be hard felt by the ostracized African American community and, doubly so, by their children.[7]

Children from ethnic and other regional communities suffered equally harsh circumstances if their parents were recent arrivals to the United States or if they worked as wage laborers. For example, on the west side of New York City, known as "Hell's Kitchen," a progression of poor ethnic and racial tenants led to overcrowding, filthy living conditions, persistent substance abuse, and crime within the community. By the 1910s, the Irish were there and suffered the most from the neglect of tenement owners and poor sanitation. Children were easy prey for the indifference and hopelessness that bred in this slum. As one middle-class reformer remarked, showing the class biases that were common, when the children got sick their

mothers could not afford doctors and seemed too lackadaisical to carry their babies to the nearby clinics and too lazy or too indifferent to carry out the instructions you might give them. I do not mean that they were callous when their babies died. Then they cried like mothers, for a change. They were just horribly fatalistic about it while it was going on. Babies always died in the summer and there was no point in trying to do anything about it.[8]

Similar conditions and responses were recorded in most major industrial regions throughout the United States during the decade.

It was not only the urban child who suffered, but those in rural regions as well. Farm work for both boys and girls was a constant. Often the tasks were hazardous. Moreover, contrary to the popular notion of the robust and healthy farm lifestyle, rural life for economically marginal families often resulted in many of the same conditions experienced by their urban cousins. When, in 1920, a study of 149 Appalachian children was released, it showed that less than a quarter of them had adequate diets and that half still obtained their water from streams which also served as communal sewers.[9] Clearly, region, race, and ethnicity had dramatic and often negative consequences for many youths.

SEEING THE CHILD

When these conditions were made public, the impulse for Progressive reform was aroused. While clearly influenced by racial, class, and nationalistic biases, the middle-class axioms of morality and progress were the dominant themes of the mission. Their moral evaluations were guided by religious assumptions, which supported pronouncements of "good" and "bad" social behavior. Seeking greater control over "bad" behavior, many Progressives justified their efforts through the dominant Protestant ethics. Progress, as the word implies, looked to science, technology, higher education (the so-called experts), and especially the controlling, rational oversight of a large bureaucracy to design institutional solutions that would rectify society's ills. The outrage over child neglect expressed by many reformers alternated between these two governing concepts which, in turn, limited their ability to find resolutions to the thorny problems of modernization.

Still, the Progressives' obvious empathy for the suffering of others should not be overlooked. Drawing upon a deep historical respect for commonwealth and republicanism in American society, reformers were able to articulate the clear choices demanded of a modern citizenry. Again, Jane Addams effectively summarized this position when she wrote that we "may listen to the young voices rising clear above the roar of industrialism and the prudent councils of commerce, or we may become hypnotized by the sudden new emphasis placed upon wealth and power, and forget the supremacy of spiritual forces in men's affairs."[10] Reformers like Addams demanded accountability. Improved institutional care for children, more programs to aid and strengthen the family, and greater sensitivity by the courts, governmental agencies, and the professions to environmental problems must accompany industrial growth and urban sophistication. Accordingly, experts in the fields of education, law, child psychology, and medicine—the disciples of progress, control, science, and bureaucracy—were called upon to address these challenges.

The reason that Progressive reform was successfully directed toward the problems of youths was that many prevailing notions of childhood had changed. Echoing Addams' romantic notions of "youth's iridescent dreams," writer and intellectual Randolph Bourne detected a newfound respect for the energy and adventurousness of youth. According to the essayist, "nothing torments youth so much" as to have their views and opinions disregarded by adults "justified on the ground of experience." Experience, to Bourne and the young adults of the decade, was nothing more that "a slow accretion of inhibitions, a learning, at its best, not to do again something which ought not to have been done in the first place." The generation gap between the young and old, and the seemingly blatant disregard for the problems of youths by adults, insulted and infuriated many Progressives like Bourne, who questioned whether the middle-aged "acquired any impartiality or objectivity of outlook, [or] have any better standards for judging life. Their ideas are wrong, and grow progressively more wrong as they become older. Youth, therefore, has no right to be humble." While the confidence and affirmative aggressiveness of this 1912 essay has an uncanny contemporary feel about it, the writing reflects the profound changes that were in the air in the 1910s.[11]

With such creativity it is not surprising that the movement was scattered and, ironically, lacked an effective and unified rational goal. While the quality of life for many dependent children improved and many others gained a greater appreciation for the environmental causes of poverty, crime, and self-destructive behavior in youth, the piecemeal pattern of Progressive reform generated many programs but few clear objectives for the American public. Infant care was confronted by the newly formed Children's Bureau, child labor and educational laws were enacted through the Labor Department, and the court systems were reformed locally. Each of these were influenced by the strident leadership and initiative of women who regarded child welfare as a special responsibility.

YOUTH AND WAR

Ironically, while World War I had little direct effect upon American youth, it largely destroyed the progressive impulse that had led to so many changes. As historians Arthur Link and Richard McCormick noted, progressivism was "easily channeled into military actions." When the "war to end all wars" brought disillusionment instead of a new world order, "the balance tipped against organized, ameliorative reform. A progressive movement which had been merely divided became embattled."[12] The relative short duration of the war also meant that deep structural social changes were not likely to develop by the end of the decade.

Military training was of growing importance for young adults. The idea of training a generation that had been raised to treasure their youthful innocence to become an implement of death and destruction proved to be problematic. George Creel, who directed the Committee on Public

Information during the war, promoted military activity as a measure of a teen's maturity. Almost as a ritual of manhood, military training was to Creel a way for young men to "earn their stripes" as full-fledged American citizens. Much as Frederick Jackson Turner suggested in 1893 that the frontier reinvented American democracy, so too did Creel portray the war as a way to reinvigorate the meaning of being a man. He held that the "very American privilege of fighting for an individual place in the sun" supported the "equally American duty of fighting to maintain the collective rights of all American citizens. Education develops individuality; military education develops nationality."[13] Still, the changing appreciation of the rights and duties of youth during the decade made Creel's sentiment far from unanimous. In 1918, when discussing a proposal to raise the draft eligibility age from 18 to 21 (voting age), Senator James K. Vardaman of Mississippi defended a widespread belief that the young needed this time to develop fully. He concluded, "There are enough older men who under the draft system can be selected—men capable of rendering efficient service in the Army, who have had their 'swing around the circle'—and if they happen to be killed they have not lost as much as a boy who has had no chance at all"[14] at life.

More typical wartime activities by children included the many service-based associations that sprang up throughout the country. Progressives and children alike warmed to President Woodrow Wilson's call to "make the world safe for democracy." For example, a Des Moines, Iowa, newspaper editor and children's book writer, Emilie Blackmore Stapp, founded a club based on her characters developed in the book *The Trail of the Go-Hawks* (1908). Combining Native American themes with a growing appreciation for the vigor of outdoor living, Stapp started her mixed-gender clubs in 1914 based on the idea that children should do at least one good deed per day. More than 1,000 children joined local "Go-Hawk" chapters in the first year alone. The progressive impulse to reform through collective action was ingrained in the movement. During the war "Go-Hawk tribes" collected more than a million pennies, organized mostly by the children, to provide relief for orphans in Belgium.

More prominent was the founding and growth of the Boy Scouts of America. Introduced first in England, the Scouts were chartered in the United States in 1910. The standardized rules, fixed organization, uniforms, and age limits (12 to 18) allowed many similar and existing institutions easy access to the Boy Scouts of America. For example, Ernest Thompson Seton, who formed an association in Connecticut much like the Go-Hawks, merged his institution with the Scouts, bringing in more than 200,000 members. The Scout movement, which expanded to include girls with the founding of the Camp Fire Girls, by Luther and Charlotte Gulick in 1910, and the Girl Scouts of America in 1912 by Juliette Gordon Lowe, used the gang instinct in teens to build comradery between the middle- and working-class children who made up the bulk of the members. Again, the war did little to change these institutions. Rather, men such as Creel used the organizations (and the revived notion that militarism is analogous to manhood) to sell war bonds and boost morale at home during the conflict.

EDUCATION

The war had little lasting effect on the traditional assumptions regarding children in American society but a great effect on educational reforms. As one historian noted, "Never was more expected of American schools"[15] than during the 1910s. Increasingly, Progressive educators, legislators, and most important, parents and voters poured resources and meaning into the primary institution for the child's long-range development. The investment in kindergartens, grade schools, and high schools throughout the decade was phenomenal. Teachers were hired at an accelerated rate. At the start of the century, the nation's 21.4 million school-age children were being served by 423,000 educators; ten years later, 24.2 million children were being taught by 523,200 teachers (an increase of nearly 24 percent); by 1920, 27.7 million students were being instructed by 679,500. To put it another way, enough new teachers were hired so that the student-to-teacher ratio fell by ten in twenty years.[16]

Financially, these increases translated into a doubling of the money spent on children's education. The total amount expended for education at the start of the decade, the 1909–1910 school year, was approximately $426.25 million; by the 1919–1920 session, this figure exceeded one billion dollars. Per capita spending rose from $4.64 to $9.80 per student. Nor were these investments solely in salaries. By 1920 more than 14,000 high schools were in operation compared to 6,000 only twenty years earlier. These contributions soon paid dividends. The number of high school graduates increased to nearly a fifth of all 17-year-olds, and fully 61.6 percent of those eligible for high school were attending classes by the end of the decade.[17]

What did this explosion in public financing and higher education mean for young people? Clearly, reformers wanted to do away with what they saw as inefficient and outdated programs. For example, the notion of the one-room schoolhouse that served all children equally, regardless of age or developmental needs, was a thing of the past. Many school districts formerly independent of centralized control, were pressured to consolidate their students into age-appropriate learning centers. The hiring of teachers by local school boards was now regarded by many as disorganized at best and corrupt at worst. Many instructors doubtlessly did not belong in the classroom. When school reform advocate Helen Todd asked 500 working-class children, in 1909, if they would want to continue to attend school if their families were wealthy enough so that they did not have to work, 412 responded that they preferred to work in the factory. One wrote, "What ye learn in school ain't no good. Ye git paid just as much in the factory if ye never was there." More than half reported that they liked the factory better than school because they were not hit at the job. In the future, educators were required to show credentials, approved by Progressive reformers, such as a college degree, before they were given access to youths. Finally, curricular reforms sought to expand the scope of education beyond the traditional needs of spelling, grammar, basic mathematics, and reading.[18]

These reforms, while complex and multifaceted, certainly demonstrate that the nature of schooling in America had undergone a transformation. In the past the school was largely a local, community institution, but by 1920 children's education had emerged as an issue of national importance. Where previous institutions might defer to the wishes of parents, who might want their children to work in the fields or factories, the model schools of the Progressive Era demanded that each child master a set of basic education aptitudes before being allowed to sell their skills in the open marketplace. The fact that the urban school system was now home to a growing population of immigrant children led impetus to these reforms, as educators claimed to be providing the necessary social skills needed to survive and participate as "good" Americans.

Serving as the point man for setting the agenda for reform was philosopher and professor of education John Dewey. First at the University of Chicago and later at Columbia University in New York City, Dewey advocated a school system that created miniature versions of society (what he termed "embryotic communities") in which citizens were asked to think creatively rather than by rules and force. Accordingly, Dewey imagined classrooms that discarded rote learning and structure for interaction and creativity. Building on an intellectual tradition, which included the important work of Joseph Mayer Rice, who published *The Public School System of the United States* in 1893, Dewey advocated the training of professional educators armed with the latest tools and modern classrooms. He wrote that "the center of gravity" of good education "is outside the child. It is in the teacher, the text-book, anywhere and everywhere you please except in the immediate instincts and activities of the child himself."[19] Dewey and his allies in higher education undermined the traditional assumptions of social Darwinism (that children of the poor were mentally inferior to those of economically successful parents) by suggesting that the environment of education was as critical, if not more, as the subject matter. While no doubt the focus on basic English, history, and math skills, as well as rewards for punctuality, obedience, and precision, convinced many native-born, middle-class citizens of the benefits of better socialization, the belief that school provided an opportunity for social renewal was a monumental change in the minds of most Americans.

By 1910 Dewey was joined by powerful interest groups, including the NAACP, many labor leaders, Social Gospel Progressives (such as Jane Addams), farm groups (such as the National Patrons of Husbandry), and business groups (such as the National Association of Manufacturers), in pressing for change. While reform, such as compulsory education laws, was widespread, there is little evidence to suggest that life for the average child was immediately altered in any substantial way. More obvious was the institutional organization that had been effected by the close of the decade. For example, in Chicago, Ella Flagg Young changed both the content and structure of the city's public school system. Trained with Dewey's "New Education" methods, Young became superintendent of the Chicago schools in 1909 and enacted sweeping reforms throughout the 1910s. Increasing the organization and reporting structure of each school, Young also split each district into elementary, junior, and senior high schools, and founded a number of junior colleges. She introduced the practice of standardized testing to evaluate student progress, revised the curriculum of each grade, kept detailed records of each student, and sought ways to meet the needs of exceptional children.

It would be wrong, however, to conclude that the educational reforms of the era were simply administrative in nature. In two key areas—preschool and vocational training—reforms clearly changed the lives of the youths enrolled. Kindergartens, which originated in Germany in the late nineteenth century, spread throughout the United States largely as a result of the efforts made by local settlement workers. By the end of the 1910s, kindergartens were well established throughout the country, providing many working mothers with safe and developmentally rich environments for their preschoolers. The changing perception that young children were not barbarians but merely unsocialized members of society was greatly advanced by the writing of Maria Montessori. Championing a child-centered learning environment termed the Montessori Childhood Education Method, she showed in her 1912 book that learning was a fun experience for children and that, properly structured, education was easiest among the very young because of their desire to understand the world around them. Aided by sympathetic treatments of her schools in the most popular ladies magazines, Montessori schools bloomed in communities across the United States throughout the decade.

Vocational training also developed in the 1910s. For young men, skills taught in vocational schools ranged from carpentry and metal trades to machine tools and repair. For girls, training provided opportunities to master clerical skills such as typing and bookkeeping as well as home economic expertise which was no longer being passed along by their busy working mothers. While the number of vocational students was far

less than the number of grade-schoolers, these institutions of higher education lent credence to the idea that schools prepared students for the
real, workaday world. In Illinois, the state legislature debated the Coo-
ley Bill, which would have established a dual system of vocational and
general education that was favored by many business leaders. The passage of the federal Smith-Hughes Vocational Education Act in 1917 provided money to found many of the nation's first professional vocational
schools.

Yet opinions differed over the intended use of vocational training.
While providing needed skills for those uninterested in other forms of
higher education, clearly some students were shepherded into vocational
training due to class, racial, or ethnic categorizations established by Progressive reformers. School reform in general suffered from a similar critique. The movement throughout the decade was dominated by white,
male, Protestant, native-born professionals. Historian David Tyack,
among others, has suggested that the school consolidation and administrative centralization served to combat the fear of these professionals
of their diminishing social control and their disdain for the electorate
and the political machines that previously had controlled the schools.
According to Tyack, "By 1913, the new set of experts had become quite
cohesive and well linked with influential lay centralizers." The corporate
model chosen by reformers was therefore no accident.[20]

These biases, which were expressed in a number of ways, had long-
term consequences for the children being educated. For example, John
Dewey took a prominent role in spreading the use of standardized tests
to evaluate student progress. While intending to avoid what we today
call "social promotion," or the practice of advancing pupils through the
grades regardless of the skills mastered, it is highly questionable as to
what these standardized tests, in fact, measured. Based on the model
provided by French psychologists Alfred Binet and Théodore Simon,
who developed Intelligence Quotient or IQ tests in the nineteenth century (an ascending scale of difficult problems graded against a norm of
intelligence levels), Dewey and others at Columbia's Teachers College,
Stanford University, and the University of Chicago originated more than
100 similar evaluations for a variety of subjects and grade levels by 1919.
Unfortunately, professionals' understanding of the results of these tests
lagged behind the ability to create and administer them. Are knowledge
and critical thinking really measurable quantities? Did one need to learn
certain skills at a certain point in life to ensure future success? Standardized tests assumed that the answer to both of these questions was an
unqualified "yes," and adherents to the method unhesitatingly labeled
students successes or failures based on their "scientific results." Low
scores indicated to Progressives a moral failing on the part of the student;
not a need for educators to improve their teaching skills.

Regional and racial biases in education were also obvious during the decade. The states of the former Confederacy were aggressive in constructing new schools and changing to the new methods. Building upon administrative protocols established by the 1901 Southern Education Board, Southern grade schools and high schools made rapid and much needed progress in the 1910s. In conjunction with leading businesses, the states of North Carolina, Florida, South Carolina, and Georgia almost completely remade their grade school and high school systems. Unfortunately, these reforms were limited to white students. Jim Crow laws, establishing "separate but equal" facilities, ensured that African Americans continued to lose control over the education of their young. Nor did blacks fare much better when they migrated out of the South. The combination of inherently poor schools, racism, and standardized tests led many educators to create additional institutional barriers to their success. A New York social investigator concluded, in 1915, that "there was a general belief among school principals, social workers, and colored clergymen that the restrictions of industrial opportunities because of their race was sapping the ambition of the colored boys and girls, and that they were not making the effort put out by their parents and grandparents to secure an education." A 1921 study of 393 black men in San Francisco found that almost all worked at unskilled jobs, including the nearly 20 percent who had completed high school and the nearly 10 percent with college degrees.[21] Adding to the problem was a general lack of black men and women hired to counsel and teach youths, a problem that would exist well into the 1940s. The work begun in 1912 by philanthropists such as Julius Rosenwald, an executive at Sears, Roebuck and Company, to channel funds directly into the rural South for the construction of schools, and the strong support by accomodationist educators like Booker T. Washington, were some of the few bright spots in a generally bleak outlook for the African American youths of the era.

All told, for American students, the era was both a starting point for modern reforms and a culmination of past biases. Some of the changes started during the 1910s were long-lasting—such as the willingness to improve the curriculum to meet the needs of everyday life—others were more fleeting. The holistic approach of Progressives seeking to effect a change in the environment of youths is reflected in a report issued in 1918 by the National Education Association. Titled "Cardinal Principles of Secondary Education," it concluded that the five goals of education were to improve the health of the student, to give command of the "fundamental processes" (e.g., reading, math), to support citizenship, to promote ethics, and to encourage "worthy home membership."[22] Clearly these last three were based on norms established by the reformers.

DEPENDENCY, INSTITUTIONS, AND "CHILD SAVING"

While the institutional changes to schools certainly affected American youth, more subtle shifts in the definition of child dependency occurred throughout the decade. The fact that children were dependent (according to Webster, someone is dependent if they are influenced, controlled, or their actions are determined by someone else) was not new. Rather, it was an appreciation for the level and type of influence that children were subjected to that became of critical importance to reformers. Fundamental to this transformation was the increased frequency with which Americans came to see the problem before them. Muckraking photojournalists, such as Jacob Riis and Lewis Hine, and sociologists and activists, including Robert Hunter, Florence Kelley, and Jane Addams, put before the nation the abysmal environmental conditions facing most youths in the modern era. By 1910 more than 110,000 children were reportedly housed in 1,151 institutions across the United States; most of these children were classified as orphans, foundlings, homeless, neglected, or indigent. In addition, at least 120,000 infants lived in the streets with their destitute families. Historian LeRoy Ashby contends that these appalling figures underestimated reality by nearly a factor of ten. The fact that orphans of U.S. veterans were treated as paupers and placed in almshouses or that factory owners routinely refused to install safety equipment as long as healthy, full-bodied children were available to replace those who had fallen simply was not registered by many middle-class Americans until activists publicized these conditions.[23]

Once aroused, however, reformers were quick to examine the assumptions of institutional care in both new and traditional ways. While opposed by many existing parochial and state agencies charged with the care of dependent children, Progressives were successful in passing legislation that ensured licensing, provided periodic state inspections, and set standards of conditions and performance for many child agencies. Central to these efforts was the overarching belief that the best place for the child was in the home. As a result, efforts focused on providing assistance and guidance for families in need as well as in reforming or creating new organizations, which reflected the family model. In many ways, it was the "problem of the child" that first led Americans to believe that the state *could* play an active and beneficial role in alleviating the economic, environmental, and social obstacles that developed in this dynamic capitalist country.

The White House Conference on Dependent Children announced the arrival of coordinated efforts to bring about such change. President Roosevelt invited 216 of the nation's most prominent child welfare workers and social activists for two days of discussion, reflection, and proposals. The basic findings of the conference set the trajectory of reform for the subsequent decade. They concluded that, first, home life was the "supreme institution of civilization," and they vowed to make public foundations more like the home as well as to work to keep the child within their natural families as long as possible. Second, the group suggested that the state provide resources for needy mothers to care properly for their children at home—an important first step in developing a modern welfare state in this country. Of course, defining those who were truly needy would prove to be problematic.

The advocacy by the White House unleashed a torrent of activity in many states. For example, in 1914, the New York State Commission on Relief for Widowed Mothers set a policy agenda that was remarkably consistent with the findings in Washington. The state held that the mother was the "best guardian of her children," that poverty was too big a problem for private philanthropy alone, that no woman could be "both the home-maker and the bread-winner of her family," that prevention and intervention were better than reacting to emergencies, and that "[n]ormal family life is the foundation of the State, and its conservation an inherent duty of government." Ideas such as these soon turned to substantial policies and actions throughout the nation. While hampered by courts unsympathetic to state activity, by 1931 only the states of South Carolina, Georgia, New Mexico, and Alabama lacked formal mothers' aid or child-saving welfare agencies.[24]

While the notion of direct financial support for widowed mothers is clear, the idea of "child saving" may be less apparent to modern readers. As the term implies, child saving appealed to the Progressive concept of service, efficiency, and civic responsibility. Decent and moral citizens were required to stand up against corrupting influences when it came to the future generation of American citizens. From this perspective, then, the fragile nature of the child was reinforced, providing even greater impetus for early detection and intervention—some may say interference—by the state. If a child was like a sponge, absorbing from his or her environment both the good and bad qualities that life and society had to offer, were not those who knew better *compelled* to step in when danger loomed?

Activist Mary McDowell believed so. She wrote about the ethnic and working-class neighborhood known as the "back of the yards" in Chicago, around 1910, and concluded that each child was unique, "each new comer is loved and is an ever new object of interest." Yet an interesting dynamic was observed by McDowell: it was the children of immigrant laborers, and not the adults, who more readily turned to criminal or antisocial behavior. She believed this happened because the child more quickly understood the United States, more quickly spoke the language, and more quickly grasped the local customs. The child became "the authority" in the immigrant, working-class family. Stripped of parental controls and moral reasoning, children came to assume that violence and crime were logical responses to the adversity surrounding them. By contrast, "parents are displaced because they are helpless, and must trust the children." It is here that reformers believed they were most needed. If "children's ideals are formed by the teachers, the politicians and often the saloonkeepers" and if the immigrant parents' ideals are "discredited . . . [as] old fashioned," then policies need to be developed to support and nurture the family and local community as a means of supporting the child. Said another way, state and local social services were needed *for the parents* if the child were to be protected by a moral society.[25]

The formation of social service agencies, which are special programs intended to change the environmental conditions at the source of many problems, was based on just such logic. Powered by the special consideration now paid to child development issues, as well as the newfound activism of women's clubs throughout many American cities, agencies worked to link current trends in education, health, and hygiene with normative concepts of motherhood. As early as 1897, Alice McLellan Birney and Phoebe Apperson Hearst had founded the National Congress of Mothers to instruct women on proper child-rearing techniques. By 1915 more than 60,000 local chapters (expanding to more than 190,000 by the end of the decade) distributed pamphlets and books in an effort to educate poor mothers. Again, it is important to recognize the strong class and religious biases imbedded in these activities.[26]

THE CHILDREN'S BUREAU

By far, the most important welfare service established during the decade was the U.S. Children's Bureau. Combining the efforts of settlement workers and activists, such as Lillian Wald and Florence Kelley, the idea for a national clearinghouse of information on child welfare was presented to President Roosevelt in 1906 and was a leading reason for his calling the 1909 conference. When formally established by Congress, in 1912, as part of the Department of Commerce and Labor, the bureau and its first director, Julia Lathrop, were asked to oversee and evaluate the work of the many state and local agencies concerned with the health, labor, and general welfare of the child. Lathrop, a veteran of Jane Addams' Hull House, Chicago-area settlement house, was pivotal as she steered the highly visible program through uncharted and turbulent waters. For example, it was unclear what responsibilities and powers the bureau actually had and which were retained by the existing Bureaus of Education, Public Health Service, and the National Child Labor Com-

Julia Lathrop. Courtesy of the Library of
Congress.

mittee. More important, assuming that clear lines of responsibility could
be established in Washington, the national bureau posed a direct threat
to the autonomy of the many existing state and local initiatives. That
Lathrop succeeded, with an initial budget of less than $25,000, is a tes-
tament to her judgment and the commitment of many women supporters
throughout the country.[27]

The bureau's lasting legacy was twofold. First, through grants-in-aid
to local and state agencies, it determinedly gathered vital information
such as infant mortality, maternal deaths, juvenile delinquency, and il-
legitimacy to quantify and substantiate with "scientific data" most of the
anecdotal observations of earlier activists. Armed with facts, sympathetic
legislators could and now did proceed with substantive legal change.
Second, the Children's Bureau published a variety of informational booklets intended to inform poor and working mothers of the most pressing

problems facing the development of their children; effectively creating a set of national standards for child rearing. Because the activities of the parent could now be judged as either good or bad, based on these objective scientific criteria, these standards became an important part of the rationale used to remove children from the home, something most Progressives hesitated to do.

The educational materials are the easiest to examine to look for the inherent biases of such a proposal. Commissioned by the Children's Bureau, writer Mary Mills West authored three of the most successful booklets published by the bureau: *Parental Care* (1914), *Infant Care* (1915), and *Child Care: The Preschool Age* (1918). The importance of these books cannot be overstated. Mothers, doctors, and educators alike looked to the books as the authority in children's health. As late as 1955, *Infant Care* was still the government document in greatest circulation, with 35 million copies in print. By and large, the publication deferred to the new health professionals who had emerged by 1910. West advised mothers to contact doctors early and often for any chronic ailments in their children, to deliver their children in the hospital and not in the home, and to demand perfect cleanliness in all things that children did. Much of the advice still makes sense today—the bureau advocated a mixed diet, the eating of fresh vegetables, and vigorous, healthy play. Other suggestions, such as strict feeding regimens, a fixation against "over-stimulating" the baby, and the breaking of "bad habits" at all cost, strike modern readers as too inhibiting for the passions of a developing child.

The manner in which West wrote added to the power of her message. By stressing simple habits and by using catchy phrases, she attempted to allay the fears of young mothers who were often pressured to make compromises as a result of their socioeconomic conditions. West wrote, "Perhaps the first and most essential good habit is that of regularity . . . [it] applies to all the physical functions of the baby—eating, sleeping, and bowel movements. The care of a baby is readily reduced to a system unless he is sick." Many of her adages, such as "Don't mind your house—mind your children," were, according to the thousands of letters sent to bureau each month, proudly displayed in many American homes.[28]

The biases and assumptions of West reflected those of the larger institution and cut to the heart of the decade's approach to American youth. Her primary concern was in relieving the anxiety and toil of the mother, not necessarily in addressing the developmental needs of the child (the very approach rejected by writers such as Dr. Benjamin Spock decades later). The strict feeding rules and stern toilet training were intended to free the mother from the countless hours of food preparation and diaper care. Moreover, many of these prescriptions were layered with class and ethnic assumptions about proper behavior in children.

Thumb sucking and childhood masturbation, "the most injurious of all these bad habits," were regarded as signs that the child lacked self-control. Good homes were ones that provided not only constant supervision to prevent these mortal sins, but also sunny and spacious rooms and yards for the little ones to learn and grow—conditions not typical of working-class tenements where both men and women worked. Certainly, West based most of her advice on the latest medical information of the age. The leading cause of infant mortality was digestive ailments. Calling for cleanliness, good nutrition, and exercise to help children's bowel movements made perfect sense. Yet her rigid guidelines left little room for improvisation and real-world advice which came from economic need. Poor mothers were often, by definition, bad mothers.[29]

The work of West and the Children's Bureau supported a second key advance in social services for children: health education. Sanitary Boards of Health were not new in the 1910s, as most Eastern cities had established these services by the late nineteenth century. The American Pediatric Society was founded in 1888 to investigate and publish findings concerning the health concerns of children. During the 1910s these early studies were put into wide practice. For example, tuberculosis, a leading killer of children, was found to spread as a result of bacterial contamination in cow's milk. In response, health experts succeeded in having laws enacted throughout the country that required suppliers to pasteurize (or sterilize) the milk. Municipal nurses were also placed throughout the public school system as a means to detect infections and other health issues that might be missed by overworked or undereducated parents. In both cases, the formal knowledge gained over the previous decades, in this case about "germ theory," was put into action in order to protect children and society. Still, it was not until the 1920s that these early reforms could claim to have been enforced throughout much of the country. The work of the Children's Bureau drastically lowered the horrific number of mothers and infants who perished during childbirth. While it should not strike modern readers as unusual that these efforts were underfunded and poorly staffed, the drive to enhance the health and safety of children was significantly strengthened during the decade.

Finally, a survey of child welfare services must not overlook the creation of direct payments to poor mothers intended to alleviate the environmental conditions of poverty. Termed "Mothers pensions," public funds were redistributed to the needy as early as 1911 in Illinois and Missouri. By 1919, 37 of the 48 states had similar laws on the books. While underfunded due to limited state resources (the inclusion of Aid to Dependent Children in the Social Security Act provided much needed federal assistance in 1935), these programs gave monetary proof that Progressives believed that the best place for a child's development was at home. The pension plans led to many innovations. Day-care facilities proliferated. Efforts to curb child labor were strengthened as recipients were required to show proof that their dependent children were not working in order to receive funds. Moreover, the movement led to a greater acceptance of the fact that society indeed had a stake in seeing children develop in healthy home settings. If the redistribution of personal property was needed to accomplish this task, a growing percentage of American seemed willing to accept it.

Yet with additional funding came moral judgment of those in need. If earlier generations accepted poverty and child dependency as a sorry fact of life, they too granted the "lower sorts" a certain kind of privacy (or at least benign neglect). This practice began to erode in the modern era. For example Mary Mills West, in *Infant Care*, was clear that a "good mother" must be "a proper person, physically, mentally, and morally fit to bring up her children."[30] The fact that children (now seen as the fragile vessels of America's democratic future) were at risk seemed to justify an unparalleled increase in state intervention and societal discrimination. Social workers, psychologists, academics, politicians, and businessmen caught up in their own prejudices and assumptions felt free to judge and alter less powerful American communities by virtue of the child's welfare. Moreover, the professionalization of these experts—as seen through the growth of associations and accredited college programs—resulted in better salaries and a heightened sense of autonomy by which to act. Cloaked in science, which validated their supposed nonpartisanship, experts began to confuse and combine notions of child neglect, dependency, and delinquency based on their own personal views rather than trying to understand the complexities of poverty and a life of need. Some reformers began to assume that intervention was warranted if a child entered a pool hall, was found out-of-doors after dark, or was exposed to any amount of alcohol in the home.

CHILD LABOR AND JUVENILE DELINQUENCY

In two conspicuous ways, these normative biases directly influenced how children were affected by reform in the 1910s. Definitions of acceptable child labor and juvenile delinquency took up a great deal of time and effort of activists. In a very real sense, both encapsulated the major themes of youth reform during the decade. Changes to child labor statutes were an effort made by the state to revise the country's views on the nature of children (as a special class of citizen) and to negotiate a new relationship between government and private property (business owners). The delinquency statutes and the juvenile courts that were founded to arbitrate conflict further developed the special status that came to protect young people in this country.

Of all the reforms that affected children in the 1910s, none was more

Fourteen-year-old spinner, Berkshire
Cotton Mills, Adams, Massachusetts.
Courtesy of the Library of Congress.

revolutionary than the effort to ban child labor. As late as 1900, child
labor was still viewed as both useful and morally justifiable. Concentrated in poorer families and communities, child laborers constituted
nearly one-third of all workers in the South and one-sixth of all workers
nationally by the turn of the century. In many states, laws already existed
to protect the right of a child to secure an education and to be protected
from exploitation, but little enforcement or alternatives to starvation
were offered to give such promises any substance. Parents could easily
sign waivers (readily supplied by the employer) or obtain false proof of
age to neutralize many of these statutes. But as the Progressive critique
sharpened against America's treatment of child laborers, so too did the
opposition to child labor grow.

Practical considerations were important to this rising opposition. Not only did child laborers lower the wages of adults, but they were more easily exploited at the workplace because of their inability collectively to protest unfair and unsafe working conditions. While many children worked near or around their homes, this was no protection against the abuses of the marketplace. Elizabeth Shepley Sergeant, who investigated children who worked in their New York City tenement homes constructing colorful ladies' hats using dyed flowers, reported in 1910 that

the floor was dirty, and one of the babies who sat there sucking a violet with very purple lips, had sore eyes. All the children's fingers were stained green and purple. I had been told that the dye was poisonous, and I asked [the mother] if it hurt the children. She shook her head philosophically. "The doctor say it may be the dye when Pietro have his pains in his stomach. But what can I do?"[31]

The tone of Sergeant's article made it clear that she expected no change would be made by the children's mother or father. State intervention and sanctions leveled against the employer were the only means of correcting such exploitation.

Reform was scattered and mixed in the first decade. The National Child Labor Committee, established in April 1904, set uniform state laws for minimum age requirements and maximum daily hours allowable for young workers. In addition, the committee established a group of state commissioners to track compliance and banned all night labor for children. Still, regulation failed to reach the farm, domestic, sweatshop, and street laborers who made up the vast majority of child workers. Congress proved unable to overcome the hesitancy by factory owners to pass more substantial reform. It was not until after 1914, when the committee's efforts were combined with those of the Children's Bureau, that tangible improvement was written by Congress. The Keating-Owen Child Labor Act, enacted in 1916, was the culmination of this marriage.

Called by some the "greatest triumph of the Progressive campaign against child labor,"[32] the Keating-Owen law extended firm federal regulations and protective standards over a host of previously unrestricted local industries. Initially opposed by President Woodrow Wilson and the National Child Labor Committee, the law soon became the cornerstone of the Wilson administration's child welfare policy and one of the ultimate examples of progressive legislation. The law banned the hiring of persons between 14 and 16 years of age and made illegal the transport of goods across state lines by firms that employed children under 14 years of age.

Ironically, the success of Keating-Owen produced the seeds of its own destruction. The U.S. government claimed that its constitutional right to regulate interstate commerce was at the root of the law. Opponents claimed that Keating-Owen was in reality an effort to regulate the conditions of labor agreements between private citizens, a right not given to the federal government in the U.S. Constitution. The effectiveness of social pressure, combined with the strong language of the law led to a host of local prosecutions. Those indicted appealed their convictions to higher courts avowing that the federal government had overstepped its jurisdiction. In a surprising move, the U.S. Supreme Court concurred with opponents to Keating-Owen in declaring, in a bitterly divided five-to-four ruling of the case *Hammer v. Dagenhart* (1918), that the Congress had indeed exceeded its legal authority. The decree made the law unconstitutional. In a dissenting opinion, Justice Oliver Wendell Holmes passionately noted that the Court's majority based its decision not on legal precedent (which, in fact, supported the law) but rather on personal morals and prejudices that were in direct conflict with the democratic process. It was not until 1941 that similar legislation sustained the approval of the highest court.[33]

The meaning of child labor reform efforts during the 1910s supports the elements of youth culture already examined in this chapter. In order for the state to gain the legal authority to protect children in the United States, American citizens needed first to address and admit that the environmental conditions that caused misery—poverty, laissez-faire business regulation, and poor sanitation and housing, for example—were legitimate targets for Progressive reform. In order for children to be protected, citizens must allow the state access to areas once regarded as private and sacrosanct. As education, labor, health, mothers' pensions, and other children's reforms became interrelated, these questions became increasingly prominent in the minds of many Americans.

A final consideration was what to do with youths who had broken the law. Could they be corrected and uplifted by the new Progressive ideals and policies? Clearly the old system did not distinguish between young and old criminals. Juvenile delinquents in the nineteenth century could expect a penal system that relied upon coercion and violence to punish and remove offenders from society, rather than to rehabilitate them. As late as 1900, it was not uncommon to find eight-year-olds confined in adult prisons. Nor were the old asylums and reformatories working, as was made clear from the reports issued by the newly instituted state inspectors.

The development of a juvenile court system, intended to protect the interests of children rather than punish them for their alleged offenses to society, happened relatively quickly between 1899 and 1910. As with most reforms discussed herein, state and local bodies acted first. The first local juvenile court was created in 1899 in Cook County, Illinois (which contains the city of Chicago). By 1912, 22 states had recognized the need for *parens patriae*, or state parenting, for children who were deemed without proper home guardians. Building on the findings of the 1909 Conference on Dependent Children, most courts committed themselves to the premise that the child was best left in the home, in foster settings where needed, and in institutions such as reform schools and prisons only as a last resort.

With this commitment came the need for investigators and specialists, such as juvenile judges, who were able to reach out to troubled youths. Denver's "Kid's Judge" Benjamin Barr Lindsey, for example, used his charisma and easygoing courtroom style to encourage children (overwhelmingly boys) to explain the circumstances of their arrest and to suggest methods for self-improvement. Judges such as Lindsey needed to be able to separate the criminal act, which society must oppose, from the perpetrator, who may or may not be criminally liable for his or her actions. Children, now recognized as having special developmental needs, merited a new set of legal principles to suit their unique place in society. The need for probation officers to examine the home lives of state wards and to ensure the enforcement of the courts's novel rulings was also new. The heavy loads and low pay for both judge and officer sapped the efficacy of these programs, but clearly they were in keeping with the style and substance of the many other reforms of the era.

Again, the normative values of the middle class greatly affected the ways in which the state assumed responsibility for dependent children. The close examination of home life bared the raw materials of dependancy: poverty, desertion, alcohol addiction, physical abuse. Correction officers, who cared little for the constitutional rights of parents, usually gained entry into the homes and private affairs of American citizens without legal justification ("probable cause") for such intrusions. Predictably, the juvenile court system instead of focusing on the source of the problems, often attacked the parents of the child. The guardians were regarded as lax and immoral if they allowed their children to play in the city streets or at night, clearly not an illegal activity. In one case, a Polish immigrant in Milwaukee was charged with neglect because she spent too much time caring for her dying husband. Brought to court, the distressed woman claimed, "I ain't no sinner, no drinker; I support my children so long, and I want to stay with them." The court found that she was a neglectful parent, however, and placed her family under formal supervision by a state probation officer. As one recent scholar concluded, "Instead of eliminating all trappings of criminal procedure, especially the concern of guilt or innocence, the juvenile court eliminated mainly those due process safeguards with which children and parents could defend themselves."[34]

The inefficiency of the system soon became apparent to reformers focused on just such outcomes. Thomas D. Eliot, secretary of the Pacific Coast office of the American Social Hygiene Association and a professor of sociology at Northwestern University, wrote a book titled *The Juvenile Court and the Community* (1914), which exposed the many problems associated with a program that relied too heavily on underpaid probationary officers to solve society's ills. Eliot concluded, "It is obviously impossible for every court and probation office to attempt to undertake all these functions." Many of the problem children, he reasoned, could easily "have been kept normal had the community shouldered the task in time."[35]

The work of John and Alice Gunckel of Toledo, Ohio, lend support to Eliot's call for greater social involvement in the general welfare of dependent children. The Gunckels' concern was the small army of newsboys employed by the local papers to distribute their product. Moved by the pictures of Lewis Hine and their own observations of children curled up under their papers in the bitter cold, the couple decided to form an association for junior street vendors in 1892. It grew, by 1913, into the National Newsboys' Association boasting more than 28,000 members in 200 branch associations. Their efforts were, in many ways, private versions of the state-financed reform that dominated the era; complete with conflicting notions of proper behavior and tinged with distinct middle-class values.[36]

Newsboys certainly were not criminals. Yet their life in the streets, to the Gunckels, was the slippery slope that would lead to a life of self-destructive behavior. Ranging in age from 10 to 14, the "newsies" usually spent the night out-of-doors in order to hit the morning sales period. The association began when John Gunckel began inviting the children into his office to warm up and rest throughout the evenings. By 1900 these informal gatherings had transformed into a well-organized association of youths. They kept tabs on each other, demanded that each followed a set of rules intended to instill "respectful" behavior (such as looking clean and neat), and even wrote a constitution to uphold democratic elections among the members. An oath was recited claiming that the boys did "not approve of swearing, lying, stealing, gambling, drinking intoxicating liquors or smoking cigarettes."[37] Newsboy courts were created to fine or, in some cases, expel unrepentant or repeat offenders.

By 1912 the association had grown to become a voluntary auxiliary to Toledo's juvenile justice system. Working as unpaid probationary officers, in their off-hours the youths followed and reported on the activities of their colleagues. One report announced that 1,230 boys and 13 girls had frequented at least one of the city's 108 saloons. It concluded, "The boys were bad enough; but oh, my, the girls were terrible. We took home twenty-one boys too drunk to know their names."[38] Names of those found in pool halls and sleeping in the streets at night were also forwarded to municipal authorities. Prevention of crime, not a coercive network of informants, was the intended goal of the association, which

Newspaper boys selling papers in front of South Station, Boston, Massachusetts. Courtesy of the Library of Congress.

claimed to have "saved" some 450 children from jail time. As historian LeRoy Ashby remarked in his book, *Saving the Waifs: Reformers and Dependent Children, 1890–1917*,

one of the most remarkable features of the Toledo Newsboys' Association was the extent to which so many youths found it appealing. Gunckel and his organization undeniably struck a popular chord. Boys—many of whom were clearly from poor, new-immigrant backgrounds quite different from Gunckel's middle-class, Protestant life-style—responded with extraordinary zeal to the moral imperatives of the association.[39]

The boys were highly critical of "traditional" and minor moral offenses, such as shortchanging or cursing at bothersome customers. An honor roll was created for those who were observed doing good work, like returning lost items. A certificate was presented by Gunckel to honorees stating, "You have done something good. You have sacrificed your self-interest, your own pleasure, to make some unknown person happy. You have obeyed the Commandment of God, to love your neighbors."[40]

A better homage to the progressive ideas for dependent child reform is hard to find. Fittingly, given the educational initiatives under way, Gunckel referred to his association as "a kindergarten in the great school of business and citizenship." By intervening in the lives of troubled youth, he hoped to prevent the negative consequences that he and most other Americans saw in plain view by decade's end. He was proudest of the fact that, 25 years after beginning his crusade, 27 of the 102 original members were doctors, 5 were bankers, 2 were ministers, 7 were newspaper managers, 12 were traveling salesmen, 11 were at wholesale houses, 15 were tradesmen, 11 were in the U.S. Navy, and 1 was a circus clown.[41]

CONCLUSION

Understanding and addressing the needs of youth culture had high priority during the 1910s. Adults turned to increasingly complex and intrusive solutions to the problems that faced young people, and the solutions challenged many of the country's most basic assumptions about personal privacy, legal rights, and the role of government. Steeped in the Progressive tradition, child welfare reform considered the young a special category of citizen, a stage in development that needed protection from the abuses of the adult world. Progressives also favored institutional solutions that relied heavily on new academic disciplines and structured hierarchies imbedded with strong cultural biases. By the end of the decade, although the lives of many individual children were not significantly changed, youth culture had been fundamentally and permanently altered. In areas of health, education, labor, and criminal justice, children had gained a special and, in a sense, revered status. These trends opened other areas of American society to reform. The nation, with the children themselves, grew up with the values of youth culture that were developed during the decade.

Part Two

Popular Culture
of the 1910s

3

Advertising

By contemporary standards, the appearance of advertising in every nook and cranny of American life may not be significant. Today, we are used to hearing pitches for everything from credit cards to bankruptcy attorneys in every public and some private places. Moreover, we have grown accustomed to the many forms of these pitches—audio, video, print—and the many approaches taken by advertisers—humor, information, voice of authority. Whether advertising greatly affects us or we can pass by a pitch without noticing it is ancillary to the fact that it is everywhere.

Modern advertising in our popular culture came of age in the second decade of the twentieth century. The explosive growth of ads anchored the many new forms of popular culture, reinforcing the desire to go to the ballpark, buy a new car, or see the latest movie. Modern advertising introduced a new influence in American life: Madison Avenue, which refers to a street in New York City where many of the largest ad agencies got their start, as well as the business culture of advertisers. Writing at the close of the decade, S.N. Behrman of the *New Republic* noted that the adman "does not conceal his awareness of the fact that he is the cornerstone of the most respectable American institutions; the newspapers and magazines depend on him; Literature and journalism are his handmaidens."[1]

Critics were quick to defend values seemingly missing in advertisements: modesty, fiscal self-control, and community. Behrman noted that this new business ethic measured success by how effectively one could *manipulate* the public trust. He suggested, with biting sarcasm, that only the inopportune "emergence of the League of Nations" prevented American advertisers from producing "the snappiest war publicists in the world." He declared, "The first act of a South American revolutionist [should] be to wire a New York agency for a publicity man . . . who could put a revolution over with neatness and dispatch."[2] Behrman's comments forecast the downpour of criticism that would appear in the coming decade, such as William E. Woodward's aptly titled *Bunk* in 1923, which openly resisted advertisers' glib trendiness.

The reason that the new advertising struck such a deep and negative chord in many Americans is complex, but it goes to the heart of the nature of change to popular culture in the decade. Central to the problem is our interpretation of the advertisements, which emanated in ever-increasing numbers from the nation's commercial sector. Do these ads reflect the ideals of the advertisers, the consumers, the manufacturers, or a mixture of all three? Why did some ad campaigns succeed while others failed? Moreover, how can we appreciate which of the many images and messages were being received by the consumer? As historian Roland Marchand notes, modern consumers tend to distort messages contained within advertising to fit their pre-existing needs. In this way, a certain product may address a specific need of mine while being of little or no use to others. I would certainly be receptive to such a product while others no doubt would hardly notice the pitch within the hundreds of ads that confront us every day. In the more poetic words of historian T. J. Jackson Lears, ads tend to "validate a way of being in the world."[3]

ADVERTISING MODERNITY

One thing is clear about advertising during the 1910s: it needed to address the fact that American society had modernized. Some of these changes were necessary precursors to the flowering of advertising during the decade. For example, the rapid expansion of railroads and a banking infrastructure made the possibility of a mass consumer market a fact. The constant population growth—the United States added more than 10 million new people in each decade from 1870 to 1920—sustained this marketplace while the near universality of literacy (approaching 94 percent by 1920) allowed their appeals to be read. Finally, the majority of Americans now worked and lived in the city, thereby thrusting themselves into a rapidly changing social and economic environment. Citizens no longer had a choice of whether they wanted industrial capitalism; it was now a reality and they sought means to cope with this reality.

As a result, advertising in the decade revolved around three key themes. The first was an effort to assist the individual to find meaning in this increasingly complex and bureaucratized world. Modern comforts and lifestyles were in sharp contrast to the production of basic goods— food, clothing, and utensils—which occupied the lives of most Americans before the turn of the century. Even the new industrial workers, less profoundly influenced than the growing white-collar population, found that they were less involved in creating a tangible product than in performing a mechanized routine. In such a setting, it was vital that citizens find new meaning for themselves, their work, and their lives. Advertising met a portion of this need by providing significance, however fleeting, to consumer goods.

Second, and closely linked to the first, advertising provided a form of therapy in offering "solutions" to many of modern life's newest problems. Frustrations with modernity and the faster pace of living were common, and advertisers sought to ease these psychological pressures by assuring their clients that their goods were the latest, the most progressive products available. As a result, the advertising styles changed markedly from 1910 to 1919. Promoters focused less on presenting their product in isolation and more on how their wares could provide richer and fuller lives for consumers. Ads that provided simple information about a product gave way to those that demonstrated, often visually, how the item could solve most of the basic problems of modern living.

Finally, ads helped to create a new standard of conduct—new moral codes—for the uninitiated. Urban living, industrialization, and the move toward bureaucratic hierarchy made social interactions more complex. What were the new standards of conduct? Was how one dressed as important as one's character? Behrman admonished admen as "usually young, good-looking, sartorially perfect, with sleek hair and particolored shoes."[4] But in many ways these were just the sort of guides that many were looking for when confronted with the mysteries of fast-paced urban living. According to Marchand, advertisers were the "high priests" of modernity, imparting knowledge and wisdom in their copy.[5] As is the trend today, most Americans first confronted novel technologies, fashions, and fads through national advertising. Reason and rationality were less effective appeals than emotion and the subconscious.

A brief review of the manner and scope in which advertising expanded during the 1910s is important to put these changes in style and substance in relief. While the revenues generated from advertising are inexact and probably understated, total advertising volumes in the United States nearly tripled from approximately $256 million in 1900 to about $682 million in 1914, then doubled again to $1,409 million by 1919.[6] While little is known about revenues for local newspapers, direct mail campaigns, or local publicity efforts (such as sandwich-board walkers), the numbers provide a clear indication of the rapid expansion of national advertising. The leading advertising trade journal, *Printers Ink*, declared in 1905, "Suddenly the manufacturing world has developed an intense, anxious interest in both advertising and consumers. It is glad to talk plans of advertising and discuss trade marks with solicitors, where a year ago the latter would have got no hearing."[7]

NEWSPAPERS AND BILLBOARDS

Newspapers certainly played an active role in the growth of the industry. Daily and weekly presses had, for decades, relied on the revenues from their sales copy to augment their subscription earnings. But typesetting technology limited innovation and, as a result, most ads were restricted to certain preformatted sections of paper (usually the front page), changed their copy infrequently, and used few pictures or other imagery to entice the audience. In essence, local newspaper advertisers hoped to scratch out a greater share of the existing regional demand for their clients rather than create new markets or grow the old ones on a national level.

Billboards or, more accurately, bill posters should not be overlooked as potential sources for advertising growth. Standardizing, in 1900, on three formats—three-, eight-, and sixteen-sheet displays (each sheet measuring 42 × 28 inches)—and seeking to regulate itself through the redundantly named Associated Bill Posters' Association, the industry did not suffer from lack of imagination or limited artistic formats. In fact, the reverse was true. Almost any artist could publicly display his or her pitches regardless of taste or quality. The public outrage over the more vulgar attempts, aided in no small part by monthly editorials in competing advertising forums such as magazines and newspapers, forced the industry to seek greater controls. By creating a national licensing system, a classification for bill quality, and an oversight board to suggest policies for improved public relations, the bill posters industry eliminated much of the antagonism directed against their efforts. Although active in the 1910s, particularly during the war years, billboard advertising hit its stride only in subsequent decades when Americans took the roads in their new automobiles.

MAGAZINES AND PERIODICAL ADVERTISING

The premiere advertising forum of the second decade was the periodical. By and large, the earliest magazines were financed through subscriptions by individual consumers. Readers supported three broad types of publications throughout the nineteenth century. One dealt with topics specific to a subscriber's area of interest, be it politics, industry, or contemporary issues. Business publications such as *Hunts' Merchants* magazine and *DeBow's Review* appealed to a different class of consumers than the agricultural publications, including the *American Farmer, Country Gentleman*, and *American Agriculturalist*. A second general approach was to showcase literary and artistic works in a mass publication. Long-running magazines such as the *North American Review, Southern Literary Messenger, Harper's* magazine, and *Atlantic Monthly* featured poetry, short stories, critical exposés, and serialized books and novellas for readers interested in sampling a wide variety of America's leading writers and reporters. Finally, toward the turn of the century, a growing number of publications emerged that provided advice and gossipy news for the curious reader who did not want to invest much time in an article. The editors of these magazines looked for articles and contributors who made current events accessible to a larger audience. Their styles sought to create an inner circle of knowledgeable yet friendly critics into which the reader was invited. The best of this genre included the *Ladies' Home Journal*, *Saturday Evening Post*, *Cosmopolitan*, *Munsey's*, and *McClure's*. Of course, most magazines mixed these three styles within each publication as editors attempted to balance the needs of their subscribers with those of their advertisers, a group of growing importance by 1910.

The relationship between the "typical" magazine reader, the advertisements, and the success of each publication is, predictably, difficult to gauge. Variables such as region, gender, economic status, and education make it nearly impossible to understand definitively how consumers used these publications. Thankfully, it is possible to track the decisions that advertisers made in their effort to meet these needs. As a result, we are left today with a record of what suppliers *thought* might attract consumers—an important distinction. With this in mind, some qualified conclusions can be reached about magazine advertisements for the era.

First, advertisers were convinced that active consumers were, in fact, avid readers of these publications. As indicated below, the advertising style began to mirror the editorial content of each publication reasoning, perhaps, that what attracted a reader to an article might also persuade them to purchase a new product. Second, the most prolific advertisers were those who sold relatively common products (such as soap, shirt collars, or cigarettes) to a broad yet selective audience. The gossipy, casual publications such as *Cosmopolitan*, *Ladies' Home Journal*, and *Saturday Evening Post* seemed the most logical choice for such advertisements. Provided access to an urban middle class eager to understand trends quickly and cope with the complexities of modern life, advertisers soon poured millions of dollars into the glossy monthlies. In 1917 alone, the *Saturday Evening Post* earned more than $17 million in advertising revenues.[8] More than half of the pages of the typical magazine, which usually extended to one hundred pages per issue, were devoted to advertisements.

The influx of advertising revenues had a profound effect on all periodicals during the decade. The vast sums allowed publishers to sell their journals at nearly the same cost that it took to print them—and occasionally below cost. The subsidization of magazines by national advertisers made the publications even more affordable, thereby expanding circulation, and, in an upward spiral, compelled other advertisers to spend their money likewise. Ad executive James Collins told a congressional committee in 1907,

There is still an illusion to the effect that a magazine is a periodical in which advertising is incidental. But we don't look at it that way. A magazine is simply a device to induce people to read advertising. It is a large booklet with two departments—entertainment and business. The entertainment department finds stories, pictures, verses, etc. to interest the public. The business department makes the money.[9]

Occasionally demand outstripped supply, and many publications lost money by undercharging advertisers for access. As a result, magazines and advertising agencies became closely linked in their goals.

Ladies' Home Journal

The best example of this symbiosis can be found in the phenomenal success of the *Ladies' Home Journal*. The magazine was born when publisher Cyrus H.K. Curtis expanded a column titled "Women and the Home," written by his wife, Louisa Knapp, in one of Curtis's existing magazines, into a free-standing publication in 1883. The popularity of the column rested on Knapp's no-nonsense approach to middle-class women's duties in the modern family. Contributions might include a melodramatic short story, several topical essays on items ranging from health to cosmetics, hints and tips on running a well-organized home, or a brief and often humorous analysis of current events from the perspective of "the ladies." A "typical" reader might examine two or three essays, scan a few others, and generally browse the pages in her spare time looking for items of interest. Significantly, the spread of visual (rather than verbal) advertisements suited this glancing reading style very well. From the outset, Curtis intended the new publication to appeal to both subscribers and to the advertisers who wanted access to this vital group of active consumers. The strategy proved wildly successful. Claiming 270,000 subscribers in 1886, the number expanded to more than 400,000 only three years later; 800,000 by 1900; and more than one million, the first magazine to do so, by 1903.[10]

Much of the success of the magazine was due to the keen editorial talents of Edward W. Bok. Born in the Netherlands, Bok immigrated to the United States at the age of seven, where he became experienced in publishing and by 1889, at 25 years of age, assumed the editor's post at the *Ladies' Home Journal*, a position that Bok would hold until his retirement in 1919. Bok's contribution to women's periodicals is legendary. He sought out and included many of the era's leading writers, championed many Progressive reforms (such as his fight against outdoor advertising), and directed the *Ladies' Home Journal* toward his goal of making the magazine "a great clearing-house of information" for his female readers.[11]

But it was Bok's development of standards for magazine advertising that made him so significant. He was instrumental in designing an advertising code that became the standard for all Curtis publications (including the mammoth *Saturday Evening Post*) and, by default, for most of the industry. Based on the facts that came to light following the Pure Food and Drug Act (1906), the Curtis Advertising Code sought to defend subscribers from advertisers who made false or exorbitant claims. Of course all patent medicines were banned, being little more than a promise, colored water, and alcohol or opiates. Bok also excluded tobacco products, playing cards, financial deals, and all liquor. The ban was absolute; advertisers were even prevented from showing glasses, bottles, or cigarettes in their advertising copy.

Bok certainly understood the close link between advertising and his publication. In his Pulitzer Prize–winning autobiography, he rhetorically asked,

Do you know why we publish the *Ladies' Home Journal*? The Editor thinks it is for the benefit of American women. That is an illusion, but a very proper one for him to have . . . the real reason, the publisher's reason, is to give you people who manufacture things that American women want and buy a chance to tell them about your products.[12]

The industry leader also recognized that the publications acted as a sentinel for many female consumers.

African American Magazines

Bok's charitable demeanor was a luxury few other publications could afford. Many periodicals intended for non-middle-class and white audiences struggled to find the necessary sponsorship that would propel circulation. For example, magazines intended for the African American community repeatedly struggled, usually in vain, for survival. Up to 1910 the two biggest of these were *The Colored American* and *Voices of the Negro*. Neither journal claimed more than 20,000 paid subscribers. While divisive debates surrounding Booker T. Washington's accommodation of Jim Crow legislation did not help, it was the lack of advertising subsidies that kept most magazines running at the bare margins. When W.E.B. Du Bois, a professor at Atlanta University, took the post of director of the newly founded National Association for the Advancement of Colored People (NAACP), in 1910, he founded probably the strongest African American publication of the era: *Crisis: A Record of the Darker Races*. Circulation grew from 9,000 in 1911 to more than 35,000 by 1915, but Du Bois could rely on little outside support beyond the subscription funds funneled to him by the NAACP. The eventual commercial success of black-owned, black-operated popular magazines, such *Ebony* and *Jet*, were decades away.[13]

REFORMING MADISON AVENUE

While newspapers, billboards, and magazines were clearly essential in the spread of advertising, it was the evolution of professional advertising agencies, especially their new advertising styles, that truly revolutionized the industry in the 1910s. A chicken-and-egg dilemma exists when comparing the media and the message, but it is certain that the large agencies, centered in New York, Chicago, and Philadelphia, were the driving force behind the modernization of the pitches presented to the public. The earliest agencies date back to the 1850s, when they simply brokered advertising space for the many newly emerging urban newspapers. As middlemen serving both the newspaper—from whom they bought bulked space at a discount—and the product provider—from whom they sold portions of that space for a profit—these agencies were almost without concern over the content of the ads. It was not until 1869, when Francis Wayland Ayer, founder of the prominent advertising firm of N.W. Ayer and Son (named for his father), established a direct connection between his copywriters and the suppliers. Ayer performed early market analyses; followed sales trends; categorized subscribers by wealth, age, and ethnicity; and developed stylized advertising campaigns. His close ties to the Curtis publications, particularly the *Ladies' Home Journal* and *Saturday Evening Post*, reinforced his firm's position as the industry leader (just as his burgeoning ad revenues did for Curtis). Other prominent concerns, most notably the J. Walter Thompson Company and Lord & Thomas, filled in behind N.W. Ayer and Son by 1910.

The chief obstacle threatening the success of these agencies was the pervasive fear that advertising was little more than trickery. Americans distrust "fancy talk," and when P.T. Barnum suggested that it was possible to separate the average citizen from his cash by using trick promotions, the industry was saddled with an almost terminal reputation. Tensions mounted in the first decade of the twentieth century as muckrakers and other Progressive reformers exposed the impurities and toxic additives routinely contained within the nation's food and drug supply. Advertisers, who up to this point had been extolling the virtues of many of the worst offenders, were connected with these villainies. While legislation like the Pure Food and Drug Act demanded some accountability on the part of the advertisers, regulators were apt to focus their energies on the easy-to-spot small-time providers. They, according to historian Jackson Lears, "dismissed national advertisers with a tolerant smile."[14]

The Progressive crusades in the 1900s did two things to help advertisers in the following decade. First, the largest advertising firms came to follow the editorial lead of the most prominent periodicals. Editors such as Edward Bok dictated many of the products that they were willing to market on their pages. With the forced exclusion of many of the most egregious offenders, such as alcohol products and patent medicines, the largest agencies were able to free themselves quite easily from the negative connotations associated with these products. Second, and following from this first point, self-regulation such as the Associated Advertising Clubs of America (1911) was begun for the express purpose of freeing the medium from falsehoods and deceptions. The strong connections between editors and publishers created an unwritten, but powerful layer of censorship, which served as reform for the decade. Just as the *Ladies' Home Journal* could set the boundaries for polite—or what we might today term politically correct—discussion, so too could advertisers now claim to be acting in the best interests of the consumer. This new public legitimacy freed agencies to experiment with new and aggressive advertising styles in the 1910s, ones that would have been largely unthinkable only a few short years earlier. When, during World War I, the U.S. government added its blessing to advertising, it set the final tumbler into place, unlocking the trust and confidence of willing consumers.

COMMUNICATING THROUGH ADVERTISEMENTS

The function of advertising is to persuade skeptics and to sell merchandise. Traditionally, this role was given to salesmen who vended their wares either directly to the consumer or to regional stores which were patronized by shoppers. Advertising circumvented salesmen by printing their arguments and conveying its message to a wide spectrum of potential consumers. Even though most nineteenth-century advertisers were limited by the print technology, early promoters effectively created strong reason-why, or hard-sell, advertisements (discussed more fully below) through the use of images and words loaded with meaning. Moreover, unlike a human salesperson, abstract words printed in newspapers and magazines allowed consumers to pour their own hopes, fears, and illusions into the products. For example, a hair tonic advertisement might not *claim* to be able to restore one's lost hair fully, but willing consumers may see only the pictures of men and women with flowing locks or prominently highlighted words, such as "guarantee" and "amazing results," to draw their own conclusions. Moreover, advertisers and manufacturers soon realized that modern society was creating a seemingly bottomless pit of insecurities and uncertainties upon which they could base their appeals. Linked to the common symbols of our culture, advertising created a tighter bond between buyer and seller than could otherwise exist by traditional sales methods.

Unique to the 1910s was the widespread use of images, pictures, and icons to facilitate this new form of communication. Michael Schudson, in his book *Advertising: The Uneasy Persuasion* (1984), calls these new symbolic pictures "Capitalist Realism." Unlike traditional ads, which promoted a specific product, sales event, or price (in other words, promotions that were tied to a concrete reality), new, largely national advertising avoided any mention of specifics and focused their appeal on abstractions. The people shown in ads were characterizations representing people how they wanted to be seen rather than how they appeared in reality. According to Schudson, advertising became "a distinctive and central *symbolic* structure" in American culture. Ironically, many of these soft-sell ads during the 1910s suggested that they did, in fact, portray reality, but it was from a curious and artificial third-party perspective.[15]

A more pointed analysis of these two dominant styles of advertising is useful in examining promotions during the decade. The more common of the two forms used was the reason-why or hard-sell approach. Based on "plain speaking," these pitches hoped to cloak their products in honesty and virtue, dispelling the fear that one might be taken in by fancy sales talk. They suggested that suppliers were simply in the business of meeting consumer demand, not creating demand as many had begun to fear. Reason-why advertising was often referred to as "salesmanship on paper" because it supposedly conveyed the same information a hired representative might convey if given the opportunity to meet with every consumer. The modern use of the hard sell is often credited to John E. Kennedy, a Canadian who joined a leading Chicago advertising firm in 1903, and later to prominent copywriter Claude C. Hopkins. Kennedy later wrote that his ads should be "easier to *understand* than to *misunderstand*."[16]

Typical to reason-why ads was the prominent display of the product at the center of the pitch. Little time was wasted in elaborate or unclear imagery that did not directly reflect upon the product. An example of such an approach is evident in the Ivory Soap campaign from 1907 to 1909. The bar of soap literally became the foundation for such well-known structures as the Washington Monument, the Great Pyramid, and the Arch de Triumphe. The ad copy is presented as straightforward and "honest." In the 1909 promotion, the manufacturers, Procter & Gamble, asked a series of questions,

Who wants pure soap?
Pretty nearly everybody.

Why do they want it?
Because it *is* pure.

Where can they get it?
At any grocery store.

How?
By asking for Ivory soap.

Is Ivory Soap absolutely pure?
No.

How nearly pure is it?
99 44/100 per cent. pure.

Is there a purer soap than Ivory?
No. Not one.

Clearly Procter & Gamble hoped to present their advertisement as simple information which any consumer might ask of a salesperson. The ad's plain talk provides straight answers while the product is prominently displayed. Clearly consumers could feel confident that Procter & Gamble had a high level of trust and confidence in Ivory Soap and, by extension, so should they.

The soft-sell, or impressionistic, approach was, by contrast, laden with atmosphere and meaning. Extensive artwork, detailed layouts, and clear associations between the product and human feeling characterize the ads. It had long been recognized that emotions are key to closing a sale, but it was not until the work of Walter Dill Scott, a professor of advertising at the Northwesten School of Business, that appeals to these psychological desires gained widespread acceptance in many agencies. In 1911 Scott wrote *Influencing Men in Business*, in which he argued that advertisements that offered goods "as a means of gaining social prestige make their appeals to one of the most profound of the human instincts."[17] Generally these promotions placed human actors at the center of the ad, showing how the product might be used to benefit the consumer. While Marchand cautions that impressionistic ads of the 1910s "rarely invited the reader's engagement and empathy with detailed vignettes of group conversations, family activities, or moments of social triumph or humiliation," as they would more effectively in the 1930s and 1940s, soft-sell advertisements were a new and profoundly revolutionary form of commercial expression during the 1910s.[18]

The work of Theodore MacManus was probably the best example from the 1910s of the soft-sell approach. Born into a working-class, Irish Catholic family in Toledo, Ohio, MacManus worked his way through a variety of newspaper and advertising positions before writing copy for

General Motors for the upscale Buick and Cadillac lines. Here was a product that consumers took time to evaluate. The expense of these automobiles made them poor choices for the hard sell. Up to 1914, MacManus was successful in creating a solid image of quality and dependability, which was important in an era where many auto manufacturers were falling by the wayside. In the fall of 1914, General Motors was faced with a public relations nightmare. A year earlier, their chief rival, Packard, had come out with a new six-cylinder engine which overpowered Cadillac's four-cylinder effort. In a hurried response, Cadillac announced an eight-cylinder model that almost immediately ran into problems. Cadillac's hard-earned aura of quality was under attack—most notably in ads for Packard products.

MacManus's response, titled the "The Penalty of Leadership," is a classic soft-sell response to the crisis. The spot, which ran only once, on January 2, 1915, in the *Saturday Evening Post*, does not mention the difficulties that precipitated the response, the Packard criticism, or even the Cadillac line itself. Instead, MacManus, who dictated the copy, wrote about geniuses like composer Richard Wagner, American artist Thomas Whistler, and Thomas Fulton, the inventor of the steamboat. According to MacManus, "In every field of human endeavor, he that is first must perpetually live in the white light of publicity." Implying both Cadillac and Packard, respectively, MacManus concluded, "When a man's work becomes a standard for the whole world, it also becomes a target for the shafts of the envious few." Although he feared that the campaign would not reach enough of the public, requests for reprints from salesman and clients alike came pouring into General Motors. In the end, more than 10,000 copies of the ad were distributed each year by the relieved auto maker. MacManus later suggested why he thought the soft-sell approach was so effective in this case: "The real explanation of this astonishing popularity is that almost every man considers himself a leader and secretly suspects that he is a victim of enmity and injustice."[19]

More than any other format, the atmosphere advertising style was best able to take advantage of the complexity and insecurity generated by modern living. For example, Arrow collars and shirts were sold with little more than pictures of men smugly secure within this new society. Others, such as the advertisers of Pebesco Tooth Paste, Woodbury's Facial Soap, and Odorono, took a more threatening stance. Promising to prevent "Acid-Mouth," which inevitably leads to the loss of teeth, a Pebesco ad shows a young woman smiling in disbelief as an old toothless man warns, "I once had good teeth like yours my dear." Woodbury's Facial Soap informed unsuspecting women of the social problems associated with "enlarged nose pores," but, thankfully, offered them a solution that protected "Complections otherwise flawless" from being "ruined by conspicuous nose pores." The laughably titled Odorono, an

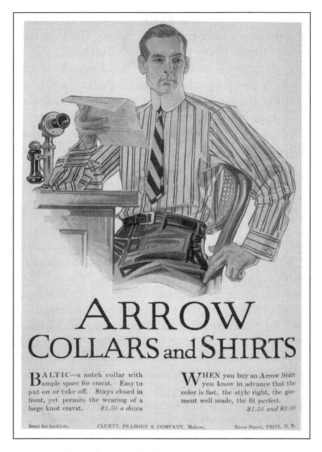

ARROW
COLLARS and SHIRTS

BALTIC—a notch collar with ample space for cravat. Easy to put on or take off. Stays closed in front, yet permits the wearing of a large knot cravat.   *$1.50 a dozen*

WHEN you buy an Arrow Shirt you know in advance that the color is fast, the style right, the garment well made, the fit perfect.   *$1.50 and $2.00*

Send for booklets.   CLUETT, PEABODY & COMPANY, Makers,   River Street, TROY. N. Y.

Impressionistic advertising for Arrow Collars and
Shirts. © Bettmann/CORBIS.

antiperspirant for women, humorlessly provides "a frank discussion of a subject too often avoided." Showing an attractive woman in close contact with a dashing suitor, the copy warns that "fastidious women who want to be absolutely sure of their daintiness have found that they could not trust to their own consciousness." Instead, "a physician formulated Odorono" to ensure a woman's "perfect daintiness." In each case, the product offers a solution to a modern problem that most became aware of only by reading these ads.

While the novelty of the impressionistic sales pitch left many doubters, the style hit its first full expression during the 1910s. Although the pattern seemed to have worked best for expensive or durable items, where consumers needed greater reassurance, or to have their opinions confirmed before making such momentous purchases, many commodity

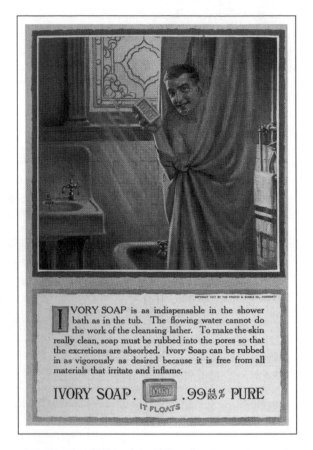

Impressionistic advertising for Ivory soap. ©
Bettmann/CORBIS.

goods such as toothpaste, cigarettes, and soap delved into the consumer subconscious. Even salesmen for Ivory Soap sampled impressionistic copy. Contending that their product "carrie[d] with it the Spirit of Cleanliness" or that it formed a special bond between athletes after a "hard game," the adventuresome advertisers of Procter & Gamble perfected the soft sell while maintaining the more factual "99 and 44/100 per cent. pure" tag line that remains to this day.

EFFECTIVENESS OF ADVERTISING

In actual practice, most advertising agencies and manufacturers in the 1910s were more comfortable with a mixture of both styles of advertising. Reason-why promotions existed within the more subtle impressionistic format. In many ways, promoters themselves still had no clear sense of what was most effective in swaying the average consumer. Many suppliers were wary of spending ever-increasing sums needed to stay in the public eye. Henry Ford, for example, alternated between a grudging acceptance of mass advertising and outright hostility. In the 1920s, Ford twice attempted to survive without national ads only to twice return to the game with more expensive and lavish promotions.

Another problem for suppliers during the decade was the relative novelty of their wares. For example, a whole gamut of electrically powered products were introduced for home use, including refrigerators, toasters, irons, fans, sewing machines, washing machines, and even dishwashers. Electricity, however, was available in only a small number of homes. It was not until 1910 that a standard electrical current was agreed upon by power providers. These limitations did not stop manufacturers, such as the Hoover Suction Sweeper Company, who constantly advertised their new electric vacuums in the most important national magazines. Stressing modernity, cleanliness (a point of growing importance for many advertisers), and ease of use, the Hoover ads were, in a sense, preparing a marketplace for their products as electrification came to more homes. Even products that did not rely on new technologies could often pose challenges to marketeers in the 1910s. For example, ready-made foods, such as the Franco-American line of canned soups, or unfamiliar baking products, such as cake flour, pancake flour, and biscuit flour, advertised in ways that reflected both the reason-why hard-sell style as well as the more impressionistic settings. An examination of the ad campaigns conducted by three new and significant products of the 1910s—Coca-Cola, the Model T, and Camel Cigarettes—sheds more light on how and why advertisers made their stylistic choices.

Coca-Cola

Soft drinks originated as inexpensive consumer indulgences. Made to order at drugstores and specialty soda fountains, the drinks were a combination of ice, carbonated water, and sweetened syrups often concocted by local druggists. Initially, most of these syrups were the result of failed experiments at creating useful medicines. Pharmacist John Pemberton created just such a potion, sometime between 1880 and 1886, to cure headaches. In 1886 Willis E. Venable began serving Pemberton's creation at his soda fountain in Atlanta, which he named Coca-Cola Syrup and Extract. Two years later, wholesale druggist Asa Chandler, also from Atlanta, took control over production and began exporting and advertising the popular syrup around the country. When Chandler retired from the firm in 1916, his net worth exceeded $50 million.

As a product that originated as a patent medicine, Coca-Cola was susceptible to the consumer pressures that resulted from the 1906 Pure Food and Drug Act. While the firm claimed in 1916 that the soft drink contained only "Pure water sterilized by boiling,"[20] sugar, flavoring extracts, caramel, caffeine, and citric and phosphoric acids, regulators were concerned that the drink included other substances ranging from cocaine (which was present in small quantities until the turn of the century) to alcohol (which had never been used). The name Coca-Cola referred to coca and cola leaves, which were the source of the extracts. By the 1910s, however, most of these constituents were far removed from the production of the syrup. Other products also relied on these seemingly simple naming conventions: Pepsi-Cola was thought to contain pepsin to aid digestion; Palmolive soaps were taken from the oils of, obviously enough, palm and olive plants. Still, in 1909, Dr. Harvey Wiley, head of the Bureau of Chemistry of the Department of Agriculture, accused Coca-Cola, whom he termed "dope peddlers," of violating the Pure Food and Drug Act because their product contained *no* coca and very little cola.[21] The suit bounced through the courts until 1918 when the case was settled in the soft drink company's favor.

This background is important in making sense of the advertising strategy of the firm in the 1910s. Coca-Cola, as with any food containing calories, was certainly nutritious and, equally true, did not contain alcohol. Moreover, the firm clearly believed that its product, which contained caffeine, provided a functional relief from headaches and drowsiness. The evolution of Coca-Cola advertising captures the spirit of the transformation of the industry as the firm moved from strong, reason-why promotions to more subtle and effervescent ones. Reflecting their roots as a soothing and inexpensive indulgence, ads from the first decade of the twentieth century provided brief and well-reasoned justifications for its consumption. In 1903, one spot proclaimed Coca-Cola as simply "Delicious, Refreshing." In 1904, "Coca-Cola is a delightful, palatable, healthful beverage." The following year, the product was hailed because it "revives and sustains." By the 1910s, however, the promotions began to appeal to more esoteric feelings. For example, advertisements asked consumers to "Enjoy a glass of liquid laughter" (1911), drink "The Best beverage under the sun" or "The Best drink anyone can buy" (1913), because the beverage was "Pure and wholesome" (1914). A longer promotion, in 1910, ties together many of these themes contained in their traditionally short ads:

When you feel all hot and sticky and tired and "head-achy," when the life and energy seems to be oozing out of your pores with each drop of perspiration and it just seems you can't go a step further or do a lick more of work, step into any place and Drink a Bottle of Coca-Cola. You'll wonder first thing who turned on the cool wave—your headache will disappear—that nervous, exhausted feeling will be replaced by a general all 'round "brace up," the rough spots will be smoothed out of your temper and you'll feel refreshed and exhilarated. The great temperance, tonic beverage for men, women, and children—now try a bottle today.[22]

While maintaining contact with their earlier rational, reason-why appeals, Coca-Cola advertisers in the 1910s willfully expanded their product's attraction to include the more emotional, less factual benefits of consumption.

Model T

Automobile advertisements also used both the hard- and soft-sell approaches. The growth of the industry drove the need for greater product differentiation. When little more than 4,100 cars were manufactured in 1900, there was not a great need to distinguish a Packard from a Chalmer from a Pierce. Beginning in 1910, however, as these production figures began to balloon—from 181,000 cars at the start of the decade, to 895,500 five years later, to almost 2 million units by 1920—manufacturers turned to advertising to spur their sales.[23] Appealing to the consumers of such expensive and durable goods was more difficult than convincing Americans to spend a nickel for a cold soda. Were the purchasing decisions of consumers influenced more by technology—in which case a reason-why approach might be more useful—or did people buy for prestige?

Impressionistic copy seemed to predominate in the minds of most suppliers. Moreover, many seemed willing to turn much of their sales pitch over to these emotional appeals. The Jordan Automobile Company, for example, claimed their car allowed modern drivers freedom to yield "to the whims of the moment," and gave access to a host of new sensations. They wanted their consumers to "Picture it all. Picture your car . . . answering to your slightest touch."[24] In 1917, the Overland Car Company explicitly pictured the "Four Greatest Events" in the life of the average American as getting married, buying a home, having a baby, "and buying your Overland." Interestingly, Ford Motor Company went the farthest from this industry trend in its advertising between 1910 and 1919.

The source of this difference can generally be attributed to Henry Ford's goal to provide a truly low-cost yet quality product. Ford's development of the interchangeable assembly-line production process was key to this approach. In 1910 it took his firm an average of 12 hours and 28 minutes to complete work on one auto. With the completion of his new Highland Park assembly plant in 1913, however, this number fell dramatically. By 1914 it took Ford only 1 hour, and 33 minutes to construct a Model T. As a result, more than 300,000 cars were manufactured that year, half a million the following year, and more than two million

Henry Ford. Courtesy of the Library of
Congress.

in 1923. With mass production came lowered costs, and the Model T fell
from $440 in 1915 to $290 in ten years.[25]

Logically, then, Henry Ford believed that it was his "better car," not
some esoteric and psychological need on the part of consumers, that
would move his inventory. In a 1912 ad placed in the *Saturday Evening
Post*, Ford asked rhetorically,

What is it that is selling 75,000 Ford cars in 1912? Is it unusually clever advertising? NO! Ford advertising never attempts to be "clever"—never aims at the

First and ten millionth Ford. Courtesy of the Library of Congress.

spectacular—never dallies with the English language—merely states the facts of
the case so that he who runs may read, and, reading, stop running and buy a
FORD.

If not impressionistic advertising, then "WHAT IS IT? Nothing but this—
the guarantee of accomplishment. . . . Satisfied buyers are the backbone
of the Ford success."[26]

Ford also looked to benefit by free publicity which, in essence, did
much of the emotional promotion for him. For example, his well-noted
and liberal minimum wage and maximum daily hour policies, com-
mencing in 1914, earned the firm much public praise. Moreover, Ford
successfully battled the Association of Licensed Automobile Manufacturers, a trust consisting of such heavyweights as Cadillac, Oldsmobile,
and Packard, to obtain the rights for a gasoline-powered engine. This
image of Ford as trustbuster and populist, combined with the car's low
cost and reliability (a later slogan by Ford Motor Company suggested
that "Nobody mortgages his house to buy a Ford," while apparently
others did to afford more luxurious wheels) freed the firm to pursue
more hard-hitting reason-why promotions when the competition was
headed in the opposite direction. According to historian James D. Norris,
by 1915 "when Ford's advertisement for the Model T simply showed a

picture of the 'Tin Lizzie' touring car model with the caption 'BUY IT BECAUSE IT IS A BETTER CAR,' most Americans believed him." Many auto makers were forced to rely on ads that highlighted the social status and prestige of their cars because of Ford's dominance at the low-end of the market spectrum. The high rate of failure for many of these firms suggests the power of reason-why advertising when coupled with strong products and low price.[27]

Camel Cigarettes

The appearance of cigarettes as a new and inexpensive "convenience" good of the 1910s provides a third useful example of the competition within advertising. Tobacco consumption in the United States was not significant before 1920. Most consumers either chewed plug tobacco or smoked the shredded leaves in a pipe. The "small cigar," or cigarette, was probably introduced via England, whose troops learned to roll Turkish tobacco during quiet spells of the Crimean War. Even the growing passion for cigars during the Gilded Age was offset by the faster pace of life in the modern era which made it harder to find time for a leisurely smoke. Cigarettes benefited greatly from the mechanization of the rolling process. Hand rolled until 1881, the mechanized roller first used by James B. Duke could produce more than 100,000 cigarettes per day. "Buck" Duke parlayed his production advantage into market dominance when he formed the American Tobacco Company (ATC) in 1890. As a trust, ATC was busted in 1911 into the new American Tobacco Company, Liggett & Meyers, R.J. Reynolds Tobacco, and P. Lorillard and Company, but these four maintained a clear market dominance throughout the decade.

As with soft drinks and automobiles, cigarettes were advertised both for the rational reasons to smoke them as well as the emotional ones. The most common reason why consumers were asked to try American cigarettes was that they were milder on the throat than the Turkish varieties while, being prerolled, they were convenient enough to smoke during life's more trying moments. George Washington Hill, who controlled the new American Tobacco Company, began to market his Lucky Strike brand in 1917 with the slogan "It's Toasted," referring to the drying process that all tobacco leaves undergo in processing, as a means of creating a rational reason for preferring his product over the others. For each of these claims, however, critics were already charging that cigarette usage was unhealthy and unappealing. Noteworthy individuals and groups—including Henry Ford, Thomas Edison, the Women's Christian Temperance Union, and Marshall Field—were undermining much of the reason-why ads of the decade.

Rather than continue in what was a losing campaign over the health benefits derived from smoking, many suppliers turned with impressive results to impressionistic appeals. The makers of Pall Mall cigarettes pitched their brand as the smoke of the rich globe-trotter. R.J. Reynolds came up with one of the most successful campaigns for their brand Camel. Beginning in newspapers, Reynolds started a cryptic campaign of announcing, in 1915, "The CAMELS are coming." Modeled after a smiling dromedary named "Old Joe" from the Barnum and Bailey circus, the camel became an emblem of an inexpensive, mild cigarette made from Turkish and domestic tobaccos intended for a mass audience. Reynolds completed the picture of brand loyalty with the slogan, "I'd walk a mile for a Camel," combined with showing numerous people willing to go to great lengths to ensure that they obtained their one true choice. These appeals had their intended effect. By 1919 Camel was the most popular ready-rolled cigarette in the world. Liggett & Meyers, ATC, and R.J. Reynolds controlled more than 82 percent of the market by 1925.[28]

ADVERTISING THE WAR

American advertising was certainly modern by the time the United States entered World War I. As a result, the great conflict did not transform advertising as much as it promoted its efficacy in the larger business community. According to Lears, "The coming of World War I gave agency people a superb chance to demonstrate their respectability and reaffirm their ties to other aspiring professionals."[29] Moreover, as manufacturers shifted to wartime production and lost opportunities to sell to the public, they had an even greater need for subtle advertising to remain visible without appearing to be callous.

It is ironic that, while manufacturers increasingly soft sold their products during the war, the U.S. government turned to advertising to hard sell the conflict to the American public. In the first days after war had been declared, President Woodrow Wilson selected George Creel to head the Committee on Public Information to accomplish this task. Creel, a muckraker from Kansas City and Denver was so effective that his name became synonymous with the committee. Most notable were Creel's "four-minute men," a veritable army of propagandists who gave more than 75,000 short, patriotic public lectures. The Creel Committee was also responsible for generating nearly 75 million pamphlets and more than 6,000 press releases.[30] Creel's enthusiasm was not intended to censor Americans, but rather to encourage their support of the war. The Red Scare and ethnic and racial intolerance evidenced after the war suggest that there were a few unintended consequences of his powerful messages.

The modern advertising styles were most obvious in the Division of Pictorial Publicity headed by artist Charles Dana Gibson, but also in-

George Creel. Courtesy of the Library of Congress.

cluding such notables as Howard Chandler Christy and James Montgomery Flagg. Playing off the hardest sell of all—human life—the poster artists tugged repeatedly at Americans' sense of duty, patriotism, and humanitarianism. Flagg's legendary portrayal of "Uncle Sam" unflinchingly demanding "I Want You" leaves little to the imagination and almost defies the viewer to not buy into the war effort. While most war art played off of these positive values, a great deal also keyed off of the not-very-subtle racial and ethnic biases of most American citizens.

Creel later claimed, "The work, as a whole, was nothing more than an advertising campaign, and I freely admit that success was won by close imitation of American advertising methods and through the generous and inspirational cooperation of the advertising profession." Advertisers, "by virtue of government recognition as a vital force in American life," were finally "recognized as a profession."[31] In 1918 the trade journal

Printers Ink agreed when they concluded, "The war has been won by advertising, as well as by soldiers and munitions. It has been a four year strife between the powers of repression and concealment and the powers of expression and enlightenment."[32]

CONCLUSION

While it is easy to argue that advertising in the 1910s did little to forward the powers of enlightenment, it most certainly expanded the means of expression. At the start of the decade, ad campaigns were primitive, hit-or-miss affairs relying on little more than the gut instincts of the copywriters or manufacturers; following the war, many national promotions involved intensive market analysis, the services of dozens of professionals, and up to half a million dollars in investments. The total advertising expenses for the nation *doubled* from $1.5 billion to more than $3 billion only ten years after the war.[33] The real question remains whether all this effort was made to meet consumer demand or to create it. Critics of modern advertising, who stress the second, conclude that modern advertising was simply the lie used to cover the abuses of mass industrial capitalism, not a democratic and popular expression of the needs of the people. While it is hard to escape this conclusion—if for no other reason than the agencies were in the direct pay of manufacturers—it is important to keep in mind the fact that consumers were often willing accomplices to this development. New products and advertising styles did provide Americans with the means, however controlled and directed by corporate managers, to address modernity. Historians have been hard-pressed to find any sources that validate claims of either a sinister manipulation by advertisers or a demand-based control over the marketplace. The reality was likely to have been a little bit of both.

The 1910s

4

Architecture

Of all architectural forms, the skyscraper is undeniably the most American. Introduced in the late nineteenth century, high-rise buildings not only were perfected in the United States but also represented a unique American blend of progress, commerce, culture, and democracy. The stunning heights of these massive structures, rising more than 800 feet from the ground by the 1910s, became a symbol of American optimism and ingenuity. Louis Sullivan, a pioneer in tall-building design and construction, wrote that the skyscraper

must be tall, every inch of it tall. The force and power of altitude must be in it. It must be every inch a proud and soaring thing, rising in sheer exultation that from bottom to top is a unit without a single dissenting line—that it is the new, the unexpected, the eloquent peroration [i.e., summation] of most bald, most sinister, most forbidding conditions.[1]

Sullivan's vision of the skyscraper suggests that architecture needed to meet a variety of demands. In one sense, a building was constructed to address the specific necessities of those who paid for its construction. Businesses needed to house their executives and employees, residences needed to provide pleasant yet efficient space for their occupants, and the public needed practical access to governmental and other institutional services such as libraries, schools, and transportation. In another sense, the building should be part of a coherent plan of design for a specific region or locale. One would no more place a 50-story apartment complex in the middle of the countryside than a free-standing single-family home in the heart of a city's business district. The environment in which the building existed was as important a design consideration as any other. Finally, good architecture required that designers be sensitive to the emotional or artistic impression that the "constructed environment" has on the people who live in and near to these creations. Like it or not, building forms communicate messages to the public, be they the solid and respectable image of the downtown bank or insurance company, the cozy domesticity of a suburban bungalow, or even the seemingly trivial yet always happy exteriors of our fast-food restaurants. In the words of New York architects Henry Cleveland and William Backus,

[T]he perception of beauty and deformity, of refinement and grossness, of decency and vulgarity, of propriety and indecorum, is the first thing which influences man to escape from a groveling, brutish character. . . . In most persons, this perception is awakened by what may be called the exterior of society, particularly by the mode of building.[2]

FORM AND MEANING

Louis Sullivan is also credited with the often-quoted yet poorly appreciated phrase "form follows function" to describe this central tension in architecture. According to the adage, and most designers who followed Sullivan, the ornamentation and style of a building was subordinate to the intended use of the structure. In fact, by the 1930s, a majority of American architects thought that traditional forms of expression were merely worn-out clichés—meaningless if not bothersome to the modern citizen. To other designers, many of whom were highly influential in the years immediately before the decade of the 1910s, the external message conveyed by a building was more important than its use. The artistry of the structure and the connections that were made between it and past architectural marvels became the true goals. Yet, as with all binary distinctions, the contrast between form and function was never absolute. Unlike almost all other artists, building designers understood that their creations must be both innovative as well as familiar—fresh while also connected to common experience. As a result, American architects in the 1910s found themselves torn between providing a building that was serviceable for the people who would use it and the desire to make a lasting artistic impression.

The type of structure under consideration figured greatly in the amount of latitude a designer had between these two poles. For example, vernacular or folk architecture, which relied on tried and true methods of construction, passed on informally from generation to generation using readily available materials (not ordered specifically for the job), produced little artistic variation in form. Barns, stores, and most early nineteenth-century houses, for example, are quite uniform throughout

the country. People resisted experimentation to ensure that their investment would do the job required of it. By contrast, academic or high-art
architecture looked for particular ideas and emotions to be delivered by
buildings specifically commissioned for construction. Relying on historical motifs, these designers used the symbols of the Gothic cathedral or
the Greek and Roman temple, for example, to signify a particular theme
of the new structure. By the 1910s, American architects confidently mixed
and matched these well-known emblems to create a style all their own.
The rise of mass production and, especially, the use of modern building
materials in both vernacular and academic design blended the relationship between form and function even further. While academic architecture remains the focus of this chapter and most critics of the era,
vernacular design increasingly influenced and redirected the efforts of
draftsmen during the 1910s.

The best term to describe the architectural style of the 1910s is eclectic,
meaning something that is a selection of components from various other
sources. To critics, this characteristic suggests that there was no particular style of the 1910s. One prominent author termed the architectural
period from 1900 to 1930 an "esthetic wasteland"[3] because of its strong
and often overpowering reliance on preexisting styles (disdainfully
termed "derivative" because it emanates or is derived from the work of
others); however, by focusing on the *shifts* in historical design we can
truly appreciate the creative and, at times, revolutionary changes that
took place during the decade. In actuality, the eclectic style was a distinct
method of design in that it avoided *one specific* historical model. The
decade saw a greater tolerance of vernacular and informal design elements that many connoisseurs found distasteful. Spanish influences from
California and Florida, Pueblo motifs from the Southwest, and Creole
styles from New Orleans, for example, were all added to the palettes of
architects throughout the decade. Traditional vernacular and academic
designs remained strong, but it was now much more likely for a suburb
or city to contain a hodgepodge of styles rather than merely variations
on a central theme.

Because most Americans are familiar with this eclectic style, distinguishing between these traditional architectural themes is relatively easy.
The four mainstays of the era were Classical, Gothic, Renaissance, and
Romanesque design. Each had its own specialized treatments, such as
the neoclassical and beaux arts classical or the Victorian and Richardsonian Romanesque (described below). The Classical style refers to a
Roman temple design that raises the base of the foundation off the level
of the ground, uses a four-column portico or entryway, and has simple,
unadorned moldings. The Gothic style is noted for its steeply pitched
roofs, multiple dormers, relatively simple lines (depending on one's
point of reference), and use of stone exteriors. Renaissance and Roman-

esque architecture are decidedly more formal and academic in composition. The Renaissance style is characterized by a strictly repeated
regularity in rectangular window and door designs and strong horizontal belts for each floor. Each floor is also distinguished by a slight but
noticeable change in the treatment of the brick exterior. The roof line is
either flat or augmented by a balustrade or railing. By contrast, Romanesque design is set off by the repeated use of archways, brick or stone
exteriors, towers at the corners, and, in the case of the Richardsonian
Romanesque, an intentional sense of great mass and volume. The famil-
iarity of each form suggests how prevalent these design elements had
become by the turn of the century. The willingness of architects during
the 1910s to mix and match these elements, often within single buildings,
attests to the respect that was and is afforded to these patterns by American builders.

These standard forms provided not only guidance for designers but,
equally important, a "standard vocabulary" for the public. When comparing the Classical, Gothic, Renaissance, and Romanesque forms above,
one might just as easily have called these, respectively, the bank, church,
townhouse, and university styles, respectively. Designers relied on these
familiar forms to place their building immediately within an established
tradition. As a result, the new space was given credibility and importance. Both academic and vernacular design responded to the spread of
this shared vocabulary. Increasingly in the 1910s, architects used standard materials, shapes, ornamentation, and proportions to experiment
with new combinations. When modern architecture, often called the International Style, was introduced in the 1920s and 1930s, it was this
shared vocabulary that was questioned by many designers. Modernists
argued, for example, that the Roman or Renaissance European models
used by most architects had no meaning to contemporary Americans;
the vocabulary made no sense. Designs based on these principles, they
claimed, were simply boring, unimaginative, and false. It is important to
keep this link between public meaning and design in mind when con-
sidering architectural eclecticism during the 1910s.

ECLECTIC ARCHITECTURE AND
MODERN MATERIALS

Of course critics had ample room to complain about the eclectic style.
When used without restraint, eclecticism tends to degenerate into mad
collections of styles and ornamentation. As early as the 1870s, when
eclecticism gained its first footing in America, Victorian homes tended
to be dark, overly ornamented, and almost maniacally stuffed with curios and keepsakes. As one historian wrote, interiors became a "murky

obstacle course" with "fashionable oddments," turning the house "into a kind of bandit's cave."[4] Well into the twentieth century, chintzy mass-produced woodwork and other accessories gave historical design elements an embarrassing pretentiousness—like hanging a paint-by-the-numbers rendition of the Mona Lisa in an art gallery—which undermined the academic architects' claim that historical design uplifted and educated the citizenry. When, from 1900 to 1920, elite draftsmen began to downplay and soften the historical elements of their buildings, the road was paved for modernists to discard them completely. Eclecticism became "a mere bad habit that needed breaking."[5]

That the eclectic style became a habit at all was due to several powerful forces that were changing the architectural and social landscape of America. The first of these was the development of new and better building materials. For example, by 1900, most suppliers of wood had standardized their millwork. Rather than relying on local mills and traditional goods (as in vernacular design), architects could now begin to order a wider variety of wood types with the assurance that a "two-by-four" or standard joist was the same regardless of the lumberyard. Mechanized millwork also improved, so that moldings, doors, shutters, blinds, gables, and trim all arrived at the job site in a much more polished and uniform state. Brick presses, used to fashion masonry in a variety of designs and colors, were also developed to give architects a wider selection for their exteriors. Finally, the spread of affordable pane glass literally opened buildings (particularly homes) to the outside and reduced the traditional reliance upon the small and expensive rows of glass, called "sash-type" or "six over nine" windows (to denote the number of individual panes), seen in many preindustrial structures. Providers often combined these services, selling completely framed windows and doors, trimmed in the specific style requested by the designer.

More important, for larger structures, was the increased availability of affordable steel. Although in general use before 1880, steel had become the overwhelming material of choice for most buildings by the turn of the century. Not only was it stronger than masonry, steel allowed designers to support the weight of the structure on the *external* frame rather than with the exterior *and* interior walls. Stone base walls needed to be twelve inches thick to support the weight of a single floor, with an additional four inches of thickness for each additional story. A steel frame distributed the load throughout the structure and practically eliminated height constraints. The use of steel support beams also meant that internal spaces could now be opened, allowing for larger rooms without walls (well suited to the growing army of clerical workers in many of America's largest businesses). The change was like building a cube using toothpicks rather than six square ceramic tiles; the resulting structure was lighter and therefore could be built higher, and it was also more open to air and light, making it more enjoyable within. When terra cotta blocks and mortar were used to cover the steel, thereby insulating the metal to prevent heat buckling, the new buildings became nearly fireproof. Appropriately, the first skyscraper to be built was constructed with a metal frame: The Home Insurance Building designed by William LeBaron Jenney, was erected in 1885 in Chicago.

New machinery and electronics had also been introduced by 1910. Most notable was the safety elevator. It was generally assumed that five floors was the reasonable limit one could ask workers or residents to climb. When, in 1870, the first safety elevator was used in a high-rise building, designers were freed to expand upward. Telephones, electricity, and incandescent lighting made these vast interior spaces functional, as employees or apartment dwellers could now communicate better within the building. By 1910 architects relied heavily on these basic technical and engineering innovations in their construction.

While technological and social changes help answer how and why academic architects began to construct urban skyscrapers, it does not explain why the eclectic style became so widely employed by the most influential designers. To explain how eclecticism became so dominant by 1910, it is necessary briefly to trace the historical development of the training methods employed in American architecture. As noted above, a building exists not only to serve a useful function but also to provide a physical space within an existing environment. Accordingly, building designers needed to consider at least three key aspects of their projects.

The first, obviously, was the plans for the building itself. Most nineteenth-century American architects were trained informally, apprenticed at an established firm, in studios, or with construction companies. Here they absorbed the basic historical vocabulary of design which included, for example, when to introduce domes or columns or how best to use distinctive windows, moldings, or other recognizable symbols. The principles of rational balance at the heart of Classical, Renaissance, Romanesque, and Gothic design, for example, were also picked up by some novices. It was not until the latter part of the century that standard skills were developed by the American Institute of Architects and formal training was provided by such universities as M.I.T., Yale, the University of Illinois, and Cornell.

In addition to building design, landscape architecture was a key piece of the puzzle. Seeking to place a structure within a "proper" environmental setting, natural designers, such as Frederick Law Olmsted, Calvert Vaux, and Charles Adams Platt, formed the American Society of Landscape Architects in 1899 to help designers to see the totality of their plans—to see the building within its "natural setting" (which were quite often completely manufactured, as in the case of Central Park in New

York City). The connection between the structure and its immediate environment had been recognized by most academic architects by 1910.

Finally, good architecture fit into and augmented a larger, citywide plan. Dating back to America's inception, city planning was not a new concept by 1910. Beginning around 1900, however, the trend was formalized, and noteworthy commissions were formed in Cleveland, Ohio; Hartford, Connecticut; Chicago, Illinois; Washington, D.C.; and San Francisco, California, to name a few. In 1910 the National City Planning Association was founded to help designers incorporate their plans better into the larger needs of the metropolis. Led by Charles Mumford Robinson, advocates believed in a "science" of city design, which provided tangible benefits to the citizens who lived there. In accordance with this new science, by 1916, New York City became the first municipality to zone its space for specific purposes (e.g., residential, commercial), a trend, which spread rapidly to other towns and, later, the suburbs.

ÉCOLE DES BEAUX-ARTS

While these three components—architecture, landscape design, and city planning—were clearly well understood by most architects, no American institution had the cultural or intellectual authority to unify designers into a single school of thought. As had been the case throughout the nineteenth century, the best and brightest American architects turned to Europe, in particular to France, for guidance and leadership. The École des Beaux-Arts, in Paris, became the most influential institution in American architectural design. Many of the most prominent American designers either attended the Beaux-Arts or worked in partnership with architects who had. While it too changed over time, the central mission of the French school was to unify the theory of the design (called the *parti*) with both the rational needs of the structure and city and the emotional or artistic desires of the architects and patrons.

While formalism and respect for historical design were highly valued, American students seemed intent on fashioning their own, unique solutions while using the traditional methods countenanced by their European masters. It was here that the eclectic style was born. For example, the influential architect Ernest Flagg was one of the scores of American designers who studied at the Beaux-Arts. After attending for nearly three years, Flagg felt he had absorbed as much academic classicism and structural rationalism as possible. As an American, however, Flagg had no interest in remaining in Europe or in earning any of the prestigious prizes awarded to the most accomplished students. What Flagg and the other Americans seemed most impressed with was the *parti*, which, according to Flagg, was "the logical solution of the problem, and as every true architect must have two natures, the practical and the artistic, the *parti* must be the logical solution of the problem from his dual standpoint as constructor and artist."[6]

Probably the best example of an American architect's interpretation of the Beaux-Arts and its influence in U.S. design was the career of Henry Hobson Richardson. Born in Louisiana, trained at Harvard and in France, and living in Boston, Richardson fused many of the traditions of European design with the republican spirit of the United States. Rejecting the strict Gothic revival, which was dominant in the 1870s and 1880s, Richardson simplified and Americanized much of the formalism that was so characteristic of the Beaux-Arts. His unique style, called Richardsonian Romanesque, imparted a sense of strength and simple honesty to his buildings when others turned to excessive ornamentation. A string of significant and prominent commissions, from 1877 to his early death in 1886, made Richardson one of the most influential designers of the era. In addition to the high-rise, Richardson pioneered the construction of buildings that spanned entire city blocks (also termed a Van Zant block). Under his guidance, these massive structures conveyed a sense of harmony and solid tranquility to the business district, an effect intended by most designers still to this day. His distinctive style shaped the careers of such luminaries as Louis Sullivan, Frank Lloyd Wright, and even the International Style which would overthrow eclecticism in the coming years.

Even if American architects' experiences at the Beaux-Arts were the only lasting by-products of their education, the training would still be noted for its deep influence on design in this country. In reality, the work of these French-influenced draftsmen were soon generalized across the country through a variety of popular and trade presses. Frank Lloyd Wright and the basics of "Prairie style" architecture were introduced to most Americans through a 1901 issue of the *Ladies' Home Journal*. By 1910 only the most isolated vernacular architects were unaware of the *parti* and the freedom of eclectic design. Periodicals included the *American Architect and Building News, American Architect*, the *Architectural Record*, the *Brickbuilder, American Builder's Companion*, and the *Modern Builder's Guide*. The last two of these are noteworthy in that they addressed the needs of builders and contractors rather than those of the design artists. Mass magazines, such as the *Ladies' Home Journal* and *Better Homes and Gardens*, began to highlight "ideal homes" and designs, further popularizing and supporting eclecticism and the architects who favored it. Many popular writers and critics, such as Russell Sturgis, Mariana Griswold Van Rensselaer, Harry Demond, Herbert Croly, and Montgomery Schuyler, gained their fame by popularizing and critiquing the latest designs. Finally, the vernacular pattern books, which provided pictorial indexes of most of the major styles of exterior and interior treatments, were wildly popular with the public.

PARTNERS AND ARCHITECTS

Regional variations accounted for the leading partnerships that formed between 1890 and 1910. In New York, the firm of McKim, Mead, and White wielded the greatest influence. Trained at the Beaux-Arts and studying under Henry Richardson, Charles F. McKim founded the partnership in 1879 with William Mead and the ill-fated Stanford White (killed by an enraged husband who alleged that White was having a tawdry affair with his wife). Unlike Richardson, but typical of many Eastern designers, the firm stayed closer to the Classical and Renaissance models advanced by Beaux-Arts than rebels such as Richardson or Flagg, who borrowed European ideas but relied on their own native architectural intuitions. By 1910 the firm's influence was largely unchallenged in New York, and their leading designs became the standard against which all others were measured.

In Chicago, the firm of Burham and Root provides a good example of the growing independence from the Beaux-Arts style displayed by many designers in the Midwest. Pioneers of the Chicago School of high-rise construction, Daniel Burnham and John Root innovated with materials and designs in ways that were true to the nature of the *parti*, but free from the constraints of historical forms. Their best example of their style was the Reliance Building, built in Chicago in 1895. Constructed of steel and glass, with large "Chicago windows" to bring in air and light, the structure reflects the lightness and grace that are so vital to model skyscraper design. The exteriors were simple and functional appendages to the metal skeleton, not needlessly pretentious.

In California, farthest removed from the cultural influence of the East Coast, designers gradually took an even greater latitude in their use of vernacular, American-born characteristics. Prominent early architects practicing in San Francisco, Pasadena, and Palo Alto, such as Arthur Page Brown and Frederick Law Olmsted, stayed closer to their Eastern roots. Brown, trained by McKim, Mead, and White, and informally connected to the Beaux-Arts, worked on a number of residential and private commissions, such as the noted mausoleum for Charles and Mary Crocker, before his own accidental death in 1896. Olmsted, commissioned by railroad magnate Senator Leland Stanford to lay out the Palo Alto campus of Stanford University, began to expand the realm of acceptable architectural forms when he chose a Spanish mission style for the California State Building at the 1893 Columbian Exposition. Both designers were hesitant to make too radical a shift in their design characteristics. Still, the seeds for a unique California style, planted in the late nineteenth century, would come to maturity in the residential architecture of the 1910s.

Perhaps no single architect played a greater role in the transition from the Beaux-Arts to the eclectic style than Louis Sullivan. The man who wrote in 1896 that "form follows function" was no modern minimalist—in fact, his most significant creation, the Chicago Auditorium, is chock full of ornamentation specifically designed by the architect—but rather one who believed that a building must be true to both its environment and its intended use. The Auditorium's form, constructed between 1886 and 1890, was largely based on the fact that it covered an entire square block. Sullivan used simplified design elements to create a sense of unity at the street level, which was missing in most urban spaces which were broken up by smaller, uncoordinated designs. Sullivan's exposure to the Japanese Pavilion at the 1876 Centennial in Philadelphia, and later to the Ho-o-Den at the Columbian Exposition, gave him and other advocates of the Chicago School a sense of the open interior spaces and simple lines of Japanese construction.

Sullivan is most influential in that he saw and publicized his view that buildings must be part of an organic whole. Dating back at least as far as Hellenic Greece, the notion of an ideal form for a particular place was pivotal in changing the thinking patterns of many designers. Clearly, if an architect needed to take into account both the environment and the city plan in his or her design, it was impossible to copy European styles wholly in the unique circumstances afforded by American cities. Midwestern cities such as Chicago, for example, were much more open to redesign and experimentation than the older, Eastern municipalities (partly because Chicago's business district and nearly 17,000 structures burned to the ground in 1871). Armed with the simplistic mantra of "form follows function" and blessed with a freedom unavailable in the East and in Europe, the Chicago School exploded across the country between 1890 and 1910 giving expression to the eclectic style in new and forceful ways.

PUBLIC BUILDINGS

The most forceful American architectural expression of the decade was clearly the skyscraper. As historian Carter Wideman cleverly noted, "They are, after all, the way Americans explain how high Superman can leap in a single bound." While height is, in itself, an impressive characteristic of building design, very often early designers lost sight of proportion. Schooled in the need to connect to historical motifs, architects often force fitted or exaggerated styles in ways that clearly detracted from the overall effect.[7]

New York's Singer Tower was an unfortunate example of this type of problem. Designed by Ernest Flagg and completed in 1908, the 47-floor, 612-foot structure was for a short time the tallest building in the world (and later the tallest building ever torn down, in 1968). Constructed in large part to steal attention away from Chicago's more celebrated sky-scrapers, Flagg appended a needlelike tower to his conventional, mansard-roofed, Beaux-Arts design. The exaggerated French Baroque design was highlighted by a garish green and red terra cotta exterior. The effect looked more like a village clock tower on steroids than a modern American office space.

If the Singer Tower has any place in the pantheon of American architecture, it is more for its role in bringing about new urban zoning laws than for its questionable adherence to European standards of beauty. While construction for Singer Tower was still under way, neighboring City Investing Company began work on an equally tall structure on the same block. It soon became apparent to both the executives at the Singer Sewing Machine Company and Ernest Flagg that the two buildings would not only crowd each other out for attention, but also for the much-needed natural light and breezes used to keep employees comfortable. Flagg approached city planners with a proposal to limit such vertical competition. Briefly stated, his plan would restrict the amount of vertical space a building could claim based on the area of the structure at the ground level and the width of the streets servicing the region. Opposed by prominent designer D. Knickerbocker Boyd, who wanted shorter but more spacious towers, discussion continued at the Heights of Buildings Commission of New York City from 1913 until 1916. When a resolution was passed by the planners, the city's unique set-back or wedding-cake building design became law. Developers could now build up to three-quarters of their lots to a height not to exceed one and half that of the city street. For the remaining quarter, there were no height restrictions. The New York zoning law was soon copied by many other cities, giving the American urban landscape a unique, ziggurat-like appearance that would last until the 1960s.

If the Singer Tower provided an example of the excesses of eclecticism coupled with modern technology, then the Woolworth Building demonstrated how the same style could result in a true work of art. Financed entirely in cash by retailing mogul Frank Woolworth (and retained by the company until 1998), the structure was designed by Cass Gilbert and engineered by Gunvald Aus from 1910 to 1913. Unlike the Singer Building, which relied on embellishments for dramatic effect, the Woolworth Building used a seemingly traditional Gothic motif to soar 57 stories, or 792 feet, above the streets of New York. Gilbert, as Richardson had before him, softened the heavier elements of the Gothic style, removing most of the horizontal breaks that would prevent an observer's eye from rising with it. At the top, the Gothic finials, gargoyles, and flying buttresses were oversized so as to be seen and experienced from the streets below. The Gothic theme is carried into the interiors, lending a sense of wholeness to the structure and leading Reverend S. Parkes Cadman, who at-

New Pennsylvania Station, New York City. Courtesy of the Library of Congress.

tended the opening ceremonies with a host of dignitaries including President Woodrow Wilson, to dub the Woolworth Building the "Cathedral of Commerce," a name no doubt pleasing to both the architect and the owner.[8] In many ways, the Woolworth Building was the fulfillment of the eclectic style. Employing the most modern technology (including a bank of 30 elevators that could take occupants to the top floors in less than a minute) and built with contemporary materials, the building could be stripped of its Gothic exterior and be indistinguishable from the emerging International Style.

In addition to the more prominent skyscrapers, other public buildings of note were either constructed or completed in the 1910s. In a very real sense, the architectural innovation that fueled the spread of high-rises had slowed. By 1910 many of the most interesting structures were those designed for broader public use. Pennsylvania Station, designed by McKim, Mead, and White, suggested that in the proper hands neoclassicism could still provide utility while conferring beauty and tranquility to an important civic space. Massive in size, measuring more than 300 feet in length, 150 feet from the ground, and covering two entire city blocks, the central rail station of New York relied on the same steel girder construction as did its loftier neighbors. The external colonnade design, completed in 1911, complemented the internal vaults which took passengers and visitors more than 45 feet below street level. For the nation's largest rail station to remain functional, McKim varied the internal spaces so

New York Public Library Building. Courtesy of the Library of Congress.

that areas that were to provide swift passage were small and low-ceilinged while the ticketing and debarkation points, places where people might linger, were large and high. As historian Richard Guy Wilson noted, "In catching or meeting a train at Pennsylvania Station one became part of a pageant—actions and movements gained significance while processing through such grand spaces."[9] As the threshold to Gotham, no functional building could better instill a sense of urban dignity and order. Razed in 1963, the site is now occupied by Madison Square Garden. Pennsylvania Station's less impressive relation, Grand Central Terminal (in essence, an inner-city depot of the station), constructed in 1913, was recently designated a historic site.

The New York Public Library also came into its own during the decade. Founded in 1886 by the largess of Samuel J. Tilden, who bequeathed about $2.4 million to create and maintain a public reading resource, the city library merged with two semiprivate collections in 1895 to form the base of the current institution. Headed by John Shaw Billings, the library immediately sought a permanent home to accommodate the immense collection (now second only to the Library of Congress). The retreat was found on Fifth Avenue between 40th and 42nd Streets when the Croton Reservoir was converted to a construction site. Although the foundation was laid in 1902, the final constitution of the library, including the placement of the now famous lions, was not completed until 1911. Commissioned to the relatively obscure firm of Carrère and Hastings, the exterior was patterned along the relatively traditional Beaux-Arts style. It was the public nature of the space, providing access to books to tens of thousands of readers and visitors on its very first day, that makes the New York Public Library such an extraordinary building.

Finally, the architecture of many semipublic institutions was also greatly shaped by American eclecticism. Higher education, in particular, was coming into its own in the United States during the 1910s, and a host of newer facilities were either opening or augmenting their campus facilities. The eclectic genre melded nicely with the needs of the university as developers were asked to design unified campuses showing both a deference to the timeless past as well as a confidence in the cosmopolitan future. European models helped to provide the former need while the American liberalism in Beaux-Arts application filled the latter need. Both Rice University in Houston, Texas, and the Massachusetts Institute of Technology, in Boston, provide excellent examples of this widespread architectural trend in the 1910s; however, perhaps American eclecticism was best applied at the U.S. Military Academy at West Point, New York. Ralph Adams Cram won the commission for the academy in 1903, and construction continued until it was completed in 1910. Cram's selection of a neo-Gothic motif for the main hall and chapel gave West Point a clean, spartan, and decidedly masculine atmosphere.

Public monuments were also key architectural legacies of the decade. Most prominent among these was the Lincoln Memorial, commissioned in 1911 by Congress and constructed between 1914 and 1922. Henry Bacon's design, like that of Charles McKim for Pennsylvania Station, used traditional Classical motifs, in this case a Greek, Doric-columned temple. As was the case with the eclectic style, Bacon modified the form to keep the best elements—giving the structure an openness and serenity that was suitable to Abraham Lincoln's memory—while maintaining functional access for the public. Such simple modifications as rotating the axis of the building by 90 degrees to allow for a more dramatic facade to face the reflecting pool, also under construction, created a symmetry with the existing Washington Monument and anchored the Washington Mall area. The massive sculpture of a seated and peaceful Lincoln, completed by Daniel Chester French, was assembled at the site near the end of 1919. Combined with the beloved president's two most cited speeches (the Gettysburg Address and his Second Inaugural) and symbolic references to the Union that Lincoln helped to preserve, Bacon's memorial became one of the most popular and solemn public places in the nation's capital.

While skyscrapers are rightly identified as lasting and important contributions by architects in the 1910s, these other forms—public transpor-

Lincoln Memorial, East Front, from the Northeast. Courtesy of the Library of Congress.

tation facilities, higher education buildings, and civic memorials, for example—are equally valid examples of the eclectic style that dominated the decade. Designers such as McKim, Cram, Bacon, and Sullivan sought to merge their experiences at the École des Beaux-Arts with the unique needs of Americans. As a decade dedicated to both progress and stability, the 1910s supported and gave greater meaning to this debate. Naturally, the degree to which they highlighted either aspect of form and function varied by man, commission, and location. While, using historical hindsight, it is now clear that eclecticism was to give way to the minimalist or functional International Style in the coming years, the brightest and most talented designers of the era remained committed to finding this elusive proportion. Ironically, it was in private residences, and not public buildings and showy skyscrapers, that most designers were able to come closest to this ideal.

PRIVATE BUILDINGS

The balance between form and function is not a new one to home design in America. Dating back to the colonial period, people have been seeking to merge useful space with a meaningful style. Early in the 1800s, the limits on materials and the essential needs of life dictated much of the vernacular style seen in houses. With the fireplace stationed at the middle of the home for the greatest conservation of heat, most structures followed a simple plan of having a great room (also called the hall, dwelling room, or fireroom) for most family activities and a smaller chamber room for sleeping. A rear or side lean-to was usually appended to the building in later years to add a formal kitchen or additional sleeping space. The American balloon frame, which employed a light timber frame using corner posts, joists, and studs secured by nails, allowed for some creative expression on the building's exterior. Early Greek Revival, Colonial, and Georgian styles echoed the internal honesty, seriousness, and (ideally) serenity of these simple homes. By the turn of the century, home ownership had become, and remains today, an important civic characteristic of the middle class. Tenement-style living was still rare, and the single-family detached home accounted for from between half and three-quarters of all housing starts from 1890 to 1930. The styles employed in designing these homes were the visible markers of an owner's relative "respectibility."

What had changed by the twentieth century was the rapid growth of suburbs in America. While many of these regions became places where citizens of moderate or even meager means might own a home, the earliest suburbs to the nation's largest cities drew families disproportionately from the upper economic categories. As noted by influential historian Kenneth T. Jackson, by 1900, the new affluent suburban residents were rejecting the inner city and "expressing a determination to control the physical and social environment in which they lived."[10] Towns such as Oak Park or Evanston, near Chicago, and Brookline, near Boston, declined offers by the major cities to annex them. This growing population of wealthy clients offered architects new and pristine places for them to design their ideal structures. Moreover, the advent of new technologies—such as electricity and indoor plumbing—removed many of the restraints to design that led developers to accept the limits of vernacular design without challenge.

Unfortunately for many creative architects, by 1900 the Victorian home design was dominated by the heavily ornamented and visually complex Eastlake and Queen Anne styles. These "painted ladies" came to the fore largely because they meshed with the, by then, dominant upper-middle-class notions of family and female domesticity. The Victorian home, with its many rooms, was suitable to the changing needs of the family, such as a sick room or a nursery. The style allowed for live-in servants and their easy and undetectable access to work areas in the large kitchen and a back stairs to the many bedrooms. The multiple exits and entrances to the home also allowed greater access by servants, children, and guests, without unintentionally disturbing other members of the family. The larger, first-floor rooms encouraged family togetherness. The Victorian home was, and in some cases remains, popular precisely because it was a new way to meet the needs of its contemporary residents.

By the 1910s, however, the many suburban Queen Anne and Eastlake homes were beginning to look dated. The vain affectations of domesticity seemed silly in an era when modernity was quickly outdating old traditions. The consumer revolution brought new, disposable products and ready-made foods which eliminated the need for large work spaces in the home. The Victorians suddenly seemed too large, pretentious, and, ironically, not cozy enough. Parlors and large hallways seemed foolish in an era when formal private visitations were disappearing in favor of more public entertainments. In the new decade, simplicity had replaced formality, and the Victorians were most certainly not simple.

The search for this simplicity consumed residential architects for most of the 1910s. The focus on honesty in form and presentation was termed by practitioners an "organic" style, which looked to build structures appropriate for the owners, the site, and the community—a goal, we have seen, that closely resembles that of the commercial architects of the decade. Organic architectural styles favored lightly treated natural surfaces, such as wood and stone, and intrinsic colors rather than the ornate and painted millwork that festooned most Victorian homes. Minimalism was also a quality of organic home design, as architects tried to reduce the need for expensive upkeep and cleaning while making each room multifunctional (a factor less influenced by the cost of a live-in maid than the fact that these women were now rapidly leaving domestic service for work in the factories). Floor patterns also changed significantly. Most first-floor patterns were now based on a circular design, allowing easy access to every room and a better awareness by mothers of the actions of their young children. Kitchens were dramatically reduced in size, and back staircases and servants quarters were eliminated. Upstairs, it was rare to find homes with more than three simple bedrooms, instead of the four or five bedrooms typical of the Victorian. Even for the least expensive new homes, built-ins were used wherever possible, including closets, which replaced free-standing armoires, laundry chutes, and bathroom fixtures. Such a house was less of a social statement and more a place for a family to care for its needs efficiently so that they might make their statements elsewhere in the increasingly public American life. These trends in organic and minimalist styles led directly to a standardization of home production and, as a result, a lowering of the cost for home ownership.

FRANK LLOYD WRIGHT

Frank Lloyd Wright stood alone as the avatar of organic design. A Midwesterner by birth, Wright was ambitious, self-assured, hypocritical in his thoughts and actions, and most definitely an architectural genius. Trained informally as a commercial architect with some of the era's greatest designers, Wright won international fame largely on the basis of his residential structures, which came to define the "Prairie school" of design. While the esthetic of the Prairie school is profound, it is important to recognize that Wright was equally capable as a pioneer in using the newest technologies and building theories. The Tokyo Imperial Hotel, built from 1916 to 1920, is a case in point. Designed using a floating foundation which simply rested on reinforced concrete, the structure was one of the few in the city to withstand the massive earthquake that struck the city in 1923. Wright's use of steel and concrete opened the doors for uncounted innovations in a multitude of buildings.

Frank Lloyd Wright and the Prairie style provided a fundamentally new and organic theory of design which met many of the basic functions of a home while providing a serene and unified form. According to Widerman, Wright's style "can be seen as a unique expression of the recurrent American conflict between wanting to expand to new horizons, while at the same time establishing some sense of permanence. Never before or since has an architect so fully and empathetically embraced this fundamental American dualism toward the idea of the home."[11] He achieved this solution by borrowing many of the time-honored practices of international home design while maintaining an absolute fidelity to the natural environment of his predominantly Midwestern clientele (hence, Prairie). Wright homes seemed to hug the flat earth, reveling in the horizontal sweep of the land. His ornamentation flowed naturally from the tones of the wood, glass, stone, stucco, and concrete that became his primary building materials. The interior spaces, supported by central steel beams, were as open as the those of the traditional Japanese structures that had impressed American architects when displayed at the 1876 and 1893 expositions. He almost invariably centered his homes around the construction of a massive hearth at the core of the structure, a tribute to one of the most basic vernacular designs. Finally, Wright invited the natural surroundings into the home through an extensive use of windows—sometime constituting entire walls—and his trademark cantilevered eaves which provided shelter near the home. Wright had seemingly invented a new vocabulary for American architecture.

While Wright's personal life prevented his active involvement in American architecture throughout most of the 1910s, he was able to construct a number of significant structures. The Robie house, built from 1908 to 1910, is considered one of his masterworks. Commissioned by a friend in Chicago to make an urban retreat, Wright was challenged by the thin, city lot and busy sidewalks and streets. His solution was to hide the front door, slightly raise the main level, and unify the structure using an extended hip roof with significant eaves. Wright's use of steel and

Frederick C. Robie House, Chicago, Illinois. Courtesy of the Library of Congress.

glass allowed for significant openness in the interior, but the elongated lot was also inevitably transferred within. A beautiful example of the Prairie design, the Robie house, however, was never an ideal domestic retreat.

Wright designed and erected Taliesin, his home, studio, and retreat, in 1911 at his family's estate near Spring Green, Wisconsin. At 37,000 square feet, Wright had ample space and a strong emotional connection to the land, which allowed his architectural imagination to run free. Significantly, he placed his home not on the crest of the hill (which would have lifted the structure away from its natural environment) but on the "brow" of the hill. According to the designer, "Taliesin was to be an abstract combination of stone and wood . . . the lines of the hills were the lines of the roofs, the slopes of the hills their slopes."[12] Unfortunately, several fires have left little of the original structure intact. As Wright rebuilt, he remained true to his vision of an organic structure that was both part of nature and also the product of a man's hand.

If Frank Lloyd Wright was less than prominent during the 1910s, the Prairie school design principles were well demonstrated by a host of Wright's apprentices. George Elmslie, Dwight H. Perkins, George Maher, and Walter Burley Griffin, to name only a few, continued and expanded the new style in places well outside of Wright's Midwest. The basic characteristics of these homes remained relatively consistent, and included a minimal number of rooms, a close integration between site and structure, few interior walls, exterior walls replaced with windows whenever possible, built-in utilities and many built-in furnishings, minimal extraneous ornamentation, and no "fashionable" (i.e., non-Prairie) decor within the structure.

While examples of the Prairie school abound from the 1910s, George Elmslie and William Purcell's 1912 construction of the Bradley Bungalow or "Airplane House" in Woods Hole, Massachusetts, merits special praise. While true to their teacher's original vision, Elmslie and Purcell clearly departed from the nestled look of the Midwestern home for this seaside lot. The steel-supported, cantilevered floors (often pictured with an ornamentally walled porch below the main house that was, sadly, added by later tenants) give the impression of flight from both within and beyond the building. The partners retained a low hip roof and a central masonry hearth, and they added a large, semicircular dining room and conservatory surrounded by a wall of windows to support the Prairie feel to the home.

GUSTAV STICKLEY, THE ARTS AND CRAFTS MOVEMENT, AND THE BUNGALOW

In recent decades it has been made abundantly clear that Wright and the Prairie school of design were not the only ones discovering the simple, organic forms of natural materials. The Arts and Crafts movement, begun in England but championed by Gustav Stickley in the United States, mirrored many of the same trends of the Prairie school but traced a different lineage. Stickley, a furniture maker who founded and edited the journal *The Craftsman*, favored a building design that championed mechanical skills over machine-made goods or milled wood. His home and studio, called Craftsman Farms, was built in 1910 near Morris Plains, New Jersey, as homage to the movement. While his simply hewn furniture remained popular during the decade, it was easily copied by those less committed to hand craftsmanship. Stickley's influence, as well as that of the Prairie school, would also be felt on the West Coast. As with commercial structures in California, residential design in the Far West veered farthest from the traditionally accepted practices of the East. While not immediately recognizable as a Stickley- or Wright-inspired design, the California style of the 1910s soon gave birth to one of the most novel, most popular home designs of the twentieth century: the American bungalow.

Architects and brothers Henry and Charles Greene were certainly influenced by the work of Wright, Stickley, and the other leading Eastern designers. Trained at M.I.T. and suffused with Beaux-Arts classicism, the Greenes designed mostly Colonial and Queen Anne homes for the wealthy until the turn of the century. Near the end of the first decade, the brothers were confident enough to begin experimenting with canti-levered eaves and historical craftsmanship (an expensive vice for a de-signer). The David B. Gamble house, built in Pasadena in 1907 and 1908, was softer in tone that a Wright home but clearly displayed such Prairie and Stickley axioms as an elongated roof line, natural or lightly finished materials, and exposed beams. By the time the partners had created the D.L. James house in Carmel Highlands, California, in 1918, the design had matured from being a derivation of others' ideas into a more natural, native creation.

The fusion of styles visible in the Greenes' work was typical of early vernacular design in California. Entire communities, such as Pasadena, imbued the Arts and Crafts style in uniquely Western ways. The inclu-sion of Arroyo Seco cultural objects such as blankets, pottery, and jew-elry, or the use of natural forms from the desert were just two of the ways in which the California style differentiated itself. One of the state's most important residential architects, Irving Gill, drew deeply upon the multicultural history of Southern California. By mixing reinforced steel with traditional adobe, Gill constructed a number of homes for both the elite and the masses. The Dodge house, built between 1914 and 1916 in Los Angeles, captures a sense of the regional identity that made the California movement so different.

These native historical traditions, academic eclecticism, and vernacular design elements all merged in the 1910s to produce a veritable boom in California bungalow construction. Dating back at least a decade, and relying on forms first pioneered by the British in colonial India (the name comes from the Bengal province in India where regional dwellings were termed bangla or bangala by the locals), the bungalow was the ideal California home. Simple, versatile, casual, inexpensive, and closely linked to the Californians' love of the outdoors, the style became an instant hit across the country. Architect and critic Charles V. Boyd wrote in 1919 that "the bungalow is of all American home types that most truly nationalistic."[13] In its ideal form, the bungalow featured a low-pitched roof, an ample porch, and an open, single-floor interior. Popularized by Henry L. Wilson's *Bungalow Book* (1908) and Henry H. Saylor's *Bungalows* (1911), the bungalow was appreciated for its low cost and basic useful-ness. The few rooms were spacious but easy to clean and maintain by working couples. The basic design was readily modified through the use of dormers, chimneys, roof lines, and windows to encourage a sense of individuality in a society that was rapidly homogenizing. By the end of the decade, developers could design and build a simple bungalow for as little as $900 (larger bungalows sold for four times that amount), mak-

Typical California Bungalow. Courtesy of the Library of Congress.

ing home ownership and middle-class respectability a reality for millions of working families.

With such democratic advantages, the bungalow quickly became the favorite style of real estate developers and even mail-order houses. The Southern California Standard Building Company, for example, sold and financed hundreds of standard bungalow designs on small lots. California speculators also originated bungalow courts, consisting of a ring of homes surrounding a central grassy area. Bowen Courts in Pasadena contained 23 small bungalows when constructed in 1910 according to the plans of Arthur and Alfred Heineman. Prefabricated bungalows were hot sellers for the Sears, Roebuck and Montgomery Ward mail-order firms after 1910. In 1918, Sears offered a 146-page catalog of various bungalow styles from which to chose. These mail-order bungalows were prefabricated and quickly assembled, often in less than a day. Other large national suppliers included Pacific Ready-Cut; the Aladdin Company of Bay City, Michigan; Harris Brothers, in Chicago; and the Gordon-Van Tine Company of Davenport, Iowa.

While seemingly never a vital concern for most architects, California designers did show an extraordinary interest in providing inexpensive and functional housing for low-income Americans. For example, Irving Gill developed Lewis Courts, in Sierra Madre, California, in 1910, to house 11 moderate-income families. The prefabricated homes were placed within a common, terraced courtyard which highlighted a communal play area for children and a large public porch. These small neighborhoods soon became so successful that developers were able to raise rents, which drove away tenants of modest means.

In addition, no region in America displayed a greater willingness to experiment with communal living in the 1910s. Most noteworthy were the attempts made by Charlotte Perkins Gilman and Alice Constance Austin to employ modern feminist designs in residential homes. According to historian Dolores Hayden, feminist design by 1910 sought to build homes that neutralized the cultural biases that maintained the belief that women were solely responsible for cooking, cleaning, and laundry, to name only three typical domestic chores. Gilman wrote, "It is not that women are really smaller-minded, weaker-minded, more timid and vacillating; but that whosoever, man or woman, lives always in a small, dark place, is always guarded, protected, directed and restrained, will become inevitably narrowed and weakened by it."[14] Communal, campus-style homes could free women from their isolation and lighten the work load.

What set the California movement apart from the Eastern tradition was the willingness and ability to build single-family homes while planning for communal cooperation. Unfortunately for the hopes of Gilman and others, the same conditions that allowed the construction of low-cost housing (cheap land, prefabricated bungalows, easy transportation to the suburbs) made it less likely that tenants would be willing to make such fundamental changes to their lifestyles. Moreover, the ease of development led to a glut of housing options, and landlords proved to be unwilling to risk their rental income for the sake of feminist principles. Individual kitchens and laundry rooms soon replaced many of the communal rooms found in the earliest experimental communities. Austin came closest to creating a truly cooperative village when, in 1916, she designed and built 900 residential units in Llano del Rio, California, for lawyer and social activist Lob Harriman. Planned for more than 10,000 people, Austin created communal eating and day-care areas, minimized interior decorations to alleviate housework, and even proposed an underground railway to ferry commuters, laundry, and supplies. While never actualized, these ideal California communities entered the "vocabulary" of residential architects nationwide and have influenced their designs ever since.

CONCLUSION

The rise of affordable housing communities, such as those in Passaic, New Jersey (called Allwood) or Goodyear Heights and Firestone Park in

Akron, Ohio, and the growing availability of the private automobile in the 1910s had long-term implications for domestic architecture. Less obvious reforms, such as the 1913 Constitutional amendment creating a graduated income tax, which sapped the unlimited spending of many of the very wealthy, left many professional architects searching for a new balance between form and function. Finally, the war cut many of the ties between the American and European branches of the profession, and many fewer aspiring designers traveled to the École des Beaux-Arts after 1914.

Were the 1910s an "esthetic wasteland" for American academic design? If one seeks to answer this question by the events that followed, it is possible to reply in the affirmative. Much of the historical deference paid by architects to established European schools (Classic, Gothic, etc.) was abandoned in subsequent decades. One might be tempted to regard Pennsylvania Station or the Woolworth Building as beautiful epitaphs for a way of thinking which had little connection to the needs of modern Americans. However, if we place the decade within a broader sweep of history, eclecticism proved to be much more lasting and influential. As historian Walter C. Kidney playfully wrote, "Eclecticism today is like a person who has almost lived down an ancient scandal, a person whose crime was once exposed, but who is now regarded merely as old and harmless, if not quite respectable."[15] The desire to preserve and update traditional motifs has survived the International Style. The desire for *both* originality and historical connectivity remain valid. If nothing else, the lasting influence of designers such as Gustav Stickley, Frank Lloyd Wright, and the Prairie school, and the popularity of the bungalow give testament to the power of eclectic architecture. While a definitive answer to the question posed above can never really be made, it is clear that architectural trends during the 1910s remained faithful to both the past and the future.

The 1910s

5

Fashion

Fashion, or the types and styles of clothing worn by people, has proven to be one of the most rapidly changing—some might say fickle—of all forms of popular culture. Perhaps because Americans are hesitant to define themselves by strict economic classes, we are more likely to use subtle visual cues such as style and appearance to define our relative place in society. Indeed, in the 1910s—part of the Age of Opulence, or what the French termed La Belle Epoque—the newly rich sought ways to flaunt their material good fortune conspicuously through their clothing and accessories. Unlike many of the other forms of popular culture during the era, staying current with the latest fashions required quite a bit of money. Styles included the use of expensive ornamentation and equally costly accessories. While department stores and mail-order catalogs provided knockoff styles for the masses, those without disposable income did not strive for fashion, but rather function, in their clothing.

Ironically, by the close of the decade, fashion trends had abandoned much of clothing's layered garishness for a newfound freedom of movement and expression. The rise of international fashion trends and the expansion of popular entertainment made much of the old bundled look seem obsolete. Brought about by both World War I and the changes to notions of women in America, fashion by 1919 was wholly distinct from that displayed ten years earlier.

THE BASICS

While men claimed no less extensive of a wardrobe than women, the cut of their clothing was certainly less varied. As a result, stylishness and fashion became even more important to distinguish a man from his peers, all of whom wore similar clothing to similar events. This probably made men's fashion more conservative, as one might be hesitant to experiment too wildly with styles lest they be seen as being frivolous or "slick." Unlike women, most men were not viewed as backward or old-fashioned if they were seen in public wearing last year's styles (the lone exception was the very wealthy, who remained quite sensitive to the latest styles).

The typical combination of trousers, shirt, collar, tie, and jacket was the uniform of the average American male. For formal occasions—ranging from funerals to state dinners—gentlemen were required to wear black morning coats (including tails which fell to the back of the knees), a heavily starched white shirt with studs and a high collar (some approaching three inches), a double-breasted waistcoat (vest), and striped grey or blue trousers, with a top hat, white gloves, and grey or black frock coat for any outdoor activity. The frocks, which were also double-breasted, fell to or slightly below the knee and were made of a warm, durable material such as wool. Highly polished black patent leather shoes were worn by nearly all to formal occasions. An ornate cane, white boutonniere, or tightly wound umbrella often completed the ensemble for the well-dressed gentleman. Some men still affected monocles, held by long and finely worked gold chains, but the practice was rare and certainly past by 1919.

The style of lapels, the shape of collars, the number of buttons (on the coat and shirt), the cut of the cuffs (on shirts and pants), and the cut of the leg (baggy or straight) modified only slightly throughout the decade. Generally, men's attire became less formal and less physically restrictive over the years. For example, the tighter lines of the double-breasted suit gave way, on informal occasions only, to the lounging suit (today called a business suit), which was tailored using a single-breasted style, without a vest, often with pants made of matching fabric. Tweed jackets and blazers were increasingly worn out of the house. These loose-fitting, heavily pocketed lounge jackets remained popular in the United States despite being shunned by most men in Europe. The terms "Yankee swank" or, more directly, the "freak American suit" were used by Europeans to deride this American style. Pants remained simple and were generally cut narrow with small, one-half-inch cuffs. Even the nearly sacred formal attire was toned down by Americans, who came to prefer the short and looser dinner jacket—today called the tuxedo but then referred to as the Monte Carlo—to the vest and morning coat combination.

Men were required to dress appropriately to the event. When about town on business—and not attending formal gatherings—most men wore fur-collared Chesterfield overcoats or capes to keep warm in cold weather. The Mackintosh, a raincoat imported from England, was popular not only because the garment was waterproof but also because it did not exude the oily, rubber smell associated with other waterproof coats. The automobile duster, which consisted of a light cotton overcoat which usually extended to the ankles, was worn with matching caps, goggles, and gloves. Younger men began to wear the duster even when they were not driving. Sporting events, too, required a specific outfit depending upon the activity. Combinations of flannel trousers, blazers, knitted wool sweaters, and cotton shirts were used for outdoor casual entertainment. While men did not have a formal "tea" outfit, as did women, they wore velvet smoking jackets embellished with gold frogging (braided cord) on the shoulders to lend the coats a more masculine, military look. Typical fashion accessories for men in the 1910s included leather shoes of many colors but nearly invariably laced and sporting a rounded toe. Silk ascot ties and cravats were still common before 1914, but rarely worn by the end of the decade. In their place were small, patterned bow ties and neckties made of silk or wool and tied with a small, undistinguished knot. Most men also carried a pocket watch (maintaining the need for vests), but by 1920 the trend was clearly moving toward the wristwatch.

Women's attire was altogether more formal but also more daring. Unlike men, whose clothing varied around a common theme, nonworking women from families of more than modest means could expect to change their clothes three or four times a day in 1910. The phases were divided among specific duties that these women might perform, and they were regular enough that many people timed their day not by a clock but rather by the styles they saw these women wearing as they passed them in public. In the morning, coordinated outfits of shirts and short jackets were worn to provide functional yet stylish cover while ladies shopped, managed their homes, and made frequent yet informal social visits around the neighborhood. In the early afternoon, tea dresses were donned. These were made of lighter fabrics and had long, free-flowing skirts that did not require corsets or other bulky undergarments. Women formally received guests in their tea gowns, but it was also a time for them to be more relaxed without the need to act in a certain way or to be seen in public (in most romance novels of the era, it was during tea time and in tea dresses that married women entertained their lovers). The afternoon break divided the day and led to the third and possibly fourth change of clothes. Women and men dressed for dinner. If there were guests or after-dinner activities were planned, wives often changed after eating. Here were the most exciting and alluring fashion styles for women. Many such dresses highlighted low necklines, pleats, satin, silk, taffeta, extensive costume and real jewelry, elaborate beadwork, feathers, furs, and anything else that might catch the eye. Hemlines rose throughout the decade, revealing ankles that had traditionally remained concealed. Tight sleeves and bodices showed a greater willingness by women in the 1910s to reveal their forms more accurately. The wardrobe of a truly wealthy woman might contain scores of outfits complete with matching accessories. Even for those of moderate means, a young woman would expect to begin her adult life with at least "[t]welve evening gowns, two to three evening wraps, two to four street costumes, two coats, twelve hats and four to ten house dresses." It was also "understood that shoes and stocking would be bought in the dozens."[1] The evening gown was the most public form of fashion for women and, as a result, it varied greatly throughout the years.

Before reviewing these trends, however, it is important to note how, in the 1910s, women's undergarments were almost an outfit in themselves. These clothes were restrictive and often painful to wear (by contrast, men's undergarments invariably consisted of a sleeveless T-shirt, boxer shorts, and hose supporters or garters to hold up their socks, which did not yet contain elastic bands). Women's undergarments took quite a bit of time and, for the most, required the assistance of another woman (family member, friend, or servant) to fasten and align them properly. When they were through, women were literally encased in clothing from their head to their toes. The first layer consisted of white cotton drawers and a short silk slip (chemise). Fastened behind with dainty ribbons and adorned with lace and embroidery, these underclothes certainly could not be seen by men but were an important part in making a woman feel feminine. From here, however, the real work began.

A corset was made of a heavyweight cotton twill, reinforced with steel or whalebone, and held together with hefty stud and loop fasteners. With almost the slightest activity, corsets made the body feel heavy, hot, and itchy. Women put on these devices each day in order to contour their bodies artificially to meet the standards of beauty that ruled the fashion world. What was desired was an "S-shape," which accentuated the bust, flattened or minimized the stomach, and highlighted the rear. Achieving this "natural look" through the use of corsets led not only to discomfort but disfigurement. Bones could break and internal organs were known to have been malformed as a result of these bindings. The best corset makers could tailor their product as to avoid these problems with the very wealthy. For those who had to rely on over-the-counter varieties, however, an ill-fitting corset could mean hours of slow torture.

Rounding out these hidden outfits were supporters or suspenders which kept the hose from falling. These were undoubtedly practical additions since once corseted a women could not bend to reach her stockings. The hose, made of cotton, wool, or silk, were often elaborately decorated with inlays and embroideries, making them one of the more provocative components of a woman's ensemble. Given that most of the leg remained hidden from view, the designs were usually concentrated on the foot and ankle, and they were closely coordinated with the cut, style, and color of the shoe.

With the unmerciful demands of the corset literally pressing upon women, it should come as no surprise that many hailed the introduction of the brassiere as a revolutionary improvement in ladies' underwear. Mary Phelps Jacob, a New York socialite, found that her wardrobe was limited by the bulk of the corset. Prevented from using the latest sheer fabrics being used in evening wear, in 1913 Jacob, with the help of her maid, devised a rudimentary brassiere using handkerchiefs, ribbon, and some cord. By November of the following year, after multiple requests from her friends for a similar article, Jacob patented the Backless Brassiere (it was not called a "bra" until the 1930s), but due to her lack of business acumen she could not profit from its manufacture and sale. She sold the patent to the Connecticut-based Warner Brothers Corset Company who began to market the product successfully throughout the country. By 1920 there were dozens of suppliers—all using slightly modified designs. Women, especially young women, opted to forego the form-shaping "benefits" of the corset in favor of the lighter, cooler, more natural, and less constraining brassiere.

Equally important for the fashionably dressed female were the accessories that coordinated an outfit, providing the appropriate focus on the many colors, textures, and styles of attire. Affordable jewelry included hair combs made of tortoiseshell and adorned with feathers. Paste diamond (rhinestone) or glass earrings, tiaras, and choker necklaces were also common. Silver and bronze adornments such as buttons, lockets, and brooches were worn, but bracelets and rings were rarely worn. Purses, shoes, gloves, and bags were required in the 1910s to coordinate or accentuate evening wear. Always matching the dress in color, purses were small and often made of delicate, impractical fabrics. Shoes rose just above the ankle and were secured with straps or buckles (never laces) and had heels of middling height (no more than an inch; the lone and unconventional exception was the "High Louis" heel). Leather and suede gloves, also colored to match the dress, were either short or barely reached the elbow and often included modest glass, paste, or buttoned detail. For the true elite, such as members of Mrs. John Jacob Astor's social register in New York City, these accessories were required for each of a woman's many outfits; extending to include furs, umbrellas, parasols, walking sticks, and fans. Rounding out the outfit of almost all women, regardless of economic status, were hats. Usually large (measuring nearly a yard across for the most radical), women's hats in the 1910s were adorned with a wide variety of plumage, beads, fringe, and pom-poms. The rage for feathers went so far as to prompt bird lovers, such as those of the Audubon Society, to begin to limit the number and types of animals harvested to feed the fickle fashion industry.

INTENDED EFFECTS

If the basics of men's and women's clothing were predictable in the 1910s, the new styles suggested that the intended effects of their ensembles were changing in significant ways. By the start of the decade, the "Gibson Girl" look was still the rage for most young women. Established by magazine illustrator Charles Dana Gibson in the 1890s, the look, popularized in periodicals such as *Life* and *Collier's*, focused on the elegant and refined beauty of the well-dressed female. To Gibson, and the dozens of other illustrators who soon copied his well-paying style, fashionable clothing created beauty from the raw material of the female form. Corsets and other undergarments were required to generate the typical S-shaped curves given such prominence. Hats, high collars, gloves, and other accessories framed a woman's face and body in ways that highlighted the "appropriate" features. All in all, while certainly comfortable with the greater sex appeal of women in public, the Gibson Girl was hopelessly reliant upon her clothing to create notions of beauty.

In the 1910s, this constructed image began to simplify in significant and long-lasting ways. Young women were increasingly unwilling to submit themselves to the tortures of the corset, turning instead to more liberating undergarments. The "New Woman" was one who was active, mobile, and more comfortable with her place in society. As a result, many felt less need to conform to, or manufacture, a visage that was impractical, uncomfortable, and foolish. Some subtle shifts in the behavior of women added to this fashion trend. For example, the spread of automobile travel gave rise to the need for female passengers to enter, sit, and exit the vehicles. As with men, comfortable dusters, caps, and goggles were developed for women that soon became symbols of the active and youthful life. Sporting attire, which became popular for golf, tennis, croquet, and skating, allowed movement and flattered a woman's natural body shape, which the steel-and-whalebone construction of the Gibson look did not.

Ironically, one of the more prominent fashion crazes of the decade was the "hobble skirt." With very tight gatherings at the knees and ankles, the dress earned its name for the way in which women were forced to walk when they wore them. While most of society shunned the hobble skirt, young urban women remained loyal consumers until the middle of the decade. The connection to youthfulness propelled the hobble skirt as long as the outfit remained practical for the young. When, by 1915, public dancing became the rage for this population, the hobble skirt faded from view. Dance also doomed the large hats, corsets, and volu-minous dresses that had dominated women's fashions.

Hairstyles and cosmetics may not be articles of clothing but they did contribute greatly to the intended effects of fashion in the 1910s. While men's styles were mainly conservative, grooming was very important. Hair was kept short and well trimmed. Moustaches were typical for young men and beards only for older gentlemen. Barbers were quick to apply dyes to color grey hair, and a variety of techniques were used to hide baldness or thinning hair. By contrast, women's coiffures were more creative. Girls invariably grew and wore their hair long until reaching their eighteenth birthdays. After "coming out" in society, young ladies curled, braided, and otherwise sculpted their long locks in ways that made them a fashion accessory. For women who had thin hair, a postiche (hairpiece) was considered acceptable. These small wigs, often called "rats" by critics, were attached with ornate pins and combs. With the demise of large hats, hairstyles became of even greater importance by the close of the decade.

Cosmetics and perfumes were also intended to be used as fashion accessories by the modern woman. As historian Kathy Piess has shown, the rise of cosmetics use in the United States followed a lengthy cultural battle over whether it was proper for a woman to "paint" herself or "put on a face" for public display; something, it was thought, that only pros-titutes or lower-class women did. Ironically, it was the heightened public presence of women in everyday life, including the stage, screen, and the many images and advertisements which filled the pages of magazines and newspapers, that led women to turn to makeup to achieve this new look. The cosmetics industry used medical terms to promote "beauty aids" that would highlight "natural" tone. Cosmetics thus became an acceptable way in which to alter one's complexion or hair. According to Piess, it was the women themselves who forced society to accept these new standards of attractiveness. Moreover, women such as Elizabeth Ar-den, Helena Rubenstein, Annie Turnbo, and the famous Sarah Breedlove (known to most by her marketing name of Madame C.J. Walker) were pioneers in the promotion, sales, and expansion of cosmetics in the mod-ern era. Breedlove, an African American entrepreneur, created an eco-nomic empire through her employment of females who traveled door to door to meet the needs of the underserviced black population. Her pyr-amid marketing relied on trained saleswomen, often neighbors and fam-ily members, to lend legitimacy to the use of cosmetics in a large number of skeptical consumers. By the 1920s, cosmetics were enshrined in female culture and, according to Piess, "promoted as a tool for women to ex-plore and portray their individuality in the modern world."[2]

Madame C.J. Walker (Sarah Breedlove).
Courtesy of the Library of Congress.

CONSUMING FASHION

The consumption of fashion took place at several levels. The most basic were the styles that were regularly seen and worn by members of one's immediate social set. These trends tended to create ensembles and accessories which then became standardized for at least the season (cold and warm weather months). Such visual consumption was augmented by the many popular magazines and newspapers of the era. Periodical illustrators were keen to detail new fashion styles. Entire publications, such as *Life*, *McClure's*, *Good Housekeeping*, and *Ladies' Home Journal*, were dedicated to helping Americans become comfortable with the quicker pace of change in the modern era. Many of their images highlighted the increased freedom in women's attire (men's fashion changed little throughout the decade) and suggested that the properly clad lady could achieve considerable social mobility. Fashionable women were viewed both as objects of desire and as individuals who had gained considerable control over men through their sexual power.

More traditional outlets for fashions were local dress shops, mail-order catalogs, and department stores, which had become common to American life by 1910. Dressmakers showed considerable adaptability in their provision of the fashion styles portrayed in the publications and copied by those lucky enough to shop in Paris. Tailors to the very elite could command great prices, and access to their studios became limited by social status and time. In less elite settings, the dressmakers did the best they could to copy the latest styles, convince their patrons of the need for change, and adapt these patterns to the many different body shapes of their customers. Even homemade dresses tended to conform to popular shifts in taste. Paper patterns and complex written instructions were dutifully followed to allow women to present themselves in a manner current to the times. Mail-order catalogs provided ready-made dresses and accessories for the masses. Focusing on quantity and low cost, mail-order firms supplied basic styles which could be amended at home to fit the needs of the consumer. "Trimming" stores were common, offering ladies a variety of bows, ribbons, buttons, feathers, and other accessories with which to personalize their wardrobes. For poorer consumers, secondhand shops and alteration tailors provided the best solution for those times when fashion was required. Rarely did the lower classes fully copy the styles of the elite. Not only were these fashions impractical and expensive, many people regarded dressing beyond "one's station in life" as presumptuous and in "bad taste."

The most important source of fashion for the typical shopper was the department store. By 1910 stores such as Marshall Field and Company, the Boston Store, and Wanamaker's had dedicated several floors of their massive emporiums to providing consumers with clothing and accessories. B. Altman and Company's Fifth Avenue showcase was typical. Their first floor—the most public space of the building—housed silk and velvet goods, laces, embroideries, women's neckware, gloves, hose, millinery, notions, umbrellas, handkerchiefs, and jewelry, as well as men's hats, coats, and shoes. On the upper floors, Altman's reserved space for ready-made clothing, attire for children and infants, outfits for maids and nurses, coats, furs, shoes, undergarments, and specialty sports or active wear. The busy hive of activity on each floor, complete with floorwalkers, salespeople, and patrons, only added to the excitement felt by consumers when perusing the racks.

B. Altman Building, New York City. Courtesy of the Library of Congress.

TRENDS AND FADS IN FASHION

While it can be problematic to discuss trends and fads in fashion (fashion, by definition, *is* a trend or fad in clothing), some shifts in taste came quite suddenly and were sparked by events traditionally not seen as part of the fashion world. For example, the rise of automobile travel for the average American led to entirely new outfits comprising dusters, gloves, caps, and goggles for both men and women. The success of the Ballet Russe, which toured the country throughout the decade, and the Post-impressionist art movement led to a variety of fads, including a simplified "Greek look" which valued straight lines, a lack of adornment, and

Irene and Vernon Castle in dancing
position. Courtesy of the Library of
Congress.

wild, vibrant, or shocking colors. The movies popularized new styles that
mirrored the childlike innocence of Mary Pickford or the sensual exoti-
cism of Theda Bara. Even cigarette makers set fashion trends when they
included picture postcards in their packs. While these tended to reinforce
traditional styles such as the Gibson girl look, some introduced a more
active, aggressive, and adventuresome female attire suppliers thought
more fitting for the woman who smoked.

The phenomenal national popularity of dance partners Irene and Vernon Castle, after 1913, led to several unintended changes to American
fashion. In particular, the freedom and grace of Irene Castle's dancing

provided women with new standards of beauty. Gone were the staid looks of society matrons, who donned expensive clothing and accessories like overloaded coat racks, in favor of less constricting, certainly less layered styles. Castle's lithe body shape and youth added to the new look. As noted by historian Lewis Erenberg, "She believed that the power of the dance would force cruel corsets, tight shoes, hats like peach baskets, heavy petticoats, and stiff-boned collars to give way to easy-moving skirts with slits in them, collarless frocks, and subtly cut, freely flowing gowns."[3] As a result, younger consumers followed every change in her wardrobe through the style magazines and copied her hairstyles. When Irene Castle decided to cut her hair short before she underwent surgery, thousands of girls followed suit.

Such fashion trends had important social consequences in the United States. Women became much more comfortable displaying their sexuality in public. While most sought to emulate the "wholesome and fresh" looks of the new woman portrayed in the popular periodicals, the looser clothing certainly emancipated many women from the constricting confines of the corset. Even though most female performers, such as Irene Castle, maintained a studied pose of elegance while on stage (largely to separate themselves from the more "degenerate" forms of popular culture performed by women of color), their style allowed for a new sensuality that came with public dancing. Even Vernon Castle, who rarely deviated from black formal wear, influenced men's wear by showing how the male dancer could be debonair without losing his masculinity. The trend toward wearing wristwatches (often considered bracelets by men) was accelerated when it was clear that Vernon wore his at all times.

Formal fashion designers also became increasingly important during the decade by giving direction and legitimacy to these new trends. Most notable were Paul Poiret, a Parisian and the most influential fashion designer of the decade, and London's Lady Duff Gordon, also known as Lucille. Poiret, who began in 1903, popularized the leaner look of the 1910s, simplifying dress design, and added to the move toward more natural beauty. His design house is credited with helping to end the reign of corsets in women's fashion and initiating the use of new colors and patterns. Poiret broke the monopoly of the color schemes that relied on traditional cream or white, pastel mauve, pink, or sky blue, and black, grey, and purple for all serious occasions. His palette included a wide range of hues, including the natural tones that are more common today. Lucille, too, while less dramatic than Poiret (she kept the corsets), erased many of the more artificial curves in women's designs in favor of more flowing, drape-like dresses. Both designers deepened the tradition of seasonal fashion shows—attended by the world's fashion press—by hosting lavish parties where their creations were unveiled. Poiret introduced formal fashion photography as both a promotional and artistic tool for designers. London and Paris solidified their claim to be the fashion capitals of the world.

In the United States, fashion-conscious women such as Edna Woolman Chase, editor in chief of *Vogue*, helped promote these designers through their publications and social contacts. After the outbreak of war, in 1914, Chase held a series of fashion fêtes to raise money for the stricken fashion houses of Europe. Held at Henri Bendel's New York department store, the gatherings did more to advance the work of young American-based designers, including Maison Jacqueline, Tappé, Gunther, Kurzman, and Mollie O'Hara, than they helped the French industry. While the war lowered the output of European fashion designers, Poiret, Lucille, Gabrielle "Coco" Chanel, and others remained active and largely unchallenged in their world leadership.

FASHION TRENDS: YEAR BY YEAR

With the changing seasons, fashion trends fell into a regular pattern. Each year new styles were introduced in the spring and fall and were adopted, rejected, or modified by the coming season. As a result, a year-by-year account of the decade provides a useful guide for the alterations that were made. Clearly, not every American had the interest or the means to change his or her wardrobe with every new design. It was possible, through the use of embroidery, appliqués, and accessories, however, to modify one's existing wardrobe. Still, by 1910, it was considered wise for most women not to have too large an inventory of clothing going into late summer, as the fashions were no doubt about to change.

In 1910, as noted, the Gibson girl S-shaped silhouette still held sway in American women's fashion. Designers highlighted small waists, large bosoms, and curved rears through the use of corsets and multiple layers of heavy fabrics. By the following year, the style was clearly on the decline as Poiret's work focused on a lighter, more natural look. The hobble skirt enjoyed a brief popularity owing to its controversial design and, in no small part, aided by a censure from the pope. In 1911 necklines were lowered, the "Greek" style was introduced, and full-length fur coats became popular in the wealthier crowds. Influenced by the movies, turbans and "tray hats" adorned with plumage were considered fashionable. Throughout these early years of the decade, men's fashion remained predictable: striped pants, vests, starched shirts, and high collars. Tweed jackets and other blazers were more common, but gloves, hats, a gold watch with chain, a cane or walking stick, studs, and tie pins were still required for all occasions.

In 1913 several new trends injected variety into women's fashion. The rise of Oriental and Turkish prints and the looser "Ballet Russe" look allowed the adventuresome to experiment with new, often clashing, combinations of styles and colors, including brighter shades of red, pink, green, and purple. Slits appeared on the sides of day skirts and on the backs of evening dresses—possibly in response to the inconveniences of the hobble skirt—which exposed more of the leg and led to more interesting and comfortable stockings and hosiery. In the last season before World War I, the dance craze (led by the tango) had pioneered new "sensible" shoes, a flounced skirt, and pantaloon suits (with looser arms and legs to ease movement). Controversy raged between the fuller, corseted silhouette and the cooler, yet more revealing, natural bodice.

With the start of hostilities in Europe, Americans turned to more conservative fashion statements—clearly a reflection of native tastes and the relatively constrained efforts of such industry leaders as Poiret. As a result, the 1915 San Francisco Exhibition of Fashion highlighted lower hemlines, natural waists, broader skirts and jackets, and simpler colors and prints. Military themes and khaki colors were also introduced. Clothing that was "smart," a term that would ironically be used later to denote fashion consciousness, was that which would not soon become obsolete. By 1916 the leading trendsetters were the American female suffragists, who popularized dresses, suits, and coats with multiple pockets (much like the military). The focus on ease and comfort remained. The jumper-blouse (called simply a jumper by 1919) could be worn with a skirt or suit. It was usually pulled over the head without fasteners, and, as a result, women's blouses began to highlight wider collars. In addition, men's fashion also became more relaxed. Jackets were rarely padded, trousers were slimmer, slash pockets replaced patch pockets, and, overall, there were fewer pleats. The term "natty" was frequently used to refer to the more natural styles in men's attire.

In 1917 and 1918, with the war draining resources and spirits on both continents, fashion was nearly nonexistent. Both men and women wore what was available and were less likely to buy new, seasonal clothing if indeed any could be found. The styles were dominated by function and comfort, and the colors were almost entirely muted (forced upon them by a lack of German-made dyes). After the war and into 1919, fashion trends were slow to rebound. Still, the return of brighter colors and patterns, the use of formerly scare materials such as wool, leather, and silk, and the availability once again of ribbons, fringes, or feathers set the stage for a rebound in fashion in the next decade.

CONCLUSION

While the fashion changes of the 1910s were significant, it should not be assumed that they fundamentally altered American popular culture or society. More than anything, because of its erratic nature and because it was a marketable product, fashion tended to reflect and reinforce changes introduced by other components of society rather than act as a pioneer. The rise of an active and mobile lifestyle and World War I, for example, did more to shape the fashion industry than fashion changed of its own accord. As a result, popular clothing should be seen as an important indicator of social evolution. Clearly the drive toward more natural and free-fitting attire reflects an American culture which was deviating from the norms that had been dominant for more than a generation. In many ways, the introduction of the brassiere was a better indicator of social change for women than the burning of them, half a century later.

6

Food

The role of food in American popular culture of the 1910s was subtle, but it masked a more profound and deeply ironic significance. Throughout the decade, the ways in which food was appraised, prepared, served, and consumed certainly changed. While these alterations were, at times, new departures for many Americans, they generally were the result of trends that dated back generations. Moreover, the routine of eating three times a day (sometimes more), every day of the year, eroded the importance or novelty of food to culture in the minds of many Americans.

It should not be overlooked that the biological need for food to survive made eating a vitally influential component of American popular culture. While citizens might only go to the movies once a week, read books periodically, or appreciate the latest in architecture rarely, most did eat every day. Where they might be hesitant to try new types of prepared foods, such as Hellmann's mayonnaise or Ocean Spray cranberry sauce, by doing so, and by getting into the habit of doing so, they were changing the basic relationship between themselves and the broader marketplace. This change was slow and usually without conscious thought or effort, but its cumulative effect on the United States was lasting. It is the universality of food, like clothing, that makes it an important component of popular culture in the 1910s.

UNDERSTANDING FOOD IN THE 1910s

While a review of the basic nutritional needs of human beings is unnecessary for an understanding of food's role in culture, Americans during the 1910s came to appreciate food in new and highly modern ways.

In particular, the nutritional value of foods—including calories, compositions, and benefits—was of increasing interest to researchers looking for the best diet. The most noteworthy new discovery was that of vitamins—naturally occurring chemical compounds found in most foods which either directly contributed to health or were key catalysts in the process of life. A wide variety of diseases, including scurvy, rickets, beriberi, and pellagra, were caused not by infection but, it was learned, by the lack of certain nutrients in the diet. Work in Europe led the research into vitamin nutrition, but American biochemists like Casimir Funk also contributed in significant ways to the identification of both the water- and fat-soluble varieties of these compounds. Funk isolated the chemicals known as B1, B2, C, and D between 1912 and 1915. Later, he connected vitamins with hormones in identifying several other common diseases and maladies. When World War I broke out, in 1914, the knowledge of vitamins was incorporated into the food rationing that was soon required by many European nations. Hoping to prevent widespread malnutrition in their populations—it was found that 41 percent of English recruits were considered in poor health as a result of nutritional deficiencies— governments were better able to balance the types of foods needed to provide an adequate amount of calories, proteins, minerals, and vitamins. Historian Reay Tannahill noted, "Nutrition became a political issue" in the 1910s as a result of vitamin research. It was not until the 1950s, however, that nutritional research was underwritten by the U.S. government and that food analysis was professionalized in this country.[1]

More typical, for the decade and the country, were nostrums and pseudo-scientific studies of proper nutritional and eating habits. For example, author and popular lecturer Horace Fletcher made his claim to fame as a noted healer of dyspepsia (indigestion and associated stomach ailments). Born in Lawrence, Massachusetts, Fletcher later lived and wrote in San Francisco. There, in 1913, he found a "cure" for his obesity and stomach ailments through the Fletcher method, also called Fletcherism, which advocated exactly 100 chews before his "patients" were allowed to swallow their food.

As with many popular cures, Fletcher's ideas had a loose connection to well-reasoned physiology and nutrition. The digestion of food begins in the mouth, where the enzymes present in saliva begin breaking down complex carbohydrates. The process of chewing pulverizes the food (providing more surface area for the enzymes to work) and releases saliva into the mouth. Fletcher correctly reasoned, without the benefit of clinical proof, that by chewing their food more fully Americans would be better able to digest it. While it is doubtful that many were willing to count to 100 after every bite, the net effect of his regimen was to slow down the eater. This alone could have benefited many Americans, but Fletcher also included a set of selected staples that included less fatty and starchy foods. These, no doubt, helped in a patient's weight loss and proper digestion.

Diet and nutritional books were not nearly as common as they became after World War II, but many suggestions were adopted by the public. The most influential, for the longer term of the twentieth century, was probably a book published by Victor Hirtzler, in 1910, titled *The St. Francis Cookbook*. Hirtzler was the head chef at the St. Francis Hotel in San Francisco where he became enamored of the lighter cuisine that was popular locally owing to the easy access to fresh fruits and vegetables. This California cuisine substituted salads, natural herbs, and vegetable and fish oils for the heavy meats, breads, and animal fats found in most existing fare. While not a best-seller, Hirtzler's contribution began the development of a uniquely American style in cooking which would become an international sensation by the end of the century.

In general, the trend toward lighter dining was in keeping with more active pastimes, like dancing, which became popular during the decade. As social role models became younger and more energetic—such as ballroom dancers Irene and Vernon Castle or actors Mary Pickford and Douglas Fairbanks—the gluttony common at the turn of the century became passé. Perhaps no single man epitomized these old ways better than railroad tycoon "Diamond Jim" Brady. Taking as many as five or six meals a day, Brady's eating (as well as his clothing, female accompaniment, and jewelry, from which came his nickname) went beyond the lavish and bordered on obscene. A typical breakfast for Brady included several quarts of orange juice, eggs, half a loaf of bread, a large steak, fried potatoes, onions, grits, bacon, muffins, coffee, and a full stack of pancakes. For Brady and his corpulent colleagues, eating was a public act intended to display their wealth. One restaurant operator was said to have quipped that Brady was the "best twenty-five customers I ever had." When Brady died, in 1917, an autopsy showed that his stomach had enlarged to over six times that of an average man his height. By contrast, the lighter breakfast of toast and a single soft-boiled egg became the traditional morning meal of most chic diners in the 1910s.

Certainly, the contingencies caused by World War I contributed toward this trend in lighter eating. Shortages and rationing in the supply of certain foods—particularly meat, eggs, and wheat—led many to plant gardens at home or to begin experimenting with newer tastes. The introduction of fresh vegetables, herbs, and meatless dishes into the diet caused, by necessity, many cooks to rethink the traditional meals that they served before the war.

DINING IN

For the most part, changes to food culture in the home during the 1910s were incremental. Nonetheless, these alterations significantly shifted how food was produced and consumed in the United States. The appearance of improved devices for food storage and cooking, new prepared foods, and the growth of suppliers able to furnish these goods all accelerated trends toward greater convenience, flexibility, and reliability in American foods.

Probably the most important change to the ways in which food was prepared in the 1910s was the spread of electric devices for the kitchen. Following the Electric Exhibition at New York City, in 1911, several new and innovative machines, including electric skillets, toasters, mixers, and waffle irons, became commonly available for affluent and upper-middle-class consumers. The KitchenAid brand of noncommercial mixers, which combined rotating beaters with a bowl that moved in the opposite direction, was the most popular but far from an everyday convenience. Priced at nearly $200 when it debuted in 1919, it was not until the 1920s that the mixer was reduced in size and cost and mass marketed to the typical homemaker. Similarly, Frigidaire and General Electric had introduced lines of electric refrigerators for domestic use by 1915. Providing convenience, freshness, and health benefits, the refrigerator was the perfect icon for the modern era. By the 1920s, advertisements highlighting the cornucopia of foods contained within these modern marvels made the products seem, in the words of one noted historian, "as spellbinding as any religious vision."[2]

New cooking devices also expanded the range of food options for the typical home cook. Thermostatic ovens, introduced in 1915, enabled bakers to maintain a constant oven temperature (either gas or electric) making it possible to follow a variety of new recipes. The introduction of new baking materials was also important. Most notable was the spread of borosilicate, or Pyrex, bakeware for the home. Pyrex, a trademark for a specific type of glass, is resistant to heat and electricity. Because its chemical properties allow Pyrex to expand about a third less than conventional glass, it is less likely to break when taken from the oven or refrigerator. These conveniences combined to give the typical cook the confidence to expand their repertoire to include a number of newer menus.

Supporting these new products was the rise of department stores and self-serve markets in which shoppers could buy fresher foods and a wider variety of products. Department stores, as well as other providers, supplied consumers with these new kitchen products through installment credit plans. While present well before the 1910s, installment credit expanded rapidly during the decade causing many to question its effects on the average consumer. While fears of excessive debt (usually by females who abused credit) and class pretentiousness (conspicuous consumption by the poor) remained, by the end of the decade most Americans felt comfortable with and had acquired many of these kitchen "necessities" through installment credit.

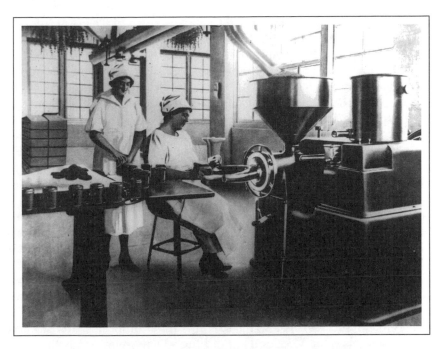

Packing peanut butter. Courtesy of the Library of Congress.

More important was the spread of the self-service grocery store. These emporiums—which today would pale by comparison to the supermarket—expanded the food options for millions of Americans while making shopping a more private and efficient process. The first of these, Piggly-Wiggly, was founded by Clarence Saunders in Memphis, Tennessee, in 1916. Saunders allowed his customers to roam the aisles of his store selecting products of their own choice rather than submitting a grocery list to be filled by a store clerk. Piggly-Wiggly developed a reputation for stocking a wide variety of named items—thousands of goods increasingly desired by America's more brand-conscious consumers. Saunders' success was quickly copied throughout the country.

Of course, these new products and outlets were only as good as the food that was available to cook, store, and sell. In the 1910s, Americans became accustomed to a wide variety of new convenience foods which made these amenities necessary. Ranging from food-preparation products to new cooking oils, the fast foods of the decade transformed what and how Americans ate.

Many of the food items first introduced in the 1910s were made popular simply because they packaged a product together in new and convenient ways. The tea bag, which premiered in 1910, allowed consumers to brew a single cup of the beverage rather than an entire pot as was customary. Other goods, such as Ocean Spray cranberry sauce (1912), fruit cocktail (1914), and Campbell's soups (Cream of Celery, 1913; Beef Vegetable, 1918), placed a perishable, time-consuming product within easy reach of the average shopper. While traveling with his family on a hunting expedition to the Labrador coast, Clarence Birdseye discovered that rapidly frozen foods (such as venison which was exposed to the Arctic air and froze in a matter of minutes) retained much of their original flavor. Birdseye perfected an artificial process which replicated these conditions, placing packaged foods in devices that could be quickly cooled to −50 degrees Fahrenheit. While several ventures failed in the 1910s—owing to the lack of freezers in most grocery stores—Birdseye's method became wildly successful in the coming decade. Frozen fish, vegetables, even entire meals were soon common fare in many homes.

While still a decade from becoming a national food sensation, peanut butter was establishing itself as a uniquely American food in the 1910s. No doubt, "nut butter" had been made by countless families before 1904, when at the World's Fair in Saint Louis, C.H. Summer introduced the spread to a wide audience. Years earlier, the brothers Dr. John and W.K. Kellogg experimented with a number of different types of peanut butter preparations with little luck (they soon turned to breakfast cereals with much greater success). The 1910s saw a number of local suppliers carve out regional markets. Most of these products were smoother, with a more refined and sweeter taste than earlier efforts. Still, it was not until the 1920s and 1930s when brand names like Skippy and Peter Pan came to dominate grocery shelf space around the country.

Other foods changed American eating and cooking habits more drastically. For example, the marketing of a granulated, "pourable" table salt by the Morton Salt Company in 1912 allowed cooks and restaurants to reduce the amount of salt used in their meals, allowing diners to salt their own food to taste. Similarly, Richard Hellmann began mass marketing his wife's Blue Ribbon mayonnaise in 1912. Hellmann, a German immigrant and deli operator on Columbus Street in New York City, had first tested his sandwich spread on customers who then rated his varieties. To meet a largely local demand for his product, Hellmann opened his first factory in Queens in 1915 and a second one in Long Island in 1920 to supply the growing regional demand. His ready-made mayonnaise allowed many to turn ordinary bread and cold cuts into an appetizing specialty sandwich. It was not until 1927, however, when Hellmann sold his concern to General Foods, that the product became truly national in scope.

By far, the introduction of Crisco in 1911 was the most profound change to America's food-preparation habits of the decade. Crisco, manufactured by Cincinnati-based Procter & Gamble, was a solidified shortening product made entirely of vegetable oils. Crisco had a unique property, obtained through a special process, which allowed the product to remain solid yet soft throughout all seasonal conditions. By contrast, before Crisco, most cooks relied on butter or animal fats (lard) which quickly spoiled or frequently became too runny for many baking needs. The product was an instant hit for both domestic and commercial bakers. Crisco was so new that Procter & Gamble actually published their own cookbooks, recipes, and tips for chefs interested in using the marvelous new product. These guides made it easy to bake "from scratch" by standardizing and making predictable the key blending product in most baked goods. With Crisco, American housewives gained the confidence to use their new kitchen gadgets more fully.

Certainly no meal was changed more drastically during the 1910s than breakfast. Typically, before this time, the morning meal consisted of leftovers from the previous night or, if one were dining out, of such favorite eye-openers as fried clams, mushrooms, grilled plover, steak, or the occasional egg. The arrival of the active, healthy lifestyle of the era expunged the desire for such heavy fare. Suppliers of nutritious, quick, and lighter breakfast alternatives quickly became popular. Cereals offered under brand names, such as Kellogg's Corn Flakes (1915), 40 percent Bran Flakes (1915), and All-Bran (1916); Quaker Puffed Rice (1913); John Campbell's Malt-O-Meal (1919); or C.W. Post's Grape Nuts (1897) and Post Toasties (1904), soon created new morning rituals throughout the United States. As made clear by the Kelloggs, and driven home by their relentless advertising campaigns, many of these breakfast cereals were promoted as "health foods," key components of a diet balanced with vitamins and natural fiber.

AMERICA'S SWEET TOOTH AND OTHER VICES

Of course, not all of America's new eating habits fostered better nutrition. During the 1910s, the nation first gave evidence of a penchant for sweet snacks between meals. Before then, most lovers of candies and cookies were content with a periodic visit to the confectioners or with a special batch of homemade treats. By contrast, the rise of "nickel candies" sold at the counters of many shops and store-bought packaged cookies made this consumption more regular, increasing the amount of empty calories in many Americans' diets. Often advertised as "instant energy," the diverse confections of chocolate, caramel, nuts, dried fruits, and a variety of other products reflected the novelty of new processed foods.

Chocolate bars were not new in 1910. As early as 1875, Henry Nestlé and Daniel Peter had perfected the manufacture of milk chocolate which could be processed, transported, stored, and sold without losing too much of its flavor. German chocolate making was displayed at the 1893 Columbian Exposition in Chicago, where Milton S. Hershey saw them and began integrating them into his caramel factory in Lancaster, Pennsylvania, in 1894.

Hershey's success in selling his milk chocolate bars in the late 1890s and early 1900s led many to experiment with ingredients and packaging in order to cash in on the new product. Some, like Frank Mars, tried a number of combinations before hitting on a successful combination. Mars introduced the Milky Way bar in 1923. Peter Paul Halajian had more immediate success with his Konabar in 1919, a candy made of dried fruit, nuts, coconut, and chocolate. In 1922, Peter Paul introduced his most successful candy, the Mounds bar, coconut dipped in bittersweet chocolate, in an effort to build on his earlier triumph. Similarly, in 1919, Christian Nelson and chocolate magnate Russell Stover experimented with other ways to apply chocolate directly to ice cream. Using cocoa butter in the preparation, Nelson premiered the Eskimo Pie in 1921 based on earlier efforts.

Non–chocolate based foods were also introduced during the decade. For example, Clarence Crane, a Cleveland-based chocolate manufacturer, was looking for a product which was not as messy as chocolate but could still satisfy America's developing sweet tooth. In 1912, he developed a hard peppermint candy which he fashioned into the shape of a circle. Crane turned his product, called Pep-O-Mint, into a commercial sensation by packaging fourteen mints in easy to dispense rolls and naming them Life Savers, after their characteristic shape. Phillip K. Wrigley, too, used aggressive advertising, sensible packaging, and low prices to expand his chewing-gum enterprise nationwide.

David Little Clark, who was selling gum to retailers in the early part of the 1910s, developed his own product, called the Clark Bar, which contained a core of roasted peanuts covered in milk chocolate. He mass marketed the candy to U.S. soldiers as a nutritious, quick energy food in 1917. The connection between candy sales and World War I was not accidental. The U.S. Army Quartermaster Corps shipped an average of 40 pounds of chocolate each week to the American bases in Europe. Broken into smaller lots on the battlefield, many servicemen grew accustomed to the easy availability of sweets. When they returned, in 1919, they not only provided a ready market for the goods but also sanctioned the practice of snacking as something that was acceptable to men of all ages. By the end of the 1920s, tens of thousands of candy bars were competing for Americans' loose change.

Perhaps the greatest novelty confection of the 1910s was the marshmallow—a gooey combination of sugar, corn syrup, and extracts from the root of the marshmallow plant. The appearance of the Moon Pie and Mallomars during the decade were the most successful of these experiments. Found primarily along the East Coast, Mallomars were first sold in 1913 as a combination of cookie, marshmallow, and dark chocolate. The Moon Pie, which was a larger version of the same medley of goods, was introduced in 1917 by the Chattanooga Bakery Company in Tennessee; it has remained the favorite of Southerners. Probably the strangest use of marshmallow was in the development of Marshmallow Fluff, a semigelatinous substance that was used on everything from ice cream and sandwiches to breakfast cereals. Developed in 1917 by Archibald Query, the product was first sold door to door around Sommerville, Massachusetts. Hard sales work by Allen Durkee and Fred Mower, who bought the recipe from Query in 1919, landed their Toot Sweet Marshmallow Fluff on the shelves of local groceries. By 1927, the product was being mass produced and sold throughout the region.

As is evident in Mallowmars and Moon Pies, packaged cookies rounded out the list of new sweets that were available to American consumers. For example, Lorne Doone cookies, a simple shortbread, premiered in 1912. Novelty cookies sold more quickly. The greatest of these during the 1910s was the Oreo chocolate sandwich cookie. Later called the King of Cookies, Oreos, which sold briskly at stores, were heavily promoted by the National Biscuit Company, later Nabisco. Probably the most novel of the new cookies was the fortune cookie, invented in the United States by David Jung, a Los Angeles noodle maker, in 1918. When production was mechanized in the 1920s, fortune cookies became standard fare at most Chinese restaurants and were soon exported from America to China and Hong Kong.

Cigarettes, which exist in a state somewhere between a food and a drug, were prone to many of the same trends seen above. At the turn of the century, Americans were already consuming more than 4 billion cigarettes per year. Unlike in the 1910s, however, opposition to tobacco use was widespread. Many were concerned that the product was adulterated, containing opium or arsenic. By 1912 Dr. I. Adler had demonstrated a strong connection between cigarette smoking and lung cancer. The following year, the American Society for the Control of Cancer, later the American Cancer Society, was founded to promote antismoking campaigns. Business leaders frowned on the use of the product by their employees and leaders such as Thomas Edison and Henry Ford openly prohibited smoking at their factories (Edison refused to hire smokers). Others feared for the safety of children and women, who were legally barred from smoking in many states. In 1909 baseball star Honus Wagner withdrew his name and image from use by cigarette companies including the baseball cards that came with their products. As a result, the Honus Wagner card remains today one of the rarest of collectibles.

Still, the tobacco industry, led by James B. Duke's American Tobacco Company, was a powerful force in American business and government. The tobacco lobby was successful at keeping nicotine off the list of controlled substances passed with the 1906 Food and Drug Act. Many began adding potency to their product by spraying the young plants with nicotine as an insecticide. Even after the American Tobacco Company was broken up as a trust into the American Tobacco Company, R.J. Reynolds, Liggett & Meyers, and Lorillard, in 1911, the industry thrived. By 1910, America averaged nearly 140 cigarettes per person per year. Driving these trends were two things. The first was the successful advertising campaigns of the 1910s. Liggett & Meyers' Chesterfield brand led the field when, in 1912, they pioneered the use of such simple slogans such as "They satisfy." In 1915 R.J. Reynolds debuted Camels and, two years later, the American Tobacco Company brought out Lucky Strikes using similarly simple yet powerful catchphrases. By 1917 cigarettes were being targeted to women as a means for suppressing the appetite. World War I provided the second key component to the success of cigarettes. Along with candy, servicemen were provided cigarettes as part of their daily rations. The boost in U.S. production of tobacco—aided by a blockade of Turkish tobaccos—provided a market advantage which allowed most producers to lower their retail charge to either a dime or fifteen cents for a pack of twenty cigarettes. By 1920 the nation was sufficiently addicted to cigarettes, a vice that was widely supported by popular culture. Reformers intent on banning the weed made little progress.

DINING OUT

Growing public amusements—including vaudeville, dance halls, and the movie theater—provided Americans with additional reasons to consume food outside of their homes. Restaurants, while still not prevalent, began to cater to the needs of a society increasingly "on the go." Their menus and style of service changed markedly during the 1910s. These trends continued to alter the traditional form of public eating in ways that laid the groundwork for the rise of many fast-food establishments in the decades to come. The fact that Nathan Handwerker opened "Nathan's" hotdog stand at Coney Island in 1916—quite possibly the most famous hotdog booth in the world—suggests that trends toward greater convenience and more fun when dining out.

Most Americans still did not frequent upscale restaurants; commonplace establishments continued to feed the majority of the nation's public. Known as chophouses, these locations typically specialized in steaks, chops, and other cuts of meat with a serving of potatoes, bread, and, nearly invariably, oysters and a schooner of beer. Many taverns offered patrons a free lunch included with the purchase of at least two drinks. Women found repast in tearooms and other ladies restaurants which typically served omelettes, light chicken dishes, and salads.

At more upscale, but still middle-class, establishments, a typical dinner, in 1910, was expected to include at least two courses. The first included either turkey, duck, or chicken, a variety of sweets, smaller dishes of fruits (usually apricots or apples), and a starchy vegetable like corn

Couple enjoying a champagne supper. Courtesy of the Library of Congress.

or peas. The second, or main, course included a choice of soups, fish, a larger portion of meat, vegetables, and breads or pastries. While tame in comparison to the meals of the upper class, these dinners indicate that the trend in lighter dining was just that—a trend that would not reach its fulfillment for another 30 years.

By far the elite dining set underwent more interesting changes. As early as 1860, wealthy Americans could find restaurants like Delmonico's where they could be treated and fed like European royalty. According to cultural historian Lewis Erenberg, by 1900 this tendency was spreading to many more establishments. In New York City alone, in the first decade of 1900, Delmonico's was joined by the Waldorf-Astoria, Martin's, Sherry's, the Holland House, the St. Regis, the Savoy, the Astor Hotel, the Knickerbocker, Shanley's, and Rector's. As with the more pedestrian, middle-class restaurants, the elite diner could expect to glut their desire for culinary excess. A typical meal might include an appetizer of clams or oysters, a clear soup, and a tray of rich hors d'oeuvres, including olives, canapes, caviar, and anchovies. A first course would be required to contain fish, potatoes, and a cucumber salad, and often included terrapin, (more) oysters, crab legs, lobster, shrimp, and frogs. Concluding the meal were large servings of roasted meat, vegetables,

The Waldorf-Astoria, New York City. Courtesy of the Library of
Congress.

bread, a fruit punch, and lighter side dishes. The postmeal desert, served
with coffee, topped off the dining experience. Many wealthy socialites
would then set off to the evening's activity only to be concluded—after
the show—with a midnight banquet of champagne and lobster at the so-
called lobster palaces that ringed the city's many theater and entertainment districts.[3]

Why the wealthy and affluent consumed food here and in this way is
related to a number of factors. Most important, food consumption was
a visible indication of one's status in society. The more one ate, and the

more luxurious were the dishes, the higher one could position himself in the social hierarchy. In addition, restaurants offered the younger elites new public places where they might interact, freed from the cloistered confines of the many balls and parties held by their economic peers. Finally, public restaurants provided new spaces for women to be freed of the confines of polite society. As Erenberg notes, the restaurants "offered rich women a place to meet, and it also provided them with a chance to pursue social leadership on a personal basis, outside the enervating round of society's all-encompassing activities."[4]

While not an era for grand cuisine, the 1910s did see the expansion of more ethnic cooking across the spectrum of restaurants. Hungarian goulash and a wide variety of Italian pastas were sampled for the first time. With the growth in immigration, until the war prevented safe passage, came Italian, German, Chinese, and Jewish cooking. Many of these styles were loosely appropriated into American cuisine. As a result, the decade saw the introduction of a number of new types of foods and preparations, including chop suey, crab Louis, fettuccine alfredo, and vichyssoise. In spite of their exotic names, all of these dishes originated in the United States. The Chinese had never prepared nor heard of chop suey. Vichyssoise, a chilled soup made from potatoes, leeks, and cream, was created by Louis Diat of the Ritz-Carlton Hotel in 1917.

CONCLUSION

Clearly, the foods and eating habits of Americans during the 1910s were not changed in any revolutionary or dramatic way. The appearance of new foods, new production methods, and new dining options were in keeping with trends that extended both before and beyond the decade. Yet it is possible to identify the rising importance of novelty and convenience in American foods. Prepackaged goods, popular sweets, and simplified cooking directions suggest that modernity was having a lasting effect on the way in which Americans fed themselves. While the pace of life seemed to be accelerating in the private sphere, restaurants still suggested that Americans wanted to experience public eating as a form of popular entertainment. While secured from the prying eyes of the nonpaying public, restaurant goers certainly were interested as much in being seen eating as in actually doing the eating. Taken together with other shifts in popular culture, food patterns of the 1910s support the notion that Americans were increasingly more comfortable with using the material culture around them to define who they were to themselves and to others.

The 1910s

7

Leisure Activities

While the broad subject of games, fads, and sports may seem inconsequential, even trivial, to popular culture in the 1910s, these facets of American life highlight then, as today, important trends. During the decade Americans displayed, through their participation in or consumption of these designations, a greater commitment to individual expression than in previous generations. In addition, these activities validated the broader Progressive ideals of fair play, democracy, and civic advancement thus redefining what it meant to *participate* in American life. The impermanence of fads and sports, by their very nature, demonstrated the values that citizens held during the 1910s. As a result, today we have a window, however indefinite, on the era that supports the claim that American culture was truly modernizing throughout the decade.

GAMES AND TOYS

In the fall of 1917, the Council of National Defense held hearings in Washington, D.C., to debate a topic that was every child's worst nightmare: whether to cancel Christmas. The council, made up of powerful industrialists and policymakers, who empaneled such notable oversight committees as the War Industries Board, was not debating the merit of observing the Christian celebration. Rather, given America's entry into World War I in April of that year, the council was questioning the rampant consumerism that had grown in conjunction with the holiday. Hoping to conserve critical war materials, such as steel and copper, as well as to instill in the populace the need for personal sacrifice, the group assumed this gesture might properly prepare the citizenry for the loss of life and daily privations that might be in store.

While doing away with the toy industry might seem like an unimaginable proposition to modern readers, it is important to remember that the production and sale of toys were not significant components of the U.S. economy in the 1910s. In 1912 less than $12 million in toys were consumed (compared to more than a billion dollars less than 40 years later). Most stores did not even carry toys regularly on their shelves; nearly two-thirds of these purchases were made around the Christmas holiday. It was the lobbyists of the scrawny toy industry, not children or their parents, who were most vocal about the potential ban.[1]

For the most part, up to 1910, typical toys and games for the American child were constructed at home or were limited to small, relatively inexpensive purchases. Homemade dolls, blocks, jigsaw puzzles, and dice were the basis for most children's toys. For girls, cutout dresses for paper dolls taken from newspaper advertisements or last year's catalogs were common. For boys, a rare figurine or wheeled miniature was standard— and these typically were handed down through the generations. By and large, at the beginning of the decade, most youth were not accustomed to seeing store-bought toys to the degree typical of today.

Most consumable toys were manufactured in Europe. As late as 1880, the United States had only the rudiments of a toy manufacturing industry. The vast majority of purchased goods were made in Germany, England, or France. There, suppliers had perfected the process of working tin (a light and malleable silvery metal) into a variety of shapes and styles. Tin plate provided a smooth, flat surface that was easy to bend and could easily be assembled using either solder or metal tabs. More important, tin allowed for metal lithographing, which applied a variety of colors and patterns to a toy's surface. By 1910 a third of all tin-plate toys were imported from Germany alone; another third came from the remaining European exporters; and American firms fought over the rest. U.S. manufacturers, such as Julius Chein & Company and the Strauss Manufacturing Company, controlled much of this domestic share.

American manufacturers did excel, however, in the production of cast-iron toys. Perhaps because of their weight, which prohibited easy overseas transport from Europe, the market for cast-iron goods remained under the control of U.S. suppliers. While these goods tended, initially at least, to be cruder than the European imports—being heavier, less articulated, and lacking ornate lithography—they were easier to mass produce and hence cheaper for the consumer. The quality of these goods varied greatly. Expensive toys were finely finished and packaged in handsome wooden boxes. Cheaper goods, much cruder, were packed in cardboard or not at all.

The American penchant for cast iron had unintended benefits in the

Children posed with bicycle and tricycles. Courtesy of the Library of Congress.

1910s. During the decade, as prices fell and casting techniques improved (allowing for greater detail), consumers became mesmerized by the sturdy mechanized banks and the spring-driven vehicles that were the stock-in-trade of the largest suppliers. Cast-iron replicas of boats, fully-functioning steam engines, miniature sewing machines, and other mementos of the machine age became increasingly easy for manufacturers to mass produce. The craze for all things on wheels, from automobiles to fire engines, helped spur the growth of sales. When the war broke out, miniature airplanes, dirigibles, and artillery pieces all cast in iron became the desire of many children. Suppliers such as the Hubley Manufacturing Company (Lancaster, Pennsylvania) and the Dayton (Ohio) Friction Toy Company expanded swiftly. By the end of the decade, the Arcade Manufacturing Company (Freeport, Illinois) was issuing an annual catalog listing over fifty pages of cast-iron toys.

Stuffed toys also were increasingly popular in the 1910s. While rag dolls and stuffed animals had always been made for children, the popularity of the teddy bear drove the markets to new heights throughout the decade. The toy, named for Teddy Roosevelt, who in 1903 refused to shoot a tethered grizzly bear cub, became the rage after the *Washington Post* promoted the incident. Typical of the period, it was a German toymaker, Margarete Steiff, who produced the first teddy bears in 1904. It was estimated that more than a million of the toys were sold by 1910. In the United States, Morris and Rose Michtom, Russian immigrants and toy retailers, began manufacturing the stuffed bears domestically in 1907. By 1910 the Michtoms had closed their store to focus on production and founded the Ideal Novelty & Toy Company, which was to become an industry bellwether. Ideal was one of the first suppliers to begin using cotton for their stuffing, rather than the traditional straw, kapok (a silky fiber imported from Malaysia), or granulated cork. As a result, they developed a reputation for quality that previously had been reserved for European imports.

Stuffed dolls kept pace with the teddy bear. Cute figurines such as Baby Bumps, Negro Baby Bumps, and dolls representing the Campbell Kids—a cherub-faced boy and girl who were depicted on the popular soup labels—were promoted forcefully by manufacturers in newspapers and the periodicals. The advertising tie-in between one product and a seemingly unrelated toy, as was the case with Campbell's campaign in 1911, was an early indication of the profound changes that were driving the consumer choices of many Americans. When Rose O'Neill began marketing her Kewpie dolls, chubby dolls with a topknot of hair, in 1911, it was not to toy stores or other retailers but rather directly to the readers of the *Ladies' Home Journal*.

No doubt the single most influential new doll of the decade was Raggedy Ann, introduced in 1918. The creation of Johnny Gruelle, a political cartoonist, Raggedy Ann (and her friend Raggedy Andy, unveiled in 1920) was patented in 1915 through a series of children's stories written and illustrated by Gruelle. The doll was based on a rag doll created by Gruelle's mother, to which the son added the characteristic button eyes and triangle nose. Gruelle found a publisher willing to package a doll with each book sold. The firm, Volland Publishing Company of Chicago, found that the product tie-in greatly enhanced their sales. By the end of the decade it was the doll, and not the story, that drove Raggedy Ann's popularity.

Board games were also played by children and young adults; but with an important difference. In the 1910s, board games were regarded as ways in which to instill proper values which would prepare youngsters for the responsibilities of adulthood. These goals included fair play, rational thought, and honest competition—meaning that the winner was determined based solely on his or her merits. For example, Milton Bradley's game the Checkered Game of Life dealt with the fleeting nature of material success (Parker Brothers' wildly successful Monopoly was still a generation away, introduced in 1935 in the heart of the Great Depression). Another was the Merchant Marine game. Edward Hurley, the chairman of the U.S. Shipping Board, proposed the board game to educate children about the complexities of overseas trade. Hurley wanted to place

ships and the sea into their daily thought and work, and making ships appeal to the imagination of everybody in the country. We want to reach the children as well as the grown ups, and, in this connection knowing how closely toys follow popular interest and what an educative value they have, it had been in my mind to have this great new national interest before the men who invent and design your goods.[2]

The Singer Sewing Machine Company did much the same thing in marketing a toy sewer that was fully functional. They advertised the child's diversion as both "Practical and Instructive." Such functional thinking was typical of the era's approach not only to games and toys, but also to children's recreation and sport.[3]

Ironically, one popular board game of the decade—Ouija—was diametrically opposed to this trend. The game was not really intended for children but rather for adults who, perhaps, had already mastered the skills needed to succeed in the modern world. The title combines the French and German words for "yes" (*oui* and *ja*). Ouija was first created in the 1880s following an occult craze. The game was played by two people who, eyes closed, placed their fingers lightly on a three-cornered device, called a planchette, which held a pencil. After asking the board (the spirits?) a question, the planchette moved across letters or to a "yes" or "no" corner to indicate a response. William Fuld, a Baltimore toy maker who marketed Ouija in the United States, sold more than a million copies of the game in 1918 alone. No doubt the uncertainty of the Great War added to the appeal of the game in the 1910s. Charles Panati, a chronicler of trends in the United States, noted that the game's popularity rose and fell with each foreign war. In 1967, for example, an updated version of the game outsold even Monopoly. In any case, the pastime was an immensely popular, highly illogical exception to the norm.[4]

The most innovative and inventive children's games of the era, however, stayed true to educational goals. Most significant was the arrival of the Erector Set. Developed by A.C. Gilbert, this construction toy was intended to allow a child to develop his imagination. Introduced in 1913, the Erector Set was sold under the slogan, Hello, Boys! Make Lots of Toys! Gilbert's eclectic past highlights the novelty of his product. Born in Salem, Oregon, Gilbert excelled at sports, including track, gymnastics, wrestling, and football, earning both an Olympic gold medal in 1908 and a scholarship to Yale. While at Yale, Gilbert focused on physical education, studied medicine, and eventually earned an M.D. Although well steeped in the Progressive values of a strenuous, healthy lifestyle, Gilbert also enjoyed practicing magic. He used this skill to earn additional money as a performer and to start a small mail-order business that catered to amateurs interested in learning a few more basic tricks. After graduating in 1909, Gilbert found that his magic supply business was prospering, and it led him to open retail establishments selling these and other toys. In 1911, while traveling from New Haven to New York City, Gilbert was intrigued by the steel girders used to support the electrical lines that propelled the streetcars. He envisioned manufacturing a set of small construction pieces, including electric motors, cogs, and other moving parts, which would allow children to build their own toys. After experimenting with a number of designs throughout 1912, he finally arrived at a working solution which he patented and began to market the following year.

Gilbert's partners in magic were unwilling to participate in this gambit. A rival construction set manufactured in England, called Meccano, had already sold poorly in the United States. Nevertheless, Gilbert believed that proper promotion and the inclusion of moving parts would ensure success. Venturing out on his own, Gilbert spent more than $12,000 to advertise the toy in such national magazines as the *American Boy, Good Housekeeping*, and *Saturday Evening Post*. Gilbert highlighted the educational features of his product, and his Erector Set became an overnight sensation. Over the next twenty years, Gilbert expanded the options available through the sets and forayed into other "educational toy" markets such as chemistry, microscope, and telescope sets.

Whether patterned after the Erector Set or not, other creative toys followed throughout the decade. Most notable was the arrival of Tinkertoys in 1914 and Lincoln Logs in 1919. The former was a construction set patented by Charles Pajeau that used wooden shafts and connectors rather than tiny steel beams. The latter, originated by John L. Wright, son of architect Frank Lloyd Wright, used small, wooden log facsimiles to build a variety of structures. Neither approached the Erector Set in popularity, but both remain successful toys today.

FADS AND HOBBIES

History has an odd effect on fads. If, through hindsight, we are able to ascertain that a novelty like the automobile or airplane had a profound effect on a culture then we are less likely to identify its early appeal as a fad. If, on the other hand, trends come and go without much bearing on society, we are quick to dismiss them. This is a good prologue to understanding fads in the 1910s, many of which were related to new technologies which did make a lasting impression on U.S. popular culture.

Several characteristics of fads during the 1910s make them stand out from those of other decades. First, they were predominantly consumer fads. That is, they appeared and were closely connected to new products or services rather than to new ideas or behaviors. If, in previous eras, fads had typically revolved around new ways of thinking, those in the 1910s were closely linked to new ways of buying. Second, probably because of the first, fads of the era quickly became absorbed by the marketplace or forgotten by consumers as new goods became commonplace. If a fad is defined as an irrational zeal over a trivial item, then the rising modern consumer culture in America was quickly making this standard operating procedure for many nondurable goods. Additionally, most of these trends appeared and expressed themselves irrespective of racial, class, and gender lines. This is not to say that they did anything to minimize these social biases, just that they were not limited by them. Finally, the 1910s witnessed, for the first time, the exportation of American fads around the globe. Americans in the 1910s developed a cultural pride, a unique sense of themselves as being separate from Europe through their unique manias. The fact that others could (belatedly) share in these passions only lent strength to their movement through U.S. society.

Given the immense popularity of the automobile, it should be no surprise that the "car culture" developed a style all its own throughout the 1910s. More important, the popularity of the universal car, Ford's Model T, turned this once elite luxury into an everyday desire. When unveiled in 1908, the Model T retailed for $850, a modest price for a typical automobile. Already more expensive vehicles had, according to Charles J. Glidden, who wrote in 1911, "completely revolutionized the life of well-to-do people." But when mass production lowered the cost of Ford's cars to $600 by 1912 (and finally to $290 by 1924), middle-class Americans and the higher-paid working class were able to join in the fun. By 1914 every other new car purchased was a Ford.[5]

While still a major acquisition, the faddishness of the Model T was more in how Americans adapted to the car than in the simple purchase. Ford's consumers quickly personalized the Model T to suit their own style. Particularly for the young, riding clothes (called dusters), goggles, running boards, rumble seats, cloth tops, picnics baskets, and other accessories became mandatory to differentiate their (or their father's) Model T from the thousands of others that were soon clattering along America's streets. More typical of a genuine fad, Model T joke books soon proliferated across the country. Commenting on the sense of helplessness often associated with learning a new skill, the jokes are less funny today than instructive in demonstrating how Americans were admitting their own anxieties. Usually they focused on the frequent breakdowns or slow speeds of the vehicle: "I hear they are going to magnetize the rear axle of the Ford. What's the idea? So it will pick up the parts that drop off" or "I understand you have just bought a Ford? Yes, I saw seven of them chasing one pedestrian the other day, and I decided that I was on the wrong end of the sport."

Another infatuation with the automobile took hold of America's imagination: speed. At first, this might seem laughable, as the poor roads and congested urban traffic limited most cars to anywhere from ten to twenty miles an hour. Still, the potential for rapid transportation captured the minds of many. As early as 1906, Fred Marriot navigated a steam-powered automobile (called the Stanley Steamer) over Daytona Beach at more than 127 miles an hour. More expensive internal combustion cars, such as Pierce Arrow or Panhards, could easily travel at over 50 miles an hour on good roads. It was no surprise, then, that the 1910s saw the development of ways to limit the eagerness of drivers to drive fast. Most cities were forced to erect speed limits (usually of 20 miles per hour); in 1914, Cleveland became the first city to employ traffic lights to force "lead foots" to yield to others at major intersections. Probably most indicative of America's love of speed was the Indianapolis 500, inaugurated in 1911 and won by Ray Harroun, who averaged an amazing 74 miles per hour around the 2.5 mile oval.

Air flights also competed in popular time trials. For example, in 1910, Glenn H. Curtiss won a thousand dollars for his record flight from Albany to New York City. Often sponsored by newspapers, such as the *New York World*, which were highly attuned to the immense popularity of such displays, flights records were repeatedly set and then broken throughout the decade, feeding the need for speed that Americans had come to love.

Airplanes provided another outlet for faddish entertainment in stunt or novelty flying. In 1911 the mail was delivered using the airplane for first time. One year later, Captain Albert Berry became the first American to jump successfully from an airplane aloft—using a parachute. In 1919 an English pilot and an American navigator became the first to perform a nonstop transatlantic flight, a feat which was finally bested in 1927 when Charles A. Lindbergh made the trip flying solo. After the war, former American aviators toured the country re-creating perilous dogfights and performing death-defying tricks with their biplanes. The fad reached its height in the decade when, in 1919, couples began taking their wedding vows while riding through the clouds.

Of course not all fads were based on such daring. Some, in fact most, were initiated by the need to be the first on one's block to experiment with the host of new products made available throughout the decade. In particular, electronic appliances such as washing machines, floor sweepers, and, in 1918, pop-up toasters each went through a brief period of consumer mania before being relegated to simple domestic necessities. Probably the most innovative was the handheld camera perfected and marketed by George Eastman. His first Kodak camera, which retailed for $25, was available for only $2 in 1913 and provided higher quality and better reliability than almost any other camera on the market.

Being the first to recognize cultural trends was also prized by many. Following the expansion of popular musical forms, ranging from Ragtime to Tin Pan Ally, dance crazes swept the country in the 1910s. By 1912 there were dozens of particular dance steps—including the fox trot, horse trot, crab step, kangaroo dip, camel walk, fish walk, chicken stretch, turkey trot, grizzly bear, and bunny hug—which rose and fell in popularity. Pacing the trends were Irene and Vernon Castle, whose grace and urbane style helped legitimize the new physicality between the sexes on the dance floor. Even the Argentinian tango, once derided as the "dance of the brothel," was accepted by many after the Castles performed it in 1914 (although many cities, including Boston and Cleveland, continued to ban the suggestive dance for years). Their roles as trendsetters extended well beyond their beautiful moves. When Irene Castle cut her hair or began wearing headbands, for example, many women followed suit. It has been suggested that Vernon Castle's penchant for wearing a wristwatch, considered effeminate by many men who refused to wear "bracelets," single-handedly (no pun intended) ended the tradition of the pocket watch.

If fads are difficult to distinguish from more important trends and directions in popular culture, then hobbies are nearly impossible to categorize. While traditional pastimes, such as retaining keepsakes and heirlooms, collecting books or antiques, and preserving customary or premodern crafts such as quilting, woodworking, and food preservation, were continued in the 1910s, little evidence exists to suggest that these activities constituted anything that we would call a hobby today. If there was one activity that did seem to approximate what we currently term a hobby, it was the growing interest in the wilderness. Increasingly, resorts and summer retreats were regarded as preferable getaways for those exhausted by the pressures of city living. The automobile gave many the freedom of movement which previously might have prevented them from acting on these impulses. Moreover, President Theodore Roosevelt's call for Americans to protect the unspoiled wilderness and to lead a "strenuous life" in the outdoors struck a chord with many in the 1910s. Although the U.S. Congress had been involved with natural preservation since the time of the Civil War, it was not until 1916 that the National Park Service was commissioned to administer these areas and to maintain the nation's parks and monuments. By 1918 the National Park Service had developed plans to provide automobile access to the most popular destinations—such as Yosemite and Yellowstone National Parks—as well as to provide hotels, museums, natural historians, and campsites within these areas. Until the arrival of the Great Depression, the National Park Service remained a well-respected, funded, and utilized agency within the public domain.

RECREATION AND SPORTS

In the 1910s, Americans continued to debate and redefine what they understood recreations and sports to mean. As Henry Adams noted in his influential work, *The Education of Henry Adams* (1907), when he was a youth "sport as a pursuit was unknown." While Adams' generation certainly found exercise in their daily lives (if from no other activity than walking), play and recreation were largely regarded as a waste of time. Most individuals who wanted to succeed avoided leisurely physical activity in favor of business or intellectual pursuits. Team and spectator sports held no virtues for these people. This interpretation began to give way, slowly in the 1890s and then much more rapidly in the new century. By 1910 play was regarded not only as a useful pursuit, but as an essential one in the training of young minds. The focus of adults on children was especially sharp, as the drive to expand recreation and sport in the United States merged with efforts made by reformers to save immigrant children from the harsh environmental conditions of the inner cities.

A key part of the redefinition of recreation and play had to do with the values that youth were supposed to absorb as they matured into responsible American citizens. Proper civic values, such as a respect for fair play, self-help, and an avoidance of class biases, were thought to be foreign to the millions of immigrants and their children who had streamed into the United States. In 1910 Otto Mallery voiced a common concern of many native-born Americans when he proclaimed the "Social Significance of Play." Mallery believed, "In the games of the street every boy is for himself. Victory belongs to the shrewd, the crafty, the strong." Well-organized (and adult-supervised) team games, by contrast, "require the submission of the individual will to the welfare of the team. Rigid rules inculcate fair play.... These standards when translated into the language of political life we call Self-government, Repect for the Law, Social Service and Good Citizenship."[6]

Armed with a greater awareness of inner-city social problems, the direct result of the reports by muckrakers and Progressives like Lewis Hine, Jane Addams, and others, advocates believed that opportunities for "organized play" would have a significantly positive effect not only on America's youth but also on the ability for others to accept these new citizens as equal members of society. When, in 1911, Milwaukee residents were asked to describe the typical day of the urban child, more than half assumed that they were "doing nothing" with their time. Two years later, a similar poll in Cleveland showed that 40 percent of respondents

Maypole dance, Central Park, New York City (c. 1905–10). Courtesy of
the Library of Congress.

also believed that youth were wasting the day, possibly leading to juvenile delinquency. Throughout the first decade of the twentieth century,
many towns and cities passed ordinances prohibiting any type of child's
play on city streets.[7]

The rising fears of gang activity also supported the need to take a
second look at recreation and sports. Social reformers had found that,
for the most part, teenagers entered into gangs as a way to achieve an
independent identity that was separate from parental (or state guardian)
authority. While in these gangs, youths were educated to believe that
their particular race, ethnicity, religion, or social status was the single
most important social characteristic in their lives. As they aged into
young adults, many gang members proved unwilling to accept their
place within a society of equal individuals because of the values instilled
by the gang. By contrast, reformers claimed, organized play and team
sports undermined the tendency to form factions and supported the idea
that fair play and respect for others were rewarded in modern society.
Individual transgressions of the rules penalized the entire group (think
of team fouls in basketball or yardage penalties in football) rather than
one person. In the words of reformer Richard T. Ely, "[H]alf of the
wrong-doings of young rascals in the cities is due to the fact that they

have no innocent outlet for their animal spirits."[8] Recreational facilities and team sports were two answers to the problem of gangs.

Finally, international events both overtly and indirectly reinforced these efforts to extol the virtues of play. The revival of the Olympic games in 1896—and especially in 1904, when the United States hosted the games at St. Louis—merged nationalism with physical skills in ways that suggested the positive good of sports. The activities of American servicemen in World War I also promoted the organized play movement. To develop physical fitness, inductees and volunteers spent countless hours at military bases playing volleyball, baseball, hockey, and basketball. The sports of boxing, wrestling, and swimming were also championed by the U.S. Army. As a result, Americans became more accepting of claims that sports and physical fitness would lead to decency and honor.

Ultimately, proponents of organized play tapped into these fears and opportunities in an effort to reform a child's "wasted time" into useful, civically beneficial activities. The play movement was essentially, therefore, a progressive reform intended to save children from the vices of the inner city and, not the least of which, to develop the civic values many believed the immigrant culture lacked. This was not an insignificant shift in the minds of many native-born Americans. Cooperation and group development ran counter to many of the intellectual trends of the past fifty years. For example, Social Darwinists championed individual achievement and argued that any limits placed on star performers merely leveled American society. In addition, many opposed the Progressive notion that environmental conditions of poverty were the leading causes of vice. The connection between mind and body, between sports and civic duty, was indeed a revolutionary shift not only in popular culture, but in society at large.

PARKS, PLAYGROUNDS, AND THE PLAY MOVEMENT

If there is a single misconception about the rise of popular recreation and sports facilities, it is that the movement was born in the country and moved to the cities. Historian Steven A. Riess clearly disputes this: "The evolution of the city, more than any other single factor, influenced the development of organized sport and recreational athletic pastimes in America."[9] More than anything, it was the challenge of dealing with overcrowded tenements, crime, and inner-city pollution that gave strength to the claim that America's youth were being raised in an environment that was fundamentally different than that in our rural past. In addition, according to Riess, it was the *process* of urbanization that made this shift possible. The rising value of land, industrialization, modern transportation, and the new mass media all made the formation of parks and recreational facilities possible, in fact probable, when compared to a nation which previously did not have its attention focused on overcrowding. Stephen Hardy echoed this sentiment when he concluded, for the city of Boston, that the "park movement . . . was part of an active, conscious search for order amid the environmental, political, social, and cultural dislocations" of the modern city.[10]

Certainly, some efforts had been made before the 1910s to develop parks and recreational facilities. Landscape architect Frederick Law Olmsted constructed New York City's Central Park in 1867 to provide contemplative, natural settings for urban citizens to relax and release their tensions. The problem was that these facilities were rarely accessible to the working class, nor were they friendly to those who wanted to use them for exercise. As late as the 1900s, many municipal parks expressly forbade walking on the grass, much less organizing a baseball game on the grounds. In 1910 Boston had only fourteen places for the public to swim and seven public gymnasiums. Similarly, small, local playgrounds were appearing in the inner city, but usually in regions that were populated by wealthier Americans and only when the land was not claimed by developers interested in erecting more housing.

Still, urban reformers convinced of the social benefits to be derived from organized play were hard at work planning facilities that could be used by those with more moderate economic means. The South Park System, begun in Chicago in 1903, was the clearest example of how such plans might proceed. South Park comprised ten separate parks, all located in the poorest parts of the city. Funds were made available for the maintenance of these grounds and for the construction of a number of playgrounds, tracks, pools, and gyms. It was estimated that in its first few years of operation, the South Park System serviced nearly five million people per year.[11]

Such concentrated efforts remained rare, however; less than 40 parks had been constructed nationwide. Moreover, the movement lacked a coordinated, national voice. This changed, in 1906, with the rise of the Playground Association of America (PAA). Led by Henry Curtis, Joseph Lee, Jane Addams, Jacob Riis, and Luther Gulick, and funded from money provided by the Russell Sage Foundation, the PAA combined the moral suasion of the settlement house movement, the medical profession (Curtis had earned his Ph.D. in child psychology and Gulick was a physician), and the "bully pulpit" of the presidency (Theodore Roosevelt acted as the honorary leader of the PAA until 1908). With its organization centered in New York City, the PAA focused their efforts on the larger, industrial cities with amazing success. By the 1910s, when the association was to be most effective, the group coordinated the work of 744 full-time and more than 5,000 part-time play directors. They oversaw the construction of thousands of playgrounds, costing localities a combined $100 million, which arranged age-specific activities for children from four to eighteen. Participation was voluntary, and it is still unclear as to which citizens took advantage of the opportunity. Still, by 1917, the PAA claimed it had initiated 3,940 playgrounds and recreational programs with 8,748 directors in 481 cities and towns throughout the country.[12]

CLASS AND THE RISE OF MODERN SPECTATOR SPORTS

The role played by class in the rise of modern sports was a significant one. Not only were middle-class and elite reformers instrumental in setting the terms of the debate over sports (i.e., the social uplift needed for inner-city youth), their activities in the first part of the twentieth century were essential to the growth of popular pastimes such as baseball and football. The sporting culture of well-to-do American men had deep roots but equally important implications for popular culture in the 1910s.

During the late Gilded Age, men of means found that they had the free time and money to pursue recreation. Whether termed hobbies or sports, these activities were secluded from the rest of American society because of where and how they held their contests. In particular, discretionary income gave elites access to the countryside where they formed a number of private country clubs and other associations. Members, who focused initially on hunting and horse racing, and later boating, polo, lawn tennis, and golf, found that they could display their wealth through their proficiency in these leisure activities.

The aspiring middle class also exerted great influence on the development of modern sports. Increasingly, by 1900, white-collar workers and professionals could find the time and money to spend on leisure pursuits. The meritocracy of sports—both for participants as well as spectators—which valued the best player on the field, not the one with the greatest social advantages, worked well with the mind-set of the increasingly confident middle class. The rationality of sports, as well as its strict organization, set rules, equality of competition, and fascination with statistics, was in keeping with the search for order craved by many new professionals. Finally, sports seemed to provide the middle class access to new and largely open opportunities for social advancement. One could hobnob with industry leaders, discussing noncontroversial sports-related topics that were the focus of such popular new magazines as *Field and Stream, Sports Afield*, and *Outing*, or demonstrate their skills on the golf course or tennis court without ever having to discuss one's parents, occupation, or country of origin.

Such activities at the highest levels of the economic spectrum had interesting and unintended consequences in the field of spectator sports. Golf was a perfect example. Long held as an elite pursuit, the game required time, equipment, and access to rural or suburban courses, which prevented most Americans from participating in the sport. But with the rise of the upper-middle-class professional, golf began to emerge as a more popular pastime in 1910. While there were no public courses before 1900, only ten years later the largest cities offered 24 courses open to all players. By the end of the decade, this number had doubled to 50 which, in addition to private clubs, handled an estimated 500,000 regular players a year.

In 1913, at the U.S. Golf Association Open, the exclusive game of golf became a national sensation. The unlikely star of the tournament was Francis Ouimet, the 20-year-old son of a recent immigrant who had learned to play golf as a caddie and by sneaking onto the exclusive Brookline Country Club, in a suburb of Boston. A hard-working and talented golfer, he had won six amateur events and legitimately qualified for the selective Open. Ouimet stunned the sports world when he tied British stars Harry Vardon and Ted Ray after three rounds. The following day, Ouimet fell behind but rallied in the final nine holes to force a fifth round the following day. Applauded for simply competing with his athletic (and possibly class) superiors, Ouimet completed the Cinderella story by besting Vardon by five strokes, and Ray by six.

Working-class Americans also had popular pastimes, but rarely were they accorded the respect given a "sport." The need for time and some disposable income were significant determinants of who participated or watched sporting events. While real wages were rising by 1910, the typical industrial laborer still needed to put in ten hours of work per day, every day but Sunday. As a result, the sports that originated in neighborhood saloons, like boxing, pool, and illegal blood sports, expanded quickly in the working-class regions of the city. The growth of pool halls throughout the decade—where for only a little money one could walk from one's apartment to talk, drink, and socialize—was phenomenal. More than 42,000 halls were legally registered by 1920. Although less numerous, bowling alleys were more popular with the upper working classes because they allowed for family entertainment by men and women who had to conserve both their time and money.

Prize fighting represented one of the rare instances in which a once disreputable working-class pastime was transformed into an accepted national spectator sport. While the era of larger-than-life ethnic legends like John L. Sullivan was not long removed (Sullivan lost his title to James Corbett in 1892 and died in 1918), the end of bare-knuckle contests in favor of the more rational Marquis of Queensbury bouts, which valued speed and, ironically, more concentrated attacks to the head (which

Jack Johnson (right) and James Jeffries (left) at the World
Championship Battle, Reno, Nevada, July 4, 1910. Courtesy of the
Library of Congress.

could result in the new and abbreviated ten-second knockout), made this
transition possible in the first decade of the twentieth century. According
to historian Elliot J. Gorn, "[B]oxing became simpler and faster-paced,
essential qualities if it was to appeal to a wide if not particularly knowledgeable audience." The emergence of respectable fighters, including
Jack Dempsey, the "Manassa Mauler," and Gene Tunney, who perfected
his boxing skills while with the American Expeditionary Force in World
War I, indicated that prizefighting had been approved as a sport.[13]

During the 1910s, the potential of prizefighting was beginning to be
realized. While largely a quiet decade, in terms of overall talent, several
men did stand out. Of these, Jack Johnson was most prominent. One of
the first black heavyweight champions of the modern era, Johnson
earned his title in 1910 with a fifteenth-round knockout of James Jeffries
(who had taken the title from Corbett). After Johnson earned $60,000 for
winning the fight, Johnson's mother proudly claimed that her son "said
he'd *bring home the bacon*, and the honey boy has gone and done it,"[14]
thereby adding a new slang phrase to the American language. In an era
of Jim Crow and overt racism, Johnson stood as a proud symbol for
African Americans: able to excel as a champion based on merit, second
to no one based on his skin tone. Johnson's much publicized drinking

and womanizing, typical for prizefighters of that era and many others, and his marriage to an 18-year-old white actress and model, Lucille Cameron, however, stoked the racial hatred of the nation. Nearly every competitor of Johnson's was labeled a "great white hope," and race riots broke out across the country when Johnson inevitably sent his opponents reeling. Johnson, exiled from the United States for supposedly violating the Mann Act through his marriage to Cameron, lost his crown in 1915 to Jess Willard while fighting in Havana, Cuba.

FOOTBALL

Boxing showed that a working-class sport could become an acceptable component of popular culture; the rise of football throughout the era confirmed that an elite sport could do the same. Football was originally a sport of the upper class; the game was the chosen recreation of most college-bound sons of America's elite. In spite of these aristocratic roots, by 1900 football was found throughout the country and was vying for recognition as *the* national game.

Football's popularity on college campuses has been ascribed to a number of factors, but a discussion need not go much further than to note that the typical college student at the turn of the century was male, young, affluent, in a relatively uncontrolled environment for the first time, and interested in demonstrating his belonging to "the team." These sons of the rich, well trained to sacrifice for the good of the group, were quite interested in showing the world that they could lead the "strenuous life" needed to take control of an emerging industrial giant like the United States. The rituals of the weekend games, either as a player or as a spectator, served to release pressure after a week's worth of classes in which one's place in the future social order was being decided. Accordingly, America's most prestigious universities became some of the fiercest and most selective football programs in the country, followed closely by the large Midwestern universities that now make up the Big 10 football conference. The popularity of football at these powerhouse programs—Harvard, Yale, Princeton, Michigan, Chicago—was remarkable. As early as 1890, contests between the best schools regularly drew between 15,000 and 30,000 spectators.[15]

Of course, a large part of the appeal of the game was the violent release of energy that occurred on the field. Keeping these collisions controlled while working in tandem with ten other teammates was, and remains, what separated the good teams from the bad. Ideally, the contest played out like a chess match—a game of war—with human pieces. Unfortunately and probably inevitably, young men driven to such levels of excitement were often unable to contain this violence. At times, the game turned deadly. In 1902, 12 collegians were killed playing football. Three

Notre Dame football squad, 1914. Courtesy of the Library of Congress.

years later, 11 died and more than 100 incurred serious (usually head) injuries. Even still, many were hesitant to lay too much blame at the feet of the game, preferring instead to extol the male virtues of such bloody competition. Notre Dame's Father John Cavenaugh "would rather see our youth playing football with the danger of a broken collarbone occasionally than to see them dedicated to croquet." Stanford president David Starr Jordan concluded simply, "It isn't a game, it's a battle." As the deaths continued, President Theodore Roosevelt threatened federal intervention and even Harvard's president, Charles Eliot, concluded, "There seems at present to be a well nigh universal consent that the present game is intolerable." [16]

Fortunately for the hundreds of student athletes, Walter Camp, the head of the American Collegiate Football Rules Committee (the precursor to the National Collegiate Athletic Association, NCAA), set to work modify the basic rules of the game. Camp, who did more to shape the current game than any other individual, wanted to create more opportunities to score. The average score for most games remained in the single digits. He legalized the forward pass and separated the teams by a line of scrimmage to give the players more time to develop complex scoring strategies. The reforms were passed in the hopes that athletes would be less likely to sacrifice themselves in order to prevent even a single point. Camp also outlawed the unstoppable, bone-snapping, flying wedge as being simply too dangerous.

Almost immediately, the procedural changes instigated by Camp had their intended effects. Deaths became less and less common, and the fans were treated to a more wide-open, enjoyable game. In some ways, scoring became too easy for the better schools. Georgia Tech's impressive 1916 and 1917 teams rolled up massive margins against their opponents, including a 41–0 win over Pennsylvania, a 98–0 pasting of Carlisle Indian School (Jim Thorpe's school), and a 222–0 nail-biter over Cumberland (Tennessee), a game in which Tech's kicker booted 18 extra points in the

first half alone. On the other hand, the rules changes also allowed innovative and daring football tacticians to take on the giants of the game. Most noteworthy was the small, wholly outmatched team from Notre Dame, a little and largely unknown Catholic college in northern Indiana, who utilized the forward pass to stun Army 35–13. Their quarterback, Gus Dorais, relied on the quickness and intelligence of his key receivers, including Knute Rockne, to befuddle the impenetrable wall that was Army's defensive line. That same year, Amos Alonzo Stagg began numbering his players' jerseys as an aid to the public, who were beginning to take an intense interest in the revived sport.

It was during the 1910s that the immense popularity of football spilled over from the college campuses onto the nation as a whole. Colleges began constructing stadiums that held many times their student populations. The newly constructed Yale Bowl, in New Haven, Connecticut, held 60,000 fans when it opened in 1914. That same year, college presidents invested over $2 million nationwide for new arenas. Harvard alone spent more than $160,000. The decade also saw the growth of football stardom for such players as Rockne, George Gipp, Jim Thorpe, and coaches including Stagg and Glen Scobie "Pop" Warner. In 1915 the second Tournament of Roses football game was played in Pasadena, California. The game was significant because the first, held thirteen years earlier, was a failure. After 1915 the Rose Bowl became an important and much discussed contest between the best teams of the East and West. It signaled the arrival of college football as a national preoccupation which continues to this day.

Jim Thorpe merits special notice for the effect he had on college football in the 1910s. While no doubt aided by the innovative tactics of his coach, "Pop" Warner, and the skills of his fellow teammates at Carlisle Indian School, Thorpe's exceptional athletic skills set him apart from all others. During his freshman year, Thorpe's smaller teams defeated such goliaths as Pennsylvania, Chicago, Army, and, in one of the greatest upsets of all time, Harvard in 1911. Thorpe solidified his reputation as "the world's greatest athlete" at the 1912 Olympic Games held in Stockholm, Sweden. There he won nearly every event in both the decathlon and pentathlon and won gold medals in both. When the king of Sweden placed the medals around his neck, he was reported to have said, "Sir, you are the greatest athlete in the world," to which Thorpe responded, "Thanks, King." When it was later reported that Thorpe had earned $15 a week for playing semi-professional baseball in the summer of 1909, a common practice for most college athletes, the Olympic Commission stripped him of his medals, an offense that was not corrected until 1980, 27 years after his death. Regardless of this slight, Thorpe popularized football as Babe Ruth did in baseball. His stellar professional football career gave incentive to many Americans to attend their first spectator sport.

THE NATIONAL PASTIME: PROFESSIONAL BASEBALL

Unlike football, baseball emerged not as an elite sport of the college campus but rather as the first true mass spectator sport intended for the average American. The travails of professional baseball are the best indication that, by the close of the decade, modern sports had carved out a permanent place in the nation's popular culture. That it did so while surviving numerous splits in the professional leagues, a world war, and a scandal that included one of its greatest players in its showcase display—the World Series—was a testament to the depth of its support throughout the country.

Contrary to American mythology, baseball was not created by Abner Doubleday in Cooperstown, New York. The game, called rounders, town-ball, or baseball, was described as early as 1744. Doubleday's contribution was largely in writing out the rules of the sport, as he understood them, in 1839. By the time of the Civil War, most Americans had either played or seen baseball being played, and almost immediately thereafter professional teams began to appear. In 1871 the Cincinnati Reds were the first touring team to pay their players. Five years later the National League was founded, including teams from New York City, Philadelphia, Hartford, Boston, Chicago, Louisville, St. Louis, and Cincinnati. By 1880 professional baseball was a solid institution in the United States.

These deep roots helped baseball weather the transition of modernization that shook the country to its foundation. Perhaps because the game was fundamentally an urban phenomenon, baseball remained relatively unchanged from 1880 to 1910. Based, as it was, on urban consumers arriving via modern mass transit systems to consume their entertainment in state-of-the-art ballparks and then read about these exploits again in the morning newspapers, baseball paved the way for other spectator sports to develop. The fact that the professional leagues grew in strength as the nation urbanized is persuasive evidence that the sport was uniquely attuned to the needs of its metropolitan fans.

Part of baseball's attraction was the nostalgia it generated for a mythic and innocent American past. Baseball's seasonality was a natural complement to these dreams. Played in a single calendar year, each team's season started as fresh as the spring, confronted hard work that required mature determination throughout the hot summer, and reaped the rewards of these efforts in the fall full of experience and wisdom. To this rhythm, the game appended a strong respect for statistics and rules which were at the heart of modern America. By season's end, it was completely possible to dissect the causes of success or failure based on hitting percentages, earned run averages, errors, or strikes. Finally, at least in the 1910s, the daily drama of the game was played out in about two hours, making it easy to fit into an afternoon schedule.

Other elements of baseball's mystique were actively created. Owners and sportswriters—men like Ring Lardner, Grantland Rice, and Damon Runyon, who well understood that by promoting the game they were promoting themselves—worked hard to accentuate baseball's rural images: the wide expanse of green grass, the sunny skies (the game was not played at night and never in foul weather), and the wholesomeness of its players (in spite of overwhelming evidence to the contrary). Two book-length histories of baseball were published during the decade: Albert G. Spalding's *America's National Game* (1911) and Francis Richter's *History and Records in Baseball* (1914), which lent credence to the mythology. Baseball owners were also quick to catch onto the ideals of organized play that were capturing the attention of reformers. It was argued that following baseball could make one a better citizen. Its rules, sense of fair play, meritocracy, and honesty made buying a ticket to the ballpark nearly a civic duty. Reporters argued that by rooting for the home team they were helping recent immigrants develop a greater sense of civic pride which would, ultimately, bring people closer and make them more cooperative both at work and at home.[17]

One important component needed by ball clubs, to make this argument more persuasive, was a sense of permanence. A club that moved from town to town soon found it was unable to attract and retain a base of fans. The construction of modern parks went far to provide this stability to local backers. The investment in new stadiums was certainly great in the 1910s. New fields in Pittsburgh (Forbes Field), Philadelphia (Shibe Park), Boston (Fenway Park), Detroit (Tiger Stadium), New York City (the Polo Grounds), Brooklyn (Ebbets Field), and Chicago (Comiskey and Wrigley Fields) were constructed throughout the decade. Comiskey Field alone cost more than $700,000 for the land and materials. These arenas were more than just monuments to the team's stability and

Baseball parks—Polo Grounds during World Series game, 1913.
Courtesy of the Library of Congress.

commitment to the locale. They also assuaged the fears of many consumers. Fires in the Chicago, Cleveland, and New York stadiums—most recently at the old Polo Grounds, in April 1911—were well chronicled in the newspapers. Old wooden stands were known to have collapsed under the weight of the crowd. These perils gave patrons pause when deciding where to spend their money. Given the heightened competition from movies, vaudeville, and dance halls, improvements were required of owners for baseball to continue growing in the 1910s.

The mammoth size of these modern arenas created a new type of public space. The Polo Fields, when opened in 1911, seated more than 32,000 people before it was expanded to hold 54,000. Twelve years later, Yankee Stadium was constructed to house more than 63,000 people.[18] One result of these large structures was that the baseball crowd tended to be more diverse and representative of America than almost any other popular sport. Women regularly attended the games, as did people of color. The arrival of the American League, in 1901, opened play on Sundays, giving access to workers who were otherwise occupied on Saturdays (leading to a middle class–working class split between the fans of National and American League teams that exists, in some cities, to the present day). While the game was still only open to white men, outsiders no doubt felt more comfortable within the anonymity of the large parks. As a result, baseball crowds tended to be much more orderly than those of almost any other sport. While the image of republican virtue cloaking the game helped in this regard, more than likely the rule changes in 1907, which protected umpires from fan intimidation, did more.

The combination of easy access, economic prosperity, newspaper publicity, and a good product resulted in an overwhelmingly positive economic outlook for professional baseball. While in 1900 there were only 13 minor leagues and one major league (concentrated in the industrial North), by 1912 there were 46 minor leagues and two major leagues with teams throughout the United States. Attendance figures for the professional leagues underscore baseball's population. Nearly 6.8 million people attended a baseball game each year by 1910 (double that of the previous decade). This grew to 9.3 million per year by the close of the decade.[19]

Still, baseball was not without its problems in the 1910s. Largely, these were structural. As the game expanded in popularity, both the minor and major leagues began to grow. With this expansion came unanticipated problems such as where to grant new franchise rights, how many clubs to allow in a single location, and how to determine the status of ballplayers who tried to jump from team to team. While the owners of the major league teams seldom acted in harmony, they were united in trying to maintain local control over these types of decisions—each club was free to act as it saw fit given its unique circumstances.

The greatest direct threat to the professional leagues came in 1913, when the Federal League was born. This new professional association was created by entrepreneurs who felt they had been excluded from the game by the current owners of National and American Leagues. By and large, the new teams were created in markets where clubs already existed. Many tried to attract the biggest talents of the established leagues through higher salaries or other incentives. This gamble proved to be too risky, and by 1915 the Federal League agreed to disband. The rapid rise and fall of the Federal League was aided in small part by the established professional club owners. They offered $600,000 to each club that agreed to fold, the possibility of buying into an established club at a discount at some future date, and admission to their league for the two most successful Federal clubs: in Chicago and St. Louis. Feeling left out, the Federal League franchise in Baltimore sued in 1919, claiming that the American and National Leagues constituted a national monopoly, or trust, over professional baseball and, as a result, should be regulated by the federal government as any other interstate business. In a landmark decision for professional baseball, the U.S. Supreme Court ruled in 1922 that while teams certainly traveled between states, the "product" of baseball (i.e., games) did not cross state lines. Baseball was not subject to federal oversight.

A second potential problem during the decade, never fully sorted out by professional baseball, was the owners themselves. While each certainly intended for his program to make money, their commitment to winning and sharing their success with the players varied greatly. For example, Frank Farrell and Colonel (hon.) Jacob Ruppert were both owners of the New York Highlanders, soon to be renamed Yankees, during the 1910s. Farrell bought into the new American League using the proceeds from his network of more than 200 gambling outlets and pool halls. While he proved to be one of the most financially resourceful of all owners, many suspected that his connections to illegal wagering held potentially explosive problems for the game. When Ruppert, a millionaire socialite and brewing magnate, purchased the team from Farrell, for $460,000 in 1915, he originally wanted to rename it after a line of his beer. In the end, both men proved to be beneficial to the Highlander/ Yankee organization. Indeed, Ruppert's lavish spending on his players and facilities—for example, on January 5, 1920, he "purchased" George Herman "Babe" Ruth from the Boston Red Sox for $125,000 and in 1923 he built Yankee Stadium for $2.5 million—created the baseball dynasty that has come to dominate the professional leagues. Owners who were less liberal or who did not have the financial resources of a Farrell or Ruppert soon found themselves at a disadvantage. Moreover, they ruled without opposition and, as was the case with the Chicago White Sox, their personal biases and intransigence could have disastrous consequences for the good of the game.[20]

Ultimately, it was the rise of the star system in baseball that secured its success. As with the movies, star players put fans in the seats and filled columns in the newspapers. With the arrival, in 1901, of the American League and then, in 1913, of the Federal League, the best ball players found they could market their services to a larger pool of bidders. By 1910 the average major leaguer was making a respectable $3,000 per year; the best players' salaries topped $10,000 per year, on a par with more elite professionals like doctors and lawyers. Each year, individual contracts kept driving the prices higher. Honus Wagner signed with Pittsburgh for $18,000 in 1910, Ty Cobb was paid $20,000 annually by Detroit, and in 1922 Babe Ruth made $56,000 for his year's service to the Yankees. While the average salary also rose to around $5,000 by the end of the decade, it was nothing compared to rapid increase for elite players.[21]

From the record book, it appears that these salaries were well spent. The 1910s saw some of the best players in the game, including Cobb, Wagner, Ruth, Christy Mathewson (New York Giants), and Walter Johnson (Washington Senators). In 1919 Ruth hit 29 homers, shattering the old record (the next year he hit 54, more than any single *team* had previously) and become a national sensation. Many consider Johnson to have been the greatest pitcher in the game. While Cy Young won more games throughout his career (he retired in 1911 with 511 wins), Johnson earned his victories with a team that was a perennial loser (in fact, he still owns the record for most 1–0 *losses* in the major leagues). Johnson had ten consecutive 20-win seasons and twice topped 30. In 1913 his record was an astonishing 36–7; he pitched 56 consecutive scoreless innings, delivered 243 strikeouts, gave up 38 walks and an average of 1.09 runs per nine innings. Mathewson's career numbers were less impressive (although he was still an outstanding pitcher), but his behavior as a professional on and off the field made him a role model for baseball. At the peak of his career, Mathewson volunteered for duty in World War I, was gassed in combat, and died, in 1925, largely as a result of related injuries. One eulogist remarked, "Such men have a very real value above and beyond the achievements of brawn and sporting skill. They realize and typify in a fashion the ideal of sport—clean power in the hands of a clean and vigorous personality." When the Baseball Hall of Fame was established in 1936, the five "Immortals" selected on the first ballot were Cobb, Wagner, Ruth, Mathewson, and Johnson—all but Ruth made their most lasting mark playing during the 1910s.[22]

Stars, high pay, and modern stadiums led to a cycle of escalating interest and attendance. Good players were increasingly lauded for how well they exemplified American values. Rising salaries and, in 1912, the formation of a new player's union (Base Ball Player Fraternity) gave strong encouragement for others to avoid embarrassing brawls and the more obvious examples of alcohol abuse. Managers, too, began to require that their players dress and act as professionals while in the public eye. Clubs looked to hire college-educated athletes, many of whom—like Jim Thorpe—had already made a name for themselves nationwide. By 1920 nearly 20 percent of all rookies came from the college ranks.[23] Umpires were now being paid better and abused less. Professionalism only boosted the faith that middle-class Americans put into baseball. Not only was it seen as a healthy and exciting sport, but one that was worthy of respect and emulation.

When viewed in this light, the 1919 "Black Sox" scandal could have been potentially lethal to the fortunes of professional baseball. Given the structure of baseball ownership, the crisis could have been predicted. The Chicago White Sox were owned by Charles Comiskey, a former player and manager who toiled all his life under cheap owners. When Comiskey himself became an owner, first in Sioux City, Iowa, and then, in 1900, in Chicago, he proved to be even more petty. Joining the fledgling American League in 1901, Comiskey's team (which took the name White Sox after it had been discarded by the National League team in that city, which shifted from White Sox, to Nationals, to Colts, and finally the Cubs) was an instant sensation, winning pennants in 1901, 1906, 1917, and 1919. While the team was well supported by the city, Comiskey paid his players less than half of the national average and much less to his star players. The greatest player of the White Sox was "Shoeless" Joe Jackson. A lifetime .356 hitter, Jackson came to Chicago in 1916 after a stellar career in Cleveland. His batting stance was thought to be nearly perfect, and numerous major league players (including Babe Ruth) patterned themselves after the consummate hitter. His skills were so well regarded that Comiskey was forced, in 1919, to extend a three-year guaranteed contract to Jackson. That year, supported by a strong team, Jackson propelled the White Sox to the World Series where they were heavy favorites to beat the Cincinnati Reds.

The links among organized crime, professional gamblers, and baseball had always been close. As noted above, Frank Farrell's chummy connections to bettors and the New York Yankees gave many pause for concern when his teams displayed unexpected slumps throughout the year. Baseball offered gamblers many ways to wager, and collusion by only a few players could have great consequence to a game or series. After winning the pennant, White Sox first baseman Chick Gandil was approached by a professional gambler named Arnold Rothstein and offered $100,000 to throw the series. Gandil agreed and was helped by seven of his teammates, including Jackson, who later admitted to taking $5,000. While Jackson played well, batting .375 and driving in six runs, it was not enough to win, and the White Sox lost the World Series three games to five (in a best of nine contest).

Many, including Comiskey, suspected that the "fix was in" by the second game. Comiskey had evidence of a bribe only weeks after the series ended. He said nothing. It was not until 1920, after a Chicago Cubs regular-season game was thrown, that Illinois Attorney General MacClay Hoyne impaneled a grand jury to investigate gambling and baseball in the state. Hoyne subpoenaed eight suspected White Sox players. In their testimony before the grand jury, Gandil, Jackson, and the others admitted they had taken money. This was enough to convince the jurists that a felony had been committed, and Hoyne was advised to press charges. The trial had the potential to ruin the White Sox, smear the reputation of baseball, incarcerate Rothstein and the players, and drive Comiskey from the game. Yet when the trial began, the incriminating testimony mysteriously disappeared. When the eight refused to testify in open court, the prosecution was left without evidence and the "Black Sox" were acquitted.

Whether a young boy actually asked Jackson to "say it ain't so, Joe" was immaterial. The damage to the reputation of baseball went to the core of its self-professed values. Only the heavy hand of the baseball commissioner, a former federal district judge, Kenesaw Mountain Landis prevented the situation from deteriorating further. In spite of the acquittal, Landis permanently banned the players from professional baseball. Jackson was also permanently barred from admission to the Hall of

Ty Cobb, Detroit Tigers, and Joe Jackson, Cleveland Indians. Courtesy
of the Library of Congress.

Fame as a result (he has the third highest lifetime batting average in all
of baseball and the highest of any player not currently enshrined at
Cooperstown). Landis's swift and decisive action, coupled with the hitting prowess of Babe Ruth, allowed baseball to emerge relatively un-
scathed by the incident. Certainly the game would have continued
regardless. But, lacking any self-policing procedure or a reason for fans

to continue to take an interest in a corrupt game, one could easily envision the national pastime being changed substantially in the coming years.

Charles Comiskey has rightly emerged as the man in the center of the controversy. His ability to run the team without oversight by league officials brought about the conditions that enabled the scandal to develop. Had he paid his players even an average salary or treated them with the respect that entertainment professionals had earned in the United States by 1919, the team members in all likelihood would not have been tempted by the numerous gamblers who loitered around America's ballparks. Comiskey's character deficiencies were revealed more fully in 1924 when, after being sued for his failure to honor Jackson's guaranteed contract, he produced the "lost" grand jury confession. By proving that Jackson had admitted taking a bribe, Comiskey showed how Jackson had breeched his contract and therefore was not entitled to the remainder of his salary. Many have concluded that Comiskey and Rothstein planned and carried out the pilfering of these confessions in 1920. The owner never admitted his role in the crisis nor did he change his tightfisted ways with other players' contracts. Charles Comiskey never fielded another contending team.[24]

CONCLUSION

It is clear, in summarizing the nature of games and toys, fads and hobbies, and recreation and sport in the 1910s, that these activities were well developed in American popular culture. While some were new and others old, each became vital to this country only after it demonstrated a connection to the larger values held by the consuming public. Americans were quick to apply the ideals of the era to even the most trivial of pastimes. Many of these continue on in American life, each demonstrating the diverse content of popular culture as well as the contingency of their success.

8

Literature

Of all the forms of popular culture, literature seems at first to be least reflective of American society. Dominated by well-educated and lettered critics, novelists, and poets, American literature seems far removed from the everyday lives of the typical citizen. Ironically, though, these artists captured a sense of the routine which, in many ways, was a more authentic picture of the 1910s than almost any other form of popular culture. The best writers used their own personal experiences and values as guides. As a result, what was saved for future generations were well-written accounts of what it *felt like* to be alive during the decade—how change was challenging society, how values were weakened and reconstructed, and how lives were lost and saved. For this reason it is common practice for historians today to assign works of literature in college courses so that students can be introduced to the strong emotions that accompanied historical change. Literature might, in the end, be the truest source of popular culture that we have.

There are problems, of course, with this assessment, not the least of which is trying to sort through the slippery relationship between historical reality and the freedom authors have to structure the world as they see it. An "American voice," as opposed to one which simply copied European styles, in literature was being consciously pursued by many authors and critics. Many readers came to be shocked by this movement toward literary independence. These new authors changed the way in which Americans read by changing the focus of their work to more modern, realistic material—the lives of everyday citizens. This rebirth was not without its vocal opponents. Still, in retrospect we can see that the best writers of the decade reflected a sense of change in American culture that was both profound and permanent.

TRENDS, CONFLICT, AND CHANGE
IN AMERICAN LITERATURE

Literary artists, unlike other artists in the 1910s, were largely free of the direct control of European stylists. Certainly, European writers were considered more refined and intellectually challenging simply because of their home, but Americans had developed their own written traditions using a language that was particularly their own. The contributions of Herman Melville, Nathaniel Hawthorne, Henry David Thoreau, and Walt Whitman did much to establish this American voice, even if local writers had done little since the 1860s to advance their cause.

While authors in the United States could claim independence from the overarching European culture, few demonstrated this in their works. The dominant interpretation of the arts in Britain during the Victorian Era (roughly the second half of the nineteenth century) carried over to the States. Termed the Genteel Tradition by philosopher George Santayana in 1911, the phrase reflected the general approach most writers took toward their craft. "Genteelists" assumed that art was the province of elites in society. Patronized and supported by the wealthy, the purpose of the arts was to uplift the electorate, refine their tastes, and, in the end, tame the savage materialism that seemed to run rampant throughout the country. Perhaps because many genteelists wrote for the popular women's periodicals of the era, most writers constructed tales that reinforced traditional values of home, independence, and propriety without bothering to examine whether these mores had validity, or even made sense, in the modern world. The genteel tradition also demanded that artwork refrain from all "offensive" subjects and language, including sex, class, race, politics, and base popular entertainment.

While remaining confident and dominant throughout the late 1800s, the genteel tradition began to look weathered and dated in the new century. The drive to avoid conflict in literature did not accurately reflect the world Americans saw around them. The new writers built upon this growing anxiety while tapping into two well-established traditions of previous transcendentalist authors. First, these earlier artists understood that change was an important component of American popular culture. Whether through commerce, technical innovation, or social evolution, U.S. citizens seemed in a constant state of "becoming," lending the optimistic view toward the future that many Americans retain to this day. Second, writers in the 1910s borrowed the strong sense of individuality that ran through the works of Melville, Ralph Waldo Emerson, Thoreau, and Whitman. This inner strength was highly democratic and rewarded those most willing to take risks. As a result, many realist writers concentrated on the very wealthy not because they were technically "better" than the rest of the public, but because they were better able to demonstrate their individual mettle since their wealth freed them from the distress of poverty.

Yet this old, romantic model was not transplanted to America in 1910 without some significant modifications. No writer more clearly demonstrated this difference than Henry Brooks Adams. His autobiography, titled *The Education of Henry Adams* (1907), balanced themes of spirituality and technological change and suggested that Americans had, in a sense, become detached from the country's founding ideals. More troubling was his suggestion that it might be impossible to rekindle these original fires. Adams's own journey revealed that even the most well-heeled and sophisticated citizens were unable to absorb the rapid fluctuations that were becoming standard in the modern world. If an American voice was to be found, according to Adams, it would not be merely an echo of a previous generation.

Trying to discover the "new," which Adams might conclude was an impossibility given the divisions he identified, became the mission of many artists and activists in the 1910s. Indeed, from Woodrow Wilson's New Freedom and Theodore Roosevelt's New Nationalism to New Poetry and New Criticism, novelty seemed more certain a guide for the future than the writings and ideas of past generations. These trends toward innovation led one historian to conclude that the "early 1910s were a promethean moment in Western art."[1]

The list of writers and literary publications that came of age under these conditions is truly remarkable. In fiction, they include Willa Cather, Sherwood Anderson, Gertrude Stein, and Theodore Dreiser. In criticism, publications like the *Masses* (1911), *Poetry* (1912), the *Smart Set* (1914), and the *New Republic* (1914) were founded, and writers such as John (Jack) Reed, Max Eastman, and H.L. Mencken gained wide circulation. In poetry, Ezra Pound, T.S. Eliot, Robert Frost, Carl Sandburg, and Edgar Lee Masters were first published. Commentators like Mabel Dodge Luhan were understandably awed when she reported that "barriers went down" in the 1910s "and people reached each other who had never been in touch before." Gertrude Stein later claimed that all of the literary change "since 1910 [was] due almost wholly to Americans."[2]

Yet it would be incorrect to conclude that these trends overturned American literature overnight. The reasons for the subtle shift are complex but can be attributed to a number of factors. First, the contrast between the soaring optimism in the world in 1910 and the bleak reality of world war knocked the breath out of the movement in its earliest years. Stein would later call the group of writers most directly affected by the war a "lost generation," hinting at their alienation and disillusionment. Second, many of these creative authors chose to emigrate from the United States and live abroad in Europe. While connected through their publications, the dilution of talent had an unintended effect of slowing the pace of literary change in the United States. Dwarfing these factors was the realist tradition in American letters which kept writers grounded in everyday life. Realism absorbed, modified, and pacified many of the most revolutionary artistic innovations of the decade, but it also changed significantly throughout the decade.

REALISM, NONFICTION, AND MODERNISM IN THE 1910s

Literary realism was both a revolutionary reappraisal of life in America and a simple acceptance of the forces of industrial capitalism. As artists, writers focused on the complexities of mass society (the "environment") and created fictional worlds where impersonal forces overwhelmed the hopes and dreams of their subjects. Typically, the drama of a realist work flowed from everyday events such as losing or taking a job, moving to a city, or making money, rather than contrived, overly emotional plot devices. Significantly, the setting of these works was almost always modern and, as a result, readers found the narratives familiar and very powerful.

The appearance of a number of influential nonfiction works supported this overall trend in the 1910s. Spanning from descriptions of the working poor to the education of preschoolers, nonfiction writing focused on the concrete reality of life in the United States. The leading books of the decade include *Twenty-Years at Hull-House* by Jane Addams (1910), *My First Summer in the Sierra* by John Muir (1911), *The Montessori Method* by Maria Montessori (1912), *An Economic Interpretation of the Constitution* by Charles and Mary Beard (1913), *Drift and Mastery* by Walter Lippmann (1914), *The Negro* by W.E.B. Du Bois (1915), and *America's Coming of Age* by Van Wyck Brooks (1915).

In like fashion, fictional works set an equally realistic pattern. Typically, a narrative introduced a young and idealistic hero who was then thrown into a setting that overwhelmed his or her ability to respond. Try as he or she might to strike out against conformity, by the end of the novel, short story, or poem, the character was usually broken in spirit and incapable of further resistance. As noted above, the focus on the very wealthy was common in the works of early realists like William Dean Howells, Theodore Dreiser, and Frank Norris. Here were men who had the inner drive to succeed in the new economy yet who ultimately had to face the reality that they could not control the markets that had made them rich. While earlier writers like Howells (in works such as *The Rise of Silas Lapham* [1885]) tended to focus on the moral apprehensions that accompanied the newly rich, later realists were more interested in how these men abused their phenomenal power.

Modernization, clearly, was a central component of realism. But here our understanding of literature in the 1910s again becomes problematic. "Modernism" is a recognized literary style separate from realism. Where realists usually depict characters struggling mightily (if unsuccessfully) to employ traditional moral values to their environmental problems, modernists suggested that these values were no longer valid. As a result, the dramatic tension realists portrayed *between* different members of society and their values was transformed to the dramatic tension *within* a single person torn between his or her own values. In short, realists suggested the need to adapt traditional morality to modernity while modernists hinted that the old views of morality no longer even applied.

During the 1910s, there was no clear distinction between the two. Stylistically, modernists tended to rely more upon everyday language, portrayed less balanced characters (both emotionally and economically), and blurred the traditional linear narrative progression of their works (i.e., telling a story from beginning to end along a fixed time line of events). The classic modern hero, F. Scott Fitzgerald's Jay Gatsby, was a man who bounced from one event to the next with little or no control over the outcomes. Well-versed in the norms of American society, he found no significance in their application in the contemporary world. Again, it is important to temper these changes with the realities of the 1910s. American writers were in the process of making adjustments, as were their fellow citizens, throughout the decade.

NEW CRITICISM, THE CRITICAL PRESS, AND H.L. MENCKEN

Contained within both realism and modernism, if indeed we can separate the two during the 1910s, was a new aesthetic in criticizing literature. Before this time, critics usually overlooked the values contained within a work provided that the artist conformed to traditional literary rules. If a verse was constructed in the proper meter or if prose developed an emotionally moving drama, the author was rarely held accountable for his or her views on society. By contrast, New Criticism and the host of publications, which sprang up in the 1910s, that published these reviews, focused intently on the cultural assumptions of the writer and directly challenged works that were based on values that they felt were unsupported in the modern era.

The birth of the *Masses*, a magazine of social and artistic criticism, in

1911, reflected this trend in New Criticism. Founded by Piet Vlag to "attack old systems, old morals, [and] old prejudices," the magazine began tentatively by humorously needling the genteel values that were already struggling to survive in the twentieth century. The magazine was soon reconstructed by Art Young and John Sloan to address explicitly the role of art in the modern industrial world. By 1913, Eastman believed that *Masses* should be

a magazine with a sense of humor and no respect for the respectable: frank, arrogant, impertinent, searching for true causes: a magazine directed against rigidity and dogma wherever it is found: printing what is too naked or true for a money-making press: a magazine whose final policy is to do as it pleases and conciliate nobody, not even its readers—there is a field for this publication in America.[3]

The *Masses*, then, is a good example of the mixture of realist and modernist trends during the 1910s.

Critical to the success of the *Masses* was its dedicated stable of talented contributors, all of whom varied in their commitment to the cause of socialism. Many of these, including Charlotte Perkins Gilman, Colonel Edward House, and Mary Heaton Vorse, are more correctly seen as Progressive reformers and muckrakers interested in popularizing the plight of the working poor in the United States. Others, like Upton Sinclair and Jack Reed, were more committed to the militant and inspired actions of the Industrial Workers of the World (IWW) and a true socialist government. Reed, in particular, seemed to live for the class struggles that were so apparent throughout the decade. The son of a wealthy Oregon family, educated at the best schools, Reed reveled in the violent strikes in Paterson, New Jersey, and Ludlow, Colorado. His passionate writing was instrumental in providing a human face to the threatening revolutions in Mexico and Russia (*Ten Days That Shook the World* was published in 1919). Reed's activism led him to the Soviet Union, where he died in 1920.

While the *Masses* staked a claim as representative of the enlightened worker, other publications sought less rigid ideological ground. Most notable was the *New Republic*, a "journal of opinion" started in 1914 by Herbert Croly with funding by heiress Dorothy Straight. More centrist in tone, the *New Republic* advocated neutrality in the war and backed the modest reforms put forth by Theodore Roosevelt's Progressive Party. While buffeted by the rise and fall of progressive politics (as was the *Masses* with socialism), the periodical maintained its focus on cultural expression and, in particular, literature. Like the *Masses*, the *New Republic* hoped to enlighten its readers with writing and criticism that expressly connected literary trends—which advanced a new understanding of one's place and role in society—and the intense political activity of the decade.

Finally, the decade saw the growth of more sophisticated and discerning literary magazines. For decades, such popular publications as the *Ladies' Home Journal*, the *Saturday Evening Post, Cosmopolitan, Munsey's*, and *McClure's* had offered middle-class readers a taste of the newest fashions in literature. Some of the contributions to these publications were significant. For example, the magazines greatly aided in the development of the short story in America. Unlike novels that tried to relate entire life histories, short pieces attempted to capture critical "moments" in a character's life. This trend grew in American literature, as writers expanded and deepened these vignettes into more psychologically intense works. As Sherwood Anderson later wrote, "I have come to think that the true history of life is but a history of moments. It is only the rare moments that we live."[4] The popular press did much to advance this trend in American letters.

Still, by and large, commercial publishers shied away from the more experimental works that propelled the medium forward into the modernist style. As a result, many specialty magazines were founded to cater to these needs. *Poetry: A Magazine of Verse* was started by Harriet Monroe in 1912 in Chicago to provide a forum for modernist poets, publishing such writers as Joyce Kilmer, Vachel Lindsay, and Carl Sandburg. Two years later, Margaret Anderson's the *Little Review*, also from Chicago, gave voice to an even more experimental style of writing. Throughout the decade, publications like *Others* (1915), the *Seven Arts* (1916), and the *Dial* (1916) provided authors with the space and freedom needed to be heard in a market dominated by commercial publications. More important, these magazines opened the public to a more pressing criticism of modern literature. In addition to Eastman and Croly, George Jean Nathan, Mencken, John Jay Chapman, Lippmann, and Lewis Mumford all began the process of critically assessing the direction and meaning of American writing. Of these, Mencken's work most certainly looms the largest.

H.L. MENCKEN

Henry Louis Mencken was born, raised, and lived most of his life in Baltimore, Maryland. As a journalist, critic, and editor, Mencken used his corrosive but humorous wit to dissolve pretentiousness, inequality, and ignorance wherever he found it. While frequently contemptuous of democracy and impatient with those of lesser intellectual capacity, Mencken was always honest and straightforward in his writing. His attacks sliced deeply, but they were never in the back. In his review of Sinclair Lewis's *Babbitt* (1922), Mencken wrote that the salient thing about [Lewis was his] complete lack of originality—and that is precisely the salient mark of every American in his class. What he feels and thinks is what it is currently proper to feel and think. Only once [in the novel does Babbitt] . . . venture upon an idea that is even remotely original—and that time the heresy almost ruins him. If he lives, he will not offend again.[5]

Such criticism was hard and made Mencken some bitter enemies, but it was also pointed at how he thought literature should serve the public (or be rejected if it did not).

Mencken was not without his flaws. He had little use for female reformers or the Women's Suffrage movement. For African Americans he had even less tolerance, partly due to his Southern upbringing, but also because he believed blacks were undereducated as a result of their own lack of resolve, a common error of the day. Moreover, he was an unabashed supporter of science and a critic of organized religions, seeing the former as completely objective and the latter as completely useless. Ironically, given his oft-quoted adage that Puritans were those who had "the haunting fear that someone, somewhere, may be happy," he lived his life as if he were a solid Christian, controlling himself in ways of money, vices, and the flesh.

Mencken wrote prolifically for newspapers and journals (such as the *Smart Set*, which he began editing with George Nathan in 1914) and in his own books. As a critic he wrote 182 book reviews spanning a wide range of offerings. He loved the works of such realist novelists as Theodore Dreiser, Sherwood Anderson, and Willa Cather, and he advanced the poetry of Edgar Lee Masters and Ezra Pound. Still, he was suspect of any strong stylistic patterns, noting honestly, "When I hear a theory I suspect a quack." More than anything, Mencken justified the practice of evaluating texts based on their applicability to modern times. He believed it was the critic's "business to provoke the reaction between the work of art and the spectator. The spectator, untutored, stands unmoved; he sees the work of art, but it fails to make any intelligible impression on him; if he were spontaneously sensitive to it, there would be no need for criticism."[6]

REALIST AND MODERNIST NOVELS

Critics like Mencken had ample opportunity to ply their trade throughout the decade. The era saw the creation of some of the best realistic, popular, and modern novels of any decade in American history, including works by Upton Sinclair, Jack London, Edith Wharton, Willa Cather, and Ellen Glasgow. In trying to make sense of this variety, however, it is important to recognize the distinctions between genres and the guiding principles of the realist movement.

Probably Theodore Dreiser's works are the best examples of the American realist style. Mencken certainly believed that, by 1914, Dreiser's style was "now every serious American novelist's formula. They all try to write better than Dreiser ... but they all follow him in his fundamental purpose—to make the novel true."[7] Raised in poverty, the twelfth of thirteen children, Dreiser left home for Chicago in 1886 when he was fifteen years old. There he developed his talents as a journalist and began to look closely at the environmental causes of poverty and the ways in which people escaped from these forces. In the 1890s he turned from journalism to writing novels.

Dreiser's breakthrough came in 1900 with the publication of *Sister Carrie*, a gritty account of how people followed the sensual pleasures on obvious display in the large cities. In the 1910s, Dreiser continued to explore the darker, more determined aspects of contemporary life. In *Jennie Gerhardt* (1911), a best-seller, and his trilogy based on the life of railroad magnate Charles T. Yerkes—*The Financier* (1912), *The Titan* (1914), and *The Stoics* (written c. 1916 but not published until 1947)—Dreiser polished his heavy-handed prose while tightening his focus on the materialism that drove so many. Objects were magical possessions and people like Yerkes, who had so much and wanted so much more, became superhuman—unburdened by pointless middle-class morals and fears of sin, lacking human warmth, and wholly manipulative of others—of intense interest to a determinist like Dreiser. His most critically acclaimed novel, *An American Tragedy*, did not come until 1925. While clearly his best work of writing, the ponderous style no longer suited the tastes of readers who now preferred the freer-flowing narratives of Fitzgerald and Ernest Hemingway.

The experimental modernism of Gertrude Stein was certainly as influential Dreiser's realism. Born in 1874, educated at Radcliffe College and then medical school at Johns Hopkins University, Stein left the United States in 1902 to live in Europe. She returned only for visits until her death in 1946, but she always considered herself a Yankee: "America is my country and Paris is my home town."[8] As a novelist, Stein was an adventuresome writer who willingly sacrificed book sales for greater freedom in her prose. In *Three Lives* (1909) and then *Tender Buttons* (1913), she experimented with repetitive sentences and new speech patterns. She largely abandoned traditional narratives for an immediacy of presentation—shifting tenses within her writing so that all action (whether intended for the past, present, or future) was directly connected to the psyche of her characters. Fond of the movies, Stein saw the stream-of-consciousness style of the projections as typically modern and more typically American. As a critic, Stein strongly supported the work of Hemingway, William Faulkner, Eliot, and others. Moreover, Stein established the "modern" characteristics in literature at a time when modernist artwork was first gaining acceptance in the United States. That she was able to discern these new relationships suggests that, by the 1910s, American literature was poised to branch off in a variety of directions.

LITERARY TRENDS AND THE POPULAR NOVEL

While Dreiser's realism and Stein's modernism were important indicators of the direction of American literature, popular novels were more loosely associated with these schema. Writers of popular fiction, Edgar Rice Burroughs and Zane Grey, for example, understood that these more respected authors were widening the possibilities of their own craft. In addition, regional writers, particularly such Midwestern authors as Hamlin Garland, Willa Cather, and Sherwood Anderson, achieved popular acclaim while driving the realist and modernist literary movement in unforeseen directions. All told, the public taste in novels both supported and limited the more artistic trends in American literature during the 1910s.

Zane Grey, born Pearl Zane Gray [sic] in 1872, began publishing in 1903 and became a successful writer in 1910 with his book *The Heritage of the Desert*. Throughout his life, Grey published 85 books that sold more than 40 million copies. One biographer claimed that Grey's books were outsold only by the Bible from 1915 to 1920. His formula for success was simple. He used predictable melodramatic plots and simple characters speaking in flat dialog all contained within a loose, realist style. His primary focus—rugged individualism in the West—changed little over his lifetime.[9]

Grey's writing was based on a true love of the mythic West, themes he had absorbed from his numerous fishing and sightseeing excursions to Arizona's Painted Desert. *The Heritage of the Desert* was typical of his early experiences. It is the story of an Easterner who is transplanted in the West who, through a rapid series of improbable yet hair-raising events, proves his mettle to the satisfaction of the heroine and validates his claim to be a real man. The modest sum he earned from this book allowed Grey to travel more extensively in the West. The result was a string of Westerns that pigeonholed the author but secured him an avid and loyal following by the public. In *Riders of the Purple Sage* (1912), Grey pilloried Mormonism to show how institutional religion and traditional notions of community undermined the natural dignity of the cowboy. Reflecting the Darwinian struggles so important to Dreiser's work, Grey established the stock Western character of the "reluctant gunman," an honorable individual who was forced to become a killer because of encroaching civilization.

Grey's pseudo-historical novels were also popular during the decade. *The U.P. Trail* (1918) and *The Desert of Wheat* (1919) deal with the contests between man and nature in building the transcontinental railroad and supplying the world with wheat, respectively. Both novels drew upon the same cast of stock characters as in his earlier works, but he used the natural drama of history to lend gravity to his stories. The reliance upon current events and heavies like the IWW and Imperial Germany gave his work the appearance of realist literature without the complexities that gave the realists their lasting reputation. After the success of *The U.P. Trail*, Grey gave up his ambitions to write on "a higher plane of literature" and concentrated his efforts on the boilerplate Western that became his trademark.[10]

In a slightly different vein, Edgar Rice Burroughs rose to fame in the 1910s as the creator of *Tarzan of the Apes*, a novella published in the October 1912 issue of the *All-Story* magazine. By the end of Burroughs' career, he had penned 23 additional Tarzan stories (and more than 50 others).[11] Like Grey, Burroughs took advantage of the realist style to pit man against nature. Influenced by Rudyard Kipling's *Jungle Book*, Teddy Roosevelt's call for a more "strenuous life," and popular novels emerging from the colonization of Africa, Burroughs devised a scenario whereby an English aristocrat was tested by the wildest of jungles. Lord Greystoke (i.e., Tarzan) might have been raised in the jungle, but in Burroughs's hands he soon proved his evolutionary worth by teaching himself to read and laying claim to being the king of the beasts. Burroughs certainly understood that what he was writing was not "literature"; he spent most of his creative energies marketing his Tarzan stories to moviemakers and the comic books. As with Grey, his series were short on credible dialog and plots and long on action.

His rise to fame shows the fate of a typical writer more clearly than that of an author with the artistic talents of Dreiser or Stein. Short stories such as Tarzan were in great demand by the pulp fiction magazines (so called because of the coarse and inexpensive paper that was used to pump out the endless strings of words) which became popular in the 1890s and sold for a nickel or dime. By 1910 all-fiction magazines such as *Popular Stories, Short Stories, Top Notch*, and *All-Story* were commercially successful. They demanded a steady stream of authors for hackneyed but surefire plots and made a habit of burning through a writer's creative imagination in a matter of months. Still, most of these magazines had their choice of stories, generally at rock-bottom prices. By 1912 Burroughs had already submitted several short stories, including "A Princess from Mars" (1911), a thriller which combined the Old West and outer space while staying true to the formula of the pulp magazines, and "The Outlaw of Torn," a similar yarn set in thirteenth-century England. Burroughs desperately needed income and was willing to try anything to make a name for himself as an author. When he heard from *All-Story*'s editor, Thomas Metcalf, that Tarzan was "the most exciting story we

have seen in a blue moon, and about as original as they make 'em,"
accompanied by an advance of $700, Burroughs understandably leaped
at the chance to secure some financial stability through a series of similar
tales. In his sequel to the popular premiere, Greystoke battled Russian
spies in the Sahara. Originally titled "Monsieur Tarzan," the chronicle
was published as "The Return of Tarzan" in *New Story* magazine in 1912.
Two years later, Burroughs published *Tarzan of the Apes* as a novel, and
in 1918 it was transformed to the silent screen (where the character was
significantly altered from Burroughs' original conception).[12]

THE MIDWESTERN RENAISSANCE

Clearly, Grey and Burroughs willingly sacrificed their artistic realism
for commercial success. Yet it was not the subject matter but rather their
treatment of their fictional worlds that limited their potency. There is no
reason why cowboys or marooned children cannot make outstanding
fiction of high literary quality (see, for example, Larry McMurtry's *Lone-
some Dove* or William Golding's *The Lord of the Flies*). If Grey and Burroughs neglected their fiction, it was largely by failing to incorporate a
more serious analysis of the relationship of their characters to their environment, the very basis of realistic writing. The Midwestern Renaissance of the 1910s did not make this mistake. The fact that much of the
work of this group was commercially successful attests to the fact that
it was possible to merge artistry with business in popular American literature.

The success of writers emerging in the Midwest in the 1910s was phenomenal. Coupled with the arrival of the Chicago School of architecture
and the importance of Midwestern musicians, the term renaissance may
not be an overstatement. Omitting Dreiser and Stein for the moment, the
list of stellar writers included Hamlin Garland, Willa Cather, Sherwood
Anderson, Sinclair Lewis, Ernest Hemingway, Ring Lardner, F. Scott
Fitzgerald, and T.S. Eliot. The region was reaching its apogee of economic importance for the United States and, lacking any real indigenous
cultural tradition, these writers tended to create one. Focusing on the
power of the land, shared rural roots, and the unbridled economic optimism of the region, Midwestern writers provided works that were robust, confident, and wholly original to American letters. Garland, Cather,
and Anderson merit special attention if for no other reason than their
works were both critically and commercially successful during the 1910s.

Hamlin Garland

Hamlin Garland was probably the least influential of the three, largely
because he wrote in an autobiographical style that did not lend itself to

emulation by other authors. Born into rural poverty, Garland struggled with the rural myth that farm life was somehow more noble and uplifting that the degeneracy of the city. Moving from the Midwest to Boston in 1884, Garland experienced just the reverse, seeing the regionally imposed limits on his life lifted by the culture and refinement of urban America. In 1887 Garland published *Main-Traveled Roads*, a collection of short stories that began to tear down this rural ideal and replace it with a more sober, realistic picture of the hardships of farm living.

Garland's fiction did not sell well, and it was not until 1917, when he published *A Son of the Middle Border*, his autobiographical tale of life on the prairie, that he became a well-read author. Reappraising many of the themes first touched on in his earlier book, Garland added a poignancy that came directly from his experience with the land and its unintended effects upon himself and his family. Garland followed this work with three other "Middle Border" books; the series earned him the Pulitzer Prize in 1922.

Willa Cather

More influential, both commercially and critically, was Willa Cather. Unlike Zane Grey, Cather never needed to travel to pick up local color; she was emotionally and spiritually a part of it. She wrote in her first major work, *Alexander's Bridge* (1912), "When a writer once begins a work with his own material, he realizes that, no matter what his literary excursions may have been, he has been working with it from the beginning—by living it." In fact, while Cather's own "literary excursions" were extensive (she wrote poetry, prose, and criticism in a variety of styles), her body of work is hard to classify as a single school or theory. While she clearly represented the realist and modernist trends of novels in the era, she also incorporated the symbolism of poetry and the political optimism that gave life to the Progressive movement. If there is a single source of power in her words, it comes from the faith that she took from the land, for this alone was the source of her and America's regenerative spirit.[13]

Willa Cather was born in Virginia in 1873. When she was 10 years old, her family moved to Webster County, Nebraska, and settled in Red Cloud, an immigrant town where native-born Americans were a distinct minority. Cather attended the University of Nebraska where she began her professional career as a writer and teacher. She moved first to Pittsburgh and then to New York where she became an editor for *McClure's* magazine in 1906. While in New York she became close friends with a group of writers and activists (including Sarah Orne Jewett and Elizabeth Shepley Sergeant) who challenged her thinking and tightened her skills as a creative writer.

Cather was an intensely private person either in spite of, or as a result of, her national fame. Upon her death she directed that most of her private correspondence and all of her unfinished manuscripts be destroyed. Her nearly lifelong habitation with women, first Isabelle McClung and then Edith Lewis, has suggested to many researchers that Cather was a lesbian. This speculation has relevance only inasmuch as her writing reflects a strong, female-centered appreciation for the Midwest, a rarity for accomplished writers of the era. Ironically, the relative lack of biographical material has forced scholars to come to terms with Cather through her fiction alone, and it is here where she earned her distinguished reputation.

Her first major published work, *Alexander's Bridge*, does not do justice to the career that was in the offing. Cather felt that the work was too shallow and artificial—resting as it did on a highly contrived plot—to merit much attention. Still, in the novel, she began to demonstrate her infatuation with the subject of youth which coursed through her entire body of work. In the story, a young architect, Bartley Alexander, must choose between his youthful dreams and his adult responsibilities. Torn between the two, Alexander is killed when his bridge collapses from its structural instability. Perfect for *McClure's* casual readers, the work had the redeeming quality of providing Cather with enough money and encouragement to devote her full energies to writing.

These efforts paid handsome dividends in the 1910s with the publication of *O Pioneers!* (1913), *The Song of the Lark* (1915), and *My Ántonia* (1918)—the first and the last of which are plausibly considered to be part of the canon of American literature. Reflecting upon her career, Cather stated that she considered *O Pioneers!* to be her first true novel. Completed quickly after a trip to the West, the story is of an immigrant woman transplanted to Nebraska who suffers through the precarious fate of most prairie settlers. Her sparse style spends little effort in describing the plains, focusing instead on the nearly tangible spirit of the land. To Cather, the determinism of Dreiser's realism was incorrect; people could choose which forces to follow. Surrounding this immigrant girl were dozens who committed themselves to chasing the illusion of success through materialism and transient pleasures. By contrast, while the heroine was tormented in life, she was sustained by the timeless peace, cycles, and surety of the physical earth. In style and subject matter, *O Pioneers!* was unique. It established Willa Cather as an author of note.

She improved her craft in 1918 with the publication of *My Ántonia*. The most biographical of all her novels, Cather transformed her presence in the novel into a young, male, romantic, native-born railroad lawyer named James Burden. Burden narrates the novel and recounts how he came to understand a Bohemian immigrant girl from Nebraska by the name of Ántonia Shirmerda and how his Ántonia restored his faith in himself and in the world around him. Again, Cather's style is spartan and the dramatic elements completely ordinary. Ántonia is seen to go through four stages of life: a spirited youth, a troubled young woman, an abandoned mother, and, finally, a fulfilled matriarch of a stable and fertile extended family. While suffering the suicide of her romantic father, the hypocritical gossip of "respectable" society, and the lies of a native-born lover, the immigrant sees the joy of life connected to the natural and living rhythms of the land. Burden, the typical American, sees through Ántonia that he had lost this faith. By the end, however, he knows where to look to recapture his youthful optimism; he knows again that all things are possible.

Sherwood Anderson

At this same time, a third Midwestern novelist was making his presence known: Sherwood Anderson. Born in Camden, Ohio, Anderson like Cather achieved his literary fame relatively late in life with the publication of *Winesburg, Ohio* in 1919 when he was 43 years old. Before this, Anderson's career was diverse and marked by fits of melancholy. He had spent time as a laborer, served in the Spanish-American War, and worked in advertising, all the while dreaming of writing fiction. After suffering a nervous breakdown in 1912, Anderson came to Chicago and became friends with a small group of struggling writers including Floyd Dell, Edgar Lee Masters, Carl Sandburg, and Harriet Monroe. This was an auspicious time for creative writing in the city as both *Poetry* and the *Little Review* gave a forum for new and experimental poetry and prose.

Anderson experimented with novels and, in 1916, he published his first book titled *Windy McPherson's Son*. One year later, *Marching Men* was released. Both books examined small-town America, the effects of modernization, and the alienation of thinking men in such a society. Both books sold poorly so, after trying poetry and finding his talents lacking, Anderson turned to shorter, more focused studies about particular individuals. Several of his short character studies were published in the *Masses* and the *Seven Arts*. These pieces formed the core of his anthology of stories which he published under the name *Winesburg, Ohio*.

Winesburg, Ohio contains 22 separate stories, usually related by or observed through the eyes of a local reporter who represented an idealized version of the author. A town just emerging from the Civil War and going into the tempest of modernization, Winesburg has no sense of the future and no trust in the past. Most of the characters are emotionally and psychologically scarred. Their lack of self-awareness and their reliance on moral clichés only deepens these wounds in others. Anderson used modern vocabulary, a frank discussion of sex and sexual drives,

Portrait of Sherwood Anderson. Courtesy of the Library of Congress.

and a merciless focus on the tottering genteel values of small town America to lend power and substance to his work.

In spite of how many received the work, Anderson did not set out to attack village life. His characters in *Winesburg* are a mixed bag of transients, locals, the urbane, and provincials. Moreover, some of his characters display strong moral values which are developed and often reinforced through their contact with fellow citizens. What Anderson disliked was not the physical reality of small-town U.S.A. but rather the self-righteousness and lack of self-criticism that come from a population that never stops to evaluate its own morals. In *Winesburg*, characters are trapped and tortured by the very institutions and belief systems held most dear by the citizens; family, rectitude, and Christian morality. While most of his characters struggle mightily against conforming to the wishes of others, the battle leaves them broken and their individuality "grotesque." Winesburg is a claustrophobic town, where its peoples' hopes and dreams are turned into fears and nightmares from the realities of modern living.

Winesburg, Ohio was both a critical and financial success for Anderson. To his credit, he used his fame to promote the work of other talented modern writers such as Ernest Hemingway and William Faulkner. Moreover, Anderson proved that the modernist style of using colloquial speech; short, simple sentences; and poetic imagery could be fashioned into a powerful yet popular novel. The Midwest Renaissance, including the work of Cather and Garland, underscored the hypocrisy of genteel moral codes and the strong impersonal forces that buffeted America. The fact that their works were set in the Midwest—Winseburg was patterned after Anderson's home of Clyde, Ohio, and Cather's Red Cloud, Nebraska, was clearly the model for her fictional locales—gave the realist style of their writing a firm footing in both the natural and urban worlds.

EDITH WHARTON, BEST-SELLERS, AND THE GREAT WAR

Lying somewhere between the extremes of experimental modernism and the adventure stories of Burroughs and Grey, novelists Edith Wharton, Booth Tarkington, and Arthur Guy Empey filled a unique niche of American literature in the 1910s. Wharton was perhaps the most influential of these popular artists. Born to wealth in 1862, she struggled with a failed marriage and the conservative elite culture of New York City, often making it the subject of the 47 volumes she wrote before her death in 1937. Finding a home in the trans-Atlantic literary community (she was lifelong friends with Henry James and Sinclair Lewis, who dedicated *Babbitt* to her), Wharton popularized the struggles of the upper classes to retain their footing upon the shifting sands of modern society. *The House of Mirth* (1905) made her reputation as a writer, but it was in the 1910s that her prolific output found a place in America.

Ethan Frome (1911) was her most popular book of the decade. In it, she shows how the schemes of two selfish and materialistic women were able to destroy the ideals and the very life of the title character. In the critically acclaimed *The Custom of the Country* (1913), Wharton's subject was again a social climber who was trapped by the shallowness of the moneyed class. In addition, Wharton published *Tales of Men and Ghosts* (1910), *The Reef* (1913), *Xingu and Other Stories* (1917), and *Summer* (1919), most of which were popular best-sellers. While *The Age of Innocence* (1920) earned Wharton the Pulitzer Prize, many of her critics contend that her work had become nostalgic and uncritical by this date.

Other best-selling authors wrote impressive, if not long-lasting, works throughout the decade. The best of these followed traditions already in place before the decade began, such as Joel Chandler Harris's *Uncle Remus and the Little Boy* (1910) and Finley Peter Dunne's *Mr. Dooley Says* (1911) and *New Dooley Book* (1912). Booth Tarkington, too, solidified his reputation as a talented narrator with *The Turmoil* (1915)—a story of economic exploitation—and *Seventeen* (1916)—a story of teens coming of age. Finally, best-sellers included Jeffrey Farnol's *The Broad Highway* (1911), Gene Stratton Porter's *The Harvester* (1912), Winston Churchill's *Inside the Cup* (1913; not the English-born Churchill, but of Saint Louis, Missouri), Harold Bell Wright's *The Eyes of the World* (1914, concerning a painter forced to come to terms with the modern art displayed at the Armory Show), and H.G. Wells's *Mr. Britling Sees It Through* (1917).

Wells's novel, which seeks meaning from death in World War I, was typical of many popular novels during the war years. The meaning of the war became a contested terrain for writers, fought over with a ferocity that mirrored that of the battlefield. During the 1910s, the majority of these books tended to the see the conflict as a way for young men to test their sense of bravery, honor, patriotism, and masculinity. Alan Seeger was an unfortunate example of this trend. Graduating from Harvard in 1910, Seeger went to Paris in 1912 and joined the French Foreign Legion when the fighting began in 1914. Unlike in the movies, Seeger was not stationed in the desert but rather on the front. While he fought, he wrote popular dispatches for the *New York Sun* and the *New Republic*. Killed in action in 1916, his posthumous memoirs became a best-seller in 1917, as Americans marveled and wept over his selfless sacrifice for "the cause."[14]

With savage attacks on these romantic notions—by writers as skilled as Hemingway and John Dos Passos—still in the future, the field was open for a large number of guts-and-glory memoirs or fictionalized accounts. Arthur Guy Empey's *Over the Top* (1917) was typical. Telling the story of his experiences as a machine gunner, Empey used realistic descriptions and jargon (there was a 35-page appendix to translate the slang) to suggest that frontal assaults on fortified gun nests were the height of glory for young men. The book sold 350,000 copies its first year and was soon turned into a movie. Empey became a featured speaker at patriotic rallies throughout the country. Nor was Empey alone in his promotion of the war. Best-sellers included Robert W. Service's *Rhymes of a Red Cross Man* (1917), Alan Seeger's *Poems of Alan Seeger* (1917), Ian

Hay's *First Hundred Thousand* (1917), Francis W. Huard's *My Home in the Field of Honor* (1917), Edward Guest's *Over Here* (1918), James W. Gerard's *My Four Years in Germany* (1918), and Lt. Pat O'Brien's *Outwitting the Hun* (1918).

RISORGIMENTO AND REGIONALISM
IN AMERICAN POETRY

While poetry clearly has a lesser claim to popular culture, the trends in poetic verse in the 1910s were important and underscored the shifts seen in popular fiction and criticism. When Ezra Pound called for a conscious risorgimento, or reorganization of poetic styles, in 1909, he was asking poets to reformulate their approach to the craft in ways that rejected the formal complexities of traditional verse. Pound, who was born in Idaho and lived most of his early life in Pennsylvania before emigrating to England in 1908, was a great promoter of American poets who he believed were attempting to make this crossover, including T.S. Eliot, William Carlos Williams, E.E. Cummings, Hilda Doolittle (who published her works by her initials, H.D.), and Robert Frost. Historian Malcolm Bradbury concluded that Pound's "remarkably generous campaign for the *Risorgimento* is one of the formative events of modern poetry and literary culture, which changed London and, largely through the mails, the United States." His efforts almost single-handedly forced Europeans to consider American poetry in a serious light.[15]

Pound's greatest ally was Thomas Stearns (T.S.) Eliot. Born in Saint Louis and educated at Harvard, the Sorbonne, and Oxford, Eliot permanently relocated to England in 1910. Neither he nor the other expatriots abandoned their American roots; rather they regarded Europe as a cultural oasis in which they could pursue their craft more freely than in the more materialistic States. Eliot championed a symbolist style in poetry which had been gaining influence since the turn of the century. His greatest work of the decade was *The Love Song of J. Alfred Prufrock*, published as a compilation titled simply *Prufrock*, in 1917. He used common language to establish new patterns of rhythm within his text. The subject matter was expanded to include all forms of human behavior— particularly those considered too crude for Victorian poets. The mood of the piece was usually implicit, established by images and tones rather than glaring emotions or contrived dramatic flourishes. Finally, Eliot's writing was meticulously crafted, often to the point that the work became near parodies. After the release of *The Waste Land* (1922), a poem of incredible influence, Eliot actually added footnotes in an effort to guide readers to the sources of his imagery.

Concurrent with the rise of a regional voice in American novels, poets too found that their experiences in the United States granted them a unique artistic perspective. The Midwest Renaissance sparked just such a movement. Edgar Lee Masters, who was born in Kansas and raised in Illinois, came to Chicago in the 1890s to practice law but made his name as an accomplished poet with the publication of *Spoon River Anthology* in 1915, his third book of verse. In this classic, Masters introduced his readers to the ghosts of former residents of the region. Being dead afforded the narrators the freedom to be honest. In their confessions, Masters related how they believed they had wasted much of their lives on petty grievances, fleeting sexual pleasures, and a fruitless search for understanding. As with Anderson and, later, Sinclair Lewis, the work is often misconstrued as a focused attack on small-town America. In actuality, these writers used their experiences in small towns to show how these frustrations were magnified by close contact within the provincial village, but that the experiences were no less present in the city. In many ways, the small-town inhabitants were at least able to identify their frustrations.

Carl Sandburg, who like Masters was first published in the Chicago-based *Poetry* magazine, was the son of a Swedish blacksmith from Galesburg, Illinois. After moving to Chicago in 1913 and taking a series of odd jobs which brought him into contact with Chicago's polyglot society, Sandburg was able to capture the distinct regional and American values of citizens toward work, society, and the country. While often overly sentimental toward the wisdom of the public, Sandburg was able to translate the raw power of America's industrial and economic might into lyrical and moving verse. His frequently quoted description of Chicago, from *Chicago Poems* (1916), as "Hog Butcher for the World, Tool Maker, Stacker of Wheat, Player with Railroads ... Stormy, husky, brawling, City of the Big Shoulders" revels in the sweaty accomplishments of workaday living. These are again hailed in his later works, *Cornhuskers* (1918) and *Smoke and Steel* (1920).

While some critics of the Midwest Renaissance take exception to the accomplishments of these poets (one placed them only "several notches above the 'birds and flowers' school of lady poets"[16]), it is clear that regionalism had become a distinguishing characteristic of American poetry in the 1910s. The appearance and success of Robert Frost's works is telling proof of this assertion. Frost, who was born in San Francisco in 1874, moved to New Hampshire with his family when he was 11 years old. There he absorbed the local diction and environment and began writing poetry. After attending Dartmouth and then Harvard, Frost emigrated to England in 1912 where his work was noticed and supported by literary activists Pound and Stein. In England, Frost began to publish his regional American verse, first with *A Boy's Will* (1913) and then the critically acclaimed *North of Boston* (1914).[17]

Frost's work is often regarded as homage to rustic simplicity and folksy wisdom. In reality, he used the picturesque New England countryside and vernacular to examine and attack the same genteel traditions that were bombarded by other modernist poets. For example, while his popular poem "The Road Not Taken," published in *Mountain Interval* (1916), seems to cherish the man who took the road "less traveled by, and that has made all the difference," he also suggests that an American will justify *any* action in hindsight as the most adventuresome and least conforming. In "Mending Wall" (*North of Boston*), Frost seems to lament the need for boundaries between citizens but concluded, with one of his characters, that "Good fences make good neighbors." Even his titles—*A Boy's Will* and *North of Boston*—allude to the fact that America was no longer in its youth and that its real heart lies in the cities, not *north* of them. Frost's complexities added to his appeal as a modern poet.

CONCLUSION

Throughout the decade, literature connected to life in America in ways that were closer and more representative than any other form of popular culture. Realists conveyed the change and conflict which were threatening citizens. Similarly, modernist writers suggested that only individual morals and judgment could lead to fulfilled lives. Traditional or genteel values were no longer relevant in the modern era. The rise of these contrary voices did much to diffuse the cultural isolation that was, no doubt, felt by many Americans. Through vernacular language and conventional settings, writers gave Americans a richer set of images by which to understand themselves and their nation.

9

Music

Popular music was one of the first entertainment media to crossover successfully from a set of distinct, usually class, cultural, and racially influenced styles, to a more generic and inclusive American format. While musicians in later decades benefited from the introduction of mass media technologies—such as radio and television—crossover artists of the 1910s relied solely on the interest generated from fusing the old with the new. From the concert hall to the nightclub, popular musicians integrated African American musical styles while, at the same time, they built upon the rich European heritage of notation, composition, and melody.

Describing this transformation has been difficult for historians for a number of very good reasons. While most acknowledge that the decade "seems to mark the transition period between past and present in American musical life,"[1] studies tend to limit their scope to a particular artist or musical genre. As a result, we understand more about how jazzmen borrowed from the development of ragtime or the blues, for example, than how all three were part of a growing trend toward a more unified American sound. The complexities of identifying and describing popular music in the 1910s are compounded by the number of separate formats—including jazz, blues, rag, show tunes, classical, and popular orchestral—which included both academic and vernacular approaches and varied greatly depending on the eloquence of the performer, the venue, and even the audience.

Accordingly, understanding the categories and distinctions between styles is vital. As with other forms of popular culture, musical artists evidenced both academic and vernacular methods. Simply stated, an academic approach to composing music was one in which the artist was concerned with, and appreciated, the aesthetic values of the work as a whole, or how well the tune built upon and reinterpreted traditional sounds and styles. Academic, or "cultivated," music was intended to be written down. As a result, the composer needed a knowledge of both musical notation and the difficult tonal balances required in a successful composition. The academic style is usually referred to as "classical" music because of its reliance upon European models and instruments but, as described below, ragtime and show tunes were also legitimate examples of the form. By contrast, vernacular music was not usually noted, was practiced by those without formal musical training, and was intended to serve a useful function, such as entertainment or religious inspiration, rather than to tap into less tangible aesthetic goals.

Categories, too, are useful but problematic for understanding popular music. Clearly there are important differences between musical formats of the era. Each listener has a unique appreciation for sound. Some hear melody where others are more attuned to rhythm. Artists in the 1910s often incorporated familiar patterns from one style into the work of another. For example, Irving Berlin's 1911 hit song "Alexander's Ragtime Band" used hints of ragtime but was not a good example of that style. Classical artists, such as Charles Ives or Igor Stravinsky, regularly borrowed from the vernacular but were most certainly academic composers. It is difficult to describe in words the subtle differences heard in pitch, tone, meter, and rhythm which are at the core of these unique styles. While these remain challenges to our understanding of music, they help support the contention that, by 1910, composers and performers were increasingly borrowing the methods of other styles.

THE EUROPEAN INFLUENCE ON AMERICAN MUSIC

If fusion was the creative source that led to a distinctly American style in popular music, then it is critical to get beyond the argument over whether European or African traditions were more important. Both European and African modes were incorporated into the American sound, and as a result neither can be assumed to be either more or less authoritative. The American periodical *Opera Magazine* expressed this linkage in 1916, "If any musician does not feel in his heart the rhythmic complexities of the [vernacular and African American Southern reel] *Robert E. Lee*, I should not trust him to feel in his heart [those] of Brahms."[2] By definition, American music was both a product of this cultural fusion and completely distinct from either source.

European composition certainly influenced white musicians because of the cultural importance of European academic training and the classical works of masters such as Ludwig van Beethoven, W.A. Mozart, and

J.S. Bach. This approach valued formal arrangements of traditional instruments to produce an appealing melody. Significantly, by 1910, these influential European trends began to move away from the strong Romanticism of German composers such as Richard Wagner—who first introduced vernacular folk music into the academic realm—toward more subtle, impressionistic effects. French composer Claude Debussy was one of the most adventuresome of these innovators. From his first public performance in 1902 until his death in 1918, Debussy challenged European critics and audiences alike to open their ears to new styles and moods of music, which gave performers the artistic space needed to experiment with unconventional methods.

The critical distance opened up by the experimentation of Debussy and others was pivotal in lending legitimacy to the process of musical fusion. By accepting the vernacular tradition, academic composers in Europe made it possible for audiences to consider these "lesser" works as true art forms. Moreover, European arrangements forced composers to find ways to incorporate the nonconventional styles of folk music, which in the United States was driven largely by rhythm, into the highly structured and melody-based methods of academic notation. Throughout the decade, leading composers, such as Béla Bartók (*Allegro barbaro*, 1911), Arnold Schoenberg (*Pierrot Lunaire*, 1912), and especially Igor Stravinsky (*Le Sacre du Printemps*, 1913), borrowed themes taken directly from the American vernacular tradition. By contrast, American composers such as Frederick Converse and Horatio Park continued within traditional patterns and, as a result, their work is largely forgotten today. While Stravinsky was clearly distant from popular musicians in the United States—he had never even heard an authentic ragtime band before he wrote *Ragtime for Eleven Instruments* in 1918—the fact that European classicists were openly interested in American folk music gave credence to the work of public performers in the 1910s.

THE AFRICAN INFLUENCE ON AMERICAN MUSIC

African musical styles are unique in that the rhythm, and not the variation of pitch, dominates. Unlike a piano, which has a number of differing tones, the sound of percussion instruments, such as the drum, vary mostly by the beat. African performers were adept at using both hands to construct contrasting yet supportive rhythms on their instruments. In addition, artists relied upon an audience's ability to maintain a base rhythm, termed a "metronomic sense" (the best example of this is toe tapping, which keeps a beat even if the musicians do not play one), to add further complexity to their music.

The communal use of music in African culture was vital to the development of these intricate rhythms and the emerging American sound.

Africans used musical performances in rituals and ceremonies, such as births, deaths, marriages, and while at work to build cohesion in the group as well as to communicate and establish a mood. As a result, the music is both participatory and extremely powerful in evoking emotional responses. According to many musical historians, these cross rhythms are unique to African music and form the basis for the syncopated sounds that are at the core of modern American popular music, from ragtime to rock and hip-hop.

In comparison to European traditions, African styles are even more elaborate. Where European artists relied on *either* a double or triple meter pattern within a single work, African stylists routinely mixed the two. Where European artists allowed the formal and noted melody to set the emotional tone for a composition, African musicians worked within the context of a particular audience. Depending on the conditions, African performers shifted and improvised their works to respond to the audience in immediate and powerful ways. When we remember that this improvisation often included dozens of performers—all of whom needed to remain coordinated within a single performance—we can begin to appreciate the freedom and creativity brought to American music by African styles.

Making a lasting impression on European musical styles was difficult, however, until the twentieth century. Based on a seven-note, half-step European scale (doe-ray-me-fah-so-lah-tee), musicians were unfamiliar and ill-equipped to write African sounds that were rooted in a scale of five notes with no halves. While European stylists were not ignorant of rhythm (think of the famous four-note introduction to Beethoven's *Fifth Symphony*), they certainly were unaccustomed to giving over so much control—and allowing for so much uncertainty in the performance—to the whim and response of an audience. Until performers began to capture this rhythmic style through formal notation, truly fusing the African and the European traditions into a new format, the African style remained outside the mainstream of American music.

Of course it was not African, but *African American* music that directly influenced popular music in the United States. The peculiar position of blacks in late nineteenth-century America—as a vital labor force living in healthy and numerically large communities but as disenfranchised citizens who were ostracized from the mainstream culture by widespread racism—ironically nurtured their distinct musical heritage. It was segregation that allowed vernacular African American music to thrive, and it was this style that irrevocably transformed the nation's music in the modern era. By 1910, according to Eileen Southern, it was through music, "perhaps more than any other field, [that] the preeminence of the African American was acknowledged by the nation."[3]

African Americans conserved their African and Afro-Caribbean musical heritage as well as possible under slavery and through emancipation. In the latter half of the nineteenth century, blacks had perfected the ability to pass along vernacular musical skills through informal or family networks. One learned to sing or play a homemade instrument in order to provide some form of additional income or simply to earn the respect of neighbors. Such training developed skills of improvisation and a heightened ability to respond to the changing mood of an audience rather than an ability to read music or perfectly re-create a tune time after time. Spirituals and work songs, the forerunners of the blues, relied heavily on call-and-response improvisation. Both the tunes and equipment allowed blacks to build upon and enhance the skills first evidenced in African rhythms.

While African Americans fought against their second-class status in the United States, most white composers were willing to profit by the rampant racism of the era. White minstrels singing "coon songs" exaggerated the "exotic" nature of African American lives, fashioning "humorous lyrics" which played on the worst of the stereotypes. Coon songs portrayed black males as ignorant, cowardly, lazy, petty thieves, and women as shallow and sexually indiscriminate. While reprehensible and slightly pathetic, these white performers did introduce an element of African American music into the mainstream culture. The problem was that few whites were able to reproduce the African American music that was so appealing to paying audiences. White composer Thomas P. Fenner, who wrote *Cabin and Plantation Songs* in 1873, complained that black musicians employed techniques which whites "have no musical characters to represent." As the popularity of cakewalks and lively rhythmic songs grew in the 1880s and 1890s, some black artists were allowed to perform more authentic versions of the craft. Musical pioneers like W.C. Handy, Bessie Smith, and Bert Williams all got their first taste of the white entertainment business through the minstrel shows.[4]

Needless to say, it was not the white misappropriation of African American music but rather the cumulative efforts of generations of black artists that eventually led to its acceptance and success. The New Negro movement of the 1910s, a predecessor of the Black Pride movement of the 1960s, supported the work of these artists by rejecting notions of cultural inferiority and an inherent submission to white authority. Activists, inducing A. Phillip Randolph, Chandler Owen, and Hubert Henry Harrison, gave voice to a growing desire to reject assimilation and to support authentic black culture. Harrison wrote in 1917 that the decade was "essentially [a] new turning point in the path of human progress. . . . [with] new ideas of freedom, politics, industry and society at large. The new Negro living in this new world is just as responsive to these new impulses as other people are."[5] Such an approach created great conflicts within the black community and placed many middle-class African Americans in the difficult position of either supporting the advancement of their race or the economic well-being of their families. Moreover, the heightened cultural consciousness of blacks no doubt added to the paranoia of many white Americans following World War I.

African and African American styles proved to be extremely significant to the development of popular music in the United States through the widespread use of syncopation. While difficult to describe in words, syncopation refers to the musical practice of unequally dividing beats into long and short notes to create multiple cross rhythms within a musical piece. One can get a sense of syncopation in the old reel "Turkey in the Straw" by noting the irregular beats of the chorus. Alternately, try tapping your foot to a regular 4/4 count while drumming your fingers twice between these beats to get a simple sense of the feel of a syncopated rhythm. Either way, the contrasting rhythms—so typical of African styles—provided an emotional power and incentive to participate in African American music which proved irresistible to popular audiences.

THE VARIED STYLES OF ACADEMIC MUSIC IN AMERICA

By 1910 European composers had provided academic artists with some leeway in the type of materials considered acceptable for performance. Moreover, from 1890 to 1910, urban Americans invested heavily in supporting local symphonies, conservatories to train musicians, and opera houses. European conductors and musicians, such as Anton Phillip Heinrich, Louis Moreau Gottschalk, and the renowned Antonín Dvořák, came to America in search of students capable and willing to explore the rich musical folk traditions of this country. The stage was set for American composers to expand their repertoire beyond the European masters and to include newer, domestic works.

Unfortunately, few composers proved willing or able to move beyond the classic symphonies. Only a few rare exceptions during the decade provided a lasting body of work. One of these was Harry Burleigh. An African American who studied under Dvořák, Burleigh became an accomplished soloist and composer who relied upon his knowledge of spirituals. Burleigh published a number of significant compositions, including *From the Southland* (1914) and *Southland Sketches* (1916) for violin and piano, before he became the music editor for Ricordi and Company. Burleigh also published a number of songs based on these works, including "The Young Warrior" (1916), which was eventually translated into Italian and became something of an anthem for Italian troops during World War I. Burleigh's greatest work was an anthology of spirituals, published under the title *Jubilee Songs of the United States of America* (1916), which he later performed before such luminaries as President Theodore Roosevelt and King Edward VII of England. He believed that his efforts were critical in bringing African American music into the mainstream: "My desire was to preserve them in harmonies that belong to modern methods of tonal progression without robbing the melodies of their racial flavor."[6] Will Marion Cook, also a black man, studied first in Berlin and then at the National Conservatory of Music in New York City. Cook composed a series of musicals, many songs, and published *A Collection of Negro Songs* in 1912.

Perhaps it was not surprising that African Americans proved to be the most successful at adapting to the new musical trends in Europe. Barred from formal training and a legitimate hearing of their skills for so long, black composers had, according to critic Robert Nathaniel Dett, in 1918, a "wonderful store of folk music—the melodies of an enslaved people, who poured out their longings, their griefs and their aspirations in the one great, universal language." Dett also understood that "this store will be of no value" unless African American composers found ways "that it can be presented in choral form, in lyric and operatic works. . . . unless our musical architects take the rough timber of Negro themes and fashion from it music which will prove that we, too, have national feelings and characteristics, as have the European peoples whose forms we have zealously followed for so long."[7]

Lacking such a purposeful musical foundation, white academics foundered in their efforts to create a style that was not derived from their European masters. Arthur Farwell was probably the best example of a white composer who understood the limits of his European education. Born in Saint Paul, Minnesota, Farwell developed his skills as a violinist, pianist, and composer first at the Massachusetts Institute of Technology, then in Germany and France. Farwell was deeply motivated by African American, Native American, and folk Western music, but despite his best efforts, he was unable to turn his fascination into a respected academic anthology of composition. He complained, in 1912, that "What [the American composer] has to give, his country does not want; and it does not tell him what it does want. . . . In fact, there is no connection at all, in a serious way, between the American composer and his country."[8]

Edward McDowell and Charles Tomlinson Griffes also attempted to fashion a genuine indigenous classical style. MacDowell, born in New York and trained overseas, unsuccessfully sought to meld Native American songs with the romantic classics. Griffes, who like many others of the era was supported by Farwell, published a variety of tone poems throughout the decade, including *Three-Tone Pictures* (1915), *Roman Sketches* (1917), and *Five Poems of Ancient China and Japan* (1917). His efforts at symphonic composition, which resulted in *The Pleasure-Dome of Kubla Khan* (1917), were first performed by the Boston Symphony in 1919 and occasionally ever since. Still, as compositions, the works of Farwell, MacDowell, and Griffes pale by comparison with those of such modern European composers as Debussy, Stravinsky, and Modest Mussorgsky. In retrospect, they and other lesser American academic musicians seemed to lack the confidence to strike out in bold new directions that reflected their local sensibilities.

Charles Ives is the era's one true lasting classical voice, partly because he did not fear the rejection of contemporary audiences. To be fair to the other professional musicians, Ives never had to rely on music or tutoring for his livelihood. Growing up in an affluent home in Danbury, Connecticut, attending Yale University, and becoming successful as an insurance executive, Ives was free from the financial pressures that could compromise an artist's creativity. Rarely did Ives perform his works (only one was ever played in public before 1919, and he stopped composing in 1923). His isolation allowed him to develop his own unique sound and produce a vast quantity of hymns, songs, tone poems, and symphonies, but never did he have to face the criticism and rebukes of a hostile and provincial season-ticket holder.

To call Ives's work idiosyncratic is an understatement. When he was once asked why he did not compose pieces that were more pleasing to the ear, he responded, "I can't do it—I hear something else!"[9] Building on his appreciation for sounds rather than harmonious tones or melodies, Ives created works of intense contrasts and jarring musical discord. Ives sampled from others' works, scored intentionally off-key sections, and interjected passages within his works using a variety of motifs. Much as the successful European modernists, Ives intended his works to be appreciated as organic wholes, but from a multitude of perspectives. He later wrote that his music

may have something in common [with] . . . a walk up a mountain. . . . the climber looks, turns, and looks down or up. He sees the valley, but not exactly the same angle he saw it at the last look—and the summit is changing with every step. . . . Even if he stands on the same rock at the top and looks toward Heaven and Earth, he is not just the same key he started in, or in the same moment of existence.[10]

Noted music historian H. Wiley Hitchcock wrote that Ives "believed in music as a re-creation in sound of life itself . . . he accepted as source material any sort of musical idea, his own or others', cultivated or vernacular; he identified dignity with strength; he abhorred the 'nice,' the easy-sounding, and the genteel; and he was willing to try anything."[11]

ARRANGEMENTS FOR POPULAR ORCHESTRAS AND BANDS

Perhaps because public orchestras and bands were less self-consciously patterned after the European ones, popular musicians displayed a greater freedom in performing a more American variety of sound in the 1910s. No artist more closely represented this difference than John Philip Sousa. Born in 1854 to immigrant parents, Sousa reveled in his role as a representative of the American dream. Formally trained by the U.S. Marine Band, he took leadership of the ensemble in 1880 and for twelve years led the group in a number of world tours. As a composer, Sousa excelled at marches and other two-step numbers, including "Semper Fidelis," "Manhattan Beach," and his signature work, "The Stars and Stripes Forever" (1896).

Sousa's contribution to American music in the 1910s was significant largely because it demonstrated that the white public had a taste for well-performed vernacular arrangements. What he played became, almost by definition, acceptable to the American public. His concerts introduced much of the country to ragtime and African American songs. He gave "black music" a national platform and included African Americans, such as Arthur Pryor, in his band. By using unconventional orchestral instruments, such as the banjo, Sousa lent legitimacy to the smaller ethnic groups that gained popularity from 1890 to 1900. In sum, Sousa opened the door for other performers to enter upon the national stage.

Of these new performers, none were as talented and potentially revolutionary as James Reese Europe. Born in Alabama in 1881 to a musically accomplished family, Europe moved to Washington, D.C., and then to New York City as a young man where he gain both formal training and real-world experience. In 1910 Europe formed the Clef Club Symphony Orchestra, which was partly a band but also functioned as a union representing and finding work for black musicians and entertainers. As an African American, Europe was instrumental in staging authentic vernacular music played on the original instruments. For example, Europe once staged a concert, in November 1911, at the Manhattan Casino, which included 50 mandolins, 20 violins, 30 harp-guitars, 10 cellos, 10 banjos, 10 pianos, 2 organs, 5 flutes, 5 clarinets, 5 double basses, timpani, drums, and a saxophone. When he played Carnegie Hall the next year, Europe premiered ragtime marches and songs from black composer Will Marion Cook.

Europe represented the surging cultural pride of African Americans that was to take the music world by storm throughout the decade. In a defensive, yet defiantly confident interview to the *New York Evening Post*, in March 1914, Europe reported that

John Philip Sousa in band uniform with Charlie Chaplin. Courtesy of the Library of Congress.

colored people have our own music this is part of us. It's us; it's the product of our souls. . . . Our symphony orchestra never tries to play white folks' music. We should be foolish to attempt such a thing. We are no more fitted for that than a white orchestra is fitted to play our music. Whatever success I have had has come from the realization of the advantages of sticking to the music of my own people.[12]

While painfully typical of the position that many blacks were forced to take throughout the era (i.e., that African Americans were incapable of mastering European music), Europe's popularity suggested that Americans were more taken with the music of his "own people" than the tired orchestral productions of European artists.

That Europe was one of America's most successful bandleaders is hardly disputable. At the height of its popularity, the Clef Club earned more than $100,000 a year. By 1914 Europe was tapped as the bandleader for the influential dance team of Irene and Vernon Castle. The Castles credited Europe with introducing many of the songs that led to their international fame. He was one of the first African Americans to secure a record deal, with Victor Records in 1913. When he and his famed vocalist, Noble Sissle, performed overseas during the war (Europe had enlisted in the 369th U.S. Infantry), the Old World was introduced to modern *American* music for the first time. Sissle later recounted how 60-year-old French women, German prisoners, and even other orchestra members spontaneously broke into dance when they heard them play. It was then, Sissle remarked, that he was "satisfied that American music would some day be the world's music."[13]

Following his return to the United States, Europe continued to promote this new style. He either composed or cowrote such big hits as "Good Night Angeline," "On Patrol in No Man's Land," and "I Wish I Had Someone to Rock Me in the Cradle of Love." In performance, Europe was restrained and professional, rejecting the over-the-top behavior that characterized most black performers in the minds of many whites. It seemed that, by 1919, James Reese Europe was about to revise completely the role of African American artists in the United States. Unfortunately, on May 9, 1919, after performing at Mechanic's Hall in Boston, one of Europe's own musicians stabbed the bandleader with a knife after being scolded by Europe for crossing the stage during the performance. Europe either refused or was denied medical treatment, and he bled to death that evening. Songwriter and musician Eubie Blake later admitted that Europe's passing was a significant blow to the advancement of black performers: "He was our benefactor and inspiration. Even more, he was the Martin Luther King of music."[14]

TIN PAN ALLEY MINES GOLD

While Europe and Sousa were able to borrow from vernacular traditions to give life to an anemic musical field, the same process elevated show music, termed Tin Pan Alley by the turn of the century, from cultural obscurity to the pinnacle of popular music. Tin Pan Alley composers could not rely on the ready-made legitimacy afforded to writers of classical pieces. Intended to support popular theater and vaudeville acts, Tin Pan Alley artists needed first to entertain before they could be concerned with the formal arrangement or the artistic aesthetics of their music. As a result, these composers borrowed heavily from both white and African American vernacular sounds. Known for the "tinny" sound generated by the upright piano, the region (concentrated near Broadway and 28th Street in New York City) became home to the type of writers who were actively looking for ways to tap into the new, lighter, and more urbane style. Melding catchy lyrics, melodies, and toe-tapping, syncopated rhythms, the sale of Tin Pan Alley sheet music brought stardom, influence, and riches to a number of innovative writers, including Jerome Kern, Harry Von Tilzer, and Irving Berlin.

No doubt, it was the financial rewards that accompanied these performances that sustained the movement for so long. Hit songs were usually sold as sheet music in the lobbies of the theaters, clubs, and vaudeville acts that performed them. In an age when most children were taught to read music in school and when many American families owned pianos or other instruments, printed musical scores sold widely. More than 45,000 sheets were sold annually by 1880, with the number growing into the tens of millions by 1910. Charles K. Harris's hit song "After the Ball" (1892) sold more than five million copies alone, while the typical hit could expect to sell nearly 100,000 sheets. Priced from thirty to forty cents each, the royalties from the sale of a single hit sustained many performers for a lifetime. When 170 Tin Pan Alley writers organized the American Society of Composers, Authors, and Publishers (ASCAP) in 1914, the recovery of royalties for the public performance of copyrighted materials increased the monetary value of their work.

Less valuable, but of growing influence, were sales from recordings. Based on the invention of the inimitable Thomas Edison, phonographs reliably reproduced music through either recorded cylinders or discs. While technological limits slowed sales—for example, the cylinders proved to be hard to mass produce, and many of the earliest phonographs could be heard only through headphones, making it impossible for groups to dance to the music—by 1901 Emile Berliner and Eldridge Johnson had perfected the Victor Talking Machine which, for all intents, was the same as our present-day listening devices. The Victor logo of "Little Nipper," the small dog who looked into the gramaphone with a cocked head, became synonymous with American's fascination with recorded sound. By 1909 more than 27 million records and cylinders had been sold with royalties (called "mechanicals") protected by the U.S. Copyright Act of 1909. Ten years later, two million players had been sold and nearly 100 million recordings. While not as influential as the spread of radio after 1920, the sales of sheet music and recordings brought the popular musical style of Tin Pan Alley out of the theaters, nightclubs, and brothels into American homes.

The topicality of the songs was their key appeal. Unlike more structured works, popular tunes could be constructed in time to meet or anticipate the public's curiosity with current events. For example, inventions such as the airplane, telephone, and automobile became the subject of hit songs, including Fred Fisher's "Come, Josephine, in My Flying Machine" (1910), Louis Hirsch's "Hello, Frisco, Hello" (1915), and Maurice Abraham's "He'd Have to Get Under, Get Out and Get Under, to Fix Up His Automobile" (1913). World War I provided composers with a way to combine their craft with patriotism and a sort of public relations boost. War songs such as "Over There," "It's a Long Way to Tipperary," and "Keep the Home Fires Burning" were performed uncountable times on stage, at home, and in the foxholes. The third of these songs, written by Ivor Novello with lyrics from Lena Ford, implored families of servicemen to

> Keep the home-fires burning,
> While your hearts are yearning,
> Though your lads are far away
> They dream of home;
> There's a silver lining
> Through the dark clouds shining,
> Turn the dark cloud inside out,
> Till the boys come home.

While clearly not great poetry, such songs gave Americans a common touchstone by which to cope with the anxieties of war.

Several artists from this genre stand out for their influence and success. Harry Von Tilzer, known as the "man who launched a thousand hits" grew rich by writing an endless string of formulaic songs loved by the public. Introducing Latin American sounds into his tunes, such as "The Cubanola Glide" (1909), or African American styles into songs, such as "Under the Yum Yum Tree" (1910), kept Von Tilzer's compositions on the lips of millions of Americans. Jerome Kern also showed a deft hand at turning out catchy tunes with syrupy lyrics. His fame spread after a string of hit songs from 1912 to 1914. By then, Kern had moved to musical comedy at the Princess Theater: *Nobody Home* (1915), *Very Good Eddie* (1915), *Have a Heart* (1917), *Oh, Boy!* (1917), *Leave It to Jane* (1917), *Oh, Lady! Lady!* (1917), and *She's a Good Fellow* (1919). None of these have the polish or depth of emotions that Kern later would be remembered for, following the 1928 premiere of *Showboat*. While not the most talented composer of Tin Pan Alley, George M. Cohan was the most successful at turning his songs into national hits. Critics such as James S. Metcalfe regarded Cohen as "a vulgar, cheap, blatant, ill-mannered, flashily-dressed, insolent, smart Aleck, who, for some reason unexplainable on any basis of common sense, good taste, or even ordinary decency, appeals to the imagination and apparent approval of large American audiences."[15] His most popular songs, "The Little Millionaire" (1911), "Hello Broadway!" (1914), "The Voice of McConnell" (1918), and "The Royal Vagabond" (1919), were typical light entertainment of the era.

By far the greatest Tin Pan Alley composer was Irving Berlin. He was born in 1888 in Russia, as Izzy Baline, and immigrated to the United States with his family. By 1902 he was making a living in New York City as a singing waiter and piano player. Much has been made of the fact that Berlin had no formal training as a musician (he could neither read nor write music and played the piano using only a single key, F#), but by 1910 Berlin was emerging as a leading force in American popular music. Possibly because of his own rise to riches, Berlin could tap into the sentimental optimism that was so closely held by many Americans. His songs of the decade could double as a list of chart toppers: "Alexander's Ragtime Band," "Everybody's Doing It," "A Pretty Girl Is Like a Melody," and the wartime hit "Oh How I Hate to Get Up in the Morning," to name only a few. When asked to rank Berlin's place in the pantheon of American songwriters, Jerome Kern remarked, "Irving Berlin has no place in American music; he *is* American music."[16]

The question for Tin Pan Alley, then, is not whether it was an influential or popular musical style, but rather *why* it was so successful. Certainly, with the advent of phonographs, the development of the dance halls and nightclubs, and the spread of sheet music, the genre was aided by some very supportive circumstances from 1900 to 1920. The most likely reason for the success of Tin Pan Alley was that it drew upon the well-developed and mature vernacular styles that existed in the United States. The reliance upon ragtime piano pieces is a good case in point. Berlin's "Alexander's Ragtime Band" and later "The International Rag" (1913) were ragtime *songs*, but not ragtime music. The difference was not too subtle; ragtime music was formally structured, syncopated, and used conventional European harmonies. By contrast, ragtime songs were much looser, intending to give *feeling* to the music without being tied to its arrangement.

Tin Pan Alley musicians should not be considered plagiarists; taking from African American artists the heart of their music without giving credit. Rather, most simply borrowed an emotive sense of the music without attempting to create a lasting work of art. For example, when Berlin composed "Alexander's Ragtime Band," he actually revitalized the original style for a number of years. That neither Berlin nor ragtime composers were very much alike was ignored by the public's association of the music with fun, trendiness, and active entertainment—just the things that attracted Berlin to the style in the first place. The fact that most new popular musical styles emerge this way, with some nostalgic connection to the previously reigning sounds, suggests that Tin Pan Alley artists should not be blamed for "robbing" black artists any more than ragtime composers could be faulted for stealing from the marches and cakewalk compositions that proceeded them. In a very real sense, Tin Pan Alley songs aided black artists by shunning the derogatory coon-song style of previous white composers.

RAGTIME

"Ragtime" is a literal term, meaning that the timing of a traditional piece of music is "ragged" through the inclusion of syncopated rhythms and an informal playing. The style was common for unschooled African American musicians who played by ear, taking well-known melodies and performing them in their own way. Key to a rag was how well the music merged with vernacular dance, the so-called cakewalks and reels that were common to African American gatherings (the cakewalk was an exaggerated rendition of blacks imitating white dandies which later became an even more exaggerated style supposedly representing authentic black culture). Existing before the Civil War, "ragging" was informally demonstrated in coon and minstrel shows but never accurately presented as a unique musical style until the 1890s. Ragtime is not jazz, blues, or spirituals, nor is it the forerunner of these styles, but rather a combination of African American vernacular styles with European methods of notion and melodies. When innovators such as Scott Joplin, Joseph Lamb, Tom Turpin, Eubie Blake, and James Scott, began the process of writing ragtime composition, they also initiated the first true musical fusion of international styles into a uniquely American sound.

Ragtime performers were first employed in the "sporting districts" of many Southern American towns and cities. The largest of these, called Storyville in New Orleans, was home to most of the city's brothels, saloons, and, later, nightclubs. While immensely popular, ragtime remained connected to the subaltern urban cultures and, as a result, was largely ignored or overlooked by the mainstream white musical community. When ragtime emerged in the late 1890s, largely through the work of composers such as Joplin, it was a mature and muscular musical style, one that sparked a national craze which lasted until the 1920s when it was replaced by jazz.

Typical of all broadly defined genres, there are many types of ragtime music. The most academic form was the instrumental rag, such as those of Joplin, Lamb, and Scott, which were formal compositions for piano based on conventional European harmonies and using a regular, syncopated melody. Following Joplin's dictum never to play ragtime too fast, instrumental rags tend to be both cheerful and serene. By contrast, ragtime songs, often written by Tin Pan Alley artists, used many of the rag techniques, but more loosely appropriated the style of watered-down coon songs and marches which were popular in the 1880s and 1890s. Two other minor forms also existed. Ragtime waltzes were syncopated dances written largely by white composers (although Joplin also experimented with these) such as Marcella Henry's "Covent Garden: Ragtime Waltz" (1917) and George Meyer's "Wiggle-Wag Ragtime Waltz" (1913). Ragged classical pieces were also performed at public concerts. Taking a new twist on well-known works, musicians tended to ad-lib their performances. The improvisational character of these works is rightly credited as part of the foundation of modern jazz.

Combined, ragtime styles became immensely popular in the United States from 1900 to 1920. Coinciding with the growing sales of home pianos (which peaked in 1909) and the maturing sheet music industry, ragtime emerged as the sound for urban performers in a nation that was increasingly looking to cities for its evening entertainment. The development of the player piano helped ragtime, for the machines could effortlessly reproduce the difficult sound of the works. That ragtime was seen as fresh "youth music" only added to its attraction. Typical were the comments of H. K. Moderwell, who wrote in 1915 that "a person who doesn't open his heart to ragtime somehow isn't human."[17]

Because of ragtime's vernacular origins, we are limited in our understanding of who contributed the most to its development. We are able to trace who published and recorded their work, but not those whose style of rag performances were the most influential. Thankfully, several publishers were willing to extend contracts to African American artists. Most notable were John Stark, who published more than 115 rags by composers such as Joplin, Scott, and Lamb; Jerome H. Remick, who printed nearly 300 tunes by artists in Detroit and New York City; and Will Rossiter in Chicago. By the 1910s, there were numerous hit ragtime songs, including Jay Roberts's "The Entertainer's Rag" (1910), George Botsford's "Grizzly Bear Rag" (1911), Edward B. Claypoole's "Ragging the Scale" (1915), and George L. Cobb's "Russian Rag" (1918). The fact that all of these men were white and that the subject matter had shifted away from the exotic African American culture or derogatory coon songs suggests how for the medium went toward providing black artists with national respectability.

Of course this acceptance did not occur without dissent. On one hand, legitimate opponents included educators, critics, and performers who simply did not like the new musical style when compared to the old European masters. Boston Symphony Orchestra conductor Karl Murk sniffed, in 1915, "I do not believe there is such a thing as good popular music. . . . I think what you call . . . ragtime is poison. It poisons the very source of your musical growth, for it poisons the taste of the young." The ironic reality—that modern European musicians were also deeply impressed by ragtime—was obviously missed. Moreover, the line between an honest dislike of the new style and hidden racial prejudice was hard to distinguish. One piano instructor, in 1912, while never specifically mentioning race, showed his clear distaste for the source of the new sound: "ragtime will ruin your touch, disable your technic, misuse your knowledge . . . and pervert whatever sense of poetry and feeling you have into superficial, improper channels. Shun in as you would the 'Black Death.' "[18]

More common were foes who openly admitted their prejudice that the rise of African American culture posed a threat to white domination and control. Such cultural critics believed that the acceptance of black music displayed a loss of critical judgment in the public that would eventually lead to a population that could not distinguish between good and evil. One moralist concluded, "In Christian homes, where purity and morals are stressed, ragtime should find no resting place." Others asked, "Can it be said that America is falling prey to the collective soul of the Negro through the influence of what is properly known as 'rag time' music?" A collective soul where "sexual restraint is almost unknown, and the wildest latitude of moral uncertainty is conceded."[19]

Still, in spite of these concerns, ragtime succeeded in fundamentally shifting the nature of popular music in America away from European sources and toward our own domestic vernacular roots. Ragtime was the first true America genre, a fusion of Old World styles into a modern, New World sound. Moreover, it opened the doors for a host of African American performers to demonstrate their skills before an interested public who were less likely to see them as caricatures and more as cultural educators about everything from clothing styles to dance steps. Ragtime also ushered in many other modern musical styles, especially jazz and the blues, as artists such as "Jelly Roll" Morton and others took the stage as rag artists but finished their careers as jazz pioneers.

SCOTT JOPLIN

Scott Joplin sustained these goals for ragtime far more than any other single performer. Ironically, Joplin's contributions had almost been forgotten. When ragtime was "rediscovered" in 1974, following the success of the Paul Newman–Robert Redford film *The Sting*, Joplin's compositions again topped the charts. Modern filmmakers and contemporary historians can credit Scott Joplin with his accomplishments because he was able to leave a written record for musicians to reproduce. His ability to capture the African American vernacular tradition so ably, while relying on European notation and melodic methods, stands as one of the greatest achievements in the history of American popular music.

Scott Joplin was born in 1868 near the border between Texas and Arkansas to parents who were former slaves. Joplin's musical talents were honed by the rich traditions of black folk music: the church, call-and-shout spirituals, and syncopated fiddle and banjo tunes. His mother's ability to purchase a used piano and a young music teacher's willingness to take on the youth as a student provided the spark needed for Joplin to turn this lode of experience into a new creative style of written composition. From 1885 to 1893, he moved to Missouri and toured the Midwest as a professional musician and played at nearly any venue that would employ him. While in Chicago, for the Columbian Exposition, Joplin organized his first band and began seriously to compose songs for them to perform. When he returned to Missouri to enroll in the George R. Smith College for Negroes, in Sedalia, the final keys to his career were found. There, among some of the greatest and best-trained black performers in the country, he became an acknowledged star at the influential Maple Leaf Club, which earned him the notice of John Stillwell Stark, a white publisher of sheet music. Stark recognized the potential of Joplin's pieces and published the "Maple Leaf Rag" in 1899. The song was soon a hit and sold millions of copies worldwide.

What drove the "Maple Leaf Rag" to such renown was the style and polish of the tune. Joplin took his work very seriously as formal compositions for piano. In a very real sense, the work was an étude for piano, much like those of Chopin, and later Stravinsky. Joplin's melodies, however, were fully syncopated, making them easy to dance to in ways traditional marches were not. The rage for rag became an international one, as performers everywhere, including the influential John Philip Sousa, began incorporating the "Maple Leaf Rag" into their repertoires. For the next twenty years, until his death in 1917, Joplin's work spearheaded the revolution of fusion in American pop. He set the standard notation for ragtime, with four, 16-bar sections arranged to repeat themselves along a pattern described by composers as AABBACCDD. Most important, he kept the quality of his work very high.

Sadly, Joplin's life did not allow him to enjoy much of this success. His relations with the love of his life, Belle Hayden, were troubled by the death of their infant daughter and his many years on the road. He was frustrated by the cheap knockoffs of his musical innovation. Moreover, the racist American musical scene did not acknowledge the phenomenal evolution that was occurring all around them. Partly as a result, Joplin focused his waning energies on writing an African American grand opera, titled *Treemonisha*. While Joplin was able to see the work staged, funded by himself, it was never performed before an audience. Overworked, Joplin collapsed in 1916 and never recovered his health.

While Joplin's career stands for itself, it is important to highlight how influential his work was to a host of others. Most notable were James Scott and Joseph Lamb. Scott, aided by Joplin, published numerous best-sellers, including "Ragtime Oriole" (1911), "Efficiency Rag" (1917), "New Era Rag" (1919), and the most acclaimed "Pegasus: A Classic Rag" (1919). Lamb, who was white, learned ragtime from Joplin's sheet music. Lamb's style, published by John Stark (based on a recommendation by Joplin), led to a ragtime craze along the Eastern seaboard. From 1908 to 1919, Lamb published 12 rags for Stark, most notably the "Ragtime Nightingale" (1915) and "Top Liner Rag" (1916). Joseph R. Scotti, a biographer of Lamb, concluded that "Joe Lamb took for granted the very respectability of ragtime, which his black hero, Scott Joplin, died proving."[20]

While probably not the most accomplished performer, Lamb, like Joplin, left a written record of how to merge successfully the two contrasting musical traditions that predominated in the United States. As ragtime pianist and composer Ben Harney later remarked, "Real ragtime . . . [almost] cannot be put in notes [because it] is the contribution of the graduated Negro banjo-player who cannot read music." Joplin, Scott, and Lamb showed American musicians how to be successful at "playing two different tunes at once," in other words, how to fuse the two traditions into one. In the coming decades, it would prove to be a very prolific lesson indeed.[21]

RELATIVES OF RAGTIME: THE BLUES AND JAZZ

While the links between ragtime, blues, and jazz are still hotly debated (and probably always will be), it is certain that the formation of the latter two musical genres in the 1910s were influenced by the growing commercial and artistic acceptance of ragtime. Fortunately for fans, neither the blues nor jazz suffered the same fate of ragtime—that of being absorbed and weakened by commercial composers on Tin Pan Alley. This was probably true for the blues because the medium was so closely linked to African American performances. Using distinct "blue notes," a flat third and seventh, few chord changes, odd modes, and only three-line verses, the blues remained a strongly vernacular sound that was nearly impossible for composers to capture on paper. The trembling blue notes were particularly discernible in black performances, a characteristic tracing its lineage back to African and Caribbean roots.

Always deep in meaning, the style was intended to be used to combat depression, not wallow in it. Typical was Charley Patton's classic "Pony Blues,"

> Hitch up my pony, saddl' up my black mare;
> Hitch up my pony, saddl' up my black mare;
> I'm gon' find a rider, ooh, baby in the world somewhere.

The repetition of the phrases (termed an AAB pattern) and tapered singing style of black artists (which wavered on the notes at the end of each line) made the "Pony Blues" a song which many later singers would reprise, including "Big Jo" Williams, Johnny Temple, "Son" House, and Howlin' Wolf. The ability to manipulate the same song into many unique forms was typical of the improvisational character of the blues. When the blues were finally published, in 1912, the genre created a line of popular music which was both separate from and connected to that of ragtime.

William Christopher (W.C.) Handy is properly credited as being the "father of the blues" in large part because he was able to compose music that retained the ephemeral qualities of the style. Because recordings of blues performances did not begin until the 1920s, Handy's compositions provide the earliest evidence of the format free and clear of commercial influence. Handy was a formally trained musician who learned as much from his everyday performances as he did from his instructors. While he began his career playing marches, rags, and popular orchestral pieces, he soon earned local fame from his renditions of "authentic" African American music. In 1909, while performing in Memphis, he was asked to turn one of these into a campaign song for a local politician. The result, first termed "Mr. Crump," was later polished and (thankfully) rechristened "The Memphis Blues." Although not published until 1912, this date serves as a useful starting point for the birth of the blues. Throughout the decade, Handy continued to produce million-selling compositions including "St. Louis Blues"(1914), "Joe Turner Blues" (1916), and "Beale Street Blues" (1917). While these received great attention from white entertainers, Tin Pan Alley proved incapable of bottling the lightening of black performers. Anyone familiar with George Gershwin's 1924 classic composition, *Rhapsody in Blue*, is aware of the clear distinction between authentic blues performances and even the most talented imitations.

The blues were also unique in that they provided an opportunity for African American female singers to flourish. Women such as Ma Rainey, Bessie Smith, Chippie Hill, and Ida Cox dominated the early blues market. With a wider vocal range and a greater ability to shift between blues notes and traditional major notes, women were able to navigate the difficult performances while still articulating the all-important lyrics. Bessie Smith was probably the best of this strong group. One accompanyist remembered that Smith "could bring about mass hypnotism. When she was performing you could hear a pin drop." Smith's fame and fortune had to wait until the 1920s, when the recording industry began to take the genre seriously and the listening public developed an ear for the new sound.[22]

Jazz, too, first appeared in the 1910s. Whether generated from ragtime or, as many claim, more directly from the blues, jazz soon developed a style all its own. The connection to ragtime is less secure, as the formal

William Christopher Handy. Courtesy of the Library of Congress.

structure and strict composition of rags were contrary to the improvisational style of jazz performances. As "Jelly Roll" Morton once remarked, "[R]agtime [has] a certain type of syncopation and only certain tunes can be played in that idea. But jazz [has] a style that can be applied to any type of tune."[23] Other aspects also differentiated jazz from ragtime. For example, ragtime performances were limited to those who could read music and, usually, were performed before mixed or all-white audiences (thereby resulting in a "cooler," more restrained sound). By contrast, jazz musicians typically played by ear, with no two renditions exactly alike, and before crowds more likely to be dominated by African Americans. As a result, the tunes were played "hotter," with a faster pace that was, like the blues, difficult for white composers to copy and exploit on Tin Pan Alley. Still, the careers of ragtime, blues, and jazz composers hint at the intricate ways in which these three threads of African American music were at times woven together.[24]

It is far easier to date the time when jazz began to migrate across the country, around 1909, than to document its early formation. The sound certainly originated in the urban black subculture of the city of New Orleans. Based on the "hot," vernacular performances of African American musicians hired to entertain customers at the local bars and brothels of Storyville, "jazzed" tunes were highly improvised. The city aided in the development of this sound in a number of ways. The tolerance of red-light districts such as Storyville provided steady work for a large number of musicians. The Creole culture of New Orleans also gave blacks greater freedom to intermingle with whites (even if not as equals), which translated into greater access to their entertainment dollars. Finally, the port city provided a source of cheap brass instruments, many left over from the Spanish-American war, for impoverished but talented black musicians.

Musicians not native to the region had a hard time imitating the effect and would have been wise to follow the advice of jazz great Fats Waller, who once remarked, "If you don't know, don't mess with it."[25] Several characteristics of jazz remain distinct. The style favored combos containing a trombone, cornet, clarinet, drums, and piano—each capable of syncopating and improvising as easily as most people breathe air. Jazz was also a performing art rather than a written or composed one. Virtuoso performances, not sheet-music sales, were the mark of a great performer. Finally, early jazz bands developed almost accidentally as talented musicians moved from gig to gig looking for steady pay and reliable partners. As a result, most jazz bands of the 1910s rarely lasted long. It was not until 1915 that Morton cut the first jazz records, and not until the 1920s that these recordings began to provide enough money to support professional jazz bands.[26]

Around 1909, New Orleans jazz bands began to migrate north—first to Kansas City and Memphis and later to Chicago, Oklahoma City, and Detroit. When in 1917, during World War I, the U.S. Army ordered the closure of most brothels in Storyville, the slow but steady trickle of musicians became a torrent. From 1918 until the mid-1920s, distinct jazz styles (such as Chicago jazz) evolved in many of these secondary cities far removed from their New Orleans origins. It was largely from these regional expressions that white performers such as Jimmie McPartland, Lionel Hampton, Bix Beiderbecke, Gene Krupa, and Benny Goodman learned their jazz sounds.

Perhaps it was inevitable, then, that the first recorded jazz band, the Original Dixieland Jazz Band, was composed of white musicians. Leaving New Orleans in 1915, the band became a sensation in Chicago and was "discovered" in 1917 while playing at Reisenweber's Restaurant, in New York City. Recorded February 26, 1917, and led by cornetist Dominic James LaRocca, the Original Dixieland Jazz Band sold over a million copies of their songs "Livery Stable Blues" and "Dixieland Jass [sic] Band One-Step." While later recordings by the group showed little originality or improvisation, their early work certainly was the product of, and accurately reflected, the New Orleans sound. Although it may be unfair that the quintessential contribution of America to world music was originally credited to white musicians, the music that they produced was the product of African American artists.

Regardless of who was recorded first, black performers soon dominated the field. Sidney Bechet, a Creole from New Orleans, toured the country, finally settled in Chicago in 1918, and went on to Europe and worldwide fame. Joseph "King" Oliver, also a product of the Big Easy, played cornet with Storyville legends such as Bunk Johnson before achieving stardom in Chicago. Oliver's departure opened the door to a young prodigy by the name of Louis Armstrong, who redefined and further elevated the genre in the coming decades. "Jelly Roll" Morton probably best defines the African American jazz performer of the 1910s. A product of rag, blues, and jazz traditions, "Jelly" experimented with a variety of sounds, techniques, and arrangements before settling on a recognizable (and marketable) jazz style. A product of the New Orleans urban subculture—a Creole who worked as a pimp and a gambler before settling on music—Morton was a character who often claimed a greater influence over the development of jazz than was probably merited. As one historian surmised, "He was proud, he was vain, he was arrogant, sensitive, ebullient, a braggart, suspicious, superstitious—but he was nonetheless the genuine article, a true artist."[27] His first composition, "Jelly Roll Blues" (1915), was a hit that contributed to an irregular but generally productive career which lasted for the next twenty years. Still, Morton's broad-based musical background included ragtime, blues, classical, jazz, spirituals, and opera; he performed from New Orleans to California in clubs ranging from two-bit brothels to some of America's greatest halls. In all, Morton represented the cultural fusion that was at the root of American popular music.

CONCLUSION

The fusion of American popular music began in the 1910s in ways that had profound consequences. The acceptance of African American styles and performers opened opportunities for new talent which accentuated the trend in the coming years. The development of jazz, blues, big band, be-bop, swing, and rock 'n' roll music all trace some portion of their lineage back to this decade, and all retain the central qualities of the fused sound. Equally important, African Americans found a means to excel in U.S. society—means that were acceptable to dominant white tastes. Although playing at exclusive nightclubs was different than being allowed through the front door, popular music did make inroads by developing a sense of national cultural pride in the new sound and by lessening some of the more caustic racial bigotry that pervaded American society. Finally, the cultural fusion occurred more forcefully at the popular level suggesting the important role the market would play in entertainment. While it is possible to credit John Stark with an enlightened interest in good music, his financial success in publishing Scott Joplin's work provided tangible support for such efforts. With Tin Pan Alley composers, such as Kern and Berlin, making millions of dollars by popularizing vernacular music, the economic incentive for fusion was obvious and, some might say, inevitable. The arrival of radio, in 1920, was the technological breakthrough that was needed to catapult this fusion into a truly mass phenomenon.

The 1910s

10

Performing Arts

As with other forms of popular culture during the 1910s, the performing arts of drama, dance, and film seemed to both conserve and undermine many of the prevailing values and behaviors of the nativist American society. The moral simplicity of Victorianism—that good and evil are easily identified, and that poverty and social inequality were indicators of individual character—held sway in the minds of many playwrights, choreographers, and producers. The most influential movie director of the decade (and some might say of all time), David Wark Griffith, relied strongly on these values and biases while he produced some of the most important films in American history. Yet the complexities and social realities of modern life were quickly dissolving the foundation of this bias. Technology freed performers from the bounds of the traditional productions allowing artists to probe more psychologically complex issues on the stage. Modern mass entertainment carried with it a cultural and economic energy never before seen in the United States—one traditional authority figures found difficult to combat. Moreover, the silent voices of millions of ethnic, religious, and racial minorities were increasingly heard through the performing arts. Many entrepreneurial immigrants, Jews, and African Americans, for example, were able to tap into these media.

Of course, the relative success of conservative and modern traditions is not always easy to gauge. For example, the separation between art and commerce in the American performing arts is not absolute. How we differentiate between the popularity and financial success of comedians such as Charlie Chaplin, for example, and the "message" of his movies determines how revolutionary we determine drama, dance, and film to be during the 1910s. Put another way, is a pie-throwing contest by the Keystone Kops social criticism or simply funny? Did Florenz Ziegfeld's *Follies* lead Americans to a freer expression of their sexuality, or did he simply cash in on an opportunity missed by wealthy, Protestant elites to give the people what they wanted? What is certainly true is that these momentous social shifts were highly visible in the performing arts during the 1910s. Influenced heavily by scholarly and artistic trends in Europe and new technologies at home, American performers experimented with their craft in ways that would have long-lasting and significant effects on their fellow citizens.

THE EUROPEAN ROOTS OF MODERN AMERICAN DRAMA

The greatest influence on the changes that overtook the American stage in the 1910s was the new intellectual trend in European drama. Dating back nearly 50 years, European writers, producers, and patrons sought to return the theater to a place of serious contemplation. Much as the Greeks had done 2,000 years earlier, writers hoped to tackle contemporary problems in ways that reflected the complexities of modern living. Most of the tension that existed for European playwrights was due to the rising intellectual dissatisfaction with bourgeois or middle-class rationalism. This conflict, between the mind and the soul, led many to reject the clear moral distinctions suggested by Victorian thought. Mystical feelings, emotions, and a growing reverence for folk art overpowered the structured and academic formalism of earlier writers. The "expressionistic" style soon dominated the European stage.

Richard Wagner, a German composer who wrote the four-opera saga *The Rings of the Nibelung,* based upon highly sentimental Norse mythology, typifies this trend. Wagner's contribution to opera was profound, but, for the American theater, his greatest influence was in how he staged his productions. With full orchestras and magnificent set designs and costumes, Wagner's compositions united both the mind and the soul in ways that changed modern drama from dry and often preachy morality plays into emotionally powerful, symbolic touchstones for his audience. Some critics have charged that Wagner's majestic and wildly popular set designs—complete with dragons, flying Valkyries, and pyrotechnics—often drowned the emotional power of his operas in favor of entertainment; nevertheless, Wagner demonstrated to many the hollowness of the established theater.

If Wagner's operas suggested the existence of a large and untapped reservoir of passion in large audiences, Norwegian playwright Henrik Ibsen showed that the most direct way to access this force was through natural dialog. Rejecting the traditional use of stage asides (i.e., an actor talking directly to the audience), long speeches (soliloquies), and grand conclusions at the end of the typical production, Ibsen relied instead upon the natural and realistic speech patterns of everyday people. Typically, Ibsen's characters wrestled with the problems of finding individuality within an increasingly complex mass society—issues that still face us and explain why his works remain relevant. His characters faced hopelessly dysfunctional families (a common theme), sexually transmitted diseases (*Ghosts*), and the changing role of women in European society (*A Doll's House*). Nor did Ibsen offer easy answers or untangle the knots of social obligation for his audiences. Heros and heroines alike were destroyed if they failed to strike a workable balance between independence and society.

The work of two other dramatists, George Bernard Shaw and Anton Chekov, solidified Ibsen's more penetrating approach to drama. Shaw, an Irish-born literary critic and writer who was prominent from the 1890s until his death in 1950, took a more satirical and humorous approach to his early playwriting. Poking fun at the inflated smugness of Victorianism, Shaw demonstrated through his characters that a life of critical self-awareness and humanitarianism could address many of society's ills. It was not until World War I obliterated his sense of progressive optimism, and the publication of *Heartbreak House* (1919), that Shaw's work took on darker, more fatalistic tones.

Far from liberal England, Russia's Anton Chekov tapped into the social frustrations of the aristocratic, landholding elite. Incapable of accepting a place among the common people, many of Chekov's characters harbored deep-seated frustrations at the limits of modern society and the emptiness of their class system. While critical of the established order, Chekov's work found expression at the more reserved Moscow Art Theatre and from there to the rest of Europe. (The Americanized form "theater" is used in all cases except when the French-based "theatre" is specifically used in a proper noun.) Staged by Konstantin Stanislavsky and Vladimir Nemirovich-Danchenko, Chekov's plays, such as *The Sea Gull* and *The Cherry Orchard*, set a standard for modern writing that remains very much alive to this day.

The combination of Ibsen, Shaw, and Chekov, among others, opened the format of the staged play to unforeseen possibilities. Still, there remained one large and serious problem: how to produce a show which effectively related the seriousness and complexity of the written word. Theaters were designed primarily to cope with traditional repertory productions. These houses had a stable of actors (both male and female members of a cast, unless indicated otherwise) who trained for and performed a set number of classical or Shakespearean dramas. Their stages, props, and lighting facilities usually had been passed down from generations of companies. Konstantin Stanislavsky found that he needed to retrain nearly all of the Moscow Art Theatre's performers. His "actor's studio" worked to prevent artists from using their clichéd, overly dramatic outbursts (such as feinting or grotesque facial contortions to indicate anger) which previously had clued an audience into the emotional state of a character. Instead, he wanted to allow the themes and dialog to set the mood. In Paris, André Antoine and the Théâtre Libre trained its thespians to act as if there were no audience, relying instead on the reaction of fellow cast members to pace their emotions.

While Americans could not (nor did not) ignore the monumental changes to European theater in the late nineteenth century, is was not until details of the new production methods had been translated into English that these plays received serious consideration in the United States. Stage director Adolphe Appia and theater connoisseur Gordon Craig made this possible in the 1910s. The Swiss Appia wrote several influential books detailing the use of three-dimensional scenery, numerous special effects, and variations in lighting (both color and brightness) and sound to help set the emotional tone of a production. Craig, a member of one of England's most well-known theatrical families, popularized these techniques in *The Art of the Theatre* (1911), *Towards a New Theatre* (1913), *The Theatre Advancing* (1919), and in a theater periodical titled *The Mask*, which was published from 1908 to 1929. Here, in a respected and easily accessible format, Americans were able to absorb many of the lessons learned by European dramatists and stage professionals. Craig's criticism of the powerful producers who restricted the development of experimental theater (in other words, most of the men who staged shows on Broadway) gave courage to a number of less influential theater companies to produce more daring plays.

A final, and unexpected, source of change was in the world of psychology and physics. From 1900 to 1905, Sigmund Freud and his leading disciple, Carl Jung, set the scientific and medical communities on their ears by demonstrating the link between dreams, the subconscious, and human sexual behavior. To Freud, the internal battles waged between one's psyche made a mockery of Victorian notions of rational self-control. Freud's celebrated speaking tour to the United States in 1909 only heightened the public's fascination with the subconscious. Also during the early 1900s, Albert Einstein published his special theory of relativity, which posits that space and time are only concepts and have no definitive meaning. Almost overnight, the sciences seemed to abandon all systematic and absolute rules for a reality that was composed of the irrational and the relative. Just as Social Darwinists had done before them, the educated public soon took up these theoretical concepts and applied them to human society. A host of introspective and highly sub-

jective dramas—such as those of Swedish playwright August Strindberg—were soon in circulation, adding even greater impetus for change.

"ART" COMES TO THE AMERICAN DRAMA

The arrival of this new perspective toward drama was in no way uniform nor particularly widespread. Pockets of change began throughout
the country, but to call these cells a movement would be an overstatement. What is clear is that, by 1910, American critics of the theater
had begun to fashion alternatives to the commercial stage. It was not
until the late 1920s and early 1930s that these trends converged to transform drama in America.

The result of this haphazard transformation was a period of intense
experimentation in dramatic realism. Sparked by the new European attitudes, the artificiality of the traditional theater became the target of
reform. Needless to say, experimentation, at times, distracted the audience more than it enhanced the performance. As Craig wrote in *The Art
of the Theatre*, "The theatre should not be a place in which to exhibit
scenery, in which to read poems, or to preach sermons; it should be a
place in which the entire beauty of life can be unfolded . . . the inner
beauty and meaning of life." The American theater lacked the people
capable of coordinating the wide range of new artistic expressions. This
role, later called the "director," had little meaning before the introduction
of the modern European style. Previously, the closest equivalent to the
director was the stage manager, an administrator whose job responsibilities included almost everything: ticket sales, the temperature of the theater, music, and stage design. While some experienced Europeans, like
Max Reinhart, did lend their talents to the American cause it was not
until the 1920s that the current form of the stage director emerged.[1]

Equally problematic was the generally poor state of dramatic writing
in America in the 1910s, although pockets of good experimental writing
did exist. Still, truly innovative plays intended for popular audiences
were few and far between. American writers proved to be awkward in
their application of Freud or their mimicry of Ibsen and Chekov. In general, writers tended to modify existing narratives or relied on fanciful
tales of transformation. For example, Alice Gerstenberg adapted Lewis
Carroll's surrealist story of Alice in Wonderland into a play titled *Alice*
in 1915. Later that year, she staged a piece titled *Overtones* that used four
women to give expression to the internal and external voices of the two
leading characters. Slightly better was Percy MacKaye's work, *The Scare-
crow*, which examined the psychological motives that drove this imagi-
nary creature. David Belasco's *The Return of Peter Grimm* and Arthur
Hopkins's *The Fatted Calf* were equally Freudian in their exposure of
inner demons and Victorian hypocrisy. While these and other writers

were first to expose American audiences to the exciting possibilities of the new style, they bestowed little motivation for the public or producers to move American theater in this direction.

THE LITTLE THEATRE MOVEMENT

The growth of small, experimental theaters in the United States provided the necessary space and audiences for America's modern playwrights to develop their skills. Under the new rules, the barren stage designs of these small, chronically underfunded theaters became a virtue. The lack of extravagant sets, complex musical numbers, and top-named actors meant that production costs could be kept low, making it easier for the company to take risks. Poor attendance actually accentuated the intimacy, so essential to psychological drama, between the actors and the patrons. In addition, the tiny audiences were usually drawn from the local arts and academic communities, who tolerated a greater freedom of expression than those who paid top dollar for Broadway productions. Critic and writer Maurice Brown termed these noncommercial venues "Little Theatres," a name that was proudly displayed by their founders.

The Little Theatre movement was unquestionably the most influential trend in American drama during the 1910s. Aided by Craig's work, beginning in 1912, local writers, actors, and enthusiasts opened Little Theatres throughout the country, including the Toy Theatre in Boston, the Little Country Theatre in Fargo, North Dakota, and the Little Theatre Society in Indianapolis, Indiana. By 1915, in New York City alone, there existed the Neighborhood Playhouse on the Lower East Side, the Provincetown Players in Greenwich Village, the Washington Square Players, and Stuart Walker's Portmanteau Theatre. By 1917 more than 50 Little Theatres were in operation throughout the United States.

The style of the Little Theatres was a complete and intended departure from the more mainstream stage. As discussed below, the traditional and most popular shows relied heavily on melodrama, star appeal, or extravaganza. The Little Theatres brashly rejected these traits and created their own, newly named "off Broadway" qualities. Novelty and experimentation were paramount. The traditional repertoire was not abandoned but rather was reinterpreted to highlight their mental complexities. The focus on simple, quiet, and realistic stage designs stood in stark contrast to the glittering rhinestones and blaring orchestras that accosted audiences at most commercial venues. Many of this country's most influential stage designers got their start in Little Theatre, including Winthrop Ames, Joseph Urban, Robert Edmond Jones, Lee Simonson, and Sam Hume. As theater historian Oscar G. Brockett concluded, the "little theatre movement made its greatest contributions between 1912

and 1920 by preparing audiences to accept [the] new drama and production methods."[2]

Undoubtedly, the Provincetown Players was the most important Little
Theatre during the decade. Moving from Cape Cod, Massachusetts, to
Greenwich Village in 1916, the Players drew upon the vast talents of
such notables as John Reed, Robert Edmund Jones, Eugene O'Neill,
George Cram Cook, and his wife Susan Glaspell. As expected, they drew
upon a variety of sources for their inspiration, including labor radicalism,
the Armory Art Show, and August Strindberg. According to Strindberg,
the new theater should be a place "where we can be shocked at what is
horrible, where we can laugh at what is grotesque, where we can see life
without shrinking back in terror if what was hitherto lain veiled behind
theological or aesthetic conceptions is revealed to us." The intellectual
community in Greenwich Village clearly believed that it was the Victorian values so widely promoted on the commercial stage that were the
chief source of these false ideas. When disbanded in the 1920s, the company had produced 97 original plays written by 47 American authors.[3]

Certainly the most accomplished writer to come from the Provincetown Players, or the little theater movement for that matter, was Eugene
O'Neill. By the time he joined the Players, in 1916 at the age of 28,
O'Neill, the son of an acclaimed Broadway actor, James O'Neill, had
already composed 16 one-act plays that had been rejected by the commercial theater and had several years of formal training at Harvard. His
true gift was in crafting natural dialog and rhythm within plays of great
emotional depth. His work was unsparing in its attacks on those who
rationalized their feelings or attempted to develop artificial states of happiness. In one of his most acclaimed plays of the era, *Beyond the Horizon*
(1918), which won the Pulitzer Prize in 1920, O'Neill portrayed the lives
of two brothers in love with the same girl, each of whom took on the
values of the other to disastrous consequences. Based on his own painful
experiences with alcoholism and a love triangle involving himself, Louise
Bryant, and John Reed (an episode popularized in the movie *Reds*), *Beyond the Horizon* stunned critics with its emotional power, contemporary
language, lack of dramatic gimmickry, and, most of all, American au-
thorship. O'Neill later wrote, "What I am after is to get an audience to
leave the theatre with an exultant feeling from seeing somebody on the
stage facing life, fighting against eternal odds, not conquering but perhaps inevitably being conquered. The individual life is made significant
just by the struggle."[4] While with the Players, O'Neill either staged or
wrote some of his most accomplished plays, including *Long Day's Journey
into Night, Bound East for Cardiff, Anna Christie* (which also won the Pulitzer Prize), and *The Emperor Jones*. He and the Provincetown community
had created a new and powerful role for visionary writers and producers
of the American stage.

THE MAINSTREAM COMMERCIAL THEATER

Critics of commercial theater found little of value there. Susan Glaspell, founder and contributor to the Provincetown Players, recalled that when she and her fellow artists attended Broadway productions they "for the most part came away wishing we had gone somewhere else." Accessing the contribution of these large and expensive shows, Glaspell noted, "They didn't ask much of you. . . . Having paid for your seat, the thing was all done for you, and your mind came out where it went in, only tireder."[5] Innovators such as Glaspell and others were no doubt frustrated by the continued success of so many seemingly identical Broadway productions. Yet still, suggesting that no contributions were made to American drama by the Great White Way misunderstands the challenges facing commercial theater during the 1910s.

Did Broadway *consciously reject* the new methods of drama and staging? By all measures, the answer was no. The success of the daring Theatre Guild and the rising popularity and recognition of writers such as O'Neill was evident to all who made their living through drama. Experimental works and "serious" plays were produced for the commercial stage in the later half of the decade. The best of these were written by Clyde Fitch, Booth Tarkington, William Vaughan Moody, Sinclair Lewis, Martha Morton, and Josephine Preston Peabody. The problem, however, was that few of these productions (and almost no works of lesser quality) succeeded in making money for their commercial producers. The merger of commerce and art was a tricky business.

Perhaps it would have been more appropriate for Glaspell to focus her condemnation on the patrons, rather than on the providers of commercial drama. Theatergoers demonstrated little patience for complex Freudian dramas, favoring instead light comedy and trendy musicals. They usually attended plays based on the stars appearing in the production, rather than on innovative writing or staging methods. Moreover, and this point cannot be overemphasized, the arrival of the little and community theaters provided enthusiasts of the modern style the perfect forum for experimental productions. It is highly probable that the inability of the commercial theaters to profitably stage experimental dramas only added to the off-Broadway movements of the decade.

The main stages were most successful when they provided extravagant, lighthearted, and lavishly expensive productions. According to Russell Lynes, "There was a kind of healthy absurdity . . . a flamboyance combined with smugness that echoed P.T. Barnum's remarkable showmanship in the 1840s and '50s."[6] America's taste for melodrama, while widely rejected by the artistic community, remained overwhelmingly popular. Preachy morality plays and tear-jerking dramas written and performed by American artists found ready support from the public.

Daniel Frohman, brother of the powerful Broadway producer Charles Frohman, believed that a commercial play needed two qualities before it could become a hit: "cleanliness and happy endings." Mainstream producers were in the business of selling tickets, not promoting art for its own sake. As a result, light dramas and musical comedies reigned on Broadway.[7]

With this in mind, it is possible to grant the commercial theater some credit for innovations unique to the American stage. Most notably, the Broadway musical comedy became an authentic national art form in the first decades of the twentieth century. Operettas and light opera, such as those written by W.S. Gilbert and Sir Arthur Sullivan in the 1880s and 1890s, had been providing Europeans with memorable songs and soul-stirring arias well before 1910. But unlike the European stage, musical comedies in the United States were awarded both artistic prestige and commercial support. Composers and librettists, such as Reginald De Kovan (whose operetta *Robin Hood* ran for 3,000 consecutive performances), Victor Herbert (who wrote the successful *Naughty Marietta* in 1910), and Jerome Kern, were instrumental in this transition from high art to popular entertainment in the United States.

Kern's career shows this evolution most clearly. Beginning in 1912, he, like most other American composers, stayed close to the methods introduced and perfected by the Europeans. Yet Kern soon found that, in order for his work to connect with American audiences, it needed to be more accessible and believable. Kern was able to polish his popular style by writing songs for shows at the Princess Theatre and, later, for Florenz Ziegfeld's *Follies*. Supported by talented librettists, such as Guy Bolton and, after 1915, P.G. Wodehouse, Kern soon perfected an American style that established a close and direct relationship with the crowd through songs that used common language, natural humor, and believable experiences. His more artistic operettas, *Very Good Eddie* (1915) and *Sally* (1920), were commercially successful and laid the groundwork for his collaboration with Oscar Hammerstein II, which produced *Showboat* in 1927.

ORGANIZATIONAL INNOVATIONS OF BROADWAY

A second important contribution made by the major commercial theaters of the era was the organization of the entertainment industry. As with other economic endeavors of the Progressive Era, mass entertainment saw a dramatic increase in the amount of money needed to produce their product. The construction of large and expensive theaters, as well as the skyrocketing costs of modern stage technologies, required internal organization and accounting that was uncharacteristic of the medium's entrepreneurial roots. Major productions cost hundred of thousands of dollars before a single ticket was sold. Managing this uncertainty while spreading the general availability of popular shows nationwide was an important legacy of Broadway during the 1910s.

The obvious example of this management style was the operation of a group of production companies collectively called "the Syndicate." Formed in 1896 by the owners of the biggest theaters in the country—including Sam Nixon and Fred Zimmerman of Philadelphia and Charles Frohman, Al Hayman, Marc Klaw, and Abraham Erlanger of New York—the Syndicate sought to create reliable cash flows to make it easier for them to stage their extravaganzas. The Syndicate offered regional theaters a full season of high-quality, popular shows if they, in turn, would promise to stage only these productions. The trust certainly harmed those theaters that chose not to align themselves with the Syndicate. Nonconformists were blacklisted by these powerful producers, making it unlikely that named actors and writers would be willing to work for non-Syndicate members. Moreover, by guaranteeing popular plays and musicals, the Syndicate effectively blocked the introduction of the experimental dramas. But the Syndicate also benefited the industry by ensuring that high-quality works made it to the interior of the nation. The mixed blessings of such an arrangement were evident. Charles Frohman, who controlled the trust by 1910, was a tireless advocate of the public's right to patronize plays they could enjoy and to see the best actors perform. He compelled his biggest stars to make exhausting trips with his touring companies in an effort to gain acceptance for the American stage.

Still, opponents to the Syndicate began to emerge in greater force during the decade. Ironically, the success of the Syndicate in assuring the public of high-quality productions led to the growth of these rebel organizations. David Belasco, who opened the Stuyvesant Theatre in 1907 (renamed the Belasco Theatre in 1910), effectively challenged the hegemony of the Syndicate when his production of *The Governor's Lady* began to tour the country in 1912. Belasco appealed to the public's desire for spectacle when he pioneered the use of modern electric spotlights and even reconstructed a working restaurant on stage. When the Syndicate backed down, allowing regional affiliates to show *The Governor's Lady* in spite of Belasco's opposition, the end of their control was near. The rise of national chains of theaters, such as those owned by brothers Lee and Jacob J. Shubert, gave writers and actors viable alternatives to the Syndicate by 1913. When Frohman died in the sinking of the *Lusitania*, in 1915, the trust lost its most effective advocate. In less than a year, the Syndicate was broken.

While it is foolish to mourn the death of an oligarchy like the Syndicate, the organization did significantly advance the interests of commercial theater in the United States. In addition to stabilizing and augmenting the cash flow into the dramatic arts, the Syndicate encouraged the construction of new theaters and the implementation of new technologies—such as high-wattage electric lighting and multiuse stages. The Syndicate also demonstrated the viability of the touring company in the United States. Anyone who has seen a major theatrical production touring outside of New York City has benefited by practices started by the Syndicate in the 1910s.

The downfall of the Syndicate had unforeseen consequences on the labor relations among actors, directors, and managers on the New York stage. These three components of the theater had traditionally vied for control. Directors, still minor players in the 1910s, tended to wield power indirectly. Actors had influence and could compete for what were at that time astronomical salaries, if they could prove their "star power" in drawing patrons to their shows. The majority of journeyman actors, however, had virtually no leverage and were paid only for performing before an audience. If an actor worked for six weeks rehearsing for a show that ran only one night, he would be paid for one night's work. Another nightmare (partially addressed by the Syndicate) was the speculative touring company that failed to meet expenses. Managers could and did stop productions in midtour, stranding dozens of people without work or pay. In 1896 the Actor's Society was formed to pressure managers to establish a fairer, more reliable payment method. The union failed, but it was replaced in 1913 by the Actors' Equity Association which expanded demands to include Sundays off and paid layoffs during Holy Week, a traditionally slow week for theaters.

The situation came to a boil in 1919 when Equity members finally struck. Several underlying factors were responsible for the final outcome. First, by the end of the decade, theaters increasingly felt the economic drain from the rise of movies. Second, the Red Scare, which followed the Bolshevik Revolution of 1918, harassed and often silenced many of Equity's more radical members. While these variables seemed to favor management, the third change was a growing support of the union by Broadway stars. Either swayed by a sympathy for their fellow actors or the threat to their profession from the silver screen, their support provided Equity with the courage to demand fair treatment for all. When managers failed to acknowledge the legitimacy of the union, refusing even to meet, a general strike began just before the curtain was called on August 6, 1919. Walking out of the theaters in entire casts, the strike closed every major theater in New York (the cooperatively run Theatre Guild was a lone exception). Emotions ran high. Managers, led by George M. Cohan, claimed that Equity's demands would ruin the industry. Star actors, including Ethyl Barrymore, Ed Wynn, Lillian Russell, and W.C. Fields, took turns walking the picket lines and using their talents to appeal to the emotions of the public. In the end, it was the stagehands and musicians (who respected the actors' picket line and refused to fill in for minor roles) who convinced the managers that they had no alternative but to settle. The Producing Managers' Association, losing fortunes every week that the theaters remained closed, on September 6, recognized the Actors' Equity Association and signed a contract, which yielded almost every demand. The generous settlement led to nearly ideal management-labor relations for the next twenty years.

THE PEOPLE'S THEATER

In addition to trends in artistic and Broadway drama, the more widely attended popular or "people's theater" was also important to the direction of the performing arts. From minstrel shows and vaudeville to revue artists and the "girly shows" of Florenz Ziegfeld, popular theater was both independent of and closely linked to the more prestigious stage productions of the decade. Probably no form of popular theater was more representative or reprehensible than the prominent minstrel or coon shows of the 1910s. Usually starring whites wearing blackface makeup, the shows parodied and exaggerated African American culture, speech patterns, and physique. Since the 1830s, minstrel shows sold bigotry to white audiences. By 1910 the growing popularity of these performances in Northern cities suggested that the shows acted to dissipate—in a caustic, mean-spirited, but nonviolent way—much of the growing fear associated with the internal migration of blacks. By laughing at the qualities of the newcomers, something that was common to ethnic theater as well, or in painting pictures of subservient and harmless Uncle Toms or Old Aunties, the shows gave African Americans an "acceptable role" in U.S. theater.

While the minstrel performances did much to advance satire, slapstick, and ad lib comedy in the United States, they did so at great cost to the lives of the few black performers able to find employment. Bob Cole and Will Marion Cook, both classically trained musicians, found work by composing coon songs for white casts. Bert Williams and George Walker, educated black actors, were typecast into self-denigrating roles that mocked the efforts of many African Americans to assimilate into the closed, bitterly racist white culture. While sharing the stage with Williams at the Ziegfeld *Follies*, W.C. Fields remarked, "Bert Williams is the funniest man I ever saw, and the saddest man I ever knew."[7] Williams probably worked himself to death, in 1922, after performing three shows a night, every night for almost his entire career, in a futile effort to gain the respect of his audiences.

African Americans did what they could to try to combat racism on the stage. The National Association for the Advancement of Colored People (NAACP) actively promoted the work of black playwrights, helped stage their work, and openly condemned the obvious hatred that supported such plays as Edward Sheldon's *The Nigger* (1910) and, later, movies such as *The Birth of a Nation*. W.E.B. Du Bois, a driving force in the NAACP, authored *The Star of Ethiopia* in 1913, and Ridgely Torrence wrote *Three Plays for a Negro Theatre* (1917) to highlight racial tensions and inequality. African American writers and actors found a more welcome reception in the experimental Little Theatres, such as Anita Bush's Lafayette Players, who staged a number of works written by and starring blacks. Eugene O'Neill's critically acclaimed *The Emperor Jones* (1920) starred African American Charles Gilpin in the title role. Still, these were limited and largely symbolic protests against the widespread bigotry of the era. It was not until the Harlem Renaissance and Jazz Age of the 1920s that significant change in the attitudes of white audiences and artists occurred on the American stage.

Vaudeville, a French term for light theater, had deep connections to American society in the 1910s. Permanent vaudeville theaters replaced the touring revue shows around the turn of the century. Featuring a variety of stage acts, the medium provided access to the stage for thousands who otherwise could not get an audience. Most typical productions included eight or nine separate acts which included comedians, singers, dancers, acrobats, jugglers, and ventriloquists. The mixture allowed managers to offer a smorgasbord of attractions. As theater historian Robert Toll wrote, "Trained seals would not have made a satisfying evening's entertainment, but they made a fine, short vaudeville act."[8] While the vaudeville stage was as fast paced and frenetic as the new urban lifestyles, production was closely choreographed so as to provide crowds with a lasting and positive impression. The ideal show reached a crescendo twice: once before the intermission and once during the next-to-last act. Usually, these peak performances featured headliners such as W.C. Fields, Will Rogers, Eddie Cantor, the Marx Brothers, or Fanny Brice. With nine acts running from 10 to 30 minutes each, a typical evening's show might last longer than three hours.

By 1910 most major cities supported a large number of vaudeville theaters: Chicago had 22; Philadelphia, 30; and New York City, nearly 40. While chains similar to the Syndicate attempted to lock in the best acts, the need for fresh material and a surplus of unusual acts generally kept the forum open. Audiences could be ruthless in their rejection of performers, and managers did use hooks to pull failing performers from the stage. Conversely, positive audience responses could sustain a talented but repetitious act for years. While the immediacy of vaudeville could be harsh, many of those who succeeded became known for their consummate skill, attention to the smallest detail, and masterful delivery. As a result, the vaudeville stage very often was the best location for experimental European and American artists to demonstrate their craft—

especially given the cold reception by Broadway managers. In 1911 the Ballet Russe performed *Salome's Dance of the Seven Veils* on the vaudeville stage in New York. Well-known performers such as Sarah Bernhardt and Anna Pavlova also toured with vaudeville companies during the decade. Popular vaudeville actors such as Charles (soon to be Charlie) Chaplin were hesitant to turn to film because it was not considered as "respectable" as the people's theater.

Two of America's most popular vaudeville performers were Al Jolson and George M. Cohan. Jolson, known today largely as the star of the first synchronized sound film, *The Jazz Singer*, in 1927, was perhaps the most personable, energetic, and well-loved stage figure of the 1910s. Performing in a one-man show, punctuated by others during his breaks, at the Shubert's Winter Garden Theater in New York, Jolson sang, danced, performed minstrelry, and told jokes at a feverish pace which left his audiences emotionally drained. While slightly less of a performer, George M. Cohan's skills as a writer, producer, singer, and manager best embodies the spirit of popular theater. Labeling himself a "Yankee Doodle Dandy," from his hit song of 1904, he was actually born on July 3, 1878, to a family deeply connected to the theater. Performing sporadically as a child, Cohan broke onto Broadway with his siblings in 1901 and as an individual performer five years later. His songs, such as "Give My Regards to Broadway," "Yankee Doodle Dandy," and his biggest hit "Over There," were successful because he tapped into America's growing optimism and embrace of urban culture. Cohan's unique musical style fit the times, if not the critics' ideal, and his successful revues, including huge production numbers, chorus lines, and bawdy humor, became the standard of what he liked to call "show business." His ability to spot young and talented composers, such as George Gershwin, Cole Porter, and Irving Berlin, to name only a few, kept his shows lively.

The so-called girly shows also reflected the changing tastes of American theatergoers. Certainly, the appeal of young and attractive females on stage was not unique to the 1910s. Rather, it was during this decade that producers first capitalized on this temptation while remaining within the accepted norms of polite society. At the fore was Florenz Ziegfeld, born in Chicago, trained in vaudeville, and dedicated to his motto, Glorifying the American Girl. Ziegfeld's revue, called the *Ziegfeld Follies* in 1911, created a glamorous, exciting, studied, and refined stage presence for young women that would remain a standard for decades. He demanded that "his girls" have ample hips, perfect teeth, and an effervescent stage personality. The well-choreographed production numbers featured exotic costumes of feathers, chiffon, and color which often cost thousands of dollars. Despite the arduous training required, Ziegfeld received more than 15,000 applications a year from women interested in an audition—in part a reflection of the grandeur the country saw in the

Mabel Boade, *Ziegfeld Follies.* © Bettmann/CORBIS.

New York stage. While Ziegfeld had little interest in the comedy presented between dance numbers, his shows featured some of the country's most talented performers. By 1917 one could see Fanny Brice, Bert Williams, Leon Errol, Ed Wynn, W.C. Fields, Eddie Cantor, and Will Rogers in a single show performing routines they had perfected on the vaudeville stage. While the Follies continued until 1934, two years after Ziegfeld's death, the movies soon stole much of the seductive mystery and allure of his dancers. The girly show soon gave way to the motion picture sex symbol.

THE RELATIVE OBSCURITY OF AMERICAN DANCE

In contrast to the stage and screen, changes to formal American dance in the 1910s were minor. While dance numbers remained an important part of the vaudeville, theater, and film repertoire, few of these productions qualify as anything more than gloried marches parading pretty women across the stage. One noteworthy exception was the extraordinary dance team of Vernon and Irene Castle, who appeared in 1914 in the Broadway musical comedy *Watch Your Step*. The Castles' elegance and energy on stage was augmented by their willingness to coordinate their movements closely to the rhythm of the music. In addition, the Castles developed an engaging presence in the emerging nightclub and cabaret scene of New York City. Dining with the posttheater crowds, around midnight, the Castles would take control of the dance floor by their sheer grace and elegance. Adventuresome couples would slowly join the Castles until the club was awash in dance. The Castle walk was one of the first styles to be transported from the stage to the popular dance studios. The fox-trot, popularized by vaudeville comedian Harry Fox while at the *Ziegfeld Follies*, also achieved notoriety by 1913. The simplicity of the dance, plus the growing interest in ragtime music, made the fox-trot a minor fad among stage performers and their fans. With the arrival of new and dynamic musical styles, affordable recordings, and, most important, jazz in the 1920s, popular dance crazes such as the Charleston were able to take root throughout the country. The Castle walk and the fox-trot are correctly seen as harbingers of these more significant changes to American popular culture.

The popular dance crazes of mid-decade, roughly from 1912 to 1916, were particularly important because they signaled a shift in the public's values toward participatory urban nightlife. Up until 1910, theater, vaudeville, and nightclubs avoided being labeled as vulgar pastimes in large part because they successfully segregated their audience based on class, race, and gender. At that time, it would have been considered scandalous to be seen dancing in public because of the threat to these strong social norms. The cabaret settings smashed these taboos and, in

the words of historian Lewis Erenberg, "broke from the formal boundaries that had separated the entertainers from the respectable, men from
women, and upper-from lower-class culture."[9] New York clubs such as
the Folies Bergère Theater, opened by Hanery B. Harris and Jesse Lasky
in 1911, and the Sans Souci, launched by the Castles in 1913, provided
venues for women to practice public dancing during afternoon "teas"
and then for the tony late-night set to dance til dawn.

The more academic forms of public dance, such as ballet, while important in Europe since the late seventeenth century was nearly nonexistent in the United States. As with drama, ballet was experiencing a
renaissance in Europe, literally to the shrieks and howls of traditionalists.
On May 29, 1913, Russian dancer Vaslav Nijinsky's brilliant yet abrasive
interpretation of Igor Stravinsky's *Le Sacre du Printemps* (The Rite of
Spring) led to a near riot at the Paris ballet. Elsewhere, in Saint Petersburg, Moscow, and Berlin, there were equally daring changes to the classic dance format. Only rare appearances, such as the tours by the Ballet
Russe, were made in the United States, and these often were seen only
on the popular vaudeville circuit—hardly an ideal location for serious
appreciation. Some dancers did find the American markets profitable
during the 1910s, such as Anna Pavlova, Mikhail Fokine, and Mikhail
Mordin, but for the most part academic dance was noteworthy by its
absence in the United States until the 1930s.

Vernacular dance did begin to evidence some creativity during the
decade. Paralleling the changes in music and an influx of immigrants,
popular dance began the process of borrowing and synthesizing that
would lead to an explosion of creativity in the coming decade. In addition to the customary waltzes and polkas of the old country, American
barn dances, two-steps, and marches were widely known and practiced
at music halls and family gatherings throughout the country. Latin
American dances, such as the tango (which was popular in Europe as
early as 1913, but not brought back to the States for another seven years),
as well as Portuguese, Italian, and even Chinese-inspired (the Tao-Tao)
dance styles, were noted but generally ignored by the public.

Finally, the decade did see the emergence of a small number of black
tap dancers on the vaudeville stage (again proving itself to be much more
tolerant than any other medium). Tap dancing, pioneered on the stage
by men like Willie Covan, was well suited to the rapid pace of vaudeville
and the sound of modern America. Covan remarked that he "used to sit
on that curb and listen to those streetcars . . . that clickety sound, that's
where I first start hearin' it." By 1917, after a lifetime of touring, he was
accepted into many of the more popular vaudeville theaters on a regular
basis. Covan was surprised by his success because, as he well knew, "In
those days you didn't play in a white house. Only whites played in a
white theater."[10] While Covan certainly earned his privileges, the major-

ity of adult black performers rarely broke through to success at the commercial theaters.

Certainly, when compared to the changes seen in drama and film, the shift in dance was minor in the 1910s. Still, the infusion of popular routines from the stage, the growing acceptance of African American artists, the rise of cabarets and public dancing in New York City and other large urban centers, and the influence from abroad suggested that dance held great promise as a form of modern popular culture. The rapid expansion of public dance in later years was built on the subtle changes that were at work during the 1910s.

THE BUSINESS OF MOTION PICTURES
BEFORE 1910

At times, historical change can be so consequential that it is difficult to come to terms with it except by examining smaller and more manageable facts—like standing at the foot of a mountain or on the shore of an ocean, one is often left asking simply "how tall is it?" or "how many miles across?" The growth of motion pictures in the 1910s is just such an event. With the possible exception of television and the automobile, no single incident or invention has ever transformed American popular culture as quickly, as forcibly, or as permanently as the growth of the movies. Furthermore, no single decade was as consequential to American cinema as the 1910s. How tall was it? By 1910 it was estimated that more than 25 million Americans (out of a total of 92 million) attended a movie *every day* of the year. How deep? By the middle of the decade, gross annual revenues for the industry were more than $735 million, exceeding that of automobiles and trailing only the railroad, textile, steel, and oil industries. When Mary Pickford, an experienced but typical stage actress, signed with Biograph Pictures in 1909 she earned $175 per week. By 1917 First National Films had agreed to pay the shrewd actress $1 million to work in three of their pictures. Two years later, the entrepreneur joined her husband, Douglas Fairbanks, Charlie Chaplin, and D.W. Griffith to form United Artists.

These glimpses at the raw power of motion pictures are only more impressive when one considers how humbly the craft began. Early film was intended more as a parlor game for the wealthy than a new and influential mass medium. Relying on a physical phenomenon known as persistence of vision, which is responsible for our ability to see the world around us without interruption despite the fact that we close our eyes to blink every few seconds, early innovators used time-sequenced photographs in toys and spinning disk curios as early as the 1880s. American inventors Thomas Edison and William K.L. Dickson were the first to patent a machine, called a Kinetograph, which projected a series of images to create the illusion of motion, in 1889. Six years later, the Kinetoscope was introduced to show moving pictures to individuals through a peephole viewer. These coin-operated machines soon began to show up in public places, particularly hotel lobbies, but were largely ignored by Edison's influential Western Electric Company as a means of public entertainment. It was in Lyons, France, rather, that Auguste and Louis Lumière used technology from the sewing machine to perfect a public projection device in 1894. Called the Cinématographe, the mechanism was possible only because of a new and improved roll of film stock, invented by George Eastman, which could reliably withstand the threading action of the camera and projector. The first public performance by the device took place in Paris the following year.

Americans were slow to adopt the new projection device largely because of the immense popularity of the more personal Kinteoscope, but also as a result of the patent battles that emerged between rival projection and film suppliers. Edison wisely had renewed his patents and cooperated closely with both Eastman and the French, but the relative ease of manufacturing the viewers and distribution of films made it difficult for Western Electric to maintain its advantage. The firm filed suit more than 500 times for patent infringement and went to court more than 200 times to press their claims, before 1910. Seeking to unify the largest manufacturers into a trust, Edison created the Motion Picture Patents Company (MPPC) in January 1909, which included Biograph, Vitagraph, Essanay, Selig, Lubin, Kalem, two French companies, and Edison's own firm. The MPPC sought to monopolize the American market by licensing all projection equipment and by establishing an exclusive arrangement for film stock through Eastman Kodak.[11]

To understand the difficulty of MPPC's task in enforcing its legal rights, one need only appreciate the phenomenal growth and complexity of the film industry by 1910. The first projection motion picture theater opened in 1902—appropriately in Los Angeles—and by 1905 there were thousands. Operated in small storefront operations, usually with nothing more than a series of benches and a crude screen, the theaters soon took the collective name "nickelodeons" as a reflection of the typical cost for admission. By 1910 there were approximately 8,000 to 10,000 nickelodeons in daily operation across the country. Largely as a result of the entertainment "rules" established by vaudeville for popular theater, patrons demanded a variety of styles of performances in their shows. Theater owners, accordingly, wanted a reliable availability of films to rent (it made no sense to purchase a film that would be a stale floorshow within a few short weeks). Film producers, rushing in to meet the opportunity, needed to sell their products to finance the production of their next movie. As a result, distributors emerged who purchased films and circulated them for rent to the theater owners.[12]

The MPPC, in essence, hoped to standardize and control the production, distribution, and exhibition of film through their trust. The control over the production of movies seemed the easiest to secure. Preventing filmmakers from buying raw stock or cameras not controlled by the trust was fairly straightforward in most Eastern cities like Chicago and New York (where most movies were made). By contrast, some renegades successfully avoided the long reach of the MPPC by moving West to Oklahoma, Texas, and the burgeoning city of Los Angeles, which had nearly perfect natural conditions for filming as well as easy access to contraband cameras and film from Mexico. The MPPC threatened to remove exhibitors' projectors or cut off the supply of films if they were unwilling to pay the weekly licensing fees and show only MPCC movies. For distribution, the trust created a film exchange clearinghouse, called the General Film Company (1910), which circulated and underwrote the production of many films. By 1912 the Motion Pictures Patent Company controlled all but one of the 58 existing distribution companies in the United States.[13]

Not all the effects of MPPC's restricting of free trade were bad. For example, the trust increased the quality and general availability of films nationwide. They also lowered the price for most films and stabilized the acting, directing, and producing talent pools. Their willingness to remove damaged films and projectors from circulation and their ability to rent rather than sell their motion pictures supported the young industry, allowing both patrons and investors to invest their faith and resources into the medium.

Two firms were responsible for finally breaking the grip of the MPPC during the 1910s: the Greater New York Film Rental Company, the lone remaining independent distribution company, owned by William Fox, and the Independent Motion Picture (IMP) Company of Carl Laemmle. Both Fox and Laemmle were immigrants, who made their fortunes in operating strings of small nickelodeons and who understood the desires of their patrons. When, in 1912, Laemmle formed Universal Pictures, which combined IMP with a host of smaller independent producers, and moved to Los Angeles, he began to sign and promote popular movie stars and feature-length films which Americans could see only at independent theaters. Fox, too, experimented with novel production and presentation methods that appealed to moviegoers' desires for a more exciting theater experience. Both men used Americans' innate distrust of monopolics to their advantage. They filed antitrust suits and used newspapers to discredit the MPPC. By lowering costs and making better films, the two effectively undermined the power of the trust.

THE STYLE AND CONTENT OF EARLY MOVIES

When commenting upon the nature of the films, it is important to recognize the difference between movies made before and after the downfall of the MPPC. With few exceptions, movies made before 1910 were quickly forgotten. Limited to single reels, which provided less than ten minutes of screen time, and filmed in a day or two, early movies spent little time in developing good stories or sympathetic characters. Much of the material produced was vulgar, such as early shorts like *How Bridget Served the Salad Undressed*, and respectable actors generally shunned the medium until the last years of the 1900s. Most films, sold by the foot, were little more than a series of stunts, travelogs, or hackneyed melodramas pumped out at a phenomenal rate. David Wark (D.W.) Griffith, for example, directed more than 400 single-reel films between 1908 and 1913.[14] While this groundbreaking director would soon go on to completely reconfigure the style and structure of film, only rare glimpses of his genius are evident in these early offerings.

The nature of these audiences is also important to understand. While the urban working class made up a sizable percentage of those who attended films, by 1910 they were in no way the only patrons. Rural and urban middle-class citizens also frequented movies in great numbers. As with vaudeville, these diverse audiences demanded high quality, ingenuity, and excitement. One bias that exists today is that films of the 1910s suffer from poor production values—the images are scratchy, the action too fast, and, of course, there was no sound. In reality, reproductions today do not re-create how the films were originally shown. The film quality was very good, and the finished prints were often tinted with colors and used extensive in-theater sound accompaniment. The current versions that exist are only black-and-white reproductions of second or third copies of an original, which was usually saved only after a long production run in theaters. More problematic, the reproducing equipment, by the 1930s, ran at a faster pace than the original, hand-cranked cameras captured the action. When we see these speeded-up versions, remember that they are only pale copies of the originals.

Finally, movie acting and narratives took on decidedly different forms from those that were used in live theater. When the accomplished actress Sarah Bernhardt starred in the movie *Queen Elizabeth* (1912), her actions seem exaggerated and foolish. Many other early actors in film used the same overly expressive stage style with similar results. The new reality was that the closeness of camera canceled the need for dramatic embellishment. Each viewer could see the actors clearly and, of course, the words were printed for all to read. Storytelling also changed as a result of the new technology. It was now possible for writers and directors to cut scenes that did not further the plot; called "ellipses" by filmmakers.

In *The Great Train Robbery* (1903), director Edwin S. Porter was the first to experiment with cutaways to achieve this effect. When combined with the visual effects of French director, and trained magician, George Mélies, whose now famous *A Trip to the Moon* (1902) employed artificial lighting, multiple exposures, and hand-painted frames, movies were freed from the traditional narrative of the stage. American film pioneer D.W. Griffith later acknowledged his debt to Méliès when he wrote, "I owe everything to him."[15]

HOLLYWOOD, THE STAR SYSTEM, AND FEATURE FILMS

The combined growth of Hollywood, the spread of the star system, the use of feature-length (multireel) films, and the rise of the new movie theaters signaled the true emergence of modern film in the United States. While the MPPC loomed as an obstacle, by 1911, when the major independents and even some of the licensed production companies moved to California, the effective control of the trust had been broken. George Spoor and his business partner, Gilbert Anderson (known for his screen name of Bronco Billy), founders of Essenay (named after their initials), were the first to relocate in 1910, and they began to produce hundreds of traditional film shorts. By 1914, 52 companies were in town purchasing vast tracks of land from the nearby lemon and orange growers. While competition between the firms was fierce and even turned violent—director Cecil B. De Mille was shot at twice while filming *The Squaw Man* in 1913—Hollywood provided movie producers enough space, actors, and set locations for most to concentrate on reaping the windfall profits of the era.

The spread of the star system, with well-known, well-liked actors whose films were patronized by the public, also helped to undermine the MPPC. Before this, most actors were paid by the day for their service and rarely received screen credit for their work. When actors did catch the eye of the public, either for their looks or acting abilities, they received fan mail addressed to "the Vitagraph Girl," "Biograph Girl," or, nicknames such as American Sweetheart, Mary Pickford. The appearance of fan magazines added fuel to the movement. Publications such as *Motion Picture Story Magazine* and *Photoplay* helped propagate the glamour of film stars. In June 1910, the most popular Vitagraph Girl, Florence Lawrence, was labeled the first motion picture star by fan magazine *New York Dramatic Mirror*. Lawrence was also the first actor "stolen" by another producer, the rebellious Carl Laemmle, for the then unheard of sum of $175 a week. When Pickford followed from Lawrence to IMP, it signaled the start of intense bidding wars for the biggest stars.

Feature-length films also placed pressure on established producers accustomed to the mass-produced shorts. While the idea of using multiple reels to show a film was, in itself, nothing revolutionary, what producers showed on these films was new. Longer films meant more complex narratives. These, in turn, required artistic directors to tell the story visually in ways that conveyed the appropriate emotions at the designated time. Features also created stronger bonds between the audience and their stars, quickening the cycle between the public's demand for their favorite actors and the studio's production of films.

The expansion of film content allowed studios to standardize their fare while it gave artists a creative new medium. Genre or type films first appeared in the 1910s as a result of the feature. Probably the best example of this was the success of the movie serial. Each week in these serials, which literally had no ending, the stars were placed in harm's way only to be rescued in the next installment in ways that were ever more daring. With little plot development, idiotic characters, and corny morality, the serials were easy to produce and proved to be popular with the public. The most famous of these, *The Perils of Pauline* (1914), starred Pearl White in a role that she would reprise, under different character names but always blindly trusting the villain, until 1923. While cliffhangers certainly brought people back to the theater, they did little to advance the craft.

Finally, the appearance of luxurious movie palaces throughout the decade signaled a qualitative shift in how Americans experienced the movies. While the MPPC retained control over many of the smaller nickelodeons, by 1910 moviegoers were becoming increasingly dissatisfied with these small outfits. These shops were opened as inexpensive, convenient, and quick diversions, and few exhibitors had plans to invest money in more comfortable seats, better screens, or ambience. Taking a tour through several run-down, neighborhood nickelodeons, critics from the film magazine *Motion Picture World* wrote in 1911: "No wonder the societies and health authorities try to bar children from the moving picture shows!"[16] By contrast, movie houses developed during the 1910s were designed to seat hundreds of patrons comfortably in an environment of luxury. U.S. architect Thomas Lamb built the Regeant, the Strand Theater, the Rialto, and the Rivoli for his boss, S.L. "Roxy" Rothafel, from 1913 to 1918, in New York. By the end of the decade he had designed nearly 300 such "movie palaces," creating a new standard for exhibitors that few of the nickelodeon operators could match.

Certainly, the sudden appearance of Hollywood, the star system, feature films, and the new cinemas had a destabilizing effect on the MPPC organization. The trust was undermined in its efforts to control the industry by entrepreneurs who relied on the public's willingness to pay for a better form of entertainment. Yet until the end of the decade, no

Detroit, Michigan, Temple Theatre auditorium. Courtesy of the
Library of Congress.

rival structure existed to compete with the MPPC for supremacy. As a
result, the stars and film content of the 1910s played a pivotal role in the
nature and direction of motion pictures. Pioneers in both acting and directing emerged during the decade with profound consequences for
American popular culture.

THE STARS

Central to the rise of the movies in the decade was the new role of
women in them. Often playing near or beyond the edges of social acceptance, female stars both expanded the perceived boundaries of Victorian righteousness while, oddly, they also strengthened them. Dorothy
and Lilian Gish, both of whom became celebrities under the direction of
Griffith, personify this creative tension. Dorothy, the older sister, was
less popular than her sibling but, as fewer of her earliest films survive,
it is unclear who was the better actor. As late as 1964 she was performing
on stage to rave reviews. Usually Dorothy was assigned supporting roles
that built upon her ability to project warmth, mischief, and female sensuality in doses acceptable to most audiences.

Lilian Gish was one of the eminent performers of the era. When D.W.

Griffith was asked if Lilian was the world's greatest actress he retorted, "Who is greater?" Griffith certainly had confidence in a woman who played the leading female role in his most critically important films, such as *The Birth of a Nation* (1915), *Intolerance* (1916), *Hearts of the World* (1918), and *Broken Blossoms* (1920). The junior sister, who had been performing on the stage since childhood, constrained by Griffith's heavy directorial hand, was compelled to play fragile, youthful beauties with a deep but tragic strength. Ironically, she served as Griffith's unofficial and certainly uncredited assistant director throughout most of these productions. Critics contend that her greatest works lay beyond the 1910s when she was able to give full expression to her dynamic range as an actor.

If Dorothy and Lilian Gish represented the warm and demure Victorian woman-child ideal, then the mysterious Theda Bara characterized the threatening and sexually charged, liberated woman. Bara, who was born Theodosia Goodman to quiet, middle-class parents in Cincinnati, Ohio, was rumored in the fan magazines to have immigrated from northern Africa with a mixture of Egyptian and Arab blood and an ancestry that traced back to the Ptolemies. She seemingly appeared from nowhere in *A Fool There Was* (1915), as a "sexual vampire" who seduced and ruined unsuspecting men. Her role as a vamp was central to almost all of the 40 movies she made at Fox. William Fox orchestrated a publicity campaign that took full advantage of the sensational movie. It was leaked to the press that her stage name was an anagram for "Arab Death," and her hobbies were listed as astrology and alchemy. Unfortunately for Bara, her phenomenal celebrity status barred her from other, more interesting roles. She made one attempt to break out of her typecast when she played a sweet and likable lead in *Kathleen Mavoureen* (1919). It was both a critical and commercial disaster.

While female stars like Dorothy and Lilian Gish and Theda Bara enjoyed immense popularity and the financial rewards that accompany commercial success, each found herself confined by the roles she was assigned to play. While all three portrayed women who were publicly confident and intellectually capable, their screen personas contained strong support for the prevailing biases toward the "proper place" of women in American society. Sadly, it would be decades before the role of the liberated women would again approach the possibilities of these early years in Hollywood.

Mary Pickford

While these examples suggest that Hollywood's star system constrained, rather than freed, dramatic artists on the screen, the astonishing careers of Mary Pickford and Charlie Chaplin provide strong counterevidence: the "New Personality" film stars were able to puncture many of society's strongest prejudices and intolerance. Pickford was born Gladys Mary Smith in Toronto in 1893. Following her father's death, she and her siblings were allowed to perform on the stage, where they changed their names. Pickford's small frame and noble bearing gave her a strong stage presence, and she had risen to prominence in the New York theater by 1909. Facing a rare stretch of unemployment, Pickford decided to augment her stage income with performances in film. While her movie roles were similar to many other young women's, her pixielike appearance gave her a special sympathetic quality that instantly attracted audiences. Lacking any credits, she became known as "Little Mary" or the "Biograph Girl" in most of her fan mail.

Unlike many other female stars, Pickford proved quite adept at taking full advantage of the economic potential of the star system. Stolen away from Biograph by Carl Laemmle, Pickford tactfully jumped from IMP to Majestic, then back to Biograph, next to Famous Players, then American Film, and finally First National. With each new contract, her salary and creative freedom increased, from $175 per week while first at Biograph (a comfortable living for an actor) to $2,000 per week by 1915 and finally the million dollar contract from First National in 1918.

Pickford's screen characters remained fairly constant throughout the decade. While usually the unfair victim of poverty, society, or an abusive male, Mary showed strength and resilience in her ability to overcome obstacles. Because of her small size, large eyes, and curly hair, Pickford was repeatedly cast as an adolescent, causing problems later in the decade, which could be solved only by designing oversized sets and furniture to help shrink the appearance of the nearly thirty-year-old actor. Even her much publicized divorce of Owen Moore and marriage to Douglas Fairbanks in 1919 did little to damage the luster of America's Sweetheart.

While her work throughout the 1910s remained fairly even, it was her association with D.W. Griffith that solidified her star status. Early movies such as Lena and the Geese (1911), The New York Hat (1912), and even her successful stage run in The Good Little Devil (1913) established her charm and gentility. But it was with Griffith in Tess of Storm County (1914) that the Little Mary persona was firmly rooted in the minds of the viewing public. Griffith's strong direction and exceptional eye for editing captured the rebelliousness, independence, and energy of youthful freedom that was so appealing to moviegoers. In The Eternal Grind (1916), Pickford played a poor sewing machine operator who forces (at gun point) the wild son of the factory owner to wed the working-class girl whom he had impregnated. True to Griffith's style, by the end of the film, all were converted by Mary's simple virtues, resulting in Pickford's character also wedding an heir to the fortune and the rehabilitation of the greedy capitalist. While her later productions, such as Rebecca of Sunnybrook Farm

Mary Pickford. © Bettmann/CORBIS.

(1917) and *M'liss* (1918), demonstrated an actor of wide range and immense depth, she never strayed far from her central character.

In both her business dealings and screen roles, Pickford tapped into
a growing awareness by American women of their potential for independence from men. Her contract battles, public appearances, weekly
newspaper column, and national advocacy for women's suffrage demonstrated to America a new and self-aware modern woman. She ac-

knowledged, "My success has been due to the fact that women like the pictures in which I appear. I think I admire most in the world the girls who earn their own living. I am proud to be one of them."[17] While she acted in films that were written and directed within the milieu of strong Victorianism (especially under Griffith), her star power and screen presence usually overshadowed the stagy morality of the stories. Of all the stars of the 1910s—including Fairbanks, Mack Sennett, and Chaplin—none had the public's admiration more than she. By merging her real life power and popularity with a willful femininity in her films, Mary Pickford helped to recast the role of women in American society.

Charlie Chaplin

In an era that still today recognizes and cherishes the "Little Tramp" character of Charlie Chaplin, it is hard to appreciate the worldwide celebrity status and hysteria that accompanied "Charliemania" in the 1910s. As film historian Gerald Mast wrote, no one "exerted a greater cultural influence, both in America and abroad, than [Chaplin] in those first four years between 1914 and 1918."[18] In those years, Chaplin not only dominated American cinema but also appeared in popular music, children's games, cartoons, and many other forms of popular entertainment. In July 1915, New York City alone hosted 30 Chaplin amateur nights where dozens of Derby-wearing tramps waddled across local stages, and shared a dim part of the brilliant spotlight that illuminated the original. By the end of the decade, in addition to the millions worldwide, Chaplin counted among his friends and professed admirers Albert Einstein, Winston Churchill, Mahatma Gandhi, James Joyce, Pablo Picasso, and Bertolt Brecht.[19]

Like Pickford, Charles Chaplin was not born in America. He arrived in the slums of Lambeth, London, in 1889, to parents who made a living performing at local music halls. Charles and his half-brother, Sydney, soon joined them on the stage. Both boys proved talented enough to earn jobs with the celebrated Karno pantomime company, which toured the American vaudeville circuit in 1911 and 1913. Charles had earned a reputation as a tremendous acrobat and physical comedian which was good enough for Mack Sennett, in May 1913, to offer him a lucrative $150 per week contract, guaranteed for one year, which lured a hesitant Chaplin to the slightly disrespectful movie industry.

While with Keystone, Chaplin made 35 films in which his character tended to mock the stereotypic English gentleman (a role Chaplin had perfected over years of practice and, no doubt, had seen as a child). In his second film for Sennett, *Kid Auto Races at Venice* (1914), Chaplin displayed his tramp character for the first time. He assembled the outward appearance of the character, who he called "the little fellow"—false mus-

Motion picture still showing Charlie Chaplin. Courtesy of the Library of Congress.

tache, loose and ill-matched clothes, the Derby hat—from castaway props found on the Keystone lot. The character evolved from an abrasive and slightly contemptible man to the lovable and honorable free spirit that immediately captured the attention of moviegoers.

The combination of Sennett's productivity and the actor's skill established the newly christened "Charlie" Chaplin as a star. While a January

1915 poll of readers of *Motion Picture Magazine* failed to cite him in their top one hundred actors, competing production companies were quick to note the packed theaters and rising anticipation for Chaplin's work. That month, he left Sennett for Essanay for $1,250 per week and a $10,000 signing bonus. One year later, Mutual inked him for $10,000 per week and a $150,000 bonus. Chaplin later recalled that the Mutual offer came "[l]ike an avalanche," the "money and success came with increasing momentum; it was all bewildering, frightening—but wonderful." His climb was not over, however. In 1918 Chaplin signed with First National for $1 million and complete creative control as producer, director, writer, and star.[20]

While the business concerns offering him such sums were convinced of the soundness of their investment, the press was quick to question whether Chaplin, or any star, was worth it. While there is no answer to such a question, almost all of his films of the era made large profits and many today are still regarded as classics. His best work during the decade stems from the Mutual years—what he called "the happiest period of my career"—and include *One A.M.*, *The Pawnshop*, *The Rink*, *Easy Street*, *The Immigrant*, and *The Adventurer*, all released between 1916 and 1917. In each, Chaplin deepened and strengthened his character's empathy for the world around him. For example, in *Easy Street* he examines social reform movements and in *The Immigrant* the problems of capitalism. What makes the films so remarkable is that he is able to make his audience aware of class tensions and poverty without preaching or losing his ability to entertain.[21]

With an international appeal that easily transcended the strong class lines of the 1910s, intellectuals and artists began to take greater notice of the new medium. In many ways, the recognition of Chaplin's "genius" and the seemingly easy way in which he moved through society provided theorists with a living example of how to connect the arts with the masses in ways that were meaningful for both. The lack of sound probably helped Chaplin, who was so adept at using his expressions, body, and props to convey universal emotions. When sound did arrive in the movies, Chaplin was unwilling to put words in the tramp's mouth and relied on his visual communication skills to the end. It has been suggested by many that Chaplin listened too closely to his own supporters, and that his later films and public advocacy for the poor and powerless distracted rather than advanced his artistry.

Genius or not, Chaplin was able to interject a subtle criticism of American society that resonated with the experiences of millions. In many of his films, Chaplin portrayed law enforcement officials as cruel and menacing rather than agents of justice. Institutions such as businesses, the church, and government show little concern for the real suffering of the people. While Charlie does arrive to apply a bandage to the problems—

often with only a smile, some food, or a well-placed kick in the pants—frequently his movies ended with him departing honorably beaten or his character awakening from a dream. In either case, the problems were on public display and left to be solved by an audience which probably had only stopped in for a good laugh.

While Chaplin's personal life and opinions would distract from his international fame in the coming decades, in the 1910s the only dark cloud that hovered over him was World War I. As a British citizen (he never pursued U.S. citizenship) in a country that was decidedly anti-German, Chaplin was regarded as slighting his country in its hour of need. As a result, Chaplin became very active in wartime propaganda both in selling Liberty Bonds and in filmmaking. In May 1918, he released *Shoulder Arms* which had Charlie going through boot camp, in the trenches, and assaulting a German position. Significantly, Chaplin did not portray the Germans as subhuman beasts, but rather suggested that it was the war itself that was the root of human suffering.

While the star system was not the direct cause of the collapse of the MPPC, it certainly hastened its demise. Stars quickened the pace of change in Hollywood, opening doors for entrepreneurial talents like Chaplin and making it difficult for the trust to keep up with public demand. The creative freedoms afforded the actors in the 1910s were soon lost. As suggested by the frustrating career of Theda Bara, most celebrities would be forced to play roles orchestrated by studio moguls. Many of these roles were traditional and often monotonous recreations of accepted social norms: the independent and honest cowboy, the tough city kid, the morally pure but helpless woman. Still, the star system did demonstrate that public demand had a new and significant role to play in shaping the direction of modern motion pictures.

THE POWER OF THE FEATURE FILM

Feature, or multireel, films also had a decisive effect on the collapse of the MPPC. By expanding the format of film, independents opened the door to creative talents who distanced themselves from the more traditional suppliers. The shift from strict rental fees to a smaller lease with a percentage of the box-office receipts ensured exhibitors that the new, longer films would always have the interests of the ticket buyers in mind. As a result, cinematic storytelling became more complex and the characters more real. In the case of the career of D.W. Griffith, this innovation allowed for radical changes in the ways in which films could be structured as well as how the moviegoing public would receive them.

Not all feature films led to any significant change. In the case of the portrayal of African Americans, for example, the feature-length movie simply amplified many of the prevailing biases. Historian Donald Bogle tallied at least five separate categories of black stereotypes that were created or accentuated in film, including the "Uncle Tom," the "Coon," the "Tragic Mulatto," the "Mammy," and the "Brutal Black Buck." While shifts occurred from time to time, these five basic types "that were dominant black characters for the next half century were first introduced" in the 1910s.[22]

Sadly, many examples can be cited to support Bogle's observation. In *Confederate Spy* (1910), *For Massa's Sake* (1911), and, of course, the first version of *Uncle Tom's Cabin* (1914), which allowed a black stage actor to play Tom, African Americans were categorized as acceptable only when they served whites faithfully and unquestioningly, and were quick to turn to God, and not against racist America, in order to deal with their suffering. In *Ten Pickaninnies* (1904), or *How Rastus Got His Turkey* (1910), both of which spawned a host of serials, blacks were portrayed as simpletons—"coons" without a care other than the next meal or the next song and dance. The "tragic mulatto" character appeared in a number of films in which (predominantly) women tried to pass as white in spite of the fact that they carried "black blood." The catastrophic consequences of their uppity behavior, as seen in *The Debt* (1912), *In Humanity's Cause*, *In Slavery Days*, and *The Octoroon* (all 1913), was proof of God's benign wrath and nature's strict hierarchy. The mammy role, numbering almost too many to note but on display in *Coon Town Suffragettes* (1914), was the female counterpart to Tom. Finally, the "Brutal Black Buck" was used infrequently but packed the most emotional charge for white audiences. This character was male, emancipated, and interested primarily in gratifying his insatiable desires for white women, relaxation, or alcohol, in no particular order.

The significance of these stereotypes is not their novelty, which date back to the eighteenth century, but rather the power provided them by the feature film. Movies worked to create an acceptable and agreed upon mythology, in the case of African Americans, which was more accurately a description of the fears and ignorance of the white artists who gave them expression. When combined with the artistry of a director like D.W. Griffith, such imagery could be harnessed as a powerful incentive for whites to lash out at the powerless.

D.W. GRIFFITH

In ancient Greek mythology, Prometheus was a titan who stole fire from the Olympian gods for the benefit of mankind. As punishment, Zeus had Prometheus chained to a rock so that vultures could eat at his liver (which Zeus replaced each evening). D.W. Griffith was a movie director who first gave meaning and artistry to the feature film. His editorial prowess, sharp eye for talent, and, above all, willingness to take

D.W. Griffith. Courtesy of the Library of Congress.

risks in his films resulted in some of the most important movies of all time. Today Griffith is seen as the key to understanding the development of American *and* European narrative film; his movies are required viewing as sources of inspiration and enlightenment. Yet within this canon of work we also find an artist whose social agenda included racism, a rejection of the modern independent women, and an utter disregard for historical fact. When Griffith died in 1948 he was not only destitute, but

also largely ignored by the cinematic community for his outdated prejudices and sappy Victorian morality. Yet if we are to continue to play
the vultures, and pick at Griffith's faults, it is vital to understand and
credit him with the fire that so deeply changed motion pictures.

Griffith, born in Kentucky in 1875, began his career in films by accident. Intending to write melodramatic plays for the stage, he turned to
acting and screen writing out of financial necessity in 1907. Within a year,
Biograph offered him the chance to direct. Griffith's bias against the
dreary single-reel films was well justified, but the unstructured nature
of the craft allowed him to experiment as long as he continued to pump
out the product. From his tentative beginning until 1913, Griffith produced more than 450 shorts for Biograph. While the scripts he followed
were no better than others, his filming, editorial, and technical abilities
were being honed. In addition, he became an astute judge of talent, surrounding himself with natural actors such as Pickford and the Gish sis-
ters, and gifted cameramen like Billy Bitzer, who could translate his
cinematic vision into actual film scenes. As Gerald Mast wrote, "Griffith's
discoveries were empirical, not theoretical" during these early years.[23]

Soon, Griffith's experience, vision, and accomplished assistants began
to produce movies that carried a dramatic authority rivaling the stage.
It is highly ironic that Griffith, who entered the craft with a strong bias
against movies, perfected the means by which film surpassed the stage
for dramatic presentation. Admittedly, he was not alone in this movement. The Great Train Robbery had pioneered the crosscut editing style
that became a Griffith trademark. While Griffith's Enoch Arden (1911) is
credited with being the first American film to extend to two reels, Europeans had been experimenting with the "feature" even earlier. What
Griffith did do that was original was to package them all together, resulting in a greater impact than simply the sum of their parts. He frequently changed camera positions to give single-room scenes greater
depth, panned across the room, or mounted the camera on tracks to
achieve a rolling effect. He pioneered the use of closeups and faraway
shots, fades in and out, variable lighting (so that one object or character
in a scene was highlighted), and he used scenes consisting of three-
dimensional props (most earlier films used painted backgrounds), the
outdoors, buildings, and other objects to create mood. The dynamic emotional power unleashed by crosscuts, which allowed the viewer to see
action taking place at several locations at the same time, were simply
impossible to duplicate in live theater. In A Corner in Wheat (1909), he
used short crosscutting scenes to compare workers shuffling through
breadlines for handouts while industrialists stuffed themselves at a gourmet banquet. In terms of film study, Griffith changed the "grammar and
rhetoric" of movie narratives, making it easier for directors to tell com-

plex and emotional stories which did not rely on dense written or verbal communication (after all, these were silent films). When compared to stage dramas today, motion pictures move at a faster pace and are able to convey more subtle emotions more quickly in large part because of the techniques discovered by Griffith.

His novel approach to filming did not happen by accident. Griffith's experienced crews of actors and technicians remained with him for long stretches of his career. Billy Bitzer served as Griffith's chief cameraman from 1908 to 1924. Lilian Gish, as noted above, acted in most of his films of the 1910s and knew him so well that she performed many of the duties of an assistant director. Griffith pressured his film companies to retain the services of these craftsmen as their market value increased over the years. He also held scheduled, expensive, and time-consuming dress rehearsals for his films, something undreamed of in an era when most movies were shot in about a week. Moreover, beginning in 1912, Griffith began to seek out longer, more difficult scripts and subjects to film. By late 1913, while he was acknowledged as a uniquely talented director, Biograph balked at the added expense of his films. Unlike movie stars, directors did not (yet) draw patrons to the cinemas. Griffith left for the independent Mutual Company, taking with him his entire cast and crew, with an agreement giving him complete creative control over some films provided that he mass-produce others.

With his reputation as a master technical filmmaker secure, it is important to look at the types of stories Griffith selected in this second, more liberated stage of his career. In *The New York Hat* (1912), starring Mary Pickford, Griffith displayed how he was wrestling with his strong sense of sentimentality and Victorian morality. Pickford's waif character longs for a hat that might transport her from her dreary life. A young reverend (played by longtime Griffith actor Lionel Barrymore) buys Mary the hat which scandalously links her to him in the minds of the town gossips. The tension between Mary's desire for independence and her abusive father's insistence that she stay at home and remain dependent is conveniently broken when her mother dies and leaves the young girl in the care of the idealistic clergyman. In the end, the characters marry and the problems are easily solved. Certainly Griffith understood the edgy emotions and morality at work in such a film. His solution, to break the tension through a traditional melodramatic device like a mother's death or marriage, reflects his adherence to the accepted social conventions that plagued most of his films. While easy answers and moral certainty might have suited Griffith's sensibilities, they were extremely difficult to use in films that tackled complex social issues. This problem was certainly apparent in his most famous productions: *The Birth of A Nation* and *Intolerance*.

The Birth of a Nation

The Birth of a Nation (1915) was intended by Griffith to consummate the merger of his technical virtuosity with the power of a modern epic. Knowing that European directors had experimented with monumental feature films, such as the eight-reel *Quo Vadis* (1913) released in Italy with a cast of thousands, Griffith began work on a similar project intended to dramatize the historic sweep of the Civil War and Reconstruction in the United States. Griffith chose for his landmark statement in film a book written by Thomas Dixon Jr., titled *The Clansman: A Historical Romance of the Ku Klux Klan* (1905). As the name implies, the novel portrayed members of the KKK as heroes bent on returning the South to white rule. Racist to the core, the text was immensely popular with Southerners such as Griffith, whose father served in the Confederacy, sympathetic to the idea that the South had fought the war out of racial pride while knowing all along that theirs was a lost cause (a false historical pretext to begin with). Griffith shot the work in nine weeks, after six weeks of rehearsal, using no formal plan other than that devised in his own mind. Costing $110,000 and running thirteen reels, the movie was premiered in New York under the title *The Clansman* on March 3, 1915. After viewing the magnificent epic, Dixon suggested that the title be changed to reflect the importance of the film's thesis.

The critically acclaimed movie was a great financial success for Griffith. President Woodrow Wilson, who was given a private screening by Dixon, a personal friend from his days at Johns Hopkins University, proclaimed that the film was "like writing history with lightning. And my only regret is that it is all so terribly true."[24] Similar reviews nationwide suggest it was not Griffith's directoral organizational and editing, but rather the offensive racial stereotyping that affected white audiences so powerfully. The "brutal black buck" typecast was everywhere, from sex-crazed crowds of freed blacks to an armed renegade named Gus who pursued a fair woman to her death. Mulattos plotted ways in which to destroy white society while black bumpkins used their time in the state legislatures to get drunk. Central to the drama was the assumption that there were "proper places" for blacks in America, and that the mixture of races inevitably led to chaos. Only the bravery of the Klan was able to restore white supremacy, if temporarily.

The response by fair-minded Americans was, thankfully, swift and loud. Progressives such as Jane Addams labeled the film an abomination. New York activist and rabbi Stephen Wise called *The Birth of a Nation* "an indescribably foul and loathsome libel on a race of human beings." The NAACP organized massive demonstrations in Chicago and Boston. Injunctions were filed in several locations, and the movie was eventually banned in five states and fifteen cities. Griffith was stung by the criticism.

To him, it was the unnatural conditions of Reconstruction, not innate depravity in blacks, that led to the fictional and devilish behavior on the part of his characters (all played by white minstrels). That this message was equally racist, historically incorrect, and never once made explicit in the two-hour-plus movie escaped Griffith's notice. To try to set the record straight, while making a grand statement for artistic freedom, he sank all of the profits made from *Birth* into his next epic film, *Intolerance*.

Intolerance and Beyond

Seeking to distance himself from the roiling domestic politics in the United States, Griffith made *Intolerance* (1916) in order to show "how hatred and intolerance, through all the ages, have battled against love and charity."[25] Using four separate narratives—the trial and death of Jesus, the Saint Bartholomew's Day Massacre of Protestants in medieval France, the fall of Babylon, and the persecution of a reformed criminal in contemporary America—and an enigmatic mother rocking a cradle (played by Lilian Gish), Griffith hoped to draw historical connections between the common ways societies have overridden the rights of their citizens because of ignorance, hypocrisy, and, of course, intolerance. Running more than three hours, the film was amazingly complex with all four narratives combined together. The mixture proved too confusing for audiences to follow and the pacifist message ran counter to a period when the drums of war were beating loudly in the United States. The fortune that Griffith earned for *Birth* was lost in an instant.

As a piece of film history, *Intolerance* was an amazing effort by a mature artist to transform his medium. Griffith spent nearly two million dollars to film the spectacle and employed 15,000 extras for the segment on Babylon alone. His continuing mastery of editing, filming, understated acting, and lighting techniques nearly carried the film. It has been estimated that no movie even approached *Intolerance* for its visual nuance and complexity until Orson Welles made *Citizen Kane* in 1941. The international influence of the film was phenomenal, shaping both the Soviet and German styles for decades.

To say that Griffith's career after *Intolerance* was a failure would be wrong. He directed several more phenomenal films, including the wonderful *Broken Blossoms* (1919, in many ways his best picture) and *Isn't Life Wonderful?* (1924), as well as a good number of commercially successful and enjoyable movies, such as *A Romance of Happy Valley* (1918), *True Heart Susie* (1919), and *The Greatest Question* (1919). Still, after 1916, his career went into a decline that Griffith could not recover from. After 1924, he lost creative control over his projects and proved to be a less than capable studio operative. His last film, in 1931, was a commercial and financial embarrassment.

Griffith's legacy is complex. His eventual failure was largely due to the narratives he chose to film. *Birth* and *Intolerance* were stiff morality plays that favored Victorian sensibilities which were rapidly fading from memory. In addition, his movies suggested that easy answers were possible if people would simply return to these values. But was the meaning of Christ's persecution or Reconstruction really that we all should try harder to act as gentlemen, civilly and within society's rules, while in public? Griffith's *stories* failed to connect in any deep or meaningful way with his audience. Except for *Birth*, which did resonate with prevailing racial fears, most of Griffith's popular films were remembered because of the actors who appeared in them. On the other hand, *The Birth of a Nation* proved conclusively that American audiences would accept complex (and long) movies that appealed to their intellect as well as their emotions. The power of his imagery and editing skills, so evident in *Intolerance*, was soon grafted to even the most formulaic Hollywood offerings.

CONCLUSION

While the degree of change in the various performing arts during the decade varied greatly, the tensions between the artistic and commercial intent was common to drama, dance, and film. In theater this conflict resolved itself through the formation of small, experimental little theaters where the new dramatic style could flourish. In dance, prevailing racial biases against African Americans effectively prevented the introduction of modern music which, in effect, stifled the spread of newer forms of dance. Still, the connection between popular music and stage musicals was growing deeper and laid the groundwork for the introduction of new dance styles fueled by the spread of jazz in the 1920s. Artistic freedom was greatest in the movies, as the domineering Motion Pictures Patent Company lost its grip on the industry and before the rise of large conglomerates.

As in other forms of popular culture in the 1910s, the aging Victorian standards of morality lost ground to more relativistic, less absolute measurements of social acceptability. The greater breadth of expression and realism in the arts, particularly in drama and film, made simplistic solutions to deep-seated social problems appear foolish and naive. As the once silent voices of many women and minorities grew louder, the performing arts helped Americans sort through these complexities and try to build a new common culture. While their failures far out weigh their successes, this "confused period" was undeniably one of great beginnings in this direction.

The 1910s

11

Travel

A number of significant innovations and long-lasting changes were made to the ways in which Americans traveled during the 1910s. From the novelties of the airplane to the everyday travel of streetcars, citizens found that getting from one place to another was easier and quicker than at any previous time in history. The variety of transportation, which ranged from the automobile and ocean liner to traditional horse carts and railroads, allowed an immense amount of personal expression in one's choice of motion. Accordingly, the *ways* in which people traveled said as much about themselves as their final destinations. Soon, driving a car or taking an elevated train came to represent one's relative status in society. Even when disaster struck, such as during the infamous maiden voyage of RMS *Titanic* in 1912, Americans read into the tragedy criticisms about modern society and culture rather than the seaworthiness of the White Star Line's massive flagship. At root was a concern that America was moving too fast and too carelessly into the modern era.

DESTINATIONS

What had not changed in the 1910s were the destinations. People still planned weekend visits to relatives, day trips to local amusements (such as parks, museums, and other places of entertainment), and annual vacations to regional resorts. What was new was that, by the end of the decade, these visits were increasingly farther away from one's home and required more cash outlays than in previous years. For example, in 1910 a typical vacation ocean cruise could be purchased for less than $60 per

person (a price well within the range of the typical worker), which included a berth and meals for a 12-day round-trip voyage from New York
City to Halifax, Nova Scotia. Similar trips were available for runs along
the Atlantic seaboard to warm-weather ports in Florida and the Caribbean. For more money, one could travel to Europe or Latin America via
regular, and increasingly quicker, boats. Railroads provided access to a
number of popular attractions, including Niagra Falls and the Grand
Canyon, which previously had been visited by those within a relatively
small radius. In conjunction with the growth of these junkets was the
spread of hotel accommodations. For around a dollar a day, the typical
traveler could find comfortable housing in just about any American city.

The growing popularity of the automobile gave rise to a sense of personal freedom and allowed for a number of new attractions to emerge.
As historian Hal Barron noted, for America's large rural population, "the
automobile increased rural access to consumer culture and had a dramatic impact on the economic geography of rural society." Farm patron-
age at small-town attractions grew and reinforced the connection
between citizens in both rural and urban locations.[1]

Cars also gave Americans access to a growing movement known as
the Chautauqua. The Circuit Chautauqua, which first appeared in the
1870s in southwestern New York State, was like a traveling troupe of
actors, motivational speakers, and religious revivalists. Largely independent of formal associations, the Chautauquas varied greatly by region
and local economy, but in general appealed to families seeking educational and cultural entertainment throughout the decade. A typical Chautauqua might last three days and include a selection from a Shakespeare
play or a dramatization of Dickens, a noted speaker (such as William
Jennings Bryan), music, movies, poetry readings, and social commentary
by both humorists and reformers. The popularity of the events (estimates
range as high as 30 to 45 million people attending by the mid-1920s) led
to great competition between the tours. The movement had ebbed by the
1930s, largely due to radio, which provided similar entertainment in the
home, the Great Depression, and, ironically, the automobile, which provided a wider array of entertainment options.

Camping, too, became more widespread as a result of growing transportation options. The desire to experience the great outdoors became
almost a national passion in the 1910s. The combined effects of Progressive reformers, who spoke against the poor quality of life within the
cities, the growing access to unspoiled natural environments throughout
the country, increased promotion by railroad companies hoping to spur
a tourism boom, and the interest generated by the formation of a National Park system led many to load up their cars with newly purchased
camping gear and to strike out for the wilds. While Congress had set
aside parts of the Yosemite Valley in California, as well as parks in Yel-

Camping in the woods. Courtesy of the Library of Congress.

lowstone in Montana and Wyoming, in the nineteenth century, protected regions expanded greatly in the 1910s. The creation of a National Park Service, in 1916, gave control of more than 14 preserves, mostly in the West, to the Department of the Interior. The agency was charged with "conserv[ing] the scenery and the natural and historic objects and the wild life therein and to provide for the enjoyment of the same in such a manner and by such means as will leave them unimpaired for the enjoyment of future generations." In response to this mandate, the service built roads, hotels, museums, and camping facilities within these domains to control the environmental impact of the thousands of new park visitors.

THE AIRPLANE

While it would be incorrect to see air travel as widely utilized, it certainly held the interest of most Americans in the 1910s. The least developed but most modern mode of transit, the airplane had come the farthest since Orville and Wilbur Wright made the first piloted flight in a power-driven device, in 1903. By the close of the decade, air travel was no longer a novelty and, probably more indicative of its growing importance, had become a key strategic technology for modern military forces.

While the change in air travel since the 1910s is profound, the change *within* the decade was probably even greater. In 1910 most airplanes were flimsy craft allowing short journeys and carrying only a limited amount of weight. Innovations were introduced throughout the decade significantly increasing these characteristics. For example, by 1913, the biplane (which used two staggered wings) had become the standard model. The increase in lift and decrease in drag, due to the streamlined, enclosed fuselage, was accompanied by an engine that steadily increased in power. In England, in 1913, A.V. Roe and Tom Sopwith constructed the first military training aircraft, a move that furthered the drive toward greater speed and agility. By the start of the war, Sopwith's "Camel" could climb more that 15,000 feet in less than 10 minutes, carry an effective military payload, and travel at over 200 miles per hour.

Pilots quickly gained much needed experience throughout the decade. Novelty displays, which were popular with the public, led to a greater knowledge of what the plane could and could not do. Parachute drops, water landings, loop-de-loops, inverted flight, and endurance flights (of speed, distance, and height) all were pioneered in the 1910s to the gaping awe of the audience.

Public fascination with air travel remained strong in the prewar years. When, in January 1914, P.E. Fansler used a Benoist flying boat to ferry passengers and freight from Tampa and Saint Petersburg, Florida, he launched the first commercial airline. While Fansler's firm lasted less than three months, more than a thousand people were willing to pay money for the 22 mile excursion. On the ground, legal battles between the Wright brothers and Glenn H. Curtiss were being closely followed. Curtiss, a public aviator and builder, made his fame by setting speed records and winning a distinguished flying contest from Albany to New York City, in 1910, sponsored by Joseph Pulitzer's *New York World*. He also was interested in building planes (he had converted his motorcycle factory to airplane production) but was blocked by patents held by the Wrights. First in 1913 and then again in 1914, the federal courts upheld the Wright patents (in the process, recognizing them as the "first in flight"). In response, Curtiss began working closely with English and French designers, incorporating their modifications into his American planes, including the first gyroscopic automatic pilot, retractable landing gear, and a number of highly useful instruments—one of the few instances when patent laws actually spurred the spread of technology.

Of course, the outbreak of war in 1914 directly and profoundly affected the evolution of air travel. While the American military was initially hesitant to invest heavily in combat-ready aircraft (not least of all because the United States was not at war until 1917), European fighters like Frenchman Roland Garros and Germany's Lt. Manfred Von Richthofen (the "Red Baron") firmly established the lethal and strategic advantages gained by an air force. Aircraft provided direct visual reconnaissance of an enemy's movements and their reinforcements. They could deliver minor, but strategic, attacks against an enemy's most vital positions (such as supply depots or command centers). They were robust tools of war, sustaining dozens of hits while remaining aloft and capable of landing in many locations (on August 2, 1917, E.H. Dunning became the first pilot to land a plane on a *moving* ship, on the deck of HMS *Furious*). The only real threat to these aircraft were other pilots. Richthofen was credited with more than 80 kills before he was killed himself, in 1918, in a dogfight with Canadian pilot Roy Brown. American Eddie Rickenbacker shot down 26 enemies in the short time he saw action.

One of the most important decisions made by the American military during the war was in choosing a standard military training plane: the Curtiss Model JN (or Curtiss "Jenny") in 1914. The Jenny, a sturdy biplane, remained a standard for American aviation for nearly a generation. With America's entry into the war, Congress appropriated more than $640 million to "darken the skies" of Europe with more than 20,000 aircraft. While only a fraction of these were ever commissioned, the American war effort lent the aircraft industry both the technical and financial justification to begin the construction and operation of a safe, affordable, and reliable civilian air fleet in the 1920s.[2]

TRAGEDY AND CLASS IN OCEAN TRAVEL

In the decade that saw the sinking of the *Titanic*, the *Lusitania*, and the *Eastland* (which, technically, was a boat designed for lake travel and capsized rather than sank), ocean travel had become regarded by many as the ultimate example of the hubris of Progressive society. The "unsinkable" designs of these mammoth ships relied on science and technology to provide patrons with the latest in consumer conveniences, including speed, at supposedly no cost. Of course, such thinking was not confined to the great ships, as World War I proved. But still, the opulence and strong class lines reflected in these liners suggested to many that the wealthy were willing to take great risks in order to maintain their place in society.

Luxurious travel was certainly the intention of ocean liners. Repeating voyages that had been sailed for centuries (functionally, the *Titanic* was no different than the *Mayflower*), the newest liners promised passengers that they would be transported in high style and at great speed to their final destinations. Relying on multiple steam-turbine engines driving three or four screw propellers, shipping companies like the English-owned White Star and Cunard lines launched dozens of ships in the first two decades of the twentieth century to meet the growing demand for trans-Atlantic travel. The largest of these were White Star's new line which included the *Olympic*, *Gigantic*, and *Titanic*.

SS *Deutschland* library. Courtesy of the Library of Congress.

Ironically, *Titanic* was designed for safety and comfort, rather than speed. The ship could travel a respectable 22 knots but was protected by 16 watertight compartments (spanning the length of the ship) and 15 transverse bulkheads (spanning the width). Electrical generators powered emergency, watertight doors that would make the vessel nearly unsinkable in the event of a hull breach. The number of lifeboats, which figured prominently in two of the three great shipping disasters of the decade, was mandated by the tonnage of the vessel, not by the capacity. All ships of over 10,000 tons were required to carry 16 lifeboats (each capable of carrying from 60 to 80 people). These regulations were followed, but *Titanic*'s weight of more than 46,000 tons suggests how hopelessly outdated such regulations were in an era of superliners. The fact that the ill-fated ship carried four additional collapsible lifeboats was seen as further deference to the safety of its passengers. It was assumed that even the direst of emergencies would not sink the vessel, and that the added boats could handle even a large number of passengers who could then wait for a speedy rescue.

The level of comfort afforded to passengers is nearly unimaginable today. Housed in luxurious suites and dining in mahogany-lined restaurants, first- and second-class patrons enjoyed ballrooms, golf links, gymnasiums, and baths as part of the basic amenities of travel. Servants catered to their every need, from personal physicians and activities directors to valets and tailors for last-minute details. Third-class patrons were also treated better than in previous decades. While prohibited from using the elite accommodations, "steerage" passengers did enjoy modern and sanitary eating, dining, and bathroom facilities and generally were free from the overcrowding common earlier. More important, the size of the superliners made the journey smooth and tolerable even for the most claustrophobic. Still, class differences were stark. Patrons did not mix socially and were treated differently when an emergency did arise.

On its maiden voyage, *Titanic* left Southampton, England, at noon on April 10, 1912, piloted by the White Star line's most well-respected and best-liked captain, Edward J. Smith. Officially, 2,227 passengers and crew were on board when, around 11:40 P.M. ship's time on April 13, the ship struck a massive iceberg. In contact with the ship for less than 10 seconds, the iceberg ripped an opening in the hull 250 feet long that transversed six separate compartments, opening *Titanic* to the North Atlantic. One survivor later reported that the collision felt as if the ship was rolling over a million marbles. Smith, who was taking a routine nap in the chart room, awoke and ordered a visual inspection of the damage. Twenty minutes later he was apprised that the liner was terminally wounded. He gave orders to swing out the lifeboats and abandon ship only 30 minutes after contact occurred.

The unfolding tragedy, which, in a matter of hours would result in the death of 1,523 passengers and crew, was due to a series of mistakes. On the part of the ship owners and crew, certainly, the lack of rescue boats and emergency preparedness lead the list. The *Titanic* was carrying over 2,200 people, but the ship's lifeboats could safely support less than 1,200. When the last lifeboat was freed from the ship, at 2:05 in the morning, and the order was passed "every man for himself," 1,500 men, women, and children remained on board with no chance of survival. Moreover, despite Smith's reputation as an accomplished captain, *Titanic*'s navigation department was poorly run. It was common knowledge that the season had spawned a great number of large icebergs. Warnings and sighting reports (much like tornado bulletins today) were routinely broadcast over the wireless telegraph. Still, in spite of *Titanic*'s treacherous route through an iceberg "nursery," the wireless operator failed to take note of repeated warnings (a technical malfunction that afternoon led to a backlog of notes), which included another ship's report, only 50 minutes before the collision, that they had taken the extreme action of ordering a full stop due to the number and size of the icebergs in the region. It seems likely, in retrospect, that *Titanic*'s owners and crew aided in the tragedy by their actions or lack of action. Smith and nearly 500 other crew members paid for this error with their lives.

More troublesome was the role that class played in the determining who was rescued. The statistics are clear: 96 percent of the first-class women and children were saved, 89 percent of second-class women and children, and 47 percent, a minority, of steerage-class women and children. When Americans learned that "women and children first" meant the rich first, a vocal debate emerged over the meaning of the tragedy. For a discussion of travel, the *Titanic* disaster became a referendum on the shifting opportunities for those of wealth in modern society.[3]

Defending the skewed survival rates were traditional nativists and other bigots who valued the lives of the propertied classes over those of the poorer immigrants on board. When the list of wealthy victims was released, including millionaires John Jacob Astor, Benjamin Gugenheim, and Charles M. Hays, many praised their unselfish devotion to duty. Ignoring the aloof luxury chosen by these men for themselves on their journey, many suggested that the rich were actually better at making sacrifice and exhibiting valor than those without means. The *San Francisco Examiner* guessed that the "picture that invariably presents itself, in view of what is known, is of men like John Jacob Astor . . . stepping aside, bravely, gallantly remaining to die that the place he otherwise might have filled could perhaps be taken by some sabot-shod, shawl-enshrouded, illiterate and penniless peasant woman of Europe." Soon, however, columnists lamented the fact that a "disease-bitten child whose life at best is less than worthless, goes to safety with the rest of the steerage riff-raff, while the handlers of great affairs, the men who direct the destinies of hundreds of thousands of workers . . . stand unprotestingly aside." A report that the ship's band played "Nearer My God to Thee" as *Titanic* underwent its final destruction was totally fabricated (none survived to report what the band played at the last moments). Still, the story resonated with upper-class Americans who saw their kind not as pampered idlers but as the righteous enablers of God's plan for the American economy.[4]

Certainly, those less taken with the "Gospel of Wealth," such as reformer Charlotte Perkins Gilman, were appalled at the distorted death tolls as well as the cavalier way in which many poorer victims went unnoticed or, worse, were listed simply by their occupation as servants, such as "a maid," for their former employers. Working-class newspapers mocked stories of how industrialists "saved" poorer *Titanic* passengers while they were seemingly unconcerned with the thousands of workers who had toiled for them for years. Less heroic to their minds than the rich who refused to get into lifeboats (many because they did not believe that the ship would sink and therefore did not want to be inconvenienced by a cold trip in a scary lifeboat) were the boilermen and stokers who worked to keep power to the ship (which maintained electricity and prevented panic) despite their certain death as the icy water rose around them. The *Titanic* served as a symbol for many of the unfairness and idiocy of the propertied elite who were, according to the the *Masses*, driven by the "insanity of luxury, of foolish display and self-pampering even to the point of wrecking the safety and health of the luxurious themselves."[5] To these critics, it was not hymns that resonated in their ears but rather a popular tune penned after the tragedy, titled "The Titanic" or "It Was Sad When That Great Ship Went Down," which concluded,

> Oh, they sailed from England, they were almost to shore,
> When the rich refused to associate with the poor;
> So they put them down below, where they were the first to go . . . [6]

In comparison to *Titanic*, the reaction of the American public to the *Eastland* and *Lusitania* disasters was tame. The *Eastland*, another mammoth steamship, was designed for travel excursions and tourism along the Great Lakes. Unlike *Titanic*, the *Eastland* was built for speed with a narrow, streamlined hull that could cut through the relatively calm waters of the inland lakes. To make room for its nearly 2,500 passengers, the gaunt substructure of the *Eastland* was redesigned to add seating capacity above the waterline. In 1904 a fully loaded and underway *Eastland* began to list to the right (starboard) by nearly 25 degrees. While the ship remained in service, this structural instability led to rumors that the boat was unsafe. Repeated inspections, certifications, and claims by *Eastland* engineers assured the public that it was seaworthy, if a bit yielding when burdened by uneven loads. The final modification, one that quite possibly led to its fatal instability, was, ironically, the installation of additional lifeboats at the top of its maindecks.

On July 24, 1915, these faults led to the death of 841 passengers. For survivors and the public, the deaths were even more gruesome than the *Titanic* because of how common the events were that surrounded the tragedy. In the aftermath, it was clear that the victims could have been anyone, not only the elite or the poor immigrant who used intercontinental travel. The *Eastland* was one of six boats chartered by the Western Electric Company for their annual employee picnic in Chicago. Entire families, from infants to grandparents, arrived early to board the *Eastland* hoping to secure coveted window seats below deck on the recently remodeled "Speed Queen of the Lakes." Passengers first entered at 6:40 A.M. and the vessel began listing almost immediately. The crew attempted to compensate by flooding ballast tanks, but by 7:20, with 2,572 people on board, the *Eastland* began swaying from one side to the other, all while docked in a sheltered river with little or no wind. The left (port) list became so bad, nearly 30 degrees, that water began to enter in the lower level windows. Below decks, the crew worked to rebalance the human cargo while engineers worked above to do the same with the ballast. Neither knew what the other was doing. Within eight minutes, the list was nearly 45 degrees. By this time, the passengers began to realize the seriousness of the problem and a slight panic ensued. Unable to maintain their position on the tilted decks, even more people slid to the left. Those fortunate enough to remain standing on the right jumped from the ship, which only added to the imbalance. At 7:30, the *Eastland* silently rolled the final 45 degrees and settled on its left side, trapping everyone who was inside below the water line. The high concentration of people in such a small space doomed those within the ship, as there was literally not enough surface area for people to reach the air. One eyewitness reported on the ghastly scene: "A few were swimming; the rest were floundering about . . . others clutching at anything they could reach—at bits of wood, at each other, grabbing each other, pulling each other down, and screaming! The screaming was the most horrible of all." Within 20 minutes it was over. Entire families, all intending to enjoy a simple day trip on Lake Michigan, were wiped out.[7]

Unlike the *Titanic* disaster, the public outcry began immediately and centered its blame on state regulators and the *Eastland* crew. The commonness of lake travel, perhaps, made people look to these professionals as a way to justify such loss. Only inept or corrupt regulators and ballast-tank operators, specialists whose job it was to keep the public safe from technical malfunction, could possibly explain why such a horror was visited on the public. The fact that such travel—especially with capacities running in the thousands—was inherently dangerous was never admitted or discussed. The final legal outcome was resolved in 1935; no criminal or civil liability was cited.

By contrast, the sinking of the *Lusitania* earlier that same year (1915) was a premeditated act of war. Built in 1906 to win the coveted Blue Riband prize for the fastest trans-Atlantic crossing, Cunard's *Lusitania* and its sibling the *Mauretania* were the largest ships of their day and could easily achieve 25 knots in calm seas. *Lusitania* won the contest in 1907, only to be bested by the slightly upgraded *Mauretania*, which continued to set records until the outbreak of war in 1914. While christened as a luxury liner, both ships were outfitted with moorings to house 6-inch guns to serve as armored troop transports or merchant cruisers should the need arise.

In a very real sense, the neutrality of the United States in the Great War led to the destruction of the *Lusitania*. Fearing a German torpedo boat, Captain William Turner hoisted and sailed under the American flag in January 1915, prompting an international incident. Unwilling to fire upon an American liner, the Germans declared in April that ships known to be chartered by belligerent countries would no longer receive the protection of American neutrality should they again by found in contested waters. *Lusitania* left New York on May 1, 1915, after a published warn-

The wreck of the *Eastland*. Courtesy of the Library of Congress.

ing by the German government, and entered the "danger zone" off the English coast carrying nearly 2,000 passengers and crew six days later. As with *Titanic*, these patrons included a large number of wealthy and influential people who regarded the liner as the finest and fastest in service. At 2:15 P.M., as the ship approached Liverpool, *Lusitania* was probably struck by a single torpedo, which was soon followed by a powerful internal explosion, or it was hit by two torpedoes, the second being more powerful than any previously recorded torpedo then in use. According to the attacking German ship's log only a single torpedo was fired. Regardless, the blasts caused the stricken vessel to list badly to the right, rendering the port-side lifeboats inoperable (they could not be lowered) and many of the starboard boats unreachable as they swung out over the open ocean. The electrical power failed immediately, creating near total darkness within the ship, and the craft sank in 18 minutes. It is remarkable that there were any survivors at all. The severe conditions accounted for 1,193 passenger deaths, 128 of whom were Americans.[8]

Again, unlike the *Titanic*, interpretation of the disaster was without class recriminations for the passengers or their luxurious mode of travel. The German navy, rather, became a symbol of treachery and heartlessness, despite the fact that the *Lusitania* was known to be carrying war provisions and was sailing within a known corridor of U-boat activity. The fact that the 31,000-ton liner sank in less than half-an-hour after being struck by a single torpedo (compared to *Titanic*'s three-hour ordeal, which was caused by hitting a mountainous iceberg) strongly supports the theory that *Lusitania* carried munitions as well as passengers and other cargo. The United States threatened to enter the war as a result of the sinking, but it was two more years before a formal declaration was issued. Still, the tragedy galvanized moderate public opinion in the United States firmly against Germany and significantly influenced the activities of both the Allied and Central Powers during the conflict.

EVERYDAY TRAVEL

Streetcars

While less glamorous, rail travel in the 1910s was certainly more important to the average American than the gaudy opulence of the ocean liners. For the very wealthy, cross-country rail travel did not require a sacrifice of comfort. Personal cars ordered from the Pullman Company, near Chicago, offered magnates like James B. Duke all the luxuries of home without the need to ever rub shoulders with the common folk. For average Americans, rail transportation improved in quality and regularity while generally decreasing in cost (in real dollars). The introduction of a number of safety features, such as the air brake and stronger alloys for key parts, decreased the likelihood of fatal accidents.

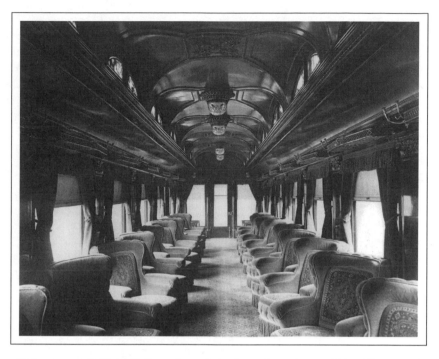

Chicago and Alton Railroad car interiors. Courtesy of the Library of Congress.

Within the cities, horse cars and cable cars transported the masses on a daily basis. Horse cars seated about 20 with more than 40 others hanging from the sides and in the aisles during peak hours. Pulled by teams of two to six horses, the service was slow, dirty, and unsanitary. It was estimated that the horses in service in a typical city the size of Milwaukee produced over 133 tons of manure a day. When the overworked beasts collapsed and died, their bodies were left along side the road for days. In 1912 the city of Chicago alone reported the destruction of nearly 10,000 draft horses per year.

Cable cars, introduced in 1883, used an underground system of steel cables to pull the attached vehicles at a fixed rate of speed. Suffering from mechanical failure, high expense, inefficiency, and an inability to speed up service during times of high usage, cable cars emerged only briefly as the popular choice for municipal mass transit. Still, more than 373 million passengers per year used cable cars throughout the country by the turn of the century.

The arrival of the electric streetcar, or trolley, in the late 1880s was a categorical boon to the growth of the modern city. According to historian Kenneth T. Jackson, "No invention, however, had greater impact on the

American city between the Civil War and World War I than the visible and noisy streetcar and the tracks that snaked down the broad avenues into undeveloped land." About half the size of a modern bus, trolleys were clean, safe, dependable, and cheap (fares quickly dropped to a nickel in most cities). At a speed of over twenty miles per hour, the streetcar was faster than other forms of urban travel, and capable of accelerating and slowing to accommodate open or congested areas. Terminating at ballparks, race tracks, beer gardens, or beaches, the trolley lines saw more than a doubling of service during the weekends, suggesting that Americans used the utility in ways that allowed them to create new usable spaces within the city.[9]

During the 1910s, America's light rail system was more developed and serviced more people than any other transportation system in the world. In 1911 New York City had ten times the mileage of Tokyo, a city that was over twice its size in population. In 1919 New York's peak year of trolley service, more than 1,344 miles of track were in use. Nationwide, more than 70,000 miles serviced billions of passengers annually.[10] In the largest cities, Americans rode the trolley an average of once every other day of the year. Unfortunately, the country was unable to capitalize on its early lead in public transportation. The pressure to retain the nickel fare overrode the need of most lines to keep up with inflation, which ran rampant during the war years. Moreover, automobiles and auto manufacturers (who purchased trolley lines only to replace service with motorized buses) soon undermined the monopoly held by electric rail in the cities. Today, horse cars, cable cars, and trolleys exist only as nostalgic reminders of a slower era. The automobile is king.

Automobiles

Unlike streetcar travel, which rose quickly after being introduced, automobile travel grew relatively slowly in the United States before 1910. The internal combustion engine was first invented in Europe in the 1860s, improved considerably by Gottlieb Daimler, Nikolaus Otto, Karl Benz, Alphonse Beau de Roches, and Jean Lenoir (hence many terms like chassis, automobile, and chauffeur are of European origin), and first tested in the United States by Charles and Frank Duryea in Springfield, Massachusetts, in 1892. Ransom E. Olds was the first American producer to target consumers of moderate means when he offered a four-cylinder, 28-horsepower car for $500 in 1900. Most cars, however, were primarily intended for use by the wealthy. As late as 1905 there was only one car for every 1,078 Americans.[11]

There were many reasons for the slow growth of the U.S. auto industry before 1910. The size of the country and the rapid growth of public transportation were certainly factors. In addition, restrictive legislation,

Traffic In Detroit, Michigan. Courtesy of the Library of Congress.

the generally poor state of roads, the lack of directional signs and maps, and the need for filling stations made automobile use inconvenient for any travel beyond one's immediate neighborhood. Instruction manuals issued warnings that were, no doubt, common errors made by new drivers. Olds cautioned not to make "improvements" to the engine or chassis, not to drive more than 100 miles on the first day as "you are green," and never to assume "your tanks of gas, oil, and water are full." A complex, preoperation checklist of duties for most drivers included an examination of the carburetor; inspection of the ignition system; lubrication of dynamo, pump, and fan; and tightening of the chains and belts.

In the 1910s, however, the relationship between Americans and their cars had fundamentally changed. By 1913 there was one car per eight people.[12] Within the state of Michigan, alone, more automobiles were registered than in all of England and Ireland. Henry Ford is properly credited with leading to this transformation. Ford, born on a farm outside Dearborn, Michigan, was a tinkerer and engineer who worked for the Edison Company in the 1880s. He built his first gasoline-powered car in 1892. After winning several prominent road races, in 1902, he started the Ford Motor Company in 1903. Owning a little more than a quarter of his firm, Ford was driven to take complete ownership over his company in the years ahead. Despite his significant impact on the

REO Mountaineer—from New York to San Francisco and back.
Courtesy of the Library of Congress.

industry, Ford actually invented little of lasting importance. Rather, it was his desire to "build a motor car for the great multitude," and his ability to do so, which made him a legend.

Early Cars, the Model T, and Fordism

Ford Motor Company's first automobile, the Model A, was not an affordable product; it sold for $1,600 in 1903 (more expensive than a Cadillac). Making matters worse, Ford found the automobile market glutted with a wide variety of manufacturers, styles, and even propulsion systems. Given these conditions, few could have predicted Ford's rapid rise to prominence. By contrast, others had established their names in the field. Probably the leading supplier of American cars was the Olds Motor Vehicle Company, begun in 1897 and absorbed into General Motors in 1908. Olds earned a reputation for quality and speed, and he was the first manufacturer to mass-produce 6- and then 12-cylinder automobiles. David Buick's firm, also soon part of General Motors, similarly projected an image of quality and simplicity. Buick introduced many technological innovations, such as the sliding-gear transmission, which allowed women to operate his cars safely. Horace and John Dodge, the

Studebaker brothers, Harry Knox, and Henry Leland, who founded the Cadillac Motor Car Company, in 1903, rounded out the list of the largest producers. These firms, who survived the 1907 financial panic and who were producing cars in the 1910s, largely imitated the European fashion for building better, more expensive, and more powerful cars for the limited markets of the very wealthy. Annual maintenance and upkeep often cost as much as the car's purchase price. Except for Olds' early efforts, an affordable, reliable car was not generally available for the average American.

In addition to such stiff competition, Ford faced an auto industry that had not standardized on a single source of power. Electric and steam-powered automobiles were widely available and offered competitive advantages that were not easily addressed by the internal combustion device. Steam cars, led by Francis and Freelan Stanley, who in 1906 built a Stanley Steamer that traveled at 127.66 mph, were simple and relatively cheap to own.[13] While inconvenient to operate, once under way, the steam car far outperformed their gasoline-powered rivals. Electric cars were quiet, clean, and favored by wealthy women, both for their ease of operation and for the status (the best electric cars ranged in price from $2,600 to $5,500). Then, as today, electric cars were limited in range and power and required a new charge every evening. The massive batteries and boilers for both styles made the cars heavy and hard to maneuver in the heavily rutted roads. In the end, neither platform met the needs of the average consumer: low cost *and* ease of operation.

Patent laws were a third obstacle to Ford's vision of a "universal car." The patent for the internal combustion engine (actually, for a two-cylinder device that was never used to power a car) was held by the Association of Licenced Automobile Manufacturers (ALAM), which charged a nominal but irksome royalty for all gasoline-powered engines. Ford, who would earn his well-known reputation as a man bent on achieving total control over his company, was bothered by the infringement and sued the ALAM in 1903. When, in 1911, he won his case (ALAM retained the rights for the nearly useless two-cylinder product), Ford Motor Company was able to develop future lines of cars without the need for prior legal approval.

Of course, by 1911, Ford had already developed his universal car in the Model T. Experimenting with a number of combinations of cylinders, chassis sizes, and production methods (termed by Ford the Models A, B, C, F, K, N, R, and S), the Model T was introduced in 1908 and was, in many ways, the culmination of Ford's engineering talents. The success of the "Tin Lizzie" or "flivver" lay less in its design or technology, and more in the fact that the car was relatively affordable (it premiered at $825), easily repaired by the average operator (a kit of tools was sold with the car), could easily traverse poor roads, and could be modified by farmers to perform a variety of tasks. In operation, the Model T does not seem to be ideal by contemporary standards. Three foot pedals, two hand levers, and a throttle switch were needed to operate the vehicle. In order to start the car, one needed to set the hand brake, set the spark and gas throttle to their "proper" positions (which varied by climate and even by car), hand crank the engine until it caught, then race back to the cabin to reset the spark and fuel mixtures. One of the endearing qualities of the "Lizzie" was its powerful reverse gear. Given that the gasoline flowed from the rear tank to the engine by gravity alone, it was common to see Ford drivers backing up hilly roads at a lively pace.

Price, of course, was what sealed the deal with the American public. While reliable, affordability made the Model T the vehicle of choice for many first-time buyers. Ford was able to lower the price of his car by developing a system of production previously unseen in American manufacturing. Called "Fordism," or the just-in-time moving assembly line, which delivered parts to workers just as they needed them in the assembly process, the technique was pioneered at his new plants in Highland Park (1910) and River Rouge (1919), Michigan. Unlike Ford's earlier efforts, which produced between 2,000 and 3,000 cars per year, the miles of conveyor belts at his new factories allowed production to multiply at a scale previously undreamed. The growth in production numbers were remarkable. In 1910, before Highland Park was in production, Ford could build only hundreds cars per day and actually had to raise the price of his cheapest car to $900. In 1914 he was producing 300,000 cars per year and the price fell to $590. By 1916 it was $345. While the war caused a brief jump in prices, by 1924 Ford Motor Company was manufacturing more than 9,000 cars per day and had lowered the price of a new car to $290.[14]

Pivotal to Fordism was the level of control Henry Ford exerted in his plants. He had bought out all other investors by 1919. This in itself was a significant feat and an indication of Ford's wealth. One minority investor, who had purchased $1,000 of stock in the original firm, sold his ownership to Ford for $30 million. Ford Motor Company remained a privately held concern until 1956, making it uniquely manageable.

Ford also recognized the need to reduce employee turnover. He wanted a labor force that could turn out quality work in record numbers. Traditionally, younger industrial laborers would often work at a firm for only a few weeks before deciding that they were unhappy or could find better wages somewhere else—often changing jobs several times per year. Summarily, in January 1914, Ford announced an eight-hour workday and a pay raise for employees with at least six months of experience on the job to $5 per day (more than double that of the best paid industrial worker).[15] The offer instantly galvanized many workers to Ford. While he demanded loyalty, and even used a variety of underhanded means by which to test this loyalty, Ford succeeded in creating a stable work-force that could produce his product the way that he wanted. The fact that the average Ford worker earned $1,500 per year, when his neighbors averaged only a third of this, and when even white-collar professionals earned only slightly more, made his employees remarkably agreeable.

CONCLUSION

While Ford would eventually be challenged, and later bested, in the marketplace by Walter C. Durant, who formed General Motors and then the Chevrolet Motor Company in 1911, he maintained his "tinkerers" vision of building universal cars. His phenomenal success in this venture nearly single-handedly changed the way in which Americans traveled in the 1910s. The drive for individuality in travel favored the growth of automobiles at the expense of the more communal forms of travel, such as the train or streetcar. The manufacturing methods and good pay fur-ther developed a consumer economy that would support America's growing love affair with the automobile. Moreover, the freedom afforded citizens to go anywhere at anytime was an appealing mixture of mo-dernity and traditional American values that obscured many of the costs associated with a highly mobile society. For good or ill, the travel trends of the decade remained the pattern followed by this country throughout the twentieth century.

12

Visual Arts

Visual arts in the 1910s displayed a tremendous variety. Ranging from the intellectual, modernist art of Stanton Macdonald-Wright to the seemingly adolescent drawings of the daily comics, visual artists used images to communicate to their audiences messages that both reinforced and challenged American society. This dialog could be friendly or hostile, easily comprehensible or ambiguous, elitist or more familiar. In any case, the images and ideas introduced by visual artists in the 1910s were more closely connected to the lives of everyday Americans than in any previous era. Whether through cubism or the comic-strip "Krazy Kat," visual artists transposed the thoughts and feelings of the average citizen onto the canvas, into magazines, or in newsprint. While disparate, these visual arts reinforced the processes of modernization that were under way throughout American culture and served to blend many of these cultural trends in new and provocative ways. The fact that today we often see high-concept abstract art in advertisements and everyday material culture in the serious arts (such as Andy Warhol's use of Campbell's soup cans) suggests just how far this consolidation has gone.

As with the other expressive humanities in the decade, realism was the dominant theme in the visual arts. The sensibilities of realism were quite provocative, given the general genteel traditions that dominated American culture in the 1910s. Showing life "as it is" meant portraying the harsher qualities of modernity, including vice, poverty, and a growing sense of alienation. Such characterizations were often seen as "vulgar" or "obscene" by moral guardians such as Anthony Comstock, who in 1906 went so far as to impound the work of an Art Students' League publication because of its display of nudes. Such opposition spanned the range of visual arts and affected everyone from the most iconoclastic painter to popular magazine illustrators.

While contemporaneous with literary realism, realism in the visual arts developed its own separate traditions and styles. As one influential painter and newspaper illustrator, John Sloan, recalled, while it was possible "to trace a connection between our work and that of [writers Theodore] Dreiser, [Frank] Norris and [Stephen] Crane. . . . there is no direct contact."[1] Sloan and many others regarded their work more as "a revolt against sentimentality and artificial subject matter and the cult 'art for art's sake'" which had come to dominate the fine arts by the 1910s. Realist painters and illustrators believed their work was a direct refutation of the fawning stance taken toward European standards by most leading American institutions. The exclusive National Academy of Design (NAD), which could make or break the career of a young artist, jealously guarded its cultural authority and passed its approval only onto those willing to follow its lead. Their conservatism led many to conclude that, by 1910, "American art was at its lowest ebb."[2] Ironically, as described below, the NAD's obstinance proved to be one of the chief reasons for the radical shift in the visual arts throughout the decade.

The more popular visual arts also wrestled with quandaries. Infusing realism into magazine and newspaper illustrations proved to be easier than getting a showing at the leading galleries, but the artists found that their craft was often tainted by commercialism. Publishers hired and retained artists who were willing to embellish and sensationalize their work. Particularly notable styles were quickly copied, leading to a standardization in the craft that threatened creative freedoms. Moreover, by the end of the decade, the most popular illustrators and cartoonists were earning millions of dollars, making it highly unlikely they would continue to innovate with untried or experimental visual forms.

What sustained the realist trend was the obvious utility of these images for the millions of readers and art patrons throughout the country. Realist portrayals provided a touchstone for citizens who were unsure of the direction their society was taking. By giving viewers easy access to art—through the use of familiar images and emotions—realists helped both educate and reassure the country. Trends, social problems, modern anxieties, and other subconscious elements of mass culture could be seen, talked about, and better understood through the realists' work. While, by 1920, the realist style was already considered obsolete, throughout the decade it remained the most influential and popular form of expression.

MAGAZINE ILLUSTRATIONS

The 1910s are seen by many as a golden era in magazine illustration. Throughout the decade, supporting trends in the industry—such as wider circulation and a commitment to print advertising—had reached their peak while those media that would soon erode the magazines' preeminence—radio and television—were still in the future. Most important, the technical process of mass-producing high-quality and often colored illustrations had been perfected by the start of the decade. While the shift from wood engravings (which manually transposed a line drawing onto a block of wood suitable for printing) to photographic engraving (which created a similar template through chemical processes) had occurred by the turn of the century, it was not until the first decade that these plates were economically reproducing the finest illustrations. Before these "line" or "halftone photoengravings" were made affordable, only a small number of the most expensive journals regularly included illustrations.

In addition to technological improvements, magazine circulation soared throughout the era providing greater exposure and more work for graphic artists. Established fiction and opinion magazines, such as *Harper's* and *Atlantic Monthly*, were joined by a host of fashionable women's and popular literary magazines, which swelled the ranks of subscribers. By 1910 the most notable illustrated magazines included *Century, Harper's, McClure's*, and *Scribner's. American, Good Housekeeping, Ladies' Home Journal, Delineator, Pictorial Review, Collier's, Saturday Evening Post, Youth's Companion*, and the humorous weeklies *Life, Puck*, and *Judge* included dozens of illustrations in each week's issue. Adding to the demand was the growth in print advertising. More than half of these 100-page monthly publications were purchased by the advertisers who invariably made use of illustrations to draw attention to their products.[3]

Finally, the literature that provided inspiration for these illustrations was becoming more engaging and lively in the 1910s. Realist writing gave artists an opportunity to delve into images and subjects thought to be beyond to staid traditions of previous illustrators like Charles Dana Gibson, whose Gibson Girls were immensely popular in the 1900s but lacked much appeal beyond their pretty faces. The strong emotions of realistic literature were captured by the illustrators as they too looked to find the essence of the work in life's highly dramatic moments.

The popularity of the best-known illustrators was significant. Illustrators received fan mail and were often considered celebrities in high society. It was not unusual for the top illustrators to earn tens or even hundreds of thousands of dollars per year. By 1919, at the age of 25, Norman Rockwell was already a millionaire as a result of his magazine and advertisement illustrations in the *Saturday Evening Post* and other popular publications.

The most prominent magazine illustrators of the 1910s included Arthur William Brown and Frederic Gruger (*Saturday Evening Post*), Coles Phillips and Jessie Smith (*Good Housekeeping*), George Plank (*Vogue*), Har-

James Montgomery Flagg and his portrait of Uncle Sam. © CORBIS.

rison Fisher (*Ladies' Home Journal*), Maxfield Parrish (*Collier's*), Wallace Morgan (*Collier's* and *Saturday Evening Post*), and James Montgomery Flagg. Gruger was probably the most influential of the lot. His long career at *Saturday Evening Post* gave him the experience to learn how to work within the confined limits of size and the reproductive technologies of mass-circulation magazines. He developed the medium to its full potential, injecting life, emotion, and meaning into his work in ways that escaped the camera. Gruger demonstrated the artistic power of illustrated literature in ways that secured the profession's position in American culture for generations. The fact that Flagg, Gruger, and many others were exhibited by the NAD as serious artists underscores the respect they provided the medium.

World War I provided unique opportunities for these illustrators. Many, like Harvey Dunn, Wallace Morgan, Harry Townsend, and Walter Jack Duncan, were commissioned in the American Expeditionary Force, lived on the Front, and conveyed to the country the striking realities and horrors of the war. Others, like James Montgomery Flagg, remained at home to lend their talents to the Committee on Public Information, a federal propaganda program intended to promote patriotism at home. Flagg's famous portrait of Uncle Sam declaring, "I Want You" (actually a self-portrait) remains the most famous of these efforts. His work also included less-obvious work on Liberty Bonds, local advertising campaigns, and billboards and posters. The power of these images, especially those depicting the brutality of the German-led enemies, was based largely on the talents of illustrators well-honed by years of magazine work.

Norman Rockwell

Certainly Norman Rockwell was the best-known magazine illustrator to get his start during the era. Born in New York City to affluent parents in 1894, Rockwell demonstrated an aptitude for drawing early in life. Following his talent, Rockwell, as an art student in 1910, studied anatomy and absorbed the artistic realism that dominated the illustrator's craft. In 1912 he was commissioned for his first professional illustrations in the newspapers. Soon, as his portfolio grew, he was contributing to the popular children's *Tell Me Why Stories* and *Boys' Life* magazine. By 1913 he was a regular contributor to *Youth's Companion, Everyland, American Boy*, and *St. Nicholas* magazines and produced more than 100 drawings for the *Boy Scouts' Hike Book*. From 1914 to 1916, Rockwell became a major illustrator garnering work in *Collier's, Life, Leslie's, Judge, Country Gentleman, Literary Digest*, and, at the tender age of 22, the cover of *Saturday Evening Post* on May 20, 1916. By 1919 Rockwell was a featured artist for the publication and began illustrating a series of Christmas covers that would continue until 1943. The illustrations were remunerative, but Rockwell made his greatest wealth as a named illustrator for such products as Maxwell House coffee, Encyclopedia Britannica, Massachusetts Mutual Life Insurance, and Interwoven Socks.

What made Rockwell's art so appealing was its simple directness. His images told stories that were easily understood by his audience and created an immediate sense of empathy for his subjects. These visual narratives were almost invariably optimistic, inoffensive, and nostalgic for an age of innocent youth that usually existed only in the yearning memories of adult subscribers. His style spotlighted the minor, awkward moments when people are faced with their own fallibility. Tempering these episodes with youthful subjects (90 percent of his *Post* covers included children before 1919), Rockwell was able to balance the painful feelings of loss with an emotional hope for learning and growth.

Rockwell's commitment to technical realism remains at the heart of his artistic legacy. On the one hand, his ability to capture an affecting moment was unparalleled. For example, his first *Post* cover depicted a boy wearing his Sunday best pushing a baby in a carriage. The youth's pained expression, as he passes his friends on their way to play baseball, those of his tormenters, and even the bottle of milk stuck hastily in his breast pocket all convey the strong yet simple emotions such a child might feel. Yet the need to reproduce photographic realism in order to achieve this effect (he began painting directly from photos of staged actors in 1937) suggests the artificiality that many critics have since condemned. While there are few who are neutral on Rockwell's work, his sentimental assemblage of stock emotions and nostalgia for family, country, and youth's innocence (or innocence lost) proved to be the most successful combination of artistic realism and commercialism of the decade.

NEWSPAPER ILLUSTRATORS AND THEIR UNIQUE VISUAL STYLE

In contrast to magazine illustrations, newspaper images remained closer to the realism that was at the heart of the print medium. Given the impermanence of each daily issue, it was not surprising that newspapers and their editors focused less on the technological improvement of the craft and the creation of lasting images—such as Rockwell's cover art—and more on the immediacy and emotional power of their work. The leading newspaper illustrators of the 1910s were committed to portraying the harsh reality of urban life which, intentionally, supported the Progressive reforms of the era. The competition from photographs, which were increasingly included in the leading dailies, led illustrators to develop a gritty, yet effective realistic style all their own.

The leading newspaper illustrators of the day, including John Sloan, George Luks, Everett Shinn, and Wallace Morgan, regarded their work as both commercially viable and aesthetically valuable. Sloan was typical in that he learned the basic skills of his craft as an art student—in his case, at the influential Pennsylvania Academy of Fine Arts—and then developed these skills into a unique realist style while meeting the daily deadlines imposed on him by Philadelphia newspapers. Illustrating articles that dealt with crime, vice, and popular entertainment, artists like

Sloan and Shinn, who worked in New York City, took a new and critical look at the coarser side of American life. Here they were able to project the strong emotions of their subjects in ways that escaped the more objective lens of the camera.

The career of William Glackens highlights the importance of this genre of visual art. Like Sloan, Shinn, Gruger, and a host of others, Glackens got his start at the Pennsylvania Academy of Fine Arts. He first began working as an illustrator for the *Philadelphia Record* before traveling to Paris to expand his knowledge of fine arts. When he returned, Glackens became a commercial artist at the *New York Herald* and *New York World*. Characteristic of the medium, Glackens illustrated fires, social unrest, parades, strikes, and other examples of dramatic urban life. Working quickly, Glackens sought to capture the essence of the moment in all of its harsh reality. He intended for his pictures to convey social relevance and the spontaneity of urban America, not some abstract notion of beauty or eternal truth, so highly regarded by the fine artists allied with the National Academy of Design.

Glackens boldly transferred this newspaper style onto the canvas in the first decade of 1900. He, along with Shinn, Sloan, Luks, and other like-minded artists, challenged the conservative and largely derivative traditions of the NAD by concentrating on the novelty of modern life. This realism used dramatic lighting and spontaneous brushwork which, in addition to its focus on everyday life, led some to call the style the Ashcan school (referring to their interest in the seamier side of life). Taking a less forgiving stance, the NAD simply referred to them as the "apostles of ugliness." It is important to note here that the newspapers provided the first venue for displaying this unique and modern American art form. Although they were ultimately unsuccessful at redefining modern art in this country, newspaper illustrators did much to weaken the artistic legitimacy of the NAD by the end of the decade.

While technically a magazine, the illustrations of the *Masses* were in keeping with this newspaper style. When, in 1912, the publication embraced a more active reformist stance, its illustrations became bolder, wittier, and more directly related to the needs of its working-class audience. George Bellows, Henry Glintenkamp, Glenn Coleman, and especially John Sloan brazenly attacked economic inequality, racism, and powerful institutions. Rejecting the sentimentality of Rockwell and the idyllic beauty of cover girls depicted by Gibson and Flagg, the *Masses* championed honesty and directness which was evident in newspaper illustrations.

The newspapers' visual style established a middle ground between the irrelevance of the "slick" magazine illustrations and the seemingly inaccessible art of the new modernists. Sloan noted, "Drawing is a human language, a way of communication between human beings."[4] As a result,

Typical realist illustration of *Masses*, "Roofs, Summer Night," by John Sloan. © Museum of the City of New York/CORBIS.

they believed that the images needed to be clear to the viewers—that figurative representation was important to the transmission of their ideas to the public. This commitment to figurative art (i.e., depicting an object or event as it appears in reality rather than through the artist's unique perspective) would become one of the greatest points of contention between American realists of the Ashcan school and the modern art depicted by Paul Gauguin, Pablo Picasso, and Paul Cézanne.

THE FUNNY PAPERS

Far from the debates of realism or modern art, but not insulated from them either, was the newspaper comic strip. While more trivial to the development of visual arts and culture in the United States, humorous drawings were by far the most popular form of illustrations throughout the decade. Moreover, the humor contained within the illustrations—both visual and written—reinforced or questioned many traditional assumptions about American society. Just as Mark Twain or, later, Will Rogers was able to use humor to address serious issues concerning the United States, so too did the comics complement the more earnest art of the era.

Regular cartoons began in the 1880s primarily in the sports and editorial sections of the newspapers. Most of these were single-panel drawings relying on verbal jokes for their humor. The characters were mostly underdeveloped and did not repeat from day to day. Some satirical magazines, such as *Puck, Judge,* and *Truth,* used illustrations and characters more regularly, but by and large these were the exceptions. Focusing on a variety of human vices, most cartoons used callow humor intended for an adult audience. As late as 1908, the *Boston Herald* predicted, "The comic section has had its day. The funnies are not funny anymore and they have become vulgar in design and tawdry in color."[5]

What helped to prevent this scenario was the growth of the regular or feature cartoon in many urban publications. As early as the 1890s, the comics became more consistent when newspapers owned by E.W. Scripps, William Randolph Hearst, and Joseph Pulitzer (whose influence was largely limited to the gargantuan *New York World*) began forming national chains, or syndicates. These affiliated dailies used wire services to standardize their editorial and reporting content and employed a regular stable of comic illustrators. By the 1910s, their comics were running in hundreds of papers, making the art form a common point of reference for many readers.

The most influential of these early cartoons, drawn by Richard Felton Outcault, was "Hogan's Alley" but known to most as the "Yellow Kid." The drawing featured a number of working-class kids, including one particularly striking child who wore only a nightshirt and was noted for his large, bald head, big ears, and gapped-tooth smile. The character, whose name was Mickey Dugan, soon sported a yellow nightshirt (color was added in 1896) and was then dubbed the Yellow Kid by an interested public.

The popularity of the character (for it really did not constitute a comic strip as we know it today) was immense. Outcault marveled years later, "I suppose I have myself made twenty thousand Yellow Kids, and when the million buttons, the innumerable toys and cigarette boxes and labels and whatnot are taken into consideration, some idea can be gleaned of how tired I am of him."[6] His publishers, however, were not tired of the public interest generated by the Yellow Kid. After Outcault left the *World* for Hearst's *New York Journal,* a circulation war, prominently featuring advertisements for the Yellow Kid, ensued. The term "yellow journalism"—which refers to the tawdry, sensationalist, tabloid style of reporting in the *World* and *Journal*—was coined as a result of the circulation war featuring Mickey Dugan. By 1910 other comics besides the Yellow Kid (now drawn for the *World* by George Luks) had become as prominent, including James Swinnerton's "Little Bears" and Rudolph Dirks's "Katzenjammer Kids."

The first true comic strip was introduced in 1907 in the *San Francisco Chronicle.* Titled "A. Mutt" and penned by Bud Fisher, the strip was a series of cartoons that told narrative and increasingly visual jokes spread out across the newspaper page. The strip was an innovation in several ways. First, by using frames, Fisher was able to introduce the comic timing that is so important in the delivery of humor. No longer required to use single, and usually dopey, punch lines, Fisher was free to develop multiple gags within a strip, which allowed character development. The use of speech balloons created a more natural dialog. It was possible now for characters to interact within each frame, rather than deliver extended speeches at the bottom of a single illustration.

Fisher's character, Mutt, was a mean-spirited, hard-edged, chronic gambler. The humor of the strip was aimed at the sporting man who read the sports pages of the *Chronicle*. It was not until 1910, with the regular appearance of a second, more sympathetic character, "Jeff," that the strip matured into an accessible and popular feature for the paper. Jeff—who appeared when Mutt was thrown into an asylum as a result of his gambling addiction—was, in fact, insane. He thought he was heavyweight boxing champion Jeff Jeffries. Jeff proved to be the perfect foil for Mutt; one an irrational idealist, softhearted and innocent, the other a crafty materialist. In 1916 the strip was retitled "Mutt and Jeff" to reflect the popularity and impact of the diminutive newcomer. Fisher had the foresight to copyright his creations. When he left the *Chronicle* for better pay at Hearst's *Examiner*, the former publication attempted to continue the strip under the same name using the same characters (as the *New York World* did with Outcault's "Hogan's Alley"). Fisher sued and won, in 1915, establishing the right of comic artists to maintain control over their intellectual property.

This creative freedom was significant and, given the direction toward pop art in the twentieth century, reinforced trends in the fine arts. For example, Cliff Sterrett's popular strip "Polly and Her Pals" (1912) told the story of Polly Perkins, a liberated "New Woman." While Sterrett's work is often noted for its focus on a mature woman as a lead character—the first of its kind—his drawing style had an important effect on loosening the rigid bounds of visual representation in the newspapers. His characters (except for Polly) were delineated using rigid geometric shapes. Sterrett's strips, as one historian noted, "Undoubtedly inspired by disciples of Futurism in the Cubist movement . . . were unparalleled in their comic distortions of reality."[7]

Strips also loosened the bounds of typical graphic humor. The need for a gag or slapstick in comics was lessened as artists sought more emotionally interesting ground to plow. George Herriman was well ahead of his contemporaries in creating abstract humorous content in "Krazy Kat" (1913). Herriman, born to a mixed-race couple in New Orleans, created a strip for Hearst's *New York Journal* that was never immensely fashionable with the public. It was featured in only 48 papers while more popular cartoons were usually syndicated in hundreds.

"Krazy Kat" remained in print solely because William Randolph Hearst liked it. When Herriman died, in 1944, the panel was discontinued because King Features thought it was not worth preserving. Still, the strip is regarded today as one of the best examples of how the visual arts both reflected and influenced popular culture.

The content of "Krazy Kat" is absurdly simple yet compellingly complex. Three central characters are involved in an unrequited love triangle, a topic that clearly indicates that, like his contemporaries, Herriman was aiming his creation at the adult reading public and not children. Krazy Kat, an androgynous (yet assumedly female) feline was is love with Ignatz the mouse. Ignatz, true to his species, hates Krazy and expressed his (he was clearly male) frustrations by hurling bricks at the confused cat who invariably assumed these to be Ignatz's expressions of love. Offissa Pup, torn between *his* love for Krazy (again, against type) and his duty to uphold the law in stopping Ignatz's behavior, stumbles between the two incapable of achieving either objective. The plot, if indeed there was one, was simply how Ignatz would find ways to lob his missiles. The humor was in how all three characters accepted the absurdity of their lives while remaining true to their hopes of love and independence. Moreover, Herriman interjected popular slang, Yiddish, Bronx accents, and even Shakespearean dialect into a surreal yet familiar speech that made reading "Krazy Kat" as much fun as following their exploits. Typical was an explanation by Krazy to the dog of their strange relationship: "And so, 'Offissa Pupp,' you & me gotta be werra watchful, & wigilint around the unlimitless etha, and from roaming around unfeathered, & loosely, y'understand?"[8] In the end, Herriman showed, love always triumphs over even the most absurd conditions.

While "Krazy Kat" offered an extreme example of the role of comics in the daily newspapers, even the most conventional strips tended to reinforce the popular culture of the day. For example, *Chicago Tribune* publisher Robert McCormick wanted his readers to become more comfortable with the automobile. As a result, illustrator Frank King was asked to create a strip in 1918, which he called "Gasoline Alley," that eventually became one of the longest running, most successful series in all cartooning. The treatment of children and youth is typical. Moving away from the tough and recalcitrant vision of inner-city children, strips began to portray kids as relatively simple and honest pranksters intent on having fun. In line with the reform of children's play, strips like Merril Blosser's "Freckles and His Friends" (1915), Gene Byrnes's "Reg'lar Fellas" (1916), and Carl Ed's "Harold Teen" (1919) all showed youth and youth culture as nonthreatening and potentially redeemable. Blooser's work ran for fifty years in more than 700 newspapers. "Harold Teen" was the first to begin identifying older children as intrinsically different from their more innocent younger siblings. Harold also provided readers, until 1959 when the strip ended, a daily dose of teen slang, humor, and trends that no doubt proved to be useful for parents confused by the growing generation gap.

Noteworthy was the phenomenal sums commanded by these popular cartoonists. George MacManus was a multimillionaire as a result of "Bringing Up Father." Former shoe salesman Gene Byrnes, who penned "Reg'lar Fellas," was making $25,000 per year by 1920. "Mutt and Jeff" creator Bud Fisher earned over $1,000 a week, hobnobbed with celebrities (he himself was one), owned a stable of horses, and was frequently seen in the company of movie starlets and showgirls. If salaries reflect social prestige, clearly cartoonists had earned an exalted place in American popular culture by the end of the decade.

THE FINE ART REVOLUTION

The fine arts witnessed what can only be described as a revolution in the 1910s. Given that the decade experienced a collision among the conservative yet powerful NAD, members of the modern American realists (the so-called Ashcan school), works by the most influential modernist painters of Europe (such as Picasso and Cézanne), the public (which was deeply involved), and a host of critics, it is no small wonder that art historians regard the 1910s as *the* decade in which modern American art was born. When the Armory Show of Modern Art was staged, on February 17, 1913, at the 69th Infantry Regiment Armory in New York City, these contradictory forces were compelled to resolve the growing gulf between their divergent aesthetic sensibilities. The drama of the Armory Show, probably the single most important exhibition of fine art in American history, was real and its effects were profound.

Of course, this clash was not foreordained but rather contingent on the efforts of a number of individuals, groups, and trends of the 1910s. Efforts by leading American artists, such as Robert Henri, Arthur B. Davies, and Alfred Stieglitz, figured greatly in determining when and how this conflict would be resolved. Moreover, World War I served as a critical backdrop to the rise of modern art in the United States—first in shaping the work of the European artists, then by validating their vision and providing U.S. artists with time to absorb these values into their own distinctive style.

Origins

The dominant European artists of the late nineteenth and early twentieth centuries were men uncomfortable with the Progressive society that had arisen around them. Starting first in France and then spreading throughout the Continent, artists rejected the self-assured and self-

View of sculpture on display at Armory Show, 1913. © Bettmann/
CORBIS.

satisfied tastes of the elites and the middle class who were quite well-
pleased with the Enlightened beauty supposedly created by industrial
capitalism. While leading painters and sculptors were tolerant of the genteel revolt fashioned by Impressionists like Édouard Manet and Pierre-
Auguste Renoir, the more brash Postimpressionists, such as Vincent van
Gogh, Georges Seurat, and Paul Cézanne (considered by many to be the
father of modern art), "poisoned the reassuring pleasures of visual aesthetics."[9] Focusing on the symbols and expressions rather than the exact
likeness of objects (such as urban scenes, nudes, haystacks, or land-
scapes), these artists exploded the range of visual expression. Accordingly, the novel approaches made by Postimpressionists were
categorized into a number of not-so-distinct styles, including symbolism,
fauvism (expressed through violent colors and misshapen forms), da-
daism (completely nihilistic and filled with disgust toward polite civilization), Orphism (depicting a realism solely defined by the artist),
expressionism (led by van Gogh and Edvard Munch who used distortions to express strong emotions or ideas), synchromism (completely abstract color designs), and cubism (called the "father of all abstract art,"
which superimposed several views of an object on a single canvas).

While American visual artists took their cue from the European art
world, rarely were they comfortable with pioneering new forms. The

NAD was no exception. First established in 1825, the NAD split into several rival groups in the 1870s, and then re-emerged united in 1906. Members of the academy were American artists whose works were deemed to best represent classical European styles: rigid compositions, strict representations of form and color, and traditional models of the past (particularly Greek mythology or biblical allegory). According to art historian Martin Green, the NAD intended its work to "beautify, dignify, and enhance the ceremonial life of [public] institutions."[10] As a result, NAD membership was required for artists to secure commissions, to be included in exhibitions, and to attract the attention of wealthy patrons. Their annual shows were "of necessity conservative and nearly always retrospective in nature. For this reason, creative and experimental works were almost invariably shunned."[11]

Not all American artists were comfortable with the NAD. Robert Henri was the single most important opponent of the NAD and the reason for the growing acceptance of realism in the fine arts by 1910. An accomplished artist, Henri studied at the Pennsylvania Academy of Art, was familiar with the Impressionist style, and had exhibited and sold his work in the Old World. In 1901, Henri joined the New York School of Art and began recruiting other promising realists to his classes. While his student lists read today like a "who's who" in American art, it is important to recognize that Henri was tapping into talents that were being developed not by the NAD but rather by the popular newspapers and magazines of the day. By 1906 these included George Luks, John Sloan, William Glackens, Everett Shinn, George Bellows, Arthur B. Davies, Rockwell Kent, Glenn Coleman, Edward Hopper, and Walter Pach.

Significantly, Henri didn't teach his students *what* to paint but rather *how*. Under his guidance, many of his apprentices got their first exposure not only to European Impressionists but also to oil painting. Henri's "soup method" (used earlier by James McNeill Whistler) was to prepaint the canvas with a neutral tone which then allowed artists to mute the colors of their inner-city subjects in ways that added emotion and depth to their brush strokes. He implored his students to simply "observe and record," to build upon the skills they had learned as newspapermen and illustrators, and to work quickly to capture the feeling of a scene rather than to worry about formal composition. Henri begged, "Have your energies alert, up and active. Finish as quickly as you can. . . . Do it all in one sitting if you can; in one minute if you can."[12]

By 1907 Henri was the most influential teacher in New York City. He hoped to get his growing corps of accomplished students shown at the NAD's spring exhibition. As an established artist and full member of the NAD, Henri was included on the 30-man panel chosen to select works from more than 1,500 entries. Despite his best efforts, which eventually included the voluntary withdrawal of his own paintings from competition (which had been accepted) and a vocal protest in the newspapers against the biases shown by many judges, none of his students' works were deemed acceptable.

Unwilling to abide by their decision, Henri organized a showing at the (William) Macbeth Gallery in New York City of "unknown and experimental" art by American painters. The show, presented in 1908, highlighted the work of Henri, Sloan, Glackens, Luks, Shinn, Davies, Ernest Lawson, and Maurice Prendergast. Known as "the Eight," the painters formed the core of what was later to be termed the Ashcan school. While critics were merciless in their censure of their work, the popularity of the show ensured that other exhibitions would be staged. By 1910 it was clear that the realists had found a way to express their vision of modern American art. Henri's students seemed to be everywhere, and the spirit of change was in the air.

Henri might have been earlier than others to call for the NAD to open its eyes to the new art, but he was not alone. Americans abroad, who were exposed to and could appreciate the trends in European Postimpressionism, like Leo and Gertrude Stein, were quite aware of the "storm on the horizon" for the visual arts in the United States. More than anyone, Alfred Stieglitz created the conditions whereby this modern art could be critically regarded by Americans. Under Stieglitz, American modern artists such as Marsden Hartley, Max Weber, John Marin, Arthur Dove, Charles Demuth, and Georgia O'Keeffe (who later married Stieglitz) were not only introduced, but also "Americanized."

Stieglitz established a magazine of photography and modern art, titled *Camera Work*, in 1903, and then, two years later, a gallery in New York City named The Little Galleries of the Photo-Secession but referred to as "291," the street address on Fifth Avenue, by almost everyone. At 291, Stieglitz found that he could express his desire to foment a "revolt against the autocracy of convention" best by showing the work of other artists who could not get an audience.[13] As a result, 291 introduced the American art community to some of the most revolutionary and influential artists of the era: the first exhibition or one-man shows of Auguste Rodin (1908), Henri Matisse (1909), Francis Picabia (1913), and Constantin Brancusi (1914). For American artists, 291 debuted John Marin and Alfred Maurer (1909), Oscar Bluemmer (1915), and Elie Nadelman (1915); staged comprehensive shows of Marsden Hartley, Arthur Dove, and Max Weber (1910), Gino Severini (1917), and Stanton Macdonald-Wright (1917); and introduced the work of Georgia O'Keeffe (1916). Following the Armory show, which led to the collapse of the NAD and the triumph of modernism, Stieglitz half-joked that he would be willing to show the work of older, conservative artists if they found no exhibition space available elsewhere.

Combined, Henri and Stieglitz prepared the ground for the arrival of

Alfred Stieglitz. Courtesy of the Library of Congress.

the Postimpressionists and suggested ways in which American artists might confidently exist within these new modes. Art historian Henry Geldzahler noted that the cultural explosion following the Armory Show "left no aftermath of involvement and acceptance." To him, the "gentler, steadier efforts" of these pioneers "were of much greater significance to the artists concerned and to American art." Still, it was the Armory Show that blew the roof off American modern art in ways that are still echoing today.[14]

The Armory Show

The Armory Show not only completely overturned the conservative NAD but also swept aside the modern American realists. The staid academic artists in America were easy targets for a style that had already overturned the European conservatives, who had enjoyed even greater social prestige than their Western counterparts. Yet Henri, the other members of the Eight, and their converts were completely unprepared for the lasting transformation that was unleashed upon them. Milton W. Brown, a distinguished historian of the era who has a generally favorable opinion of the Ashcan school, noted that, by the close of the Armory Show, the one-time mavericks were "blind to the fact that [their work] had already become irrelevant."[13]

The bitter irony was not lost on these contemporary artists. The Armory Show was organized by the Association of American Painters and Sculptors (AAPS), supporters of the Ashcan movement, to highlight the many changes wrought by American realists. It was assumed that patrons would be found for and canvases sold by these new American visionaries. Their success, as a result of the show, would force the NAD to recognize the significance of their contribution. But the intense comparison brought about by the show between the Americans and the Post-impressionist Europeans fully marginalized their work, seemingly aging the compositions overnight.

The AAPS was founded in late November 1911, by Jerome Myers, Elmer McRae, Walt Kuhn, and Henry Fitch Taylor. Joined by Henri, Glackens, Lawson, Bellows, Davies, Alden Weir, Gutzun Borglum, and Jonas Young, the association represented some of the finest and most respected artists in the country (seven of the 25 founders were also members of the NAD). They resolved to field an exhibition of the best modern works, regardless of nationality, with competition open to all, regardless of NAD membership. Fearing an open war with the powerful NAD, Weir declined the presidency in January 1912, and the office fell to Arthur B. Davies.

The choice of Davies was not accidental nor was he second-rate compared to Weir. Davies had an acclaimed portfolio and was an exhibited painter with strong connections to American and European art patrons and dealers. Davies also had surprisingly adept organizational skills. In the late summer of 1912, Davies, aided by Walter Pach, traveled throughout Europe securing the loan of modern works and the cooperation of a number of galleries in the Hague, Munich, Paris, and Berlin. Returning in November, Davies and the AAPS set about funding the project, arranging the various halls, printing more than 50,000 catalogs and pamphlets, and scheduling delivery for and hanging more than 1,300 works of art (a third of which were produced by foreign artists).

When the show opened, on February 17, 1913, more than 4,000 people attended. When it closed in New York, conservative estimates suggested that at least 75,000 had seen the exhibit. Even typically uninterested publishers like the *New York Sun* recognized that the AAPS had "wrought something very like a miracle.... an event not on any account to be missed."[16] The show's motto—The New Spirit—was plainly evident in the breadth of the display. The first galleries displayed the "Old" modern masters van Gogh, Paul Gauguin, Seurat, and Cézanne; the mood then quickly shifted toward the more daring works of Picasso, Matisse, Georges Braque, Odilon Redon, Marcel Duchamp, Francis Picabia, Constantin Brancusi, and Wassily Kandinsky. The American modernists were numerically superior and included the works of the Eight as well as such later notables as Edward Hopper, Joseph Stella, and Charles Sheeler. Still, despite their numbers, the American pieces shrank when compared to more mature, daring, and brazenly confident European offerings. By contrast, the Americans seemed even more provincial and derivative than they had realized. Given the lack of knowledge of the European movement, it was amazing that the AAPS was capable of presenting such a high quality and breadth of works.[17]

On March 15, the New York show closed and about 500 pieces moved on to the Art Institute of Chicago. The exhibit, which opened nine days later, was seen by another 200,000 people (a reflection of the critical response to the first Armory Show) in less than 25 days. By the end of April, approximately 250 works continued on to Boston's Copley Hall where they were shown to dwindling audiences. When the Boston exhibition closed, on May 19, the organizers agreed to end the tour. Internal dissent over the (generally negative) effect of the show on American artists had split the AAPS by 1916. The association never staged a second exhibition after the Armory Show. Its one production had fundamentally transformed the fine arts in America.

The Critics

It would be incorrect to conclude that every individual who attended the Armory Show was harshly critical of what he or she saw. Most were impressed by the magnitude of the display. A few were openly supportive of the new and modern aesthetics. The majority of critics, however, were simply unsure of exactly *what* to think of these creations; they had no point of reference, it was all amazingly new. In historical retrospect, it is possible to be overly derisive of these evaluations. After all, we might conclude, how could one possibly dismiss Cézanne or Picasso (one writer said tartly, "Picasso fails to impress"[18]) when compared to artists who would be forgotten in less than a decade? It is vital to understand these views, however, to appreciate how the new visual culture challenged America's tastes and personal assumptions about art. When evaluating the evaluators, then, we look not only for their artistic interpretation but also their cultural biases and reactions as a way in which to appreciate the United States during the 1910s.

Grudging acceptance or hidden bemusement might best describe the typical response of the Armory Show visitor. Characteristic was Theodore Roosevelt, who attended the New York showing on March 4, not coincidentally the very same day that his rival for the presidency in 1912, Woodrow Wilson, was being inaugurated. Roosevelt published his response in *Outlook*, titled "A Layman's View of an Art Exhibition." In the essay, Roosevelt showed considerable flexibility and a liberal spirit for most of what he saw. He loved the sense of adventure evinced by many of the works and cited the lack of "simpering, self-satisfied conventionality" as one of the show's greatest features. Roosevelt was also perceptive in (humorously) comparing one of the modernists works to a Navajo rug that hung in his bathroom—a connection of modern to "primitive" art which would soon dominate the academy. Yet Roosevelt was also uncomfortable with what he regarded as a lack of common reference points for the viewing audience. He concluded, "In this recent exhibition the lunatic fringe was fully in evidence, especially in the rooms devoted to the Cubists and the Futurists, or Near-Impressionists." For the former president, and many others, these avant-garde artists and their work had gone too far afield to even be considered art.[19]

Lacking the intelligence and subtle sophistication of Roosevelt, many other critics simply tried to laugh at what they did not understand. Correspondent Margaret Hubbard Ayer reported, "One of the best signs of the day [was] that these pictures evoke laughter instead of fear, mystery, desire, or any of the other sentiments they were expected to inspire. I am thankful to say that I have seen each woman burst into laughter or grow indignant or uncomfortable as she looked at certain of the lurid pictures." Marcel Duchamp's *Nude Descending a Staircase, No. 2* (1912) was described by many as an explosion in a shingle factory, and it inspired popular jingles and cartoons. Many came to the show simply to see the canvas and laugh.[20]

Even experienced artists showed a particular lack of gravity for the new arrivals. John Sloan drew a cartoon for the *Masses* which made a clever play of the children's rhyme "A Crooked Man." His sketch, titled "A Slight Attack of Third Dementia Brought on by Excessive Study of the Much-Talked-of Cubists Pictures in the International Exhibition at New York," showed the progression of stick men with the stanzas reading, "There was a Cubic man who walked a cubic mile, he found a cubic sixpence upon a cubic style."[21] Noted critic Gillett Burgess, who traveled regularly to Europe and was better prepared for the modernist style, asked, "If you can imagine what a particularly sanguinary little girl of eight, half-crazed with gin, would do to a white-washed wall, if left alone with a box of crayons, then you will come near to fancying what most of the work was like."[22] The conservative judge Royal Cortissoz likened Picasso's subjects to a "monstrous potato or gourd which the farmer brings to the village store to see [what] his cronies can make out in certain 'bumps.' "[23] Such humor created a circus atmosphere for the show and gave legitimacy to more mean-spirited attacks.

These onslaughts derided the works for the same reasons that others laughed; they were unusual, novel, or threatening. Many critics took special comfort in the odd personal histories of the leading artists. For example, Cézanne was known to have been an incompetent businessman before turning to painting, van Gogh had mutilated himself by cutting off an ear, and Gauguin had deserted his family and friends for a life in Tahiti. Clearly these individuals were as "mad" as their paintings suggested them to be—"failures" both as artists and men. While Frank J. Maher Jr., concurred that "this new art is very living and interesting," he suggested that the public's interest was like the "feeling on [one's] first visiting a lunatic asylum. The inmates might well seem more vivid and fascinating than the every-day companions of home and office." George De Forest Brush added that, while Matisse may be more exciting than the average American painter, "it doesn't at all follow that Matisse is the better artist. So is a vitriol-throwing suffragette more exciting than a lady."[24] Many noted that the relative sanity of the American works spoke well for this country's reputation around the globe.

By far, the responses of the instructors and students at the Art Institute of Chicago were the most acrimonious. Because of the intense criticism emanating from the New York debut, Chicago's artists were primed to hail the newcomers as "fakers," "madmen," and "degenerates." Organizer Walt Kuhn retorted that the "instructors at the Institute are mad through, one even went so far as to take a big class of the students into the French room and threw a virtual fit condemning Matisse."[25] Near the show's close, students were further incited by their teachers to burn images of Matisse, Brancusi, and Walter Pach in effigy. It was not the professionals but the laymen who believed this type of activity to be simply un-American. The *Chicago Evening Post* opined, with rare objectivity, that the city "ought to give [the show] a fair hearing and a serious consideration." To their view, the show,

already impelled many of us to arm ourselves against its novelty with weapons of ridicule. . . . This is no more than the reaction of natural conservatism. . . . We cannot laugh this new post-impressionistic . . . movement out of court. . . . however incomprehensible it may be, it at least embodies a spirit of individualistic revolt that ever wins the respect of men. The spirit of American art can least of all afford to reject. We need it keenly right here in the art schools of Chicago.[26]

Ironically, while most Americans defined themselves as an individual-istic society, modern painters earned the wrath of the American art com-munity for taking this same spirit into the visual arts.

Despite these problems, most art critics were willing to take the Ar-mory Show seriously and to try to assess the works as professionally as possible. Most of the nation's preeminent writers added their opinions, including Kenyan Cox (writing for the *New York Times*, *Century*, and *Scribner's*), Royal Cortissoz (*New York Tribune*), and Frank Jewett Mather Jr. (a Princeton professor and contributor to the *Nation*). That they rec-ognized the show to be a direct challenge to tradition and their well-trained sensibilities is indisputable. Cox wrote that the Armory display was "not amusing; it [was] heart rending and sickening."[27] Matisse fig-ured prominently in this attack, largely because of the wide variety of his work on display and the obvious zeal with which he broke the rules (and perhaps because the cubists were just *too* strange for the critics to reflect upon). Cortissoz later wrote, "I have been a traditionalist, stead-fastly opposed to the inadequacies and bizarre eccentricities of modern-ism."[28] The "oddness" of the works masked the fact that American critics were especially opposed the *subjectivity* of their content and style.

Elitism and the Fine Arts

The question of elitism has shown great longevity in the ways in which the American public embraced or rejected the fine arts since 1913. In many ways, it was (or is) the intense subjectivity in the new art that alienated many casual observers. Artists, like the critics who interpret them, had for centuries taken traditional objects and made them things of transcendent importance to the public. Whether is was the *Mona Lisa* (which was actually stolen in 1911, then recovered in Florence in 1913) or "Whistler's Mother" (in fact, titled *A Study in Grey and Black*), previous fine artists had depicted images that were accessible to all. The new styles, by contrast, seemed to be all subjectivity and perspective. More-over, for fans of the American modernist movement, these temperaments were decidedly European and undemocratic. According to painter Wil-lard Huntington Wright, "The antagonism of the masses to the artist sprang up simultaneously with the disgust of the artist for the masses." This was an "inevitable result," according to Wright, when the artist's work suggested that "the artist's mind [was] developing beyond them."[29]

Most modern artists had (and have) a different interpretation than these critics. Many would claim that the new art more clearly relates the individualistic world around them than those works that use "common images" heavily laden with symbolic meaning, often created by those in power for their benefit (for example, the use of the thin, young, white female as "the" absolute definition of beauty). The modernists' conclusion, that science and modernity had killed realistic representation, is best seen in the ready-made art of Marcel Duchamp. Calling his creations "the most important single idea to come out of my work," Duchamp displayed everyday items in galleries and at exhibitions, simply calling them works of art. His most (in)famous was *Fontaine*, displayed at 291 and the Independents' Exhibition (1917). The item was once a working urinal, but by placing it on display Duchamp hoped to show how life and art were one. The public, according to Duchamp, does not need critics, art academies, or their biased aesthetic filters to recognize that "art" surrounds them.[30] "Beauty" was literally in the eye of the beholder. In this way, the new art could claim to be radically democratic and emancipated from the control of others.

By contrast, charges of elitism emerged (and largely remain to this day). Nowhere was this sentiment more pronounced than on the pages of the *Masses*. The magazine, home to many influential American realists, believed in a clear connection between art and social uplift. Much like Stieglitz, who held that the new art could change the world, contributors to the *Masses* were concerned when they saw the Armory Show diverge so forcefully from accessible visual culture. Glackens wrote, in 1917, that "a great deal of this so-called modern art is pure materialism, the pouring out through symbols of a half-baked psychology, a suppressed adolescence."[31] If artists were simply taking stock of their own irrational, and functionally useless, opinions of the modern world, what reason would the real masses have to seek their council? Sloan believed that the "graphic artist makes a human document" displaying the "realities seen with the heart *and* mind."[32] To them, the Postimpressionists spoke in a foreign language wholly indecipherable by anyone else. Such elitism ran counter to their basic values and was soundly condemned by established American modernists.[33]

The Post-Armory Years

Of course, for the realists such misgivings were soon moot. The success of the Armory Show spawned a host of exhibitions and new modern art galleries. Large museums, such as the Carnegie Institute in Pittsburgh, the Taylor Galleries in Cleveland, and the Carroll Gallery and National Arts Club in New York City, and many smaller ones now spent their energies and resources in developing American artists with Postimpressionist styles. In 1916 the Forum Exhibition at Anderson Galleries on Park Avenue held its second major show of American modernism, followed, in 1917, by the Independents' Exhibition of more than 2,500 works by 1,300 artists. The sales figures from the Armory Show suggested the coming trend. Most of the major collectors (including John Quinn, Arthur Jerome Eddy, Lillie P. Bliss, Walter Arensberg, Albert C.

Barnes, and Stephen C. Cook) purchased aggressively during the show. Of the 250 works sold, however, more than 200 were by foreign artists. By 1918 most "official" American academies (such as the NAD) and art schools had lost their prestige and, with it, their power to control the content of exhibitions. The central fatality of this change was the modern realist style of the Ashcan school. Ostensibly the reason for the Armory Show, these artists were quickly marginalized and often forgotten in the immediate aftermath of the show.

Judging from the output, cubism, abstraction, and expressionism became the dominant form of most fine artists in America. Max Weber, Marsden Hartley, Man Ray, John Covert, and Arthur Dove were the most notable of a large group. Stuart Davis became the most original and inventive. A former Ashcan artist and contributor to the *Masses*, Davis merged expressionism with ready-mades into a form that heralded the pop art movement of the 1950s and 1960s. Thomas Hart Benton, Joseph Stella, Morgan Russell, and Stanton MacDonald-Wright all experimented with synchromatic art, and were exhibited at the Carroll Gallery in 1914. Stella's *Battle of Lights, Coney Island* (1913) and *The Bridge* (1918) remain testaments to the group's talents and ambitions. Georgia O'Keeffe, the youngest of the new artists, melded synchromism, abstraction, and Southwestern themes. She was one of the few artists who developed a particularly American style in the 1910s. Unfortunately, the brilliance of the Armory Show blinded artists to their own visions, and led many simply to copy the newer European styles. Still, the show and the subsequent war jumpstarted American modern art, enabling domestic painters to equal and then surpass their colleagues overseas. By 1930 America would become the source of most major innovations in the fine arts.

CONCLUSION

The variety ranging from comics to cubism makes it difficult to summarize the visual arts in the 1910s. Most certainly, the period witnessed one (if not two) of the greatest and most wrenching transformations in the fine arts. Other displays, by illustrators, commercial artists, and cartoonists, were also significant for the way in which they solidified the use of images in American popular culture. Ironically, it was the war that unified and validated many of these trends. For popular culture, the war provided an opportunity for commercial art to serve a useful purpose other than selling newspapers, magazines, or mouthwash; for the fine arts, the war swept away the "universal truths" many conservative artists had been clinging to. In a very real sense, the artistic community (which participated in the war in great numbers) came to believe that only personal truths were meaningful. By 1919 their artwork began to reflect this trend. The final irony was that the Armory Show did work as intended—if only for the wrong painters. America soon became the home of the most influential, original, and leading artists of the twentieth century. If the goal of the promoters was to develop a truly modern American artistic style, they succeeded on a grand scale.

Cost of Products

ENTERTAINMENT AND TRAVEL

Vacation cruise (berth and meals): 12-day round-trip from New York City to Halifax, $60.

Vacation cruise (berth and meals): round-trip from New York City to Jacksonville, Florida, $43.30.

Typical hotel room (New York City): $1.50–$3.00/evening.

Postcard: $0.02.

Personal Pullman railroad car of cigarette magnate James B. Duke: $38,050.

Average automobile: $600.

Average accessories

> Tire pump: $12.00
> Warning signal: $3.50–$6.00
> Speedometer: $10.00
> Gas gauge: $10.00

Ford Model T: $360.

Maxwell automobile: $695.

Dodge roadster: $885.

Dodge sedan: $1,350.

Cadillac automobile: $2,500–$3,250.

Taxi ride: $0.05 within the city.

Player piano: $1,050 new; $300–$425 used.

Annual salary of George M. Cohan: $1.5 million.

Ticket to see the Castles dance at Air Ice Palace, New York City: $1.50 (including dinner).

Ticket to Lavish Palace Theater (New York City): $2.00.

Ticket to typical vaudeville show: $0.50.

Ticket to typical movie: $0.05–$0.10; special features run as high as $2.00/ticket.

Daily newspaper: $0.01–$0.02

CLOTHING

Men's dressing gown (Sak's Fifth Avenue, New York City): $12.00–$40.00.

Men's suit (tailored): $13.95–$15.00.

Men's Arrow shirt: $1.50–$10.00.

Men's Hart, Shaffner & Marx overcoat: $22.50.

Men's Florshiem shoes: $5.00–$6.00/pair.

Men's hosiery, cotton: $0.06/pair.

Men's hosiery, silk: $0.23.

I. Magnin (San Francisco) women's velvet dress: $16.50–$35.00.

Gimbel's ostrich plumed hat: $0.69.

Gimbel's women's corset: $3.00.

Gimbel's Women's shoes: $1.95/pair.

Women's hosiery, cotton: $0.075/pair.

Women's hosiery, silk: $0.16–$0.25/pair.

Costs during World War I

    Dress: $39.50–$57.50
    Women's coats: $59.50–$79.50
    Women's shoes: $2.50–$8.00/pair
    Women's undergarment: $1.25–$1.50
    Child's coat: $5.98.

MISCELLANEOUS LIVING EXPENSES

Wool blanket: $1.68.

Hot water bottle: $0.59.

Dental fillings: $0.50; gold crown $3.00.

Listerene mouthwash: $0.29/pint.

Toilet paper: eight rolls for $0.25.

Push lawnmower: $1.98.

Gallon of mixed paint: $0.98.

Camel cigarettes (pack of 20): $0.10.

8 quarts of whiskey: $5.00.

Coffee percolator: $2.00–$5.00.

Sunshine biscuits: $0.10/box.

Refrigerator: $900.

Tuition, room, and board at Harvard: $700 per year.

Eggs: $0.34/dozen.

Milk: $0.08/quart.

Bread: $0.05/loaf.

Bacon: $0.26/pound.

Round steak: $0.17/pound.

Oranges: $0.48/dozen.

Coffee: $0.28/pound.

MISCELLANEOUS DEMOGRAPHIC TRENDS, 1910–1920

U.S. deaths due to World War I: 53,402 in battle, 116,516 total.

European deaths due to World War I: 10,000,000 total.

U.S. population, 1910: 92,407,000; 1920: 106,491,000.

Life expectancy male/female, 1910: 48.4/51.8 years; 1920: 53.6/54.6 years.

Births, 1910: 30.1/1,000 people; 1920: 27.7/1,000 people.

Marriage, 1910: 13.2/1,000 people; 1920: 12.0/1,000 people.

Divorce, 1910: 1.1/1,000 people; 1920: 1.6/1,000 people.

Unemployment, 1910: 2.150 million; 1920: 2.132 million.

U.S. GNP, 1910: $35.3 billion; 1920: $91.5 billion.

Average salary, 1910: $750/year; 1920: $1,236/year.

Consumer price index, 1910 (CPI, 1967 = 100): 28; 1920 (CPI, 1967 = 100): 60.

Homicides, 1910: 4.6/100,000 people; 1920: 6.8/100,000 people.

Suicides, 1910: 15.3/100,000 people; 1920: 10.2/100,000 people.

The statistical data presented in this section is compiled and taken from a number of sources, including Donald B. Dodd, comp., *Historical Statistics of the United States: Two Centuries of the Census, 1790–1990* (Westport, CT: Greenwood Publishing Group, 1993); John Milton Cooper Jr., *The Pivotal Decades: The United States, 1900–1920* (New York: W.W. Norton, 1990); Nell Irvin Painter, *Standing at Armageddon: The United States, 1877–1919* (New York: W.W. Norton, 1987); and especially from Lois Gordon and Alan Gordon, *The Columbia Chronicles of American Life, 1910–1992* (New York: Columbia University Press, 1995), 2–95.

Notes

INTRODUCTION

1. H. Wayne Morgan, *The New Muses: Art in American Culture, 1865–1920* (Norman: University of Oklahoma Press, 1978), 156.

2. James Marston Finch refers to "esthetic wasteland" in *American Building: The Historical Forces that Shaped It*. 2d ed. (Boston: Houghton Mifflin, 1966), 228.

3. Robert H. Bremner, John Barbard, Tamara K. Hareven, and Robert M. Mennel, eds., *Children and Youth in America: A Documentary History*, vol. 2 (Cambridge, MA: Harvard University Press, 1971), 86–87.

4. Irving Sablosky, *American Music* (Chicago: University of Chicago Press, 1969) 155–56.

CHAPTER 1

1. The statistical data presented in this chapter is compiled and taken from a number of sources, including Donald B. Dodd, comp., *Historical Statistics of the United States: Two Centuries of the Census, 1790–1990* (Westport, CT: Greenwood Publishing Group, 1993); John Milton Cooper Jr., *The Pivotal Decades: The United States, 1900–1920* (New York: W.W. Norton, 1990); Forrest E. Linder and Robert D. Grove, *Vital Statistics Rates in the United States, 1900–1940* (New York: Arno Press, 1976); Lois Gordon and Alan Gordon, *The Columbia Chronicles of American Life, 1910–1992* (New York: Columbia University Press, 1995); and Nell Irvin Painter, *Standing at Armageddon: The United States, 1877–1919* (New York: W.W. Norton, 1987).

2. Lois Gordon and Alan Gordon, *The Columbia Chronicles of American Life, 1910–1992* (New York: Columbia University Press, 1995), 2, 754.

3. Timothy J. Gilfoyle, *City of Eros: New York City, Prostitution, and the Commercialization of Sex, 1790–1920* (New York: W.W. Norton, 1992), 308–9.

4. John Mack Farragher et al., *Out of Many: A History of the American People*, 3d ed. (Upper Saddle River, NJ: Prentice-Hall, 2000), 657.

5. Thomas H. Johnson, *The Oxford Companion to American History* (New York: Oxford University Press, 1966), 490.

6. David M. Kennedy, *Over Here: The First World War and American Society* (New York: Oxford University Press, 1966), 10.

CHAPTER 2

1. Leroy Ashby, *Endangered Children: Dependency, Neglect, and Abuse in American History*, Twayne's History of American Childhood Series (New York: Twayne Publishers, 1997), 79.

2. Robert H. Bremner, John Barnard, Tamara K. Hareven, and Robert M. Mennel, eds., *Children and Youth in America: A Documentary History*, vol. 2 (Cambridge, MA: Harvard University Press, 1971), 83–84.

3. Lois Gordon and Alan Gordon, *The Columbia Chronicles of American Life, 1910–1992* (New York: Columbia University Press, 1995).

4. Booker T. Washington, "Destitute Colored Children of the South," Proceedings of the Conference on the Care of Dependent Children held at Washington, D.C., January 25–26, 1909 (Washington, D.C.: n.p., 1909), 114–17.

5. Lewis W. Hine, "Children or Cotton?," *Survey* 31 (February 7, 1914): 589–90.

6. Washington, "Destitute Colored Children of the South," 114–17.

7. Hine, "Children or Cotton?," 589–90; Washington, "Destitute Colored Children of the South," 114–17.

8. S. Josephine Baker, *Fighting for Life* (New York: Macmillan, 1939), 17.

9. Bremner et al., *Children and Youth in America*, 18–20.

10. Ibid., 85.

11. Ibid., 86–87.

12. Arthur S. Link and Richard L. McCormick, *Progressivism* (Arlington Heights, IL: Harlan Davison, Inc., 1983), 110.

13. Bremner et al., *Children and Youth in America*, 95.

14. Ibid., 96.

15. Ibid., 1093.

16. David B. Tyack, *The One Best System: A History of American Urban Education* (Cambridge, MA: Harvard University Press, 1974), 183; Bremner et al., *Children and Youth in America*, 1093–94.

17. Tyack, *The One Best System*, 183; Bremner et al., *Children and Youth in America*, 1094.

18. Tyack, *The One Best System*, 177–78.

19. John Dewey, *The School and Society* (Chicago: University of Chicago Press, 1900), 47–53.

20. Tyack, *The One Best System*, 137.

21. Ibid., 222.

22. Lawrence A. Cremin, *American Education: The Metropolitan Experience, 1876–1980* (New York: Harper & Row, 1988), 233.

23. LeRoy Ashby, *Saving the Waifs: Reformers and Dependent Children, 1890–1917* (Philadelphia: Temple University Press, 1984), xi.

24. Bremner et al., *Children and Youth in America*, 379.

25. Ashby, *Endangered Children*, 81.

26. Cremin, *American Education*, 2–3.

27. Bremner et al., *Children and Youth in America*, 751–55.

28. Max West, *Infant Care*, United States Children's Bureau, Pub. No. 8 (Washington, D.C., 1914), 59–63.

29. Bremner et al., *Children and Youth in America*, 36–38.

30. Cremin, *American Education*, 286–89.

31. "Toilers of the Tenements Where the Beautiful Things of the Great Shops are Made," *McClure's* magazine 35 (July 1910): 231–32.

32. Bremner et al., *Children and Youth in America*, 603.

33. Ibid.

34. Joseph Hawes, *The Children's Rights Movement: A History of Advocacy and Protection*, Twayne's Social Movement Series (Boston: Twayne Publishers, 1991), 34.

35. Thomas D. Eliot, *The Juvenile Court and the Community* (New York: n.p., 1914), 13–16.

36. Ashby, *Saving the Waifs*, 104–32.

37. Ibid., 110.

38. Ibid., 114.

39. Ibid., 115.

40. Ibid., 122.

41. Ibid., 131–32.

CHAPTER 3

1. S.N. Behrman, "The Advertising Man," *New Republic* (August 20, 1919), cited in Robert B. Luce, ed., *The Faces of Five Decades: Selections from Fifty Years of the New Republic, 1914–1964* (New York: Simon and Schuster, 1964), 49.

2. Ibid., 50.

3. For example, Roland Marchand shows how ads changed little during the Great Depression when, obviously, societal needs were diverging drastically. Roland Marchand, *Advertising the American Dream: Making Way for Modernity, 1920–1940* (Berkeley: University of California Press, 1985), xvi; Jackson Lears, *Fables of Abundance: A Cultural History of Advertising in America* (New York: Basic Books, 1995), 1.

4. Behrman, "The Advertising Man," 49.

5. Marchand, *Advertising the American Dream*, 2.

6. Lears, *Fables of Abundance*, 159–62.

7. Theodore Peterson, *Magazines in the Twentieth Century* (Urbana: University of Illinois Press, 1964), 19.

8. John Tebbel and Mary Ellen Zuckerman, *The Magazine in America: 1741–1990* (New York: Oxford University Press, 1991), 140–46.

9. Lears, *Fables of Abundance*, 201.

10. Statistics for *Ladies' Home Journal* taken from Theodore Peterson, *Magazines in the Twentieth Century*; Salme Hrju Steinberg, *Reformer in the Marketplace: Edward D. Bok and the* Ladies' Home Journal (Baton Rouge: Louisiana State University Press, 1979); and Tebbel and Zuckerman, *The Magazine in America*.

11. Tebbel and Zuckerman, *The Magazine in America*, 97.

12. James P. Wood, *The Story of Advertising* (New York: Ronald Press, 1958), 211.

13. Tebbel and Zuckerman, *The Magazine in America*, 131–39.

14. Lears, *Fables of Abundance*, 203.

15. Michael Schudson, *Advertising, the Uneasy Persuasion: Its Dubious Impact on American Society* (New York: Basic Books, 1984), 210, 214–18.

16. Stephen Fox, *The Mirror Makers: A History of American Advertising and Its Creators* (New York: William Morrow, 1984), 50.

17. Stewart Ewen, *Captains of Consciousness: Advertising and the Social Roots of Consumer Culture* (New York: McGraw-Hill Book Company, 1976), 35.

18. Marchand, *Advertising the American Dream*, 11.

19. Fox, *The Mirror Makers*, 72.

20. Cecil Munsey, *The Illustrated Guide to the Collectibles of Coca-Cola* (New York: Hawthorne Books, 1972), 8–10, 39–40.

21. Lears, *Fables of Abundance*, 159.

22. Munsey, *The Illustrated Guide to the Collectibles of Coca-Cola*, 313–18.

23. U.S. Department of Commerce, *Bureau of the Census, Historical Statistics of the United States: Colonial Times to 1970*, vol. 2 (Washington, D.C., 1975), 716.

24. Lears, *Fables of Abundance*, 212–13.

25. James D. Norris, *Advertising and the Transformation of American Society, 1865–1920*, Contributions in Economics and Economic History, no. 110 (Westport, CT: Greenwood Press, 1990), 151.

26. Charles Goodrum and Helen Dalrymple, *Advertising in America: The First 200 Years* (New York: Harry N. Abrams, 1990), 236.

27. Norris, *Advertising and the Transformation of American Society*, 161–65.

28. Ibid., 138–39, 141; Goodrum and Dalrymple, *Advertising in America*, 195.

29. Lears, *Fables of Abundance*, 219.

30. Ibid.

31. Fox, *The Mirror Makers*, 76.

32. Lears, *Fables of Abundance*, 220.

33. Marchand, *Advertising the American Dream*, 6; Ewen, *Captains of Consciousness*, 19, 31, 46.

CHAPTER 4

1. Carter Wiseman, *Shaping a Nation: Twentieth-Century American Architecture and Its Makers* (New York: W.W. Norton, 1998), 48.

2. Clifford Edward Clark Jr., *The American Family Home: 1800–1960* (Chapel Hill: University of North Carolina Press, 1986), 22.

3. James Marston Finch, *American Building: The Historical Forces That Shaped It*, 2d ed. (Boston: Houghton Mifflin, 1966), 228.

4. Walter C. Kidney, *The Architecture of Choice: Beaux-Arts Architecture and Urban Reformer* (Cambridge, MA: MIT Press, 1986), 9.

5. Kidney, *The Architecture of Choice*, vii.

6. Mardges Bacon, *Ernest Flagg: Beaux-Arts Architect and Urban Reformer* (Cambridge, MA: MIT Press, 1986), 43.

7. Wiseman, *Shaping of a Nation*, 47.

8. Bacon, *Ernest Flagg*, 187–88.

9. Richard Guy Wilson, *McKim, Mead, & White, Architects* (New York: Rizzoli, 1983), 211–12.

10. Kenneth T. Jackson, *Crabgrass Frontier: The Suburbanization of the United States* (New York: Oxford University Press, 1985), 149.

11. Wiseman, *Shaping of a Nation*, 103–4.

12. Taliesin Preservation Society, "Taliesin Residence," available online at http://www.taliesinpreservation.org/estate/residence.htm.

13. Clifford Edward Clark Jr., *The American Family Home: 1800–1960* (Chapel Hill: University of North Carolina Press, 1986), 171.

14. Dolores Hayden, *The Grand Domestic Revolution: A History of Feminist Designs for American Homes, Neighborhoods, and Cities* (Cambridge, MA: MIT Press, 1983), 183.

15. Walter C. Kidney, *The Architecture of Choice: Eclecticism in America, 1880–1930* (New York: George Braziller, 1974), 67.

CHAPTER 5

1. Valerie Mendes and Amy de la Haye, *20th Century Fashion* (London: Thames & Hudson, 1999), 28–29.

2. Kathy Piess, *Hope in a Jar: The Making of America's Beauty Culture* (New York: Henry Holt, 1998), 144.

3. Lewis Erenberg, *Steppin' Out: New York Nightlife and the Transformation of American Culture, 1890–1930* (Chicago: University of Chicago Press, 1981), 168.

CHAPTER 6

1. Reay Tannahill, *Food in History: The New, Fully Revised, and Updated Edition of the Classic Gastronomic Epic* (New York: Crown Publishers, 1988), 334.

2. Roland Marchand, *Advertising the American Dream: Making Way for Modernity, 1920–1940* (Berkeley: University of California Press, 1985), 272.

3. Lewis Erenberg, *Steppin' Out: New York Nightlife and the Transformation of American Culture, 1890–1930* (Chicago: University of Chicago Press, 1981).

4. Ibid., 37.

CHAPTER 7

1. Inez and Marshall McClintock, *Toys in America* (Washington, D.C.: Public Affairs Press, 1961), 421.

2. Bernard Mergen, "Games and Toys," in *Handbook of American Popular Culture*, ed. M. Thomas Inge, vol. 2 (Westport, CT: Greenwood Press, 1980), 166–68.

3. Blair Whitton, *The Knopf Collector's Guide to American Antiques: Toys* (New York: Alfred A. Knopf, 1984), 113.

4. Charles Panati, *Panati's Parade of Fads, Follies, and Manias: The Origins of Our Most Cherished Possessions* (New York: Harper Perennial, 1991), 92.

5. Foster Rhea Dulles, *America Learns to Play. A History of Popular Recreation, 1607–1940* (New York: Appleton-Century, 1940), 310.

6. John R. Betts, *America's Sporting Heritage, 1850–1950* (Reading, MA: Addison-Wesley, 1974), 187.

7. Mergen, "Games and Toys," 169.

8. Betts, *America's Sporting Heritage*, 179.

9. Steven A. Riess, *City Games: The Evolution of American Urban Society and the Rise of Sports* (Urbana: University of Illinois Press, 1989), 1.

10. Stephen Hardy, *How Boston Played: Sports, Recreation and Community, 1865–1915* (Boston: Northeastern University Press, 1982), 67.

11. Dominick Cavallo, *Muscles and Morals: Organized Playgrounds and Urban Reform* (Philadelphia: University of Pennsylvania Press, 1981), 29–30.

12. Ibid., 16–45.

13. Elliot J. Gorn, *The Manly Art: Bare-Knuckle Prize Fighting in America* (Ithaca, NY: Cornell University Press, 1986), 205.

14. Randy Roberts, *Papa Jack: Jack Johnson and the Era of White Hopes* (New York: The Free Press, 1983).

15. Allen Guttmann, *From Ritual to Record: The Nature of Modern Sport* (New York: Columbia University Press, 1978), 133.

16. Betts, *American's Sporting Heritage*, 127.

17. Steven A. Riess, *Touching Base: Professional Baseball and American Culture in the Progressive Era*, Contributions in American Studies, no. 48 (Westport, CT: Greenwood Press, 1980), 46–53.

18. Ibid., 220–21.

19. Ibid., 14–20.

20. Ibid., 53–66.

21. Ibid., 86–91.

22. Ibid., 24.

23. Ibid., 88–90.

24. Eliot Asinof, *Eight Men Out: The Black Sox and the 1919 World Series* (New York: Henry Holt, 1963), 226.

CHAPTER 8

1. Wendy Steiner, "The Diversity of American Fiction," in *Columbia Literary History of the United States*, ed. Emory Elliott (New York: Columbia University Press, 1988), 845.

2. Malcolm Bradbury, "The American *Risorgimento*: The United States and the Coming of the New Arts," in *American Literature Since 1900, The New History of Literature*, ed. Marcus Cunliffe (New York: Peter Bedrick Books, 1987), 9–10, 12.

3. Eugene E. Leach, "The Radicals of The Masses," in *1915: The Cultural Moment: The New Politics, the New Woman, the New Psychology, the New Art, and the New Theatre in America*, ed. Adele Heller and Lois Rudnick (New Brunswick, NJ: Rutgers University Press, 1991), 28, 29.

4. Ellen Kimbel, "The American Short Story: 1900–1920" in *The American Short Story: 1900–1945, A Critical History*, ed. Philip Stevick (Boston: Twayne Publishers, 1984), 62.

5. Charles A. Fecher, "The Comfortable Bourgeois," in *On Mencken*, ed. John Dorsey (New York: Alfred A. Knopf, 1980), 120–23.

6. William H. Nolte, "The Literary Critic," in *On Mencken*, ed. John Dorsey (New York: Alfred A. Knopf, 1980), 204, 214.

7. Ibid., 233.

8. Bradbury, "The American *Risorgimento*," 2.

9. Carlton Jackson, *Zane Grey* (Boston: Twayne Publishers, 1973), 8.

10. Ibid., 70.

11. John Taliaferro, *Tarzan Forever: The Life of Edgar Rice Burroughs, Creator of Tarzan* (New York: Scribner, 1999).

12. Ibid., 75.

13. Jamie Ambrose, *Willa Cather: Writing at the Frontier* (New York: Berg Publishers, 1988), xiii.

14. David M. Kennedy, *Over Here: The First World War and American Society* (New York: Oxford University Press, 1980), 180–81.

15. Bradbury, "The American *Risorgimento*," 21.

16. Geoffrey Moore, "American Poetry and the English Language, 1900–1945," in *American Literature Since 1900: The New History of Literature*, ed. Marcus Cunliffe (New York: Peter Bedrick Books, 1987), 91.

17. Ibid.

CHAPTER 9

1. Irving Sablosky, *American Music* (Chicago: University of Chicago Press, 1969), 135.

2. Russell Lynes, *The Lively Audience: A Social History of the Visual and Performing Arts in America, 1890–1950* (New York: Harper and Row, 1985), 102.

3. Eileen Southern, *The Music of Black Americans: A History*, 3d ed. (New York: W.W. Norton, 1997), 265.

4. James Lincoln Collier, *The Making of Jazz: A Comprehensive History* (Boston: Houghton Mifflin, 1978), 23.

5. Ernest Allen Jr., "The New Negro: Explorations in Identity and Social Consciousness, 1910–1992," in *1915: The Cultural Moment: The New Politics, the New Woman, the New Psychology, the New Art, and the New Theatre in America*, ed. Adele Heller and Lois Rudnick (New Brunswick, NJ: Rutgers University Press, 1991), 48.

6. Southern, *The Music of Black Americans*, 271.

7. Ibid., 280.

8. Gilbert Chase, *America's Music: From the Pilgrims to the Present*, 3d ed. (Urbana: University of Illinois Press, 1987), 354; Sablosky, *American Music*, 155–56.

9. Sablosky, *American Music*, 157.

10. Chase, *America's Music*, 439.

11. H. Wiley Hitchcock, *Music in the United States: A Historical Introduction* (Upper Saddle River, NJ: Prentice-Hall, 1969), 155.

12. Chase, *America's Music*, 332.

13. Ibid., 334.

14. Ibid., 335.

15. Lynes, *The Lively Audience*, 146.

16. Terry Waldo, *This Is Ragtime* (New York: Hawthorne Books, 1976), 96.

17. Chase, *America's Music*, 413.

18. Neil Leonard, "The Reaction to Ragtime," in *Ragtime: Its History, Composers, and Music*, ed. John Edward Hasse (New York: Schirmer Books, 1985), 107.

19. Ibid., 105–7.

20. Joseph R. Scotti, "The Musical Legacy of Joe Lamb," in *Ragtime: Its History, Composers, and Music*, ed. John Edward Hasse (New York: Schirmer Books, 1985), 255.

21. Chase, *America's Music*, 414.

22. Collier, *The Making of Jazz*, 114.

23. William W. Austin, *Music in the 20th Century: From Debussy Through Stravinsky* (New York: W.W. Norton, 1966), 188.

24. Lynes, *The Lively Audience*, 105–7.

25. Collier, *The Making of Jazz*, 3.

26. Lynes, *The Lively Audience*, 105.

27. Collier, *The Making of Jazz*, 95.

CHAPTER 10

1. Ethan Mordden, *The American Theater* (New York: Oxford University Press, 1981), 56.

2. Oscar G. Brockett, *History of the Theater*, 7th ed. (Boston: Allyn and Bacon, 1995), 495.

3. Adele Heller, "The New Theater," in *1915: The Cultural Moment: The New Politics, the New Woman, the New Psychology, the New Art, and the New Theatre in America*, ed. Adele Heller and Lois Rudnick (New Brunswick, NJ: Rutgers University Press, 1991), 220, 231.

4. Barbara Gelb, "Eugene O'Neill in Provincetown," in *1915: The Cultural Moment: The New Politics, the New Woman, the New Psychology, the New Art, and the New Theatre in America*, ed. Adele Heller and Lois Rudnick (New Brunswick, NJ: Rutgers University Press, 1991), 313.

5. Heller, "New Theater," 217.

6. Russell Lynes, *The Lively Audience: A Social History of the Visual and Performing Arts in America, 1890–1950* (New York: Harper & Row, 1985), 132.

7. Mordden, *The American Theater*, 66.

8. Robert C. Toll, *On With the Show: The First Century of Show Business in America* (New York: Oxford University Press, 1976), 131.

9. Ibid., 278.

10. Lewis Erenberg, *Steppin' Out: New York Nightlife and the Transformation of American Culture, 1890–1930* (Chicago: University of Chicago Press, 1981), 113.

11. Gerald Mast, *A Short History of the Movies*, 5th ed. (New York: Macmillan, 1992), 5–28.

12. Mast, *A Short History of the Movies*, 57.

13. Geoffrey Nowell-Smith, ed., *The Oxford History of World Cinema* (New York: Oxford University Press, 1996), 25–27.

14. Ibid., 30–31.

15. Rusty E. Frank, *Tap! The Greatest Tap Dance Stars and Their Stories, 1900–1955* (New York: William Morrow, 1990), 25, 28.

16. Mast, *A Short History of the Movies*, 31.

17. Lary May, "Douglass Fairbanks, Mary Pickford and the New Personality, 1914–1918, in *Hollywood's America: United States History Through Its Films*, ed. Steven Mintz and Randy Roberts (St. James, New York: Brandywine Press, 1993), 70.

18. Eileen Bowser, "The Transformation of Cinema, 1907–1915," in *History of the American Cinema*, ed. Charles Harpole (New York: Charles Scribner's Sons, 1990), 121.

19. Nowell-Smith, *The Oxford History of World Cinema*, 84–85.

20. Mast, *A Short History of the Movies*, 93.

21. Charles J. Maland, *Chaplin and American Culture: The Evolution of a Star Image* (Princeton, NJ: Princeton University Press, 1989), 25.

22. Ibid., 26.

23. Donald Bogle, *Toms, Coons, Mulattoes, Mammies, and Bucks: An Interpretive History of Blacks in American Films* (New York: Viking Press, 1973), 4.

24. Mast, *A Short History of the Movies*, 51.

25. Steven Mintz and Randy Roberts, eds., *Hollywood's America: United States History Through Its Films* (St. James, NY: Brandywine Press, 1993), 47.

CHAPTER 11

1. Hal Barron, *Mixed Harvest: The Second Great Transformation in the Rural North, 1870–1930* (Chapel Hill: University of North Carolina Press, 1997), 198.

2. James M. Morris, *America's Armed Forces: A History*, 2d ed. (Upper Saddle River, NJ: Prentice-Hall, 1996), 189–91.

3. Steven Biel, *Down With the Old Canoe: A Cultural History of the* Titanic *Disaster* (New York: W.W. Norton, 1996), 128. A complete list of victims can be accessed through the Encyclopedia Titanica project, or compiled in Lester J. Mitcham, "RMS Titanic: Passenger Numbers: The Statistics of the Disaster," available online at http://www.encyclopedia-titanica.org/articles/statistics_mitcham.shtml. For a discussion of the interpretation of the disaster, see Paul Heyer, Titanic *Legacy: Disaster as Media Event and Myth* (Westport, CT: Praeger, 1995).

4. Biel, *Down With the Old Canoe*, 38–39, 43.

5. Ibid., 126–127.

6. Heyer, Titanic *Legacy*, 163.

7. George Hilton, *Eastland: Legacy of the* Titanic (Stanford, CA: Stanford University Press, 1995).

8. Thomas H. Johnson, ed., *The Oxford Companion to American History* (New York: Oxford University Press, 1966), 490–91.

9. Kenneth T. Jackson, *Crabgrass Frontier: The Suburbanization of the United States* (New York: Oxford University Press, 1985), 103.

10. Ibid., 112.

11. Allan Nevins, *Ford: The Times, the Man, and the Company* (New York: Charles Scribner's Sons, 1954), 135–42, 252–55.

12. Jackson, *Crabgrass Frontier*, 157–58.

13. David J. Wilkie, *Esquire's American Autos and Their Makers* (New York: Esquire, Inc., 1963), 70.

14. Nevins, *Ford*, 447–80.

15. Jackson, *Crabgrass Frontier*, 160–61.

CHAPTER 12

1. Henry Geldzahler, *American Painting in the Twentieth Century* (New York: Metropolitan Museum of Art, 1965), 30.

2. Bennard B. Perlman, *The Immortal Eight: American Painting from Eakins to the Armory Show, 1870–1913* (Westport, CT: North Light Publishers, 1979), 15.

3. John Tebbel and Mary Ellen Zuckerman, *The Magazine in America: 1741–1990* (New York: Oxford University Press, 1991), 140–46.

4. Rebecca Zurier, "The *Masses* and Modernism," in *1915: The Cultural Moment: The New Politics, the New Woman, the New Psychology, the New Art, and the New Theatre in America*, ed. Adele Heller and Lois Rudnick (New Brunswick, NJ: Rutgers University Press, 1991), 209.

5. Robert C. Harvey, *Children of the Yellow Kid: The Evolution of the American Comic Strip* (Seattle: Frye Art Museum and the University of Washington Press, 1998), 10.

6. Ibid., 16.

7. Ron Goulart, ed. *The Encyclopedia of American Comics* (New York: Facts on File, 1990), 295.

8. Ibid., 223.

9. Martin Green, "The New Art," in *1915: The Cultural Moment: The New Politics, the New Woman, the New Psychology, the New Art, and the New Theatre in America*, ed. Adele Heller and Lois Rudnick (New Brunswick, NJ: Rutgers University Press, 1991), 158.

10. Ibid., 157.

11. Perlman, *The Immortal Eight*, 109.

12. Ibid., 87–88.

13. Edward Abrahams, "Alfred Stieglitz's Faith and Vision," in *1915: The Cultural Moment: The New Politics, the New Woman, the New Psychology, the New Art, and the New Theatre in America*, ed. Adele Heller and Lois Rudnick (New Brunswick, NJ: Rutgers University Press, 1991), 187.

14. Geldzahler, *American Painting in the Twentieth Century* (New York: Metropolitan Museum of Art, 1965), 51.

15. Milton W. Brown, "The Armory Show and Its Aftermath," in *1915: The Cultural Moment: The New Politics, the New Woman, the New Psychology, the New Art, and the New Theatre in America*, ed. Adele Heller and Lois Rudnick (New Brunswick, NJ: Rutgers University Press, 1991), 164.

16. Milton W. Brown, *The Story of the Armory Show*, rev. ed (New York: Abbeville Press, 1988), 86.

17. Ibid.

18. Ibid., 149.

19. Ibid., 119.

20. Ibid., 138–39.

21. *Masses* 4 (April 1913), 12.

22. H. Wayne Morgan, *The New Muses: Art in American Culture, 1865–1920* (Norman: University of Oklahoma Press, 1978), 172–173.

23. *Masses* 4 (April 1913), 12; Morgan, *The New Muses*, 172, 173.

24. Morgan, *The New Muses*, 161

25. Brown, *The Story of the Armory Show*, 178.

26. Ibid., 179–80.

27. Ibid., 132.

28. Morgan, *The New Muses*, 152.

29. Ibid., 160.

30. Abrahams, "Alfred Stieglitz's Faith and Vision," 190.

31. Morgan, *The New Muses*, 164.

32. Zurier, "The *Masses* and the Modernism," 209.

33. Morgan, *The New Muses*, 164 (italics added); Zurier, "The *Masses* and Modernism," 209.

Further Reading

Abrahams, Edward. *The Lyrical Left: Randolph Bourne, Alfred Stieglitz, and the Origins of Cultural Radicalism in America.* Charlottesville: University Press of Virginia, 1986.

Abrams, Richard M. *The Burdens of Progress, 1900–1929.* Glenview, IL: Scott, Foresman, 1978.

Allen, Ann Taylor. "Feminism, Social Science, and the Meanings of Modernity: The Debate on the Origins of the Family in Europe and the United States, 1860–1914." *American Historical Review* 104 (October 1999): 1085–113.

Ambrose, Jamie. *Willa Cather: Writing at the Frontier.* New York: Berg Publishers, 1988.

Anderson, Rudolph E. *The Story of the American Automobile.* Washington, D.C.: Public Affairs Press, 1950.

Ashby, LeRoy. *Endangered Children: Dependency, Neglect, and Abuse in American History.* Twayne's History of American Childhood Series. New York: Twayne Publishers, 1997.

———. *Saving the Waifs: Reformers and Dependent Children, 1890–1917.* Philadelphia: Temple University Press, 1984.

Asinof, Elliot. *Eight Men Out: The Black Sox and the 1919 World Series.* New York: Henry Holt, 1963.

Bacon, Mardges. *Ernest Flagg: Beaux-Arts Architect and Urban Reformer.* Cambridge, MA: MIT Press, 1986.

Banner, Lois W. *American Beauty.* New York: Knopf, 1983.

Banta, Martha. *Imaging American Women: Ideas and Ideals in Cultural History.* New York: Columbia University Press, 1987.

Barron, Hal. *Mixed Harvest: The Second Great Transformation in the Rural North, 1870–1930.* Chapel Hill: University of North Carolina Press, 1997.

Belasco, Warren. *An Appetite for Change.* New York: Pantheon, 1990.

Benson, Susan Porter. *Counter Cultures: Saleswomen, Managers, & Customers in*

American Department Stores, 1890–1940. Urbana: University of Illinois Press, 1986.

Berlin, Edward A. *Ragtime: A Musical and Cultural History*. Berkeley: University of California Press, 1980.

Betts, John R. *America's Sporting Heritage, 1850–1950*. Reading, MA: Addison-Wesley, 1974.

Biel, Steven. *Down With the Old Canoe: A Cultural History of the* Titanic *Disaster*. New York: W.W. Norton, 1996.

Bigsby, C.W.E. *A Critical Introduction to Twentieth-Century American Drama, Volume One, 1900–1940*. Cambridge, UK: Cambridge University Press, 1982.

Blaxter, Kenneth and Noel Robertson. *From Dearth to Plenty: The Modern Revolution in Food Production*. New York: Cambridge University Press, 1995.

Bogle, Donald. *Toms, Coons, Mulattoes, Mammies, and Bucks: An Interpretive History of Blacks in American Films*. New York: Viking Press, 1973.

Bowser, Eileen. *The Transformation of Cinema, 1907–1915*. New York: Charles Scribner's Sons, 1990.

Bremner, Robert H., John Barnard, Tamara K. Hareven, and Robert M. Mennel, eds. *Children and Youth in America: A Documentary History*. Volumes I and II. Cambridge, MA: Harvard University Press, 1971.

Brockett, Oscar G. *History of the Theater*. 7th Edition. Boston: Allyn and Bacon, 1995.

Bronner, Simon J. *Grasping Things: Folk Material Culture and Mass Society in America*. Lexington: University Press of Kentucky, 1986.

Brown, Milton W. *The Story of the Armory Show*. New York: Abbeville Press, 1988.

Buechner, Thomas S. *Norman Rockwell: A Sixty Year Retrospective*. New York: Harry N. Abrams, 1972.

Cavallo, Dominick. *Muscles and Morals: Organized Playgrounds and Urban Reform*. Philadelphia: University of Pennsylvania Press, 1981.

Chambers, John Whiteclay, II. *The Tyranny of Change: America in the Progressive Era, 1900–1917*. New York: St. Martin's Press, 1992.

Chandler, Alfred, Jr. *Giant Enterprise: Ford, General Motors, and the Automobile Industry*. New York: Harcourt, Brace and World, 1964.

Chase, Gilbert. *America's Music: From the Pilgrims to the Present*. 3rd Edition. Urbana: University of Illinois Press, 1987.

Clark, Clifford Edward, Jr. *The American Family Home, 1800–1960*. Chapel Hill: University of North Carolina Press, 1986.

Collier, James Lincoln. *The Making of Jazz: A Comprehensive History*. Boston: Houghton Mifflin, 1978.

Condit, Carl W. *The Chicago School of Architecture: A History of Commercial and Public Building in the Chicago Area, 1875–1925*. Chicago: University of Chicago Press, 1973.

Cooper, John Milton, Jr. *The Pivotal Decades: The United States, 1900–1920*. New York: W.W. Norton, 1990.

Cremin, Lawrence A. *American Education: The Metropolitan Experience, 1876–1980*. New York: Harper and Row, 1988.

Cunliffe, Marcus, ed. *American Literature Since 1900: The New History of Literature*. New York: Peter Bedrick Books, 1987.

Danbom, David B. *The Resisted Revolution: Urban America and the Industrialization of Agriculture, 1900–1930.* Ames: Iowa State University Press, 1979.

DiMeglio, John. *Vaudeville, USA.* Bowling Green, OH: Bowling Green University Popular Press, 1973.

Dorsey, John, ed. *On Mencken.* New York: Alfred A. Knopf, 1980.

Dulles, Foster Rhea. *America Learns to Play. A History of Popular Recreation, 1607–1940.* New York: Appleton-Century, 1940.

Elliott, Emory, ed. *Columbia Literary History of the United States.* New York: Columbia University Press, 1988.

Erenberg, Lewis. *Steppin' Out: New York Nightlife and the Transformation of American Culture, 1890–1930.* Chicago: University of Chicago Press, 1981.

Fass, Paula. *The Damned and the Beautiful.* New York: Oxford University Press, 1970.

Fields, Jill. " 'Fighting the Corsetless Evil': Shaping Corsets and Culture, 1900–1930." *Journal of Social History* 33 (Winter 1999): 355–84.

Fink, Deborah. *Agrarian Women: Wives and Mothers in Rural Nebraska, 1880–1940.* Chapel Hill: University of North Carolina Press, 1991.

Fink, James J. *America Adopts the Automobile, 1895–1910.* Cambridge, MA: MIT Press, 1975.

Fox, Stephen. *The Mirror Makers: A History of American Advertising and Its Creators.* New York: William Morrow, 1984.

Foy, Jessica H. and Thomas Schlereth, eds. *American Home Life, 1880–1930: A Social History of Spaces and Services.* Knoxville: University of Tennessee Press, 1992.

Frank, Rusty E. *Tap! The Greatest Tap Dance Stars and Their Stories, 1900–1955.* New York: William Morrow, 1990.

Fraser, James. *The American Billboard: 100 Years.* New York: Harry N. Abrams, 1991.

Gilfoyle, Timothy J. *City of Eros: New York City, Prostitution, and the Commercialization of Sex, 1790–1920.* New York: W.W. Norton, 1992.

Gioia, Ted. *The History of Jazz.* New York: Oxford University Press, 1997.

Goodrum, Charles and Helen Dalrymple. *Advertising in America: The First 200 Years.* New York: Harry N. Abrams, 1990.

Gordon, Linda. *Pitied But Not Entitled: Single Mothers and the History of Welfare, 1890–1935.* New York: Free Press, 1994.

Gordon, Lois and Alan Gordon. *The Columbia Chronicles of American Life, 1910–1992.* New York: Columbia University Press, 1995.

Gorn, Elliot J. *The Manly Art: Bare-Knuckle Prize Fighting in America.* Ithaca, NY: Cornell University Press, 1986.

Goulart, Ron, ed. *The Encyclopedia of American Comics.* New York: Facts on File, 1990.

Guttmann, Allen. *From Ritual to Record: The Nature of Modern Sport.* New York: Columbia University Press, 1978.

Hall, Lee. *Common Threads: A Parade of American Clothing.* Boston: Bulfinch Press/ Little, Brown, 1992.

Hardy, Stephen. *How Boston Played: Sports, Recreation and Community, 1865–1915.* Boston: Northeastern University Press, 1982.

Harvey, Robert C. *The Art of the Comic Book*. Meridian: University of Mississippi Press, 1996.

———. *The Art of the Funnies*. Meridian: University of Mississippi Press, 1994.

———. *Children of the Yellow Kid: The Evolution of the American Comic Strip*. Seattle: Frye Art Museum and the University of Washington Press, 1998.

Hasse, John Edward, ed. *Ragtime: Its History, Composers, and Music*. New York: Schirmer Books, 1985.

Hawes, Joseph. *The Children's Rights Movement: A History of Advocacy and Protection*. Twayne's Social Movement Series. Boston: Twayne Publishers, 1991.

Hayden, Dolores. *The Grand Domestic Revolution: A History of Feminist Designs for American Homes, Neighborhoods, and Cities*. Cambridge, MA: MIT Press, 1983.

Hays, Samuel P. *The Response to Industrialism, 1885–1914*. Chicago: University of Chicago Press, 1961.

Heller, Adele and Lois Rudnick, eds. *1915: The Cultural Moment: The New Politics, the New Woman, the New Psychology, the New Art, and the New Theatre in America*. New Brunswick, NJ: Rutgers University Press, 1991.

Heyer, Paul. Titanic *Legacy: Disaster Media Event and Myth*. Westport, CT: Praeger, 1995.

Hilton, George. *Eastland: Legacy of the* Titanic. Stanford, CA: Stanford University Press, 1995.

Hiner, N. Ray and Joseph M. Hawes, eds. *Growing Up in America: Children in Historical Perspective*. Urbana: University of Illinois Press, 1985.

Hooker, Richard. *Food and Drink in America: A History*. New York: Bobbs-Merrill, 1981.

Jackson, Carlton. *Zane Grey*. Boston: Twayne Publishers, 1973.

Jackson, Kenneth T. *Crabgrass Frontier: The Suburbanization of the United States*. New York: Oxford University Press, 1985.

Keegan, John. *The First World War*. New York: Knopf, 1999.

Kennedy, David M. *Over Here: The First World War and American Society*. New York: Oxford University Press, 1980.

Kidney, Walter C. *The Architecture of Choice: Eclecticism in America, 1880–1930*. New York: George Braziller, 1974.

Knock, Thomas J. *To End All Wars: Woodrow Wilson and the Creation of the League of Nations*. New York: Oxford University Press, 1992.

Leach, William. *Land of Desire: Merchants, Power, and the Rise of the New American Culture*. New York: Pantheon Books, 1993.

Lears, Jackson. *Fables of Abundance: A Cultural History of Advertising in America*. New York: Basic Books, 1995.

Lee, Brian. *American Fiction, 1865–1940*. New York: Longman, 1987.

Levenstein, Harvey. *Paradox of Plenty: A Social History of Eating in Modern America*. New York: Oxford University Press, 1993.

———. *Revolution at the Table: The Transformation of the American Diet*. New York: Oxford University Press, 1988.

Link, Arthur S. and Richard L. McCormick. *Progressivism*. Arlington Heights, IL: Harlan Davidson, Inc., 1983.

Lynes, Russell. *The Lively Audience: A Social History of the Visual and Performing Arts in America, 1890–1950*. New York: Harper and Row, 1985.

MacDonald, Victoria-Maria. "The Paradox of Bureaucratization: New Views on Progressive Era Teachers and the Development of a Woman's Profession." *History of Education Quarterly* 39 (Winter 1999): 427–53.

Maland, Charles J. *Chaplin and American Culture: The Evolution of a Star Image.* Princeton, NJ: Princeton University Press, 1989.

Malnig, Julie. "Athena Meets Venus: Visions of Women in Social Dance in the Teens and Early 1920s." *Dance Research Journal* 30 (Fall 1998): 34–62.

Mancini, Joanne M. " 'One Term Is as Fatuous as Another': Responses to the Armory Show Reconsidered." *American Quarterly* 51 (December 1999): 833–70.

Marchand, Roland. *Advertising the American Dream: Making Way for Modernity, 1920–1940.* Berkeley: University of California Press, 1985.

Mast, Gerald. *A Short History of the Movies.* 5th Edition. New York: Macmillan, 1992.

May, Henry F. *The End of American Innocence: A Study of the First Years of Our Own Times, 1912–1917.* Chicago: Quadrangle Press, 1964.

May, Lary. *Screening Out the Past: The Birth of Mass Culture and the Motion Picture Industry.* Chicago: University of Chicago Press, 1983.

McFarland, Dorothy Tuck. *Willa Cather.* New York: Frederick Ungar, 1972.

Mendes, Valerie and Amy de la Haye. *20th Century Fashion.* London: Thames & Hudson, 1999.

Mergen, Bernard. "Games and Toys." In *Handbook of American Popular Culture,* ed. M. Thomas Inge, Volume 2, 163–91. Westport, CT: Greenwood Press, 1980.

Meyer, Stephen, III. *The Five-Dollar Day: Labor, Management, and Social Control in the Ford Motor Company, 1908–1921.* Albany: State University of New York Press, 1981.

Mintz, Steven and Randy Roberts, eds. *Hollywood's America: United States History Through Its Films.* St. James, NY: Brandywine Press, 1993.

Mordden, Ethan. *The American Theater.* New York: Oxford University Press, 1981.

Morgan, H. Wayne. *The New Muses: Art in American Culture, 1865–1920.* Norman: University of Oklahoma Press, 1978.

Mrozek, Donald J. *Sport and American Mentality, 1880–1910.* Knoxville: University of Tennessee Press, 1983.

Mumford, Lewis. *The Brown Decades: A Study of the Arts in America, 1865–1895.* Rev. ed. New York: Dover, 1971.

Murray, Robert K. *Red Scare: A Study in National Hysteria, 1919–1920.* New York: McGraw-Hill, 1955.

Musser, Charles. *The Emergence of Cinema: The American Screen to 1907.* Berkeley: University of California Press, 1994.

Nevin, Allan and Frank Ernest Hill. *Ford: Expansion and Challenge, 1915–1933.* New York: Charles Scribner's Sons, 1962.

Norris, James D. *Advertising and the Transformation of American Society, 1865–1920.* Contributions in Economics and Economic History, no. 110. Westport, CT: Greenwood Press, 1990.

Nowell-Smith, Geoffrey, ed. *The Oxford History of World Cinema.* New York: Oxford University Press, 1996.

O'Gorman, James F. *Three American Architects: Richardson, Sullivan, and Wright, 1865–1915*. Chicago: University of Chicago Press, 1991.

Ostrander, Gilam. *America in the First Machine Age, 1890–1940*. New York: Harper and Row, 1970.

Painter, Nell Irvin. *Standing at Armageddon: The United States, 1877–1919*. New York: W.W. Norton, 1987.

Panati, Charles. *Panati's Parade of Fads, Follies, and Manias: The Origins of Our Most Cherished Possessions*. New York: Harper Perennial, 1991.

Peacock, John. *Fashion Accessories: The Complete 20th Century Sourcebook*. London: Thames and Hudson, 2000.

Perlman, Bennard B. *The Immortal Eight: American Painting from Eakins to the Armory Show, 1870–1913*. Westport, CT: North Light Publishers, 1979.

Peiss, Kathy. *Cheap Amusements: Working Women and Leisure in Turn-of-the-Century New York*. Philadelphia: Temple University Press, 1986.

———. *Hope in a Jar: The Making of America's Beauty Culture*. New York: Henry Holt, 1998.

Rae, John B. *The American Automobile: A Brief History*. Chicago: University of Chicago Press, 1965.

Rawls, Walton. *Wake Up, America! World War I and the American Poster*. New York: Abbeville Press, 1988.

Riess, Steven A. *City Games: The Evolution of American Urban Society and the Rise of Sports*. Urbana: University of Illinois Press, 1989.

———. *Sport in Industrial America, 1850–1920*. Wheeling, IL: Harlan Davidson, 1995.

———. *Touching Base: Professional Baseball and American Culture in the Progressive Era*. Contributions in American Studies, no. 48. Westport, CT: Greenwood Press, 1980.

Rosenzweig, Roy. *Eight Hours for What We Will: Workers and Leisure in an Industrial City, 1870–1920*. New York: Cambridge University Press, 1983.

Ross, Gregory. *The Origins of American Intervention in the First World War*. New York: W.W. Norton, 1971.

Schlereth, Thomas J. *Victorian America: Transformations in Everyday Life, 1876–1915*. New York: HarperCollins, 1991.

Schudson, Michael. *Advertising, the Uneasy Persuasion: Its Dubious Impact on American Society*. New York: Basic Books, 1984.

Seller, Maxine Schwartz, ed. *Ethnic Theatre in the United States*. Westport, CT: Greenwood Press, 1983.

Seward, Keith. *The Legend of Henry Ford*. New York: Russell & Russell, 1968.

Sklar, Robert. *Movie-Made America: A Cultural History of American Movies*. New York: Vintage, 1975.

Skocpol, Theda. *Protecting Soldiers and Mothers: The Political Origins of Social Policy in the United States*. Cambridge, MA: Harvard University Press, 1992.

Southern, Eileen. *The Music of Black Americans: A History*. 3rd Edition. New York: W.W. Norton, 1997.

Spindler, Michael. *American Literature and Social Change: William Dean Howells to Arthur Miller*. Bloomington: Indiana University Press, 1983.

Steinberg, Salme Hrju. *Reformer in the Marketplace: Edward W. Bok and the Ladies' Home Journal*. Baton Rouge: Louisiana State University Press, 1979.

Stevick, Philip, ed. *The American Short Story: 1900–1945. A Critical History*. Boston: Twayne Publishers, 1984.

Stokes, Melvyn and Richard Maltby, eds. *American Movie Audiences: From the Turn of the Century to the Early Sound Era*. London: British Film Institute, 1999.

Taliaferro, John. *Tarzan Forever: The Life of Edgar Rice Burroughs, Creator of Tarzan*. New York: Scribner, 1999.

Tannahill, Reay. *Food in History: The New, Fully Revised, and Updated Edition of the Classic Gastronomic Epic*. New York: Crown Publishers, 1988.

Tebbel, John and Mary Ellen Zuckerman. *The Magazine in America: 1741–1990*. New York: Oxford University Press, 1991.

Toll, Robert C. *On with the Show: The First Century of Show Business in America*. New York: Oxford University Press, 1976.

Tyack, David B. *The One Best System: A History of American Urban Education*. Cambridge, MA: Harvard University Press, 1974.

Voigt, David Quentin. *American Baseball*. Norman: University of Oklahoma Press, 1966.

West, Nancy Martha. *Kodak and the Lens of Nostalgia*. Charlottesville: University Press of Virginia, 2000.

Widick, B.J., ed. *Auto Work and Its Discontents*. Baltimore: Johns Hopkins University Press, 1976.

Wiebe, Robert H. *The Search for Order, 1877–1920*. New York: Hill and Wang, 1967.

Wik, Reynold. *Henry Ford and Grass-Roots America*. Ann Arbor: University of Michigan Press, 1972.

William, Susan. *Savory Suppers and Fashionable Feasts: Dining in Victorian America*. New York: Pantheon, 1985.

Wilson, Richard Guy. *McKim, Mead, & White, Architects*. New York: Rizzoli, 1983.

Wilson, Richard Guy, D.H. Pilgrim, and R.N. Murray. *The American Renaissance, 1876–1917*. New York: Pantheon, 1979.

Winter, J.M. and Blaine Baggett. *The Great War and the Shaping of the 20th Century*. New York: Penguin Studio, 1996.

Wiseman, Carter. *Shaping a Nation: Twentieth-Century American Architecture and Its Makers*. New York: W.W. Norton, 1998.

Wishy, Bernard. *The Child and the Republic: The Dawn of Modern American Child Nurture*. Philadelphia: University of Pennsylvania Press, 1968.

Index

("i" indicates an illustration)

About the Author

DAVID BLANKE is currently an Assistant Professor of History at Texas A&M–Corpus Christi. He is the author of *Sowing the American Dream: How Consumer Culture Took Root in the Rural Midwest.*